EMPOWERED FOR WITNESS

The Spirit in Luke–Acts

ROBERT P. MENZIES

T & T CLARK INTERNATIONAL
A Continuum imprint
LONDON • NEW YORK

To William and Doris Menzies,
Wayne and Doris Turnbull,
loving parents,
faithful witnesses

Published by T&T Clark International
A Continuum imprint
The Tower Building, 11 York Road, London SE1 7NX
15 East 26th Street, Suite 1703, New York, NY 10010

www.tandtclark.com

First published as The Development of Early Christian Pneumatology with
Special Reference to Luke–Acts by Sheffield Academic Press 1991
This edition first published as JPTS 6, © Sheffield Academic Press 1994
This edition published 2004

British Library Cataloguing-in-Publication Data
A catalogue record for this book is available from the British Library

ISBN 0-567-04190-5 (paperback)

CONTENTS

FOREWORD

The pivotal role of Luke–Acts for Pentecostal theology is well known. With the possible exception of 1 Corinthians, no other New Testament works have been as crucial in the development of Pentecostal life, thought and world-view. When Robert Menzies' book *The Development of Early Christian Pneumatology with Special Reference to Luke–Acts* (JSNTSup, 54; Sheffield: JSOT Press, 1991) first appeared, it created quite a stir within the world of New Testament scholarship as well as within Pentecostal circles and continues to call forth a number of responses in both arenas. Given its obvious importance for Lukan studies and Pentecostal theology specifically, the editors of the *Journal of Pentecostal Theology* seek to make the substance of this work available to a broader audience by adding it to the journal's supplement series of monographs. In *Empowered for Witness: The Spirit in Luke–Acts*, Menzies has revised his earlier work in two substantive ways. First, he has provided a translation of most non-biblical foreign language citations found in the first edition, and secondly, he has added two chapters which make clear the implications of this study for Pentecostal theology. The editors of *JPT* are pleased to add this work by Robert Menzies to its series of supplement volumes.

PREFACE

This book is a significantly revised edition of *The Development of Early Christian Pneumatology with Special Reference to Luke–Acts* (JSNTSup, 54; Sheffield: JSOT Press, 1991). In an effort to make the book accessible to a wider audience, numerous changes have been made: the footnotes and the discussion of secondary literature contained in them have been greatly reduced, foreign language material has been translated when appropriate, and two chapters on Paul have been replaced with chapters which seek to address contemporary questions.

This new edition has provided me with an opportunity to introduce new material developed during the course of my teaching ministry at the Asia Pacific Theological Seminary (Baguio, Philippines). I would like to express my appreciation to the students and faculty of this fine institution for their many contributions to the development of my thinking on the matters contained in this book. I would also like to thank John Christopher Thomas, the editor of the *Journal of Pentecostal Theology* Supplement Series, for his encouragement to produce this book and for his efforts on behalf of Pentecostal scholarship in general. I am excited about the emergence of the *Journal of Pentecostal Theology* and trust this book will serve as a worthy member of its Supplement Series.

Baguio City, Philippines
January 7, 1994

PREFACE TO THE FIRST EDITION

We often complain that Christian people at home have little zeal for the spread of the gospel. How can it be otherwise when our people are taught that the Holy Spirit is given, when they are taught to recognize him in their own souls, almost entirely as the sanctifier, the truth revealer, the strengthener, and in the church as the organizer and the director of counsels, whilst they are not taught in anything like the same degree that [the Spirit] is the spirit of redeeming love, active in them towards others, moving every individual soul to whom [the Spirit] comes and the church in which [the Spirit] dwells to desire and to labour for the bringing of all men everywhere to God in Jesus Christ?

—Roland Allen, 'The Revelation of the Holy Spirit in the Acts of the Apostles', *International Review of Missions* (April 1918)

ACKNOWLEDGMENTS

I would like to express my appreciation to the numerous people who, in a variety of ways, enabled me to write this book, originally penned as a PhD thesis at the University of Aberdeen. I am particularly indebted to the students and faculty of the Asia Pacific Theological Seminary (Baguio, Philippines), for the stimulus to undertake this project arose from my association with these friends and colleagues. The encouragement provided by this institution made my time of research at Aberdeen possible. For this I am most grateful.

Although the physical environment of Aberdeen is considerably different from that of Southeast Asia, I found the intellectual and spiritual climate to be equally enriching. I am especially thankful to have had the privilege of working under the supervision of Professor I. Howard Marshall, a man of incisive mind, gentle manner, and obvious enthusiasm for the study of the New Testament. I count myself doubly fortunate, for while at Aberdeen I had access to another gifted scholar, one with a special interest in the work of the Spirit, past and present, Max Turner. My fellow postgraduate students were also a major source of encouragement. Mike Nola helped a young 'rookie' feel at home. Conrad Gempf and Chuck Guth offered timely help when I encountered computer problems. And the 'lunch bunch' always provided food for thought. Although various individuals helped at the proof-reading stage, I owe a great debt to Gary Alan Long and Lynn Graham, both of whom took time from their busy schedules to read the entire manuscript. The fellowship and support of the Abbey Christian Fellowship were a constant source of strength. An Overseas Research Scholarship provided by the British Government lightened the financial load. Dr David Hill and Sheffield Academic Press have kindly made the thesis available to a wider audience. Most of all, my wife Joanne joyfully sojourned with me, provided loving companionship, and paid most of the bills during the period of study. She also provided me with a beautiful daughter, who made life interesting and fun.

ABBREVIATIONS

AB	Anchor Bible
AnBib	Analecta Biblica
AnGreg	Analecta Gregoriana
ArBib	The Aramaic Bible
ASTI	*Annual of the Swedish Theological Institute*
ATANT	Abhandlungen zur Theologie des Alten und Neuen Testaments
AThD	Acta Theologica Danica
BETL	Bibliotheca Ephemeridum Theologicarum Lovaniensium
BibLeb	*Bibel und Leben*
BTB	*Biblical Theology Bulletin*
BTS	Biblisch-Theologische Studien
BZ	*Biblische Zeitschrift*
CGTC	Cambridge Greek Testament Commentary
DL	*Doctrine and Life*
EE	*Der Evangelische Erzieher*
EHPR	Études d'Histoire et de Philosophie Religieuses
EKKNT	Evangelisch-Katholischer Kommentar zum Neuen Testament
EvQ	*The Evangelical Quarterly*
ETL	*Ephemerides Theologicae Lovanienses*
ExpTim	*Expository Times*
FRLANT	Forschungen zur Religion und Literatur des Alten und Neuen Testaments
FV	*Foi et Vie*
GCS	Die griechischen christlichen Schriftsteller der ersten drei Jahrhunderte
GNS	Good News Studies
HM	Heythrop Monographs
HNT	Handbuch zum Neuen Testament
HTKNT	Herders Theologischer Kommentar zum Neuen Testament
HTR	*Harvard Theological Review*
IBS	*Irish Biblical Studies*
IDB	*The Interpreter's Dictionary of the Bible*
Int	*Interpretation*
JBL	*Journal of Biblical Literature*
JJS	*Journal of Jewish Studies*
JPT	*Journal of Pentecostal Theology*

JSNT	*Journal for the Study of the New Testament*
JSNTSup	Journal for the Study of the New Testament Supplement Series
JSOT	*Journal for the Study of the Old Testament*
JSS	*Journal of Semitic Studies*
JTF	Jesuit Theological Forum
JTS	*Journal of Theological Studies*
KEKNT	Kritisch-exegetischer Kommentar über das Neue Testament
LCL	Loeb Classical Library
LD	Lectio Divina
NCB	New Century Bible
NICNT	The New International Commentary on the New Testament
NICOT	The New International Commentary on the Old Testament
NIGTC	The New International Greek Testament Commentary
NovT	*Novum Testamentum*
NRT	*Nouvelle Revue Théologique*
NTA	Neutestamentliche Abhandlungen
NTD	Das Neue Testament Deutsch
NTS	*New Testament Studies*
OC	*One in Christ*
ÖTKNT	Ökumenischer Taschenbuchkommentar zum Neuen Testament
PA	Philosophia Antiqua
PGM	Papyri Graecae Magicae
PTh	Le Point Théologique
PVTG	Pseudepigrapha Veteris Testamenti Graece
RB	*Revue Biblique*
RefR	*The Reformed Review*
RevQ	*Revue de Qumran*
RSR	*Revue des Sciences Religieuses*
RTR	*Reformed Theological Review*
SANT	Studien zum Alten und Neuen Testament
SBF	Studium Biblicum Franciscanum
SBL	Society of Biblical Literature
SBLDS	Society of Biblical Literature Dissertation Series
SBLMS	Society of Biblical Literature Monograph Series
SBS	Stuttgarter Bibelstudien
SBT	Studies in Biblical Theology
SH	Scripta Hierosolymitana
SJ	Studia Judaica
SJT	*Scottish Journal of Theology*
SN	Studia Neotestamentica
SNT	Studien zum Neuen Testament
SNTSMS	Society for New Testament Studies Monograph Series
StBT	*Studia Biblica et Theologica*
SUNT	Studien zur Umwelt des Neuen Testaments

TDNT	G. Kittel, G. Friedrich (eds.), *Theological Dictionary of the New Testament*
THKNT	Theologischer Handkommentar zum Neuen Testament
ThWAT	G.J. Botterweck and H. Ringgren (eds.), *Theologisches Wörterbuch zum Alten Testament*
TNTC	Tyndale New Testament Commentaries
TPQ	*Theologisch-praktische Quartalschrift*
TU	Texte und Untersuchungen zur Geschichte der altchristlichen Literatur
TynBul	*Tyndale Bulletin*
VE	*Vox Evangelica*
VT	*Vetus Testamentum*
WBKEL	Wissenschaftliche Beiträge zur kirchlich-evangelischen Lehre
WMANT	Wissenschaftliche Monographien zum Alten und Neuen Testament
WUNT	Wissenschaftliche Untersuchungen zum Neuen Testament
YJS	Yale Judaica Series
ZNW	*Zeitschrift für die neutestamentliche Wissenschaft*
ZTK	*Zeitschrift für Theologie und Kirche*

Chapter 1

INTRODUCTION

1. *The Task*

The following study is an attempt to reconstruct Luke's role in the development of early Christian pneumatology. Luke's pneumatological perspective can be elucidated through an analysis of the way in which he uses and modifies Mark and Q. For this reason Luke's perspective can be easily compared with the pneumatology of the non-Pauline primitive church reflected in Matthew, Mark and Q. Furthermore, as a historian and theologian who chronicles the emergence of the early church, Luke discusses in considerable detail the nature of early Christian experience of the Spirit. Thus Luke's perspective can be productively compared with the pneumatological insights of Paul.

I shall begin this study by reviewing the significant contributions of a century of scholarship. Each of the authors cited below, albeit in a variety of ways (some indirectly), deal with a question central to this inquiry: to what extent does Luke follow Paul in attributing soteriological significance to the gift of the Spirit? Put another way, to what extent does Luke, in a manner analogous to Paul, view reception of the Spirit as necessary for one to enter into and remain within the community of salvation: the source of cleansing (1 Cor. 6.11; Rom. 15.16), righteousness (Gal. 5.5; Rom. 2.29; 8.1-17; 14.17; Gal. 5.16-26), intimate fellowship with (Gal. 4.6; Rom. 8.14-17) and knowledge of God (1 Cor. 2.6-16; 2 Cor. 3.3-18), and ultimately eternal life through the resurrection (Rom. 8.11; 1 Cor. 15.44-45; Gal. 6.8)? In view of the importance of this question for the task at hand, I shall categorize the principal authors discussed below according to their responses to this fundamental question. Three major categories emerge: those who emphasize the continuity between Luke and Paul at this point, those who emphasize discontinuity, and those holding mediating positions.

2. The Development of Early Christian Pneumatology:
A Survey of Modern Scholarship

2.1. Discontinuity

2.1.1. Hermann Gunkel. As early as 1868 B. Weiss, in his *Lehrbuch der biblischen Theologie des Neuen Testaments*, noted the distinctiveness of Paul's pneumatology as against that of the non-Pauline sector of the early church (*Urgemeinde*).[1] According to Weiss, the concept of 'the Spirit as the God-given principle of the new life' was uniquely Pauline.[2] O. Pfleiderer, writing shortly after Weiss, came to similar conclusions in his lengthy work on Pauline theology, *Der Paulinismus*. Pfleiderer argued that the *Urgemeinde* viewed the Spirit essentially in Old Testament terms as the Spirit of revelation: a divine substance which, after coming upon humans, granted supernatural power and produced miracles. According to Pfleiderer Paul started from this conception, yet moved beyond it. For Paul, the Spirit was not simply the source of miraculous power, it was fundamentally the dynamic which shaped the entire Christian life:

> In short, the πνεῦμα is changed, in the mind of Paul, from an abstract, supernatural, ecstatic, Apocalyptic principle, to an immanent, religious, moral principle of the life of renovated humanity, to the nature of the καινὴ κτίσις.[3]

Although Weiss and Pfleiderer laid the groundwork, it was H. Gunkel who first devoted an entire monograph to the topic and initiated much of the modern discussion.[4] In *Die Wirkungen des heiligen Geistes*, first

---

1. B. Weiss and others such as O. Pfleiderer and H. Gunkel did not attempt to distinguish between the perspective of those communities represented by Matthew, Mark, and Q, and the perspective of Luke. For this reason they viewed Luke–Acts as a major resource for reconstructing the perspective of the non-Pauline early church. In the interest of precision, I shall refer to the non-Pauline early church (inclusive of Luke–Acts) as the *Urgemeinde*, and I shall refer to those early Christian communities within the *Urgemeinde* whose theological outlook is reflected in Matthew, Mark, and Q (excluding Luke–Acts) as the 'primitive church'.
2. B. Weiss, *Lehrbuch der biblischen Theologie des Neuen Testaments* (2nd edn, 1873), p. 216. ET is my own. See also pp. 338-39, 413-14, 454.
3. O. Pfleiderer, *Paulinism: A Contribution to the History of Primitive Christian Theology* (1877; orig. German edn, 1873), I, p. 200.
4. H. Gunkel, *Die Wirkungen des heiligen Geistes nach der populären Anschauung der apostolischen Zeit und nach der Lehre des Apostels Paulus* (1888).

published in 1888, Gunkel offered detailed argumentation in support of his thesis that Paul, in light of his own experience, attempted to correct the pneumatology of the *Urgemeinde*, for whom 'the Spirit was only the power which wrought wonders, the guarantor of spectacular deeds'.[1]

Emphasizing the essentially Jewish and experiential nature of the *Urgemeinde*'s understanding of the Spirit, Gunkel began by posing the central question, 'What were the symptoms by which earliest Christianity determined that a phenomenon was an activity of the Spirit?'[2] According to Gunkel the answer was not to be found in the character of normal Christian behavior, nor in relation to the purposes of God, but rather in the mysterious and powerful nature of deeds which defied natural explanation.[3] Thus, according to Gunkel, the activity most characteristic of the gift of the Spirit in the *Urgemeinde* was glossolalia.[4] In glossolalia the mysterious and powerful character of the Spirit was supremely displayed: 'In glossolalia the individual is overwhelmed by a powerful force that has taken total possession of him'.[5]

This mysterious and powerful activity was not without theological significance. Set against the background of first-century Judaism, these marvelous manifestations were indications of the in-breaking of the Kingdom of God: '"Where the Spirit is, there is the kingdom of God"... The appearance of the Spirit is the breaking in of a new age in which the kingdom of God is coming.'[6]

With this portrait of the *Urgemeinde* complete, Gunkel set out to establish the uniqueness of Paul's understanding of the Spirit. Like the *Urgemeinde*, Paul understood the Spirit to be the source of supernatural power. Yet Gunkel insisted that there were two significant differences in Paul's perspective. First, for Paul the supreme sign of the gift of the Spirit was not limited to mysterious and powerful effects; it entailed another essential ingredient: the divine purpose of the gift—the edification of the Christian community.[7] For this reason Paul, in contrast to

---

All references are from this edition unless otherwise stated. English references are from Gunkel, *The Influence of the Holy Spirit* (1979, trans. R.A. Harrisville and P.A. Quanbeck II) unless otherwise stated.

1. *Die Wirkungen* (2nd edn, 1899), p. 89. ET is my own.
2. *Die Wirkungen*, p. 5. ET from Gunkel, *The Influence*, p. 15.
3. *Die Wirkungen*, p. 22.
4. Gunkel describes glossolalia as 'ekstatische Raserei' (*Die Wirkungen*, p. 21).
5. *Die Wirkungen*, p. 21. ET from Gunkel, *The Influence*, p. 31.
6. *Die Wirkungen*, p. 59. ET from Gunkel, *The Influence*, p. 72.
7. *Die Wirkungen*, p. 74.

the primitive church, held glossolalia in relatively low esteem.[1] In this regard Paul was the first to emphasize the ethical dimension of the gift of the Spirit.[2] Secondly, Paul viewed the Spirit not simply as the source of sporadic and mysterious power, but as the source of Christian life in its totality. Thus, for Paul, the Christian life in its entirety was a sign of the presence of the eschatological Kingdom:

> The community thus regards as pneumatic what is extraordinary in Christian existence, but Paul what is usual; the community what is individual and unique, but Paul what is common to all; the community what abruptly appears, but Paul what is constant; the community what is isolated in Christian existence, but Paul the Christian life as such. And this yielded a totally different, infinitely higher evaluation of Christian conduct.[3]

Gunkel insisted that the source of Paul's unique insight into the working of the Spirit was the personal experience of the Apostle. Nothing else could adequately account for his new perspective. Arguing against H.H. Wendt, Gunkel denied that Paul had taken over from the Old Testament 'his doctrine of the moral and religious activities of the πνεῦμα'.[4] In support of his position Gunkel sought to demonstrate that 'for Judaism the piety of the ordinary man on the whole appeared to have nothing in common with the רוח'.[5] Gunkel acknowledged that there were instances where the Old Testament writers gave ethical significance to the Spirit, though he stressed that these were relatively rare.[6] According to Gunkel, the only true parallels to Paul were Pss. 51.13 and 143.10, yet the absence of similar references elsewhere proved his case.

Gunkel also rejected the view of Pfleiderer that Paul was influenced by the literature of Hellenistic Judaism, particularly Wisdom. Although superficial similarities exist between the role of the Spirit in Paul's thought and that of wisdom/Spirit in Wisdom, the differences are dramatic: 'A man learns wisdom, but the Spirit seizes him'.[7]

---

1. *Die Wirkungen*, p. 72.
2. *Die Wirkungen*, p. 77.
3. *Die Wirkungen*, p. 82. ET from Gunkel, *The Influence*, p. 96.
4. *Die Wirkungen*, p. 85. ET from Gunkel, *The Influence*, p. 99. See pp. 83-86 for arguments *contra* H.H. Wendt, *Die Begriffe Fleisch und Geist im biblischen Sprachgebrauch* (1878).
5. *Die Wirkungen*, p. 85. ET from Gunkel, *The Influence*, p. 99.
6. *Die Wirkungen*, p. 10.
7. *Die Wirkungen*, p. 87. ET from Gunkel, *The Influence*, p. 100. Gunkel

The thesis advanced by J. Gloël, that Jesus and the first apostles acknowledged the ethical character of the work of the Spirit, was also summarily dismissed.[1] Gloël's thesis rested on texts from John, 1 Peter and Acts. Gunkel responded by reversing the logic of Gloël's argument: John and 1 Peter were influenced by Paul. Gunkel had already dispensed with Gloël's interpretation of Acts in his portrait of the *Urgemeinde's* understanding of the Spirit. Although he acknowledged that the Spirit was not completely unrelated to the moral and religious sphere in Acts, Gunkel emphasized that the normal, ongoing religious life of the individual Christian was not a result of the gift of the Spirit. When ethical-religious conduct was attributed to the Spirit, it was simply a heightening of what was already present in the Christian. Thus, a connection to the moral and religious dimension of Christian life was not at the heart of the *Urgemeinde's* understanding of the Spirit—it was simply a by-product of a more fundamental perspective.[2] Gunkel concluded:

> Paul found ready-made the concept of the πνεῦμα as a wonder-working power, but on the basis of his experience, by which the Christian himself appeared to be the greatest miracle, he described the Christian life as an activity of the πνεῦμα in a completely original way.[3]

The sharpness with which Gunkel separated the pneumatology of Paul from that of the Judaism and the *Urgemeinde* which preceded him is striking. Certainly not all would allow Gunkel's wedge to be driven so deep. Indeed, his insistence that Paul was the first to give prominence to the ethical character of the Spirit has been widely challenged. On the basis of his examination of rabbinic texts F. Büchsel responded, 'There can be no doubt concerning the ethical character of the Spirit'.[4] More recently W.D. Davies concluded, 'The long-standing discussion as to whether Paul was the first to "ethicize" the Spirit can now be regarded, in light of the scrolls, as closed'.[5] It would appear that first-century

criticizes Pfleiderer's position put forth in *Das Urchristentum* (1887), pp. 86-88.

1. *Die Wirkungen*, p. 89. Gunkel criticized the viewpoint of J. Gloël expressed in *Der heilige Geist in der Heilsverkündigung des Paulus* (1888).

2. *Die Wirkungen*, p. 9.

3. *Die Wirkungen*, p. 88. ET from Gunkel, *The Influence*, p. 102.

4. F. Büchsel, *Der Geist Gottes im Neuen Testament* (1926), p. 133. ET is my own.

5. W.D. Davies, 'Paul and the Dead Sea Scrolls: Flesh and Spirit', in *The Scrolls and the New Testament* (1958), p. 177.

Judaism was not as monolithic as Gunkel judged. This raises important questions concerning Gunkel's portrait of the *Urgemeinde*.

Gunkel can also be criticized for underestimating the degree to which the *Urgemeinde* identified the work of the Spirit with the purposes of God revealed in the ministry of Jesus. Luke identifies the work of the Spirit so closely with the mission of Jesus that it is 'the Spirit of Jesus' who directs the early missionaries (Acts 16.7). In this regard it is questionable whether Gunkel presents an adequate description of the *Urgemeinde's* criteria for identifying the work of the Spirit.[1]

These criticisms in no way detract from the genius and significance of Gunkel's work. Indeed, one can only wonder how Gunkel's views would have changed if he had access to the scrolls from Qumran or to the contributions redaction criticism has brought to our understanding of the synoptic Gospels. Written in 1888, *Die Wirkungen* was remarkable for its methodological sophistication and its insightful conclusions. Gunkel's emphasis on the significance of the Jewish background for understanding the pneumatology of the *Urgemeinde*, the eschatological nature of the Spirit as a sign of the presence of the Kingdom of God, and his suggestion of Pauline influence on John and 1 Peter, anticipated perspectives of a later era. His central thesis raised many issues which are still unresolved. In short, Gunkel set the agenda for the modern discussion.

2.1.2. Eduard Schweizer. E. Schweizer marks another significant milestone in the discussion concerning the development of early Christian pneumatology. His first essay treating the topic, an article published in the July 1952 issue of *Interpretation*, was followed by his contribution to the *TDNT* article on πνεῦμα in 1956.[2] Both essays attempt to distinguish Luke's pneumatology from that of the other synoptic evangelists and Paul.[3]

According to Schweizer, Matthew and Mark viewed the Spirit largely

---

1.   Gunkel asserts that the *Urgemeinde* recognized the Spirit at work in events which were mysterious, powerful, somehow connected to the Christian community, not harmful to humans, effected by agents not unworthy of such a relationship to God (*Die Wirkungen*, p. 47).

2.   E. Schweizer, 'The Spirit of Power: The Uniformity and Diversity of the Concept of the Holy Spirit in the New Testament', *Int* 6 (1952), pp. 259-78; and 'πνεῦμα', *TDNT*, VI, pp. 389-455.

3.   Schweizer traces the development of the early church's thinking on the Spirit from the primitive pneumatologies of the primitive church (Matthew, Mark) and Luke to the more developed pneumatology of Paul.

in Old Testament terms as the source of supernatural power for the performance of miracles. Thus they differed from the Old Testament perspective only in their emphasis on the presence of the Spirit in Jesus.[1] Yet this by itself did not communicate the true significance of Jesus, for he was not simply another pneumatic or Spirit-inspired miracle worker. Therefore, whenever Matthew or Mark mentioned the Spirit it was in order to underline the uniqueness of Jesus as *the* eschatological deliverer.[2] However, the portraits they produced were not entirely clear on this point, for they did at times naïvely portray Jesus as a pneumatic.

Luke clarified this ambiguous picture. In his earthly life Jesus 'is not the object of the Spirit...He is Lord over the Spirit'.[3] As the exalted Lord he dispenses the Spirit to the eschatological community. In this way Luke stressed the distinctiveness of Jesus' experience of the Spirit as against that of the Old Testament prophets and the disciples.

Luke differed from Matthew and Mark in another way. Schweizer asserted that Luke's pneumatology, more than the other evangelists', was shaped by 'the typically Jewish idea that the Spirit is the Spirit of prophecy'.[4] For this reason, in spite of Luke's special interest in the visible manifestations of the Spirit,[5] he never attributed miraculous healings or exorcisms to the Spirit. Rather, Luke always portrayed the Spirit as the source of inspired speech, such as glossolalia or preaching.[6]

According to Schweizer, Luke also went further than Matthew and Mark with reference to the bestowal of the Spirit. Whereas Matthew and Mark, consistent with the Old Testament, viewed the gift of the Spirit as limited to a specially chosen few, Luke understood that a new age had dawned: the Spirit had been given to all of God's people.[7] However, Luke remained relatively similar to the evangelists in his assessment of

---

1. 'πνεῦμα', p. 404; 'Spirit of Power', p. 260.
2. 'Spirit of Power', p. 264.
3. 'Spirit of Power', p. 265 and 'πνεῦμα', p. 405.
4. 'πνεῦμα', p. 407; 'Spirit of Power', p. 266.
5. Schweizer attributes this interest in the visible manifestations of the Spirit to Luke's hellenistic background ('πνεῦμα', p. 407).
6. It is unfortunate that Schweizer's position has been obscured by a mistranslation. The English summary statement mistakenly includes a negative: 'Luke thus shares with Judaism the view that the Spirit is essentially the Spirit of prophecy. This does *not* prevent him from directly attributing to the πνεῦμα both the χαρίσματα ἰαμάτων on the one side and strongly ethical effects like the common life of the primitive community on the other' ('πνεῦμα', *TDNT*, VI, p. 409; italics are mine).
7. 'Spirit of Power', p. 267; 'πνεῦμα', p. 410.

the significance of the gift. Betraying his indebtedness to Judaism, Luke understood the Spirit to be a supplementary gift, not necessary for salvation:

> The Spirit is, therefore, not the power which binds a man to God and transfers him into a state of salvation; it is a supplementary power which enables him to give form to his faith in the concrete activity of the proclamation of the gospel.[1]

Distinguishing his own position from that of Gunkel, Schweizer states that for Luke 'it would be wrong to ascribe only extraordinary religious effects to the Spirit'.[2] On the one hand boldness (παρρησία) is attributed to the Spirit, on the other hand miracles are not. Yet Schweizer acknowledges that in Luke's perspective the Spirit is essentially 'the extraordinary power which makes possible unusual acts of power'.[3] This view has been modified by the Jewish tradition, which viewed the Spirit as the source of prophetic inspiration, and by Christian tradition, which viewed the Spirit as a gift given to every member of the new community.

Schweizer distinguishes sharply Paul's pneumatology from that of Luke. For Luke, since the Spirit did not bestow salvation, it could only function as a sign pointing to that which was yet to come. Yet for Paul the Spirit was much more. The Spirit revealed the true significance of the cross, and as such, bestowed salvation.

Paul's unique pneumatology was largely the result of the Hellenistic context in which he found himself. Schweizer asserted that Hellenistic society, in contrast to its Jewish counterpart, thought in terms of superimposed spheres rather than detached aeons. The Hellenist also always thought of power in terms of substance. Therefore in the Hellenistic world the Spirit could not be a sign of the age to come. It had to be a substance from the heavenly sphere. This set the stage for Paul's unique pneumatology, as well as that of the Gnostics:

> If Jesus was the bringer of the Spirit, then He was the bearer of heavenly substance with which He endowed believers and united them with the heavenly world. A radical solution thus became possible for the first time. The point of the mission of Jesus was to bring the heavenly substance πνεῦμα into the world. Attachment to Jesus is attachment to this substance of power, to the heavenly world. It is thus salvation itself.[4]

1. 'Spirit of Power', p. 268. See also 'πνεῦμα', p. 412.
2. 'πνεῦμα', p. 412.
3. 'πνεῦμα', p. 412.
4. 'πνεῦμα', p. 416.

Paul, like the gnostic, adopted these Hellenistic ideas, but unlike the gnostic, he placed them in a uniquely Christian context. Both the gnostic and Paul understood the Spirit to be the means by which one is transferred from the earthly world to the heavenly. But in contrast to the gnostic, who viewed the Spirit as a heavenly substance inherent in every one which could be rekindled by the redeemer myth, for Paul the Spirit was separate from humans and revealed to them the significance of the saving act of God in Christ.[1] Paul distinguished himself from gnostic thought by focusing on the historical necessity of the cross and resurrection and fusing these events together with the bestowal of the Spirit.

In this way Paul also distinguished himself from Luke, for the Spirit is now 'the decisive saving power which unites man with God, and thus bestows salvation upon him'.[2] This, according to Schweizer, constitutes the fundamental distinction between Luke and Paul. It is not the adoption of the ethical, nor the focus on the inner life; these are merely symptoms of a more basic distinction: '*pneuma* is now the power of God which brings a man to faith in the cross and resurrection of Jesus'.[3]

Although Schweizer accented the distinctiveness of Paul's pneumatology as Gunkel had before him, he advanced the discussion at significant points. First, building upon the work of H. von Baer, Schweizer emphasized the importance of the Jewish background for Luke's understanding of the Spirit in a unique way.[4] Arguing that Luke, more than the other synoptic writers, was influenced by the Jewish conception of the Spirit as the Spirit of prophecy, Schweizer distinguished Luke's pneumatology from that of Matthew and Mark on the one hand, and Paul on the other. In this way Schweizer was able to move beyond Gunkel. Schweizer's contention that late Judaism viewed the Spirit predominantly as the source of prophetic inspiration was undoubtedly correct; however, other perspectives existed as well. Thus Schweizer has raised an important question: to what extent was Luke's understanding shaped by the Jewish conception of the Spirit as the Spirit of prophecy?

Secondly, Schweizer argued that Luke carefully distinguished Jesus' experience of the Spirit from that of the Old Testament prophets and the disciples. Jesus was Lord of the Spirit. This is a theme which we shall meet again and with which I shall take issue.

1. 'Spirit of Power', p. 273. See also 'πνεῦμα', p. 425.
2. 'Spirit of Power', p. 272.
3. 'πνεῦμα', p. 432.
4. See §2.3.1 below for a discussion of H. von Baer.

Thirdly, Schweizer shifted the focus in his treatment of Paul's pneumatology from the ethical dimension to the dimension of faith. The uniqueness of Paul's pneumatology is not to be found in the ethical dimension he added, rather it is found in his understanding of the Spirit as the power which generates belief. In this way Paul transformed the Spirit from a supplementary gift into that which is vital for salvation. Although this element was present in Gunkel's work, Schweizer represents a shift in focus.

Fourthly, Schweizer argued that Paul's unique understanding of the Spirit resulted from Hellenistic influence. This of course runs counter to Gunkel's insistence that Paul's uniqueness was solely the product of his personal experience. Schweizer can be criticized at this point for anachronistically attributing features exhibited in second-century gnostic material to the Hellenistic world of the first century.[1]

2.1.3. David Hill. Employing the lexicographic method of the *TDNT*, D. Hill sought to uncover the significance of πνεῦμα for the various New Testament writers. The title of his work, *Greek Words and Hebrew Meanings*, suggests the major conclusion of his study: the New Testament usage of πνεῦμα is shaped by Judaism, not by Hellenism.[2]

Hill, like Schweizer before him, asserted that Luke's two-volume work was influenced largely by the prophetic character of the Jewish concept of the Spirit.[3] Building on this Jewish foundation, Luke portrayed the Spirit as the prophetic power which energized the missionary expansion of the church. The Spirit inspired the proclamation of the end-time prophets.

According to Hill, Luke does not advance significantly beyond the Old Testament and Jewish perspective which viewed the Spirit as a supplementary gift, a special endowment to fulfill a specific task. Hill notes that 'there is little reference in Acts to the presence of the Spirit as the

---

1. E. Brandenburger has argued that the origin of Paul's pneumatic mysticism is not to be found in Hellenistic-Gnostic influences, but rather in the dualistic wisdom of Hellenistic Judaism (*Fleisch und Geist: Paulus und die dualistische Weisheit* [1968]).

2. D. Hill, *Greek Words and Hebrew Meanings: Studies in the Semantics of Soteriological Terms* (1967). In this regard Hill builds on the work of W.D. Davies who emphasized the Jewish character of Paul's theology, including his pneumatology (*Paul and Rabbinic Judaism: Some Rabbinic Elements in Pauline Theology* [1948], esp. pp. 177-226).

3. *Greek Words*, pp. 261-63.

inner principle of the believer's life or as an abiding gift within the Church's life'.[1]

In contrast, Paul grasped the broader dimensions of the Spirit's work. Rather than simply being the source of prophetic activity, the Spirit for Paul was the source of the entire Christian life, including the ethical dimensions. Hill downplays Paul's uniqueness at this point by emphasizing his indebtedness to Judaism:

> In ethicising the Spirit, Paul was not an innovator: he was emphasising what had been present in the Old Testament and what was implicit (though only rarely expressed) in later Jewish thought.[2]

Hill's work is significant in that, although he accents the differences between Luke and Paul in a manner similar to Schweizer, he underlines the Jewish character of the pneumatology of both Luke and Paul. Like Schweizer, Hill maintains that for Luke the Spirit is the Spirit of prophecy. Yet Paul's uniqueness results not from his accommodation to the Hellenistic context, but rather from his appropriation of themes present in the Old Testament and contemporary Judaism.

2.2. *Continuity*

2.2.1. *Friedrich Büchsel.*

With *Der Geist Gottes im Neuen Testament* (1926), F. Büchsel added new impetus to the discussion. By stressing the relative homogeneity of the various pneumatologies represented in the New Testament, Büchsel offered an important alternative to Gunkel. If Gunkel was the father of the discontinuity perspective, Büchsel represents his counterpart for the continuity school.

According to Büchsel, the *Urgemeinde* viewed Jesus as the supreme *Pneumatiker* (Spirit-inspired person). Jesus became the *Pneumatiker par excellence* at his baptism. This perspective was shared by each of the synoptic evangelists. For although Matthew and Luke associated the Spirit with Jesus' birth, he was not yet driven by the Spirit, not yet filled with the Spirit, until his baptism.[3] Only after his reception of the Spirit at his baptism did Jesus embark on his ministry of preaching and performing wonders.[4]

---

1. *Greek Words*, p. 264.
2. *Greek Words*, p. 270.
3. According to Büchsel this did not present a problem for Matthew or Luke: 'Jesus ist Gottes Sohn seit seiner Geburt, und er ist Gottes Sohn durch den Geistempfang bei seiner Taufe' (*Der Geist Gottes*, p. 165).
4. *Der Geist Gottes*, p. 149. See also pp. 220-21..

What was the significance of Jesus' reception of the Spirit, what did it mean to become a *Pneumatiker*? Büchsel answered this question by pointing to Jesus' unique awareness that he was the son of God: 'For Jesus, possession of the Spirit is divine Sonship'.[1] Büchsel acknowledged that there was a difference between Jesus' self-understanding as Messiah and as the Son of God. Although both were mediated to Jesus by the Spirit at his baptism, Büchsel asserted that the emphasis was clearly on Sonship:

> Jesus' messianic consciousness was not the center-point of his self-understanding and effectiveness. He lived and died in devotion and obedience to God. That was of primary importance. Authority over the Jews and the world was always secondary... His messianic consciousness grew out of his filial relationship to God. Indeed, the latter gave the former uniqueness and depth.[2]

To be a *Pneumatiker* is to address God as Father. For this reason Büchsel denied that the *Urgemeinde* viewed the Spirit simply as miraculous power. On the contrary, the primitive church understood the Spirit to be the means by which humankind was brought into special relationship with God:

> One who receives the Spirit is brought into personal relationship with God. The recipient of the Spirit not only receives power for some special task, but also assurance that he is loved by God and the knowledge that he is God's son. The great difference which exists between power and a personal relationship with God is most evident in the account of Jesus' baptism.[3]

Similarly, Büchsel rejected Gunkel's suggestion that the Spirit had little ethical significance for the *Urgemeinde*. It was false to view the Spirit simply as the source of naked power, for the Spirit shaped the entire life of the supreme *Pneumatiker*, Jesus.[4]

Büchsel's analysis, as indicated, was based largely on the portrait of Jesus which emerged from the synoptic Gospels. Jesus modeled what it meant to be a *Pneumatiker*, to experience the power of the Spirit. This was not without significance for the early church. Büchsel insisted that 'the early Christians... were all, in some measure, *Pneumatiker*'.[5]

---

1. *Der Geist Gottes*, p. 165. ET is my own.
2. *Der Geist Gottes*, p. 165. ET is my own.
3. *Der Geist Gottes*, p. 168. ET is my own.
4. *Der Geist Gottes*, pp. 182, 186-87, and especially p. 223.
5. *Der Geist Gottes*, p. 230. ET is my own.

Although Jesus' disciples had not received the Spirit during his earthly ministry,[1] Jesus promised that they would receive the pneumatic gift.[2] The subsequent reception of the Spirit by the early church shaped its existence as a community of *Pneumatiker*.

The early church's experience of the Spirit not only shaped its existence, but also exerted a tremendous influence on the documents of the New Testament which it produced. The Spirit provided the church with a theme that influenced the whole of the New Testament and gave it unity.[3] The experience of the Spirit bound the early church together.

This is not to deny that Paul made a distinctive contribution. Yet, according to Büchsel, this contribution was not a radically new understanding of the Spirit. Paul was unique in two ways. First, in his epistles we have access, for the first time, to the self-reflection of a *Pneumatiker*.[4] That is, Paul, as no other New Testament writer, expressed what it meant to be a *Pneumatiker* from the perspective of personal experience. Secondly, Paul, by rejecting the necessity of obedience to the law, emphasized the significance of the Spirit in a new way. Paul placed the Spirit, as never before, at the center of the Christian life.[5] Yet this was simply a continuation, an extension of what was already present in the *Urgemeinde* before him; it does not represent a decisively new understanding of the Spirit. Indeed, possession of the Spirit meant essentially the same thing for the *Urgemeinde* as for Paul: 'The love of God has been poured out into our hearts'.[6]

Methodologically, Büchsel was significant for his emphasis on the Jewish origin of the early church's pneumatology;[7] this only a few years after Bousset and Leisegang. But Büchsel's real contribution lay elsewhere. By maintaining that the Spirit was, above all, the source of sonship with God, the power which enabled the *Pneumatiker* to address God as Father, Büchsel was able to link the pneumatology of the *Urgemeinde* with that of Paul. Written in the wake of Pfleiderer and Gunkel, it is this focus on the continuity of the early church's under-

1. *Der Geist Gottes*, p. 185.
2. Büchsel distinguishes between the gift of the Spirit as a special power to fulfil specific functions (for the apostles only) and the gift of the Spirit in the broader sense described above, granted to all (*Der Geist Gottes*, pp. 234-35).
3. *Der Geist Gottes*, pp. 228-29.
4. *Der Geist Gottes*, pp. 267-68.
5. *Der Geist Gottes*, pp. 442-48.
6. *Der Geist Gottes*, p. 333. ET is my own.
7. *Der Geist Gottes*, pp. 200-201, 239-40, 252.

standing of the Spirit that makes Büchsel's voluminous work so significant. Although I shall criticize Büchsel's interpretation of Luke, there can be no doubt that his influence has been lasting.

2.2.2. James D.G. Dunn. The prolific pen of J. Dunn has, without question, exerted the greatest influence on recent discussion concerning the pneumatology of the early church. Dunn's initial major work, *Baptism in the Holy Spirit*,[1] was a two-pronged critique of Pentecostal and sacramental interpretations of the gift of the Spirit. Dunn asserted that, in the perspective of the early church, the gift of the Spirit was neither a *donum superadditum* received subsequent to conversion nor inextricably bound to water baptism; rather it was the 'chief element in conversion initiation'.[2] The enormous influence *Baptism in the Holy Spirit* had on subsequent discussion was reflected in the decision by Westminster Press in 1977 to reprint it as a 'classic'. Dunn's sequel, *Jesus and the Spirit*, has received equal acclaim.[3] The title is somewhat misleading, for in this book Dunn analyses the religious experience of both Jesus and the early church. These works, as well as other shorter essays by Dunn,[4] follow in the tradition of Büchsel by emphasizing the underlying continuity which existed in the early church's experience and understanding of the Spirit.

Although Dunn's concerns are broader than the respective pneumatologies of Luke and Paul, he devotes considerable space, particularly in *Baptism in the Holy Spirit*, to Luke's understanding of the Spirit. Dunn argues that the gift of the Spirit for Luke, as for the early church as a whole, is that which makes a Christian truly Christian. The gift of the Spirit is the climax of conversion-initiation. The Spirit initiates believers into the new age and mediates to them the life of the new covenant.[5]

---

1. J.D.G. Dunn, *Baptism in the Holy Spirit: A Re-examination of the New Testament Teaching on the Gift of the Spirit in Relation to Pentecostalism Today* (1970).

2. *Holy Spirit*, p. 4.

3. *Jesus and the Spirit: A Study of the Religious and Charismatic Experience of Jesus and the First Christians as Reflected in the New Testament* (1975).

4. See Dunn, 'Spirit-Baptism and Pentecostalism', *SJT* 23 (1970), pp. 397-407; 'Spirit and Kingdom', *ExpTim* 82 (1970), pp. 36-40; 'The Birth of a Metaphor: Baptized in the Spirit', *ExpTim* 89 (1977), pp. 134-38, 173-75; *Unity and Diversity in the New Testament: An Inquiry into the Character of Earliest Christianity* (1977), pp. 174-202.

5. *Holy Spirit*, pp. 23-32, 47-48. Cf. *Jesus and the Spirit*, p. 6; *Unity and Diversity*, p. 183.

Dunn's case rests on three pivotal arguments. First, Dunn claims that Jesus' experience at the Jordan was not primarily an anointing for power; rather it marked his initiation into the new age.[1] Dunn, following in the steps of H. von Baer and H. Conzelmann, views Luke as portraying three distinct epochs in salvation history.[2] The decisive transition points are Jesus' Jordan experience and Pentecost. Each is said to be an initiation into the new age: Jordan for Jesus, Pentecost for the disciples.[3] Each is linked to the bestowal of the Spirit. For, as Dunn argues, the Spirit is the catalyst of the kingdom, the dynamic of the new age: 'Where the Spirit is there is the kingdom'.[4]

Dunn, like Büchsel, views Jesus' Jordan experience as the decisive point in his life. And with Büchsel, Dunn also sees Jesus' reception of the Spirit as more than simply an anointing with power. It is Jesus' entry into the new age and covenant. Dunn can even say that through his reception of the Spirit at the Jordan, Jesus entered into a 'newer and fuller phase of his messiahship and sonship'.[5] Yet Dunn is reluctant to say with Büchsel that Jesus' sense of sonship flowed from his reception of the Spirit. Spirit and sonship are two prominent aspects of Jesus' religious experience and both result from his Jordan experience, but one cannot be said to have priority over the other; rather they are 'two sides of the one coin'.[6] In this regard Dunn is more sensitive to the difficulties Büchsel's view raises for Luke's Gospel. Indeed, he denies that Luke's account of Jesus' experience at the Jordan contradicts what Luke has already written in Luke 1 and 2.[7] Dunn resolves the apparent contradiction by focusing on Luke's scheme of salvation history. The experience of Jesus at the Jordan was 'not so much of Jesus becoming what he was not before, but of Jesus entering where he was not before—a new epoch in God's plan of redemption'.[8]

A second pivotal argument for Dunn is his claim that the Spirit is the

1. *Holy Spirit*, p. 32.
2. H. von Baer, *Der heilige Geist in den Lukasschriften* (1926); H. Conzelmann, *The Theology of St Luke* (1961; German edn, 1953). However, it should be noted that these authors place the divisions between the epochs at different stages in Luke's narrative.
3. *Holy Spirit*, pp. 23-32, 40-41.
4. *Jesus and the Spirit*, p. 49. See also, 'Spirit and Kingdom', pp. 36-40.
5. *Holy Spirit*, p. 29.
6. *Jesus and the Spirit*, p. 66; see pp. 62-67.
7. *Holy Spirit*, p. 28.
8. *Holy Spirit*, p. 28.

essence and embodiment of the new covenant. This argument is particularly important for Dunn's interpretation of the gift of the Spirit at Pentecost. He asserts that Luke employs the term 'promise'[1] in the same sense as Paul to refer to the covenant promise of God to his people:

> Implicit here, therefore, is the thought of the Spirit as the new covenant fulfillment of the ancient covenant promise. The gift of the Spirit is now the means whereby men enter into the blessing of Abraham...It is very probable therefore that Luke also saw the Spirit as the essence and embodiment of the new covenant, as that which most distinguished it from the old.[2]

That Luke understood the Spirit to be the essence of the new covenant is confirmed by the fact that he presents the outpouring of the Spirit as taking place on the Feast of Pentecost. This is significant, insists Dunn, because 'Pentecost was more and more coming to be regarded as the feast which commemorated the lawgiving at Sinai'.[3] Pentecost was, for Luke, the giving of the new Torah. Thus Dunn emphasizes Luke's continuity with Ezek. 36.26, Jer. 31.33 and ultimately Paul.[4] Initiation into the new age involves incorporation into the new covenant: both are mediated through the Spirit.

The life of the new community, as well as that of the individual believer, is shaped by the Spirit. According to Dunn, the Spirit forms the corporate believers into the body of Christ, the church. Apostolic preaching and κοινωνία are a direct result of the activity of the Spirit. 'Luke's history at this point demonstrates Paul's doctrine.'[5]

A third pivot to Dunn's argument is his claim that, for Luke, 'the gift of' or 'to be baptized in' the Spirit always refers to an initiatory experience, the means by which one enters into the new age. For this reason Dunn argues that the Samaritans, Paul and the Ephesians were not considered Christians by Luke before they received the gift of the Spirit.[6]

The picture of Luke's pneumatology which emerges is, indeed, very similar to that of Paul. Certainly there are differences. Dunn criticizes

---

1. τὴν ἐπαγγελίαν τοῦ πατρός (Lk. 24.49; Acts 1.4) and ἐπαγγελίαν (Acts 2.33, 38-39).
2. *Holy Spirit*, pp. 47-48.
3. *Holy Spirit*, p. 48. See also p. 49.
4. *Holy Spirit*, p. 48.
5. *Holy Spirit*, p. 51; cf. pp. 50-51.
6. *Holy Spirit*, pp. 55-56 (Samaritans), 73-74 (Paul), 83-84 (Ephesians).

Luke for being 'crude' because 'he shares the enthusiasts' desire for tangibility'.[1] Luke's account also tends to be 'lop-sided' because it does not deal sufficiently with the broader aspects of the religious experience of the community: 'Nowhere is this lop-sidedness more evident than in his complete disregard for the experience of sonship'.[2] In contrast stands Paul, for whom the distinctive mark of the Spirit is his 'Christness'.[3] This was Paul's distinctive contribution, one born out of his personal experience.[4] Yet, in the final analysis, Dunn's work suggests an enormous amount of continuity between Paul and Luke on the Spirit: for both the Spirit initiates the believer into the new age and mediates to him new covenant existence. Thus Dunn marks the unity rather than the diversity of their thought.

Dunn's influence has not been without warrant. He has put forth a carefully argued thesis which moves significantly beyond the earlier work of Büchsel in its sophistication. Dunn integrated a wide knowledge of modern scholarship with an appreciation for some of the difficulties of Büchsel's perspective. By setting Luke's pneumatology against the backdrop of his scheme of salvation history, Dunn shifted the focus from Büchsel's emphasis on 'sonship' to 'initiation into the new age'. Although I shall criticize the major tenets of Dunn's argument,[5] one must acknowledge the significance of Dunn's achievement. He succeeded in raising the argument for continuity to a place of prominence in the modern discussion.

2.3. *Mediating Positions*

2.3.1. *Heinrich von Baer*. H. von Baer's *Der heilige Geist in den Lukasschriften* (1926) can be seen as a two-sided polemic against H. Leisegang, who argued that the pneumatology of the early church reflected widespread Hellenistic influence,[6] and against the conclusions

---

1. *Jesus and the Spirit*, p. 190.
2. *Jesus and the Spirit*, p. 191. See also *Unity and Diversity*, p. 181.
3. *Jesus and the Spirit*, pp. 301-42. See also *Unity and Diversity*, pp. 194-95.
4. *Jesus and the Spirit*, p. 201. See also *Unity and Diversity*, p. 190.
5. Note Dunn's recent reponse, 'Baptism in the Spirit: A Response to Pentecostal Scholarship on Luke-Acts', *JPT* 3 (1993), pp. 3-27. See also my reply, 'Luke and the Spirit: A Reply to James Dunn', *JPT* 4 (1994), pp. 115-38.
6. H. Leisegang, *Der heilige Geist: Das Wesen und Werden der mystisch-intuitiven Erkenntnis in der Philosophie und Religion der Griechen* (1919); and *Pneuma Hagion: Der Ursprung des Geistbegriffs der synoptischen Evangelien aus der griechischen Mystik* (1922). For von Baer's critique of Leisegang, see *Der*

of Gunkel described earlier. Yet von Baer's criticism led to a positive contribution of his own. Noting Luke's interest in the work of the Spirit and salvation history, von Baer asserted that the two themes are inter-related: the Spirit is the driving force behind Luke's scheme of salvation history. This focus on salvation history provided von Baer with a distinc-tively Jewish background against which to set Luke's pneumatology.

Anticipating the views of Hans Conzelmann, von Baer argued that Luke divides salvation history into three distinct epochs.[1] In the first epoch various figures, particularly John the Baptist, are endowed with the Spirit of prophecy in order to announce the coming of the Messiah.[2] The second epoch is inaugurated at Jesus' birth, when 'the Spirit of God as the essence of the Son of God appears in this world'.[3] The third epoch begins with Pentecost, the point at which the Spirit begins to work in the church.[4]

Although von Baer sought to distinguish between the nature of the Spirit's activity in these epochs,[5] nowhere did he work out the distinc-tive features in detail. Rather than highlighting the distinctive aspects of the Spirit's work, von Baer tended to focus on the continuity which existed, particularly in the relationship between the Spirit and proclamation:

> A characteristic of Luke's writings, especially the book of Acts, is that the activity of the Spirit is always directly or indirectly related to the proclama-tion of the gospel.[6]

When von Baer writes that 'the Spirit of Pentecost is the Spirit of mission',[7] he acknowledges that he is describing the work of the Spirit throughout Luke–Acts. This ambiguity concerning the nature of the Spirit's distinctive activity in the various epochs runs throughout von Baer's work. Here, then, is a fundamental tension which von Baer never resolves.

heilige Geist, pp. 13, 110, 138, 161; esp. pp. 112-13, 131.

1. H. Conzelmann, *The Theology of St Luke* (1961). Conzelmann acknowledges his dependence on von Baer, if somewhat inadequately (see F. Bovon, 'Aktuelle Linien lukanischer Forschung', in *Lukas in neuer Sicht* [1985], p. 10).
2. H. von Baer, *Der heilige Geist*, pp. 45-47.
3. *Der heilige Geist*, p. 49. ET is my own.
4. *Der heilige Geist*, pp. 92-93.
5. *Der heilige Geist*, pp. 4, 45, 57-58, 111.
6. *Der heilige Geist*, p. 103. ET is my own.
7. *Der heilige Geist*, p. 103. ET is my own.

This tension is illustrated in von Baer's treatment of Jesus' experience at the Jordan. According to von Baer, Luke edits his sources in order to highlight the parallels between Jesus' experience of the Spirit at his baptism and that of the disciples at Pentecost. In each case the Spirit is primarily the power to preach the gospel.[1] Yet von Baer insists that the two events must be distinguished, for they lie 'in different epochs of salvation history and therefore must be judged by different standards'.[2] Exactly how these events are to be distinguished is never clearly outlined.

The tension inherent in von Baer's work is nowhere more apparent than when he criticizes Gunkel's position.[3] In Acts 2, von Baer declares, we meet 'the Spirit of Pentecost's power for moral renewal'.[4] Support for this statement is elicited from texts where the Spirit is cited as the source of joy (Acts 4.33), fear (Acts 2.43; 5.11) and unity (4.32).[5] Yet, as I have noted, von Baer also puts the accent elsewhere: 'the Spirit of Pentecost is the Spirit of mission'.

In short, von Baer's central thrust in *Der heilige Geist* was not to define the distinctive nature of the Spirit's activity in the various epochs of salvation history, but rather to show that the Spirit is the driving force behind Luke's scheme of salvation history. This, however, produces a certain tension in von Baer's work, one that is never resolved. On the one hand von Baer insists that the Spirit's activity is distinctive in each of the various epochs, but on the other hand he emphasizes the fundamental continuity which binds Luke's pneumatology and scheme of salvation history together. Similarly, von Baer asserts that the Spirit is the source of the moral-religious life of the believer, yet he acknowledges that it is fundamentally the power to proclaim the gospel.[6] One is left with a sense of ambiguity.

In spite of the ambiguity present in von Baer's work, it is noteworthy for several reasons. First, von Baer argued persuasively against Leisegang for the Jewish origin of Luke's pneumatology. Secondly, his emphasis on the Spirit as the driving force in Luke's scheme of salvation history

---

1. *Der heilige Geist*, pp. 57-62, 98-99.
2. *Der heilige Geist*, pp. 57-58. ET is my own.
3. *Der heilige Geist*, pp. 16-19, 100-102, 186-92.
4. *Der heilige Geist*, p. 188. ET is my own.
5. *Der heilige Geist*, pp. 188-90.
6.   This same ambiguity characterizes James Shelton's recent work, *Mighty in Word and Deed* (1991). See R.P. Menzies, 'James Shelton's *Mighty in Word and Deed*: A Review Article', *JPT* 2 (1993), pp. 105-15.

anticipated the work of Conzelmann and Dunn. Thirdly, von Baer's criticisms of Gunkel, coupled with his emphasis on the Spirit as the 'Spirit of mission' (*Missionsgeist*), gave new direction to the discussion concerning the nature of Luke's pneumatology and its relationship to Paul's. Although von Baer himself did not resolve the tension inherent in his work, he did attempt to forge a middle path between Gunkel on the one hand and Büchsel on the other.

2.3.2. Gonzalo Haya-Prats. Written at approximately the same time as Dunn's *Baptism in the Holy Spirit* and independent of it, G. Haya-Prats's *L'Esprit force de l'église* offered conclusions concerning Luke's pneumatology that differed dramatically from those of Dunn.[1] Whereas Dunn portrayed the gift of the Spirit as the climax of conversion-initiation, the source of new covenant existence, Haya-Prats argued that the Spirit was directly related to neither conversion nor salvation. Yet Haya-Prats was not content to restrict Luke's pneumatology as sharply as Gunkel or Schweizer had before him. The Spirit provided more than prophetic power. In this way Haya-Prats took up the tension in von Baer's work and sought to resolve it.

Haya-Prats argues that there are three discernible levels in the history of the composition of Acts. First, there existed a record of Pentecost. Secondly, Luke, the principal author of Luke–Acts, added to this record the accounts of Stephen, Ananias and Sapphira, and Philip, in order to build up gradually to two pericopes of central importance: the record of Cornelius and the Jerusalem Council. These two accounts, shaped by Luke's pen, show the Spirit's decisive intervention in the evangelization of the Gentiles. Thirdly, the remaining sections of Acts were completed and amplified by a second redactor who attempted to imitate the style of Luke. Thus, Haya-Prats asserts that Acts consists of two distinct parts: one written by Luke, the principal author of Luke–Acts, the other produced by a later redactor.[2]

The various layers of tradition and the respective portions of Acts which they represent are distinguished by Haya-Prats according to the manner in which the Spirit's activity is described. Haya-Prats notes that

---

1. G. Haya-Prats, *L'Esprit force de l'église: Sa nature et son activité d'après les Actes des Apôtres* (1975). This work, originally written in Spanish and later published in French, shows no awareness of Dunn's work. Therefore it was probably written around 1970.

2. *Force*, pp. 73-82, 198.

in a number of passages the Spirit is described as working in co-operation with a human agent. The human agent is the subject of an action of which the Spirit is a complementary cause. Haya-Prats terms this mode of activity *influx complémentaire*.[1] However, in other passages the activity of the Spirit is emphasized so strongly that the role of the human agent all but disappears. The Spirit takes complete control, replacing the decisions and actions of the human agent. In these passages the Spirit is often the sole subject of an action. This mode of activity is termed *irruptions absorbantes*.[2] Haya-Prats argues that Luke's redaction in the first part of Acts is dominated by *influx complémentaire* activity. The second part of Acts, however, is characterized by *irruptions absorbantes*, and therefore attributed to a later redactor.[3] For this reason Luke's distinctive pneumatology emerges most clearly from the initial section of Acts and the Gospel of Luke. Above all, three passages stand out as central to Luke's theological concern: Jesus' baptism (Luke 3), the Jerusalem Pentecost (Acts 2) and the Gentile Pentecost (Acts 10).[4]

On the basis of his analysis of the initial portion of Acts, Haya-Prats asserts that Luke does not portray the gift of the Spirit as the climax of conversion-initiation. Three major arguments support Haya-Prats's thesis. First, Haya-Prats argues that Luke does not directly relate the gift of the Spirit to water baptism. Noting that the gift of the Spirit is bestowed apart from (before or after) water baptism, Haya-Prats characterizes the relationship as 'internally independent'.[5] Secondly, Haya-Prats insists that in Luke's scheme initial faith does not result from the gift of the Spirit, rather this faith is a prerequisite for reception of the Spirit.[6] Thirdly, according to Haya-Prats, the Spirit is the source of neither forgiveness nor progressive purification. Rather, 'Luke attributes the total work of salvation to Jesus'.[7]

Positively, Haya-Prats argues that for Luke the Spirit is the source of special power which heightens (*réactivation extraordinaire*) certain aspects of the Christian life already present in the believer.[8] Generally

1. *Force*, pp. 73-78.
2. *Force*, pp. 73-78.
3. *Force*, pp. 73-82.
4. *Force*, pp. 192-93, 203.
5. *Force*, p. 137. ET is my own.
6. *Force*, pp. 125-29, 130.
7. *Force*, p. 125. ET is my own. For this reason Haya-Prats, like Schweizer, does not attribute miracles of healing to the work of the Spirit (pp. 37, 147, 173).
8. *Force*, pp. 138-63. Haya-Prats acknowledges that the Spirit does, at times,

the Spirit gives prophetic direction to the people of God and in this way directs the unfolding plan of God's salvation in history.[1] Yet Haya-Prats distinguishes between two aspects of the Spirit's work: the *historique/ kérygmatic* and the *eschatologique/fruitif*.[2] The *historique/ kérygmatic* dimension of the Spirit provides special power to proclaim the gospel. Haya-Prats limits this dimension to Jesus and the apostles.[3] The *eschatologique/fruitif* dimension of the Spirit, experienced by all believers, serves as a sign or guarantee of salvation. It is an anticipation of the fullness of salvation. Haya-Prats supports these distinctions from his analysis of Lukan texts, particularly the three central passages mentioned previously: Luke 3, Acts 2 and Acts 10.

At his baptism, Jesus experienced the *historique/kérygmatic* dimension of the Spirit: he was anointed with power for his messianic mission. Yet this was not the 'promise of the Spirit'. Only at his exaltation did Jesus receive 'the promise of the Spirit'. This experience of the Spirit at his exaltation was quite different from what Jesus had previously experienced at the Jordan; for, as the Messianic King, he received 'the eschatological gift of the Spirit' and bestowed it on the people of God: Jews (Acts 2) and Gentiles (Acts 10).[4]

For this reason Haya-Prats insists that the *eschatologique/fruitif* dimension of the Spirit is most prominent at Pentecost.[5] The Spirit is received by the disciples as an anticipation of the fullness of salvation. Manifestations of this eschatological anticipation are inspired praise (glossolalia and prophecy) and joy. These manifestations testify that the recipients of the Spirit have been incorporated into the eschatological people of God. They signal the beginning of a new epoch, an end-time

---

have ethical significance for Luke. Yet he denies that the Spirit is the author of sanctification, for the Spirit merely heightens certain Christian characteristics already present in the believer and this is a special occurrence, not representative of ordinary Christian development (p. 147).

1.   *Force*, pp. 165-93. According to Haya-Prats, Luke's understanding of the Spirit is largely shaped by the OT.
2.   *Force*, pp. 165-93, 206-207.
3.   *Force*, pp. 69-70, 169-70, 174-75, 179, 182-83, 187, 193, 206-208. This dimension of the Spirit is, in a sense, also experienced by other members of the hierarchy, such as the seven; yet according to Haya-Prats, they are to be distinguished from the apostles in that they are chosen by the apostles, who remain the leaders of the expansion of the church (e.g. Peter in Acts 10). (See pp. 182-83, 207-208.)
4.   *Force*, pp. 69-70, 170-75.
5.   *Force*, pp. 173-176, 185-89.

era in which salvation is offered to all. The *historique/kérygmatic* dimension of the Spirit is not wholly absent at Pentecost, but it is limited to the apostles.[1]

According to Haya-Prats, Luke highlights the parallels between Acts 2 and Acts 10 in order to emphasize their continuity. As in Acts 2, the *eschatologique/fruitif* dimension of the Spirit is most prominent in Acts 10: 'The Spirit attests that the Gentiles have been sanctified by faith in Jesus without having to observe the law of Moses and, in this way, facilitates their entrance *en masse* into the Church'.[2]

Following von Baer, Haya-Prats views the Spirit in Luke–Acts as the driving force behind salvation history. However, in contrast to von Baer and Dunn, Haya-Prats sharply distinguishes between the work of Jesus and the Spirit in Luke's scheme: salvation is the work of Jesus; the Spirit guides the historical development of salvation history. In this way Luke separated the work of the Spirit from conversion, sanctification and salvation.[3] Thus, according to Haya-Prats, the Spirit neither initiates nor sustains the Christian life in Luke's scheme. In short, the Spirit is not the source of ordinary Christian existence.

It would appear that from Haya-Prats's perspective the pneumatologies of Luke and Paul are radically different. Yet we have seen that Haya-Prats distinguished between two aspects of the Spirit's work. Although Luke at times features the *historique/kérygmatic* dimension of the Spirit's work, the *eschatologique/fruitif* dimension represents the fundamental aspect of Luke's pneumatology.[4] Through his focus on the *eschatologique/fruitif* dimension of the Spirit, Haya-Prats found significant common ground between the pneumatologies of Luke and Paul, while at the same time maintaining that the Spirit for Luke was not the source of ordinary Christian existence. Although I shall question the validity of Haya-Prats's distinction between the *eschatologique/fruitif* and *historique/kérygmatic* dimensions of the Spirit's activity, and particularly his insistence that the latter is limited to the apostles, Haya-Prats represents a significant alternative to the position espoused by Dunn.

2.3.3. *M.M.B. Turner.* M. Turner's contribution to the current discussion comes in the form of a Cambridge PhD dissertation and

1. *Force*, p. 169. See also p. 138.
2. *Force*, p. 192. On Acts 10 see pp. 189-93.
3. *Force*, pp. 201-202.
4. *Force*, p. 200.

several published essays.[1] Like Haya-Prats and von Baer, Turner approached the issue almost exclusively from the Lukan end. Turner's work resembled that of Haya-Prats in many ways. Following Haya-Prats, Turner criticized Dunn's thesis at a number of points, particularly Dunn's insistence that the gift of the Spirit initiated the believer into the new age.[2] Both argued that Luke did not simply equate the gift of the Spirit with salvation.[3] And Turner, like Haya-Prats, insisted that the gift of the Spirit for Luke offered more than simply power to proclaim the gospel.[4] Here, however, is where the paths of Turner and Haya-Prats diverge. Haya-Prats had argued that the gift of the Spirit had two aspects, neither of which related directly to ordinary Christian existence. Turner, on the other hand, insisted that for Luke the Pentecostal gift was the means of communication between the Lord and his disciples. Therefore the gift of the Spirit was, in Luke's perspective, essential for Christian existence (after Pentecost).[5] Turner and Haya-Prats sought to resolve the tension in von Baer's work and build a bridge between the schools of Gunkel and Büchsel. Whereas Haya-Prats's solution had more

---

1. M.M.B. Turner, 'Luke and the Spirit: Studies in the Significance of Receiving the Spirit in Luke–Acts' (1980). Other works of Turner related to the subject include: 'The Significance of Spirit Endowment for Paul', *VE* 9 (1975), pp. 56-69; 'Spirit Endowment in Luke–Acts: Some Linguistic Considerations', *VE* 12 (1981), pp. 45-63; 'Jesus and the Spirit in Lucan Perspective', *TynBul* 32 (1981), pp. 3-42; 'The Spirit of Christ and Christology', in *Christ the Lord* (1982), pp. 168-90; 'Spiritual Gifts then and now', *VE* 15 (1985), pp. 7-64; 'The Spirit of Prophecy and the Power of Authoritative Preaching in Luke–Acts: A Question of Origins', *NTS* 38 (1992), pp. 66-88.

2. 'Luke and the Spirit', pp. 148-55.

3. 'Luke and the Spirit', pp. 178-79.

4. 'Luke and the Spirit', pp. 159, 183-84.

5. See 'Spirit Endowment in Luke–Acts', p. 59; 'Jesus and the Spirit', p. 39; 'Spiritual Gifts', pp. 40-41; and 'Christology', pp. 180-81. Turner's thought appears to have undergone a process of development at this point. In 'Luke and the Spirit', Turner suggests that one need not personally receive the gift of the Spirit in order to live as a Christian in relationship to God: Christian existence can be maintained through responding to the charismata manifest through others (see p. 178 and esp. p. 184). He does however assert that the gift of the Spirit is received by each individual Christian after Pentecost (p. 159). In the subsequent essays cited above Turner seems to view reception of the gift as an essential element of individual Christian experience. Thus he maintains that it is the *sine qua non* of Christian existence (e.g. 'Spiritual Gifts', p. 41).

affinities with Gunkel's school, Turner identified more closely with Büchsel and his followers.

Through detailed analysis of relevant Lukan texts, Turner sought to answer the question: 'What activity (or nexus of activities) of the divine Spirit is being thought to be communicated to the disciple (or initiated in him) when he "receives the Spirit"?'[1] Turner's answer to this question is shaped largely by his assertion that Luke thought of the Spirit in terms of the Jewish Spirit of prophecy:

> In the Spirit of prophecy the early church had a concept which could readily be adapted to speak of its new sense of immediate awareness of God, and of communication with him, and, at the same time to refer to the charismatic character of much of its corporate worship.[2]

According to Turner, the essential function of the Spirit in Judaism, as the Spirit of prophecy, was to reveal God's message to his prophet. Criticizing Schweizer's position, Turner maintains that the Spirit as the power to preach the gospel 'bears little relationship to any "typical Jewish idea" of the Spirit of prophecy'.[3] The Old Testament and the literature of late Judaism[4] indicate, according to Turner, that:

> The proper sphere of activity of the Spirit of prophecy is thus not the imparting of charismatic character or authority in the delivery of a message, but usually in the prior revelation to the prophet of the content of the message to be delivered as an oracle, or preached about. Prophecy and preaching may overlap; but the activity of the Spirit of prophecy, and the Spirit's empowering of the preacher in his preaching, are complementary, not congruent roles.[5]

Turner interprets Luke as modifying and broadening this Jewish understanding. For Luke, the function of the Spirit of prophecy is varied: the Spirit grants wisdom, reveals the will of God, edifies the community through χαρίσματα, and inspires preaching and praise.[6] On the basis of

---

1. 'Luke and the Spirit', p. 35.
2. 'Luke and the Spirit', p. 134.
3. 'Luke and the Spirit', p. 65.
4. Turner maintained that 'the Spirit of prophecy as understood by apocalyptic Judaism, Qumran, rabbinic Judaism, and even Philo, remains roughly within the guidelines of the OT concept' ('Luke and the Spirit', p. 66).
5. 'Luke and the Spirit', p. 66.
6. 'Spirit Endowment in Luke–Acts', p. 58. Turner discusses the evolution of thought concerning the Spirit of prophecy in Judaism and modifications by the early Christians in 'Luke and the Spirit', pp. 66-67, 130-34, 178-80.

his criticism of Schweizer, Turner also affirms that the Spirit is the source of miracles of healings and exorcisms.[1] The extent to which Luke, in Turner's perspective, has broadened the Jewish concept is seen most clearly in his understanding of the gift of the Spirit at Pentecost:

> Quite clearly, after the ascension, this gift promised by Peter is a *sine qua non* of Christian existence. The man who knows the presence of the Lord; who experiences Jesus speaking to him in his heart...any such man owes all this to the Spirit experienced as what Luke means by the Spirit of prophecy promised by Joel.[2]

In short, according to Turner the Spirit of prophecy is, for Luke, fundamentally 'the organ of communication' between God and humanity.[3]

Yet Turner, like Haya-Prats, distinguishes between the way in which the Spirit functions in Jesus' ministry and that of the disciples, between Jesus' experience of the Spirit at the Jordan and that of the disciples at Pentecost.

Turner asserts that Jesus' experience of the Spirit at the Jordan was essentially a prophetic anointing, an endowment of power to carry out his messianic duties.[4] Jesus' Jordan experience does not provide him with power for moral renewal or some new existential awareness of sonship. This resulted from Jesus' miraculous birth. At the Jordan, Jesus is anointed with power to fulfill his role as the eschatological herald, the end-time Moses, who announces and brings liberation to Israel.[5] Therefore, Turner argues that the primary function of the Spirit, as the Spirit of prophecy, is not to reveal divine messages to Jesus; rather, the Spirit empowers his word so that it can be revealed to others.[6] In short, Jesus receives the Spirit for others.

However, the experience of the disciples at Pentecost is not to be equated with that of Jesus at the Jordan. Speaking of the disciples, Turner writes, 'It would be hollow to assert that they receive the "same" Spirit [as Jesus]'.[7] Although, according to Turner, the disciples before

---

1.   'Luke and the Spirit', pp. 66-67, 139-46.
2.   'Spiritual Gifts', p. 41.
3.   'Spiritual Gifts', p. 40. See also 'Luke and the Spirit', p. 185, where Turner speaks of the Spirit as the 'organ of revelation' to the disciples.
4.   'Luke and the Spirit', pp. 53, 56-57, 73, 76, 81, 93, 158, 180-81.
5.   'Luke and the Spirit', p. 85: Turner, on the basis of Lk. 4.1, 14 argues that Luke portrays Jesus as the eschatological Moses. See also 'Christology', pp. 176-79.
6.   'Luke and the Spirit', pp. 180-84.
7.   'Luke and the Spirit', p. 185. See also 'Jesus and the Spirit', pp. 28-33.

Pentecost had already begun to experience the Spirit during the ministry of Jesus,[1] with the exalted Jesus' reception and subsequent bestowal of the Spirit on the disciples a new nexus of the Spirit's activity is unleashed:

> The gift of the Spirit is the means by which the now ascended Jesus can continue to bring the blessings of messianic ἄφεσις, or salvation, to his church, and through it to the world. Without such a gift there could be no christianity after the ascension except as a lingering memory of what had happened in Jesus' day. The Spirit of prophecy, as Luke understands it, is the vitality of the community both in its witness to Jesus and in its own religious life.[2]

In view of this distinction, Turner insists that the gift of the Spirit at Pentecost is not primarily an empowering for mission; this is 'merely one possible sphere... Luke places at least equal emphasis on the Spirit as the organ of revelation to the disciples'.[3] Whereas Jesus received the Spirit for others, the disciples received the Spirit, to a significant extent, for themselves.

Thus, from Pentecost on, the Spirit enlivens the community, providing the link between the ascended Lord and his church. Yet this does not mean that Luke portrays the gift of the Spirit as the source of salvation *in toto*. Turner offers detailed criticism of Dunn's thesis that, for Luke, the gift mediates to its recipient the blessings of the new covenant to the believer. The gift of the Spirit is 'not the matrix of new covenant life, but an important element within it'.[4] On the basis of his analysis of Acts 8.4-24, Turner concludes:

> The very fact of the separation of baptism from receiving the Spirit here, and the characteristics of Luke's description, favour the view that he did not identify receiving the Spirit as the gift of messianic salvation itself, but as one particular nexus within it: the christian version of judaism's hope for the Spirit of prophecy.[5]

Turner, like Schweizer and Haya-Prats before him, emphasized the importance of the Jewish concept of the Spirit of prophecy for Luke's pneumatology. Yet through his criticism of Schweizer's analysis of the Spirit of prophecy in Judaism, and his description of Luke's modification

1. 'Luke and the Spirit', pp. 96-116; especially pp. 108-109, 115-16.
2. 'Luke and the Spirit', p. 159.
3. 'Luke and the Spirit', p. 185.
4. 'Luke and the Spirit', p. 155. See pp. 148-55 for Turner's criticism of Dunn at this point.
5. 'Luke and the Spirit', p. 170.

of the concept, Turner raised new questions concerning the significance of this concept for Luke and offered a stimulating and new analysis of Luke's pneumatology. For Luke, the Spirit is neither the matrix of new covenant existence nor a *donum superadditum*. Rather the Spirit, as the Spirit of prophecy, is the means of communication between God and man: essential for Christian existence yet not identical with it.

3. *The Thesis*

The survey presented above has revealed that apart from the essays by Schweizer and Hill, which were by design general overviews and thus lacking in detailed argumentation, all of the major post-Gunkel studies have affirmed the relative homogeneity of the pneumatology of the early church. It is generally asserted that the soteriological dimension of the Spirit's activity which is so prominent in Paul's epistles was, to a significant extent, already an integral part of the pneumatology of the primitive church (Büchsel, Dunn). Furthermore, it is argued that this perspective exerted considerable influence on Luke. Thus Luke is said to have viewed the gift of the Spirit as the source of cleansing and moral transformation (Dunn, von Baer),[1] the essential bond which links the individual Christian to God (Turner), and a foretaste of the salvation to come (Haya-Prats).

In the following study I shall challenge these conclusions. I shall seek to establish that Luke never attributes soteriological functions to the Spirit and that his narrative presupposes a pneumatology which excludes this dimension (e.g. Luke 11.13; Acts 8.4-17; 19:1-7). More specifically, I shall argue that Luke consistently portrays the Spirit as the source of prophetic inspiration, which (by granting special insight and inspiring speech) empowers God's people for effective service. Two interrelated arguments will be offered in support of this thesis.

In Part One I shall argue that soteriological functions were generally not attributed to the Spirit in intertestamental Judaism. The Spirit was regarded as the source of prophetic inspiration, a *donum superadditum* granted to various individuals so they might fulfill a divinely appointed

---

1. See also J. Kremer, *Pfingstbericht und Pfingstgeschehen: Eine exegetische Untersuchung zur Apg 2,1-13* (1973), pp. 177-79, 197, 219-220, 273; G.W.H. Lampe, *God as Spirit: The Bampton Lectures, 1976* (1977), pp. 64-72; J.H.E. Hull, *The Holy Spirit in the Acts of the Apostles* (1967), pp. 45-46, 53-55, 143-68.

task. The only significant exceptions to this perspective are found in later sapiential writings (1QH, Wisdom).

In Part Two I shall argue that Luke, influenced by the dominant Jewish perception, consistently portrays the gift of the Spirit as a prophetic endowment which enables its recipient to participate effectively in the mission of God. Although the primitive church, following in the footsteps of Jesus, broadened the functions traditionally ascribed to the Spirit in first-century Judaism and thus presented the Spirit as the source of miracle-working power (as well as prophetic inspiration), Luke resisted this innovation. For Luke, the Spirit remained the source of special insight and inspired speech. The important corollary is that neither Luke nor the primitive church attributes soteriological significance to the pneumatic gift in a manner analogous to Paul. Thus I shall distinguish Luke's 'prophetic' pneumatology from the 'charismatic' perspective of the primitive church on the one hand, and Paul's 'soteriological' understanding of the Spirit on the other.

In Part Three I shall draw out the implications of my findings for questions generated by the emergence of the Pentecostal movement. Specifically, I shall discuss the significance of Luke's pneumatology for classical Pentecostal perspectives on Spirit-baptism: the doctrine that Spirit-baptism is an experience 'subsequent to and distinct from' conversion; and that glossolalia is the 'initial physical evidence' of this experience.

Finally, by way of conclusion, I shall summarize my findings.

Part I

PNEUMATOLOGICAL PERSPECTIVES
IN INTERTESTAMENTAL JUDAISM

INTRODUCTION

Articles and books extolling the virtues of Jewish studies for the interpretation of the New Testament are legion. The voluminous writings of Jacob Neusner, along with the productive pens of Geza Vermes and E.P. Sanders, have not only brought renewed interest and controversy to Jewish studies, they have also heightened the awareness of the field's significance for the study of the New Testament. Today everyone would affirm that 'Jesus was a Jew'.[1] The important corollary for this study is that the first Christians who thought through the significance of their experience of the Spirit did so in light of their Jewish background. Indeed, due to the early efforts of H. Gunkel, F. Büchsel and H. von Baer, it is now recognized that Judaism provided the conceptual framework for the pneumatological reflection of Luke and the primitive church before him. For this reason my inquiry into the character of Luke's pneumatology begins with a survey of the various pneumatological perspectives which were current in intertestamental Judaism.

In order to facilitate the analysis, I have arranged the sources into four groups: diaspora literature, Palestinian literature, Qumran literature and rabbinic literature. Although diaspora and Palestinian sources can be distinguished on the basis of language and geography, the significance of these distinctions, as will become apparent, should not be over-emphasized. Martin Hengel has established that from the middle of the third century BC 'Jewish Palestine was no hermetically sealed island in the sea of Hellenistic oriental syncretism'.[2] Clearly firm lines of demarcation cannot be drawn simply on the basis of language and geography.

1. G. Vermes, 'Jewish Studies and New Testament Interpretation', *JJS* 31 (1980), p. 1: 'It is, I am sure, no surprise to you, as it was to many readers of the great German biblical scholar Julius Wellhausen, at the beginning of this century, to hear that Jesus was not a Christian, but a Jew'. See also G. Vermes, *Jesus the Jew: A Historian's Reading of the Gospels* (1973).
2. M. Hengel, *Judaism and Hellenism* (1974), I, p. 312. See also Davies, *Paul*, pp. 1-16; and D.E. Aune, *Prophecy in Early Christianity and the Ancient Mediterranean World* (1983), p. 16.

Chapter 2

THE DIASPORA LITERATURE*

1. *The Septuagint*

With their tendency to translate רוח of the Hebrew Scriptures with πνεῦμα, the LXX translators added new dimensions to the term. Whereas in Greek thought, with the notable exception of Stoicism,

* The sources examined include those writings produced during the intertestamental period in regions outside of Palestine and written originally in Greek: Additions to Esther; Additions to Daniel (i.e. The Prayer of Azarias, The Hymn of the Three Young Men, The History of Susanna, and Bel and the Dragon); The Prayer of Manasseh; The Epistle of Jeremiah; Demetrius; Eupolemus; Artapanus; Cleodemus; Philo the Epic Poet; Theodotus; Ezekiel the Tragedian; Aristobulus; *Sibylline Oracles* 3.98-808; Pseudo-Hecataeus; Pseudo-Phocylides; *2 Enoch*; *3 Baruch*; *3 Maccabees*; *4 Maccabees*; *Letter of Aristeas*; Wisdom; the writings of Philo Judaeus; the writings of Flavius Josephus; the Alexandrian Text (K) of the Greek Old Testament (the LXX); *Treatise of Shem* (although *Treatise of Shem* was probably originally written in either Hebrew or Aramaic, I list it among the diaspora literature due to its provenance, which, according to J.H. Charlesworth, was probably Alexandria [*Pseudepigrapha*, I, p. 475]); *Apocryphon of Ezekiel*; *Apocalypse of Zephaniah*; *Testament of Job*; *Ladder of Jacob*; *Prayer of Joseph*; *Orphica*; Fragments of Pseudo-Greek Poets; Aristeas the Exegete; Pseudo-Eupolemus. *Joseph and Aseneth* has been excluded from consideration due to its possible second-century AD (or later) origin and evidence of Christian interpolations. See T. Holtz, 'Christliche Interpolationen in "Joseph und Aseneth"', *NTS* 14 (1967–1968), pp. 482-97.

Subsections which focus on a single author are arranged (with the exception of Josephus) in chronological order. These works may be dated as follows: (1) LXX (third century BC). The *Letter of Aristeas* places the writing of the LXX during the reign of King Ptolemy II Philadelphus (284–247 BC). Although the legendary nature of the account is not to be disputed, the date of composition is likely close to the mark. (2) The writings of Josephus (c. 90 AD). This date is widely recognized and confirmed by Josephus's own hand. (3) Wisdom of Solomon (first century BC). The dating of Wisdom remains a matter of dispute. Although Wisdom is generally placed in the first century BC, possible dates range from the mid-second century BC to the mid-first century AD. (4) The writings of Philo (c. 25 BC). This date is commonly accepted and substantiated by autobiographical comments.

πνεῦμα was not usually associated with God and confined to such concepts as 'wind, breath, and air', in the LXX the association with divinity becomes quite common. Similarly, although the Greeks frequently alluded to prophetic inspiration, they rarely connected this inspiration with πνεῦμα.[1] However, in the LXX the πνεῦμα of God is routinely depicted as the source of prophetic inspiration. Indeed, apart from the inspiration of the Spirit, genuine prophecy is an impossibility. For the translators of the LXX the characteristic activity of the Spirit was prophecy (e.g. Num. 11.25-26; 1 Kgdms 10.6-7; Ezek. 2.2-3). The close association between the Spirit and prophetic activity is particularly evident in two instances where πνεῦμα is inserted into the text although in the MT רוח is conspicuously absent:

1. In Num. 23.7, just before Balaam utters his prophecy, the LXX inserts the phrase: καὶ ἐγενήθη πνεῦμα θεοῦ ἐπ' αὐτῷ.[2] The phrase ותהי עליו רוח אלהים ('and the Spirit of God came upon him') does occur in the MT at 24.2 with reference to Balaam. Thus, the LXX translator has picked up this phrase and not only translated it as it appears in 24.2, but also inserted it into 23.7, showing his penchant for attributing prophecy to the Spirit.

2. In Zech. 1.6, the word of the Lord came to Zechariah: 'But do you receive my words and my decrees, all that I command by my Spirit (ἐν πνεύματί μου) to my servants the prophets?' The phrase ἐν πνεύματί μου is absent from the MT and indicates how closely this particular translator associated prophetic inspiration with the Spirit.

In short, the concept of πνεῦμα is given broader definition through its association with רוח of the MT. Of primary importance for this study is the way in which various translators of the LXX equate prophetic inspiration with the activity of the Spirit.

2. *Diaspora Judaism: Various Texts*

Although the activity of the Spirit is not a prominent theme in much of the Hellenistic Jewish literature of the intertestamental period, there are scattered references outside of Josephus, Philo and Wisdom which deserve attention.

---

1. M. Isaacs, *The Concept of Spirit* (1976), p. 15.
2. All texts of the LXX cited are from A. Rahlfs, *Septuaginta* (1979).

2.1. The Spirit as the Source of Prophetic Inspiration
When reference is made in this literature[1] to the divine πνεῦμα, it almost always appears as the source of prophetic activity (inspiring speech or granting special knowledge). For Aristobulus, prophecy and Spirit-inspiration are inextricably bound together. Eusebius records his claim that intelligent people 'marvel at the wisdom of Moses and at the divine Spirit in accordance with which he has been proclaimed as a prophet also (καθ' ὃ καὶ προφήτης ἀνακεκήρυκται)'.[2] The κατά-clause indicates that Moses was proclaimed a prophet because of the marvelous activity of the Spirit in his life.

In the History of Susanna the story is told of how young Daniel, equipped with special insight and wisdom, was able to expose the treachery of two witnesses whose false testimony had condemned Susanna of adultery. The LXX attributes this special wisdom to an Angel, who gave a 'spirit of understanding' (πνεῦμα συνέσεως) to young Daniel (LXX, Sus. 45). However, Theodotion alters the LXX reading and attributes Daniel's special insight directly to the Holy Spirit. According to Theodotion, 'God stirred the Holy Spirit' (ἐξήγειρεν ὁ θεὸς τὸ πνεῦμα τὸ ἅγιον) already present in Daniel (Theodotion, Sus. 45). There is no mention here of angelic mediation of the knowledge. Both angelic assistance (Dan. 9.21; 10.5) and the power of the Spirit (Dan. 4.9, 18; 5.11) are associated with the adult Daniel. Apparently the former tradition was picked up by the author of the LXX reading and the latter by Theodotion.[3]

One Greek manuscript of *T. Job* 43.2 attributes Eliphas's recital of a hymn to the inspiration of the Spirit.[4] Inspired praise is also associated with the Spirit in 48.3:

---

1. 'This literature' includes all those works cited as sources for diaspora Judaism in the introductory section, excluding those works dealt with separately: the LXX, Josephus, the works of Philo, and Wisdom.
2. Fragment 2 of Aristobulus in Eusebius, *Praeparatio Evangelica* 8.10.4; ET from A. Yarbro Collins, 'Aristobulus', in Charlesworth, *Pseudepigrapha*, II, p. 838; Greek text cited is from A.-M. Denis, *Fragmenta Pseudepigraphorum Quae Supersunt Graeca* (1970), p. 218.
3. This hypothesis is put forward by C.A. Moore, *Daniel, Esther, and Jeremiah: The Additions* (2nd edn, 1978), p. 108.
4. See R.P. Spittler, 'Testament of Job', in Charlesworth, *Pseudepigrapha*, I, p. 861 n. a on ch. 43.

She [Hemera] spoke ecstatically in the angelic dialect, sending up a hymn to God in accord with the hymnic style of the angels. And as she spoke ecstatically, she allowed 'The Spirit' to be inscribed on her garment.[1]

We have seen that isolated diaspora texts, in a manner consistent with the translators of the LXX, present the Spirit as the source of prophetic activity. The only exceptions depict the divine πνεῦμα as the breath of God which gives physical life to all humans. Thus we read: 'the Spirit is a loan of God (θεοῦ χρῆσις) to mortals' (Ps.-Phoc. 106).[2] *2 Enoch* lists seven components of the human being. The seventh is 'his spirit from my [God's] spirit and from wind' (30.8).[3]

The lack of Spirit references in other contexts indicates that experience of the Spirit was virtually identified with prophetic inspiration. Although *Pr. Man.* 7b-15 is similar to Ps. 51.1-14 in both structure and content,[4] the text is silent concerning the Spirit. Ps. 51.11a, 'do not banish me', is paralleled in v. 13 of the *Prayer*, but Ps. 51.11b, 'do not take your Holy Spirit from me', is remarkably absent.

2.2. Wisdom, the Law, and Reason: the Source of True Religion
Esoteric wisdom can be associated with the inspiration of the Spirit in the diaspora literature (e.g. Theodotion, Sus. 45). However, at a more fundamental level wisdom is virtually identified with rational study of the Law. This is certainly the case in the definition of wisdom we read in *4 Macc.* 1.15-19:

> Reason, I suggest, is the mind making a deliberate choice of the life of wisdom. Wisdom (σοφία), I submit, is knowledge of things divine and human, and of their causes. And this wisdom, I assume, is the culture we acquire from the Law (αὕτη δὴ τοίνυν ἐστιν ἡ τοῦ νόμου παιδεία), through which we learn the things of God reverently and the things of men to our worldly advantage. The forms of wisdom consist of prudence,

---

1. ET from Spittler, 'Testament of Job', p. 866.
2. ET from P.W. van der Horst, 'Pseudo-Phocylides', in Charlesworth, *Pseudepigrapha*, II, p. 578; Greek text from Denis, *Fragmenta Pseudepigraphorum Graeca*, p. 152.
3. ET from F.I. Andersen, '2 (Slavonic Apocalypse of) Enoch', in Charlesworth, *Pseudepigrapha*, I, p. 151. Extant manuscripts of *2 Enoch* are only available in Slavonic, therefore the underlying Greek text is unavailable.
4. For the parallels between Prayer of Manasseh and Psalm 51 see Charlesworth, *Pseudepigrapha*, II, p. 630.

justice, courage, and temperance. Of all these prudence (φρόνησις) is the most authoritative, for it is through it that reason controls the passions (ἐξ ἧς δὴ τῶν παθῶν ὁ λογισμὸς ἐπικρατεῖ).[1]

In this text the source of wisdom is the instruction of the law (ἡ τοῦ νόμου παιδεία). The most significant outworking of wisdom is φρόνησις, for through 'prudence' the passions are controlled by reason. Similarly the link between the law and the intellect (νοῦς) is made in 2.23, 'To the intellect he gave the Law, and if a man lives his life by the Law he shall reign over a kingdom that is temperate and just and good and brave'. Here again the virtues of wisdom result as the mind or intellect follows after the law.[2]

The entire book of *4 Maccabees* extols the triumph of reason over the passions. Eleazer, the seven sons and their mother, all tortured and killed by Antiochus for not eating unclean food, are offered as examples of the triumph of reason over passion, of the victory of true religion centered on the law. The martyrs are vindicated, for resurrection is the ultimate reward of such a life (17.18; 18.18; 18.23).

According to the author of *4 Maccabees*, the source of true religion is the intellect informed by the Law rather than the illumination of the Spirit. Thus, while esoteric wisdom is attributed to the Spirit in the literature, sapiential achievement at a more fundamental level is associated with rational study of Torah, independent of Spirit-illumination.

2.3. *Sources of Miraculous Power*

Although prophetic activity is frequently attributed to the agency of the Spirit, miraculous events not associated with inspired speech or special revelation are always attributed to other sources: angels, the name of God and God himself. According to the Hymn of the Three Young Men, an angel of the Lord saved the Hebrew men from the heat of the furnace (LXX: Dan. 3.49). It is also an angel who carries Enoch away into the highest heaven (*2 En.* 67.2).

Artapanus attributes miraculous power to the will of God and the divine name. He records how Moses, who had requested the release of his people, was locked in prison by the king of Egypt. When night came, according to Eusebius's account, 'all of the doors of the prison opened of themselves' (*Pr. Ev.* 9.27.23). Clement of Alexandria, however, says

---

1.   ET from H. Anderson, '4 Maccabees', in Charlesworth, *Pseudepigrapha*, II, p. 545.
2.   See also 18.1-2.

54   Empowered for Witness

the prison was opened at night 'by the will of God' (κατὰ βούλησιν
τοῦ θεοῦ; *Stromata* 1.154.2).[1] Moses went to the palace of the king and
woke him. Frightened, the king ordered Moses to declare the name of
the God who had sent him. Eusebius then records these climactic events:

> He bent forward and pronounced it [the divine name] into his ear. When
> the king heard it, he fell down speechless (ἀκούσαντα δὲ τὸν Βασιλέα
> πεσεῖν ἄφωνον) (*Pr. Ev.* 9.27.25).[2]

3. Josephus

When citing the Old Testament, Josephus retains the usage of πνεῦμα
with reference to wind and breath. However, he is reluctant to employ
πνεῦμα with reference to the spirit of humanity, and this usage virtually
disappears. When πνεῦμα refers to God, Josephus is much more apt to
retain it, although he does prefer πνεῦμα θεῖον to the πνεῦμα θεοῦ of
the LXX. Of special importance for this study is the significance Josephus
attaches to πνεῦμα as the Spirit of God. Josephus has left us important
clues concerning his own perception of the role of the Spirit of God
through his alterations of the Old Testament text. To these clues I now
turn.

3.1. Additions of πνεῦμα to the LXX and/or MT

On four occasions Josephus inserts πνεῦμα into texts where it is not
present in the MT or the LXX, but is found in the immediate context. In
Ant. 4.108, citing Num. 22.15-16, Josephus introduces the idea that
Balaam's ass was conscious of the πνεῦμα of God. The Spirit draws
near to the ass and the ass then begins to speak with a human voice.
Although the MT (24.2) and the LXX (23.7; 24.2) refer to the Spirit
coming upon Balaam, neither speaks of the Spirit with reference to the
ass. Josephus thus adds the idea that the speech of the ass, like the
prophecy of Balaam, was inspired by the divine πνεῦμα. Similarly, in
Ant. 4.119-20, Josephus alters the MT and LXX reading of Num. 23.12
so that Balaam's prophetic speech is attributed to the πνεῦμα θεοῦ
rather than to God. Josephus's text emphasizes the passivity of Balaam
and the compulsion of the Spirit. In *Ant.* 6.166, Josephus expands the

1.   ET from J.J. Collins, 'Artapanus', in Charlesworth, *Pseudepigrapha*, II, p. 901.
Greek text from Denis, *Fragmenta Pseudepigraphorum Graeca*, p. 192.
2.   The text of Clement of Alexandria at this point is almost identical. Greek text
is from Denis, *Fragmenta Pseudepigraphorum Graeca*, pp. 192-93.

account of the Spirit's transfer from Saul to David (1 Kgdms 16.13-14) by noting that David began to prophesy when the Spirit came upon him. And in an interpretative retelling of 1 Kgs 22.21-25, one of Josephus's characters declares, 'you shall know whether he is really a true prophet and has the power of the divine Spirit' (καὶ τοῦ θείου πνεύματος ἔχει τὴν δύναμιν; *Ant.* 8.408).[1]

In each addition cited above, the πνεῦμα of God is portrayed as the source of prophecy. This is even more striking when it is noted that in those passages where Josephus retains the biblical reference to the Spirit, all but one (*Ant.* 1.27 = Gen. 1.2) refer to the divine πνεῦμα as the source of prophetic inspiration.[2] However, Josephus never speaks of contemporary prophets as being inspired by the Spirit. He was undoubtedly convinced that prophecy inspired by the Spirit was a thing of the past.

There is one addition of the divine πνεῦμα into an Old Testament context in which reference to the Spirit is wholly lacking. *Ant.* 8.114 (1 Kgs 8.27-30) records Solomon's entreaty to the Lord, 'send some portion of your Spirit to dwell in the temple'. Josephus may have interpreted Solomon's request as a plea for the bestowal of the prophetic gift upon the temple priests. Or possibly, as Ernest Best suggests, Josephus replaced 'Shekinah', a term that would have been strange to Greeks, with πνεῦμα.[3]

3.2. *Omission and Interpretation of* πνεῦμα

Josephus not only adds references concerning God's πνεῦμα to Old Testament texts; he also omits such references, replacing them with interpretative comments. In a number of passages where the LXX explicitly speaks of the Spirit coming upon individuals, Josephus alters the text to say that they prophesied. Thus while in Judg. 13.25 we read of Samson, 'the Spirit of the Lord began to stir him', in *Ant.* 5.285 Josephus writes, 'it was clear...that he was to be a prophet'. Similarly Joshua (*Ant.* 4.165 = Num. 27.18), Azariah (*Ant.* 8.295 = 2 Chron.

---

1. All citations from Josephus (English and Greek) are from H.J. Thackeray (ed.), *Josephus* (LCL, 1926–1965).

2. E. Best justifiably downplays the significance of this lone exception: 'In 1. 27 πνεῦμα plays no clear role; loyalty to such an important passage of Scripture demands its retention; a Greek could easily take it to mean "wind" or "breath"' ('The Use and Non-Use of Pneuma by Josephus', *NovT* 3 [1959], p. 223).

3. Best, 'Josephus', p. 223.

15.1), Zechariah (*Ant.* 9.168 = 2 Chron. 24.20), and Jahaziel (*Ant.* 9.10 = 2 Chron. 20.14) all prophesy.

It is noteworthy that Samson, who was endowed with special strength to defeat the Philistines, is called a prophet by Josephus (*Ant.* 5.285). Here Josephus used the term 'prophet' in a rather broad way. This usage appears to suggest that Josephus attributed the working of miracles and great exploits of strength to the Spirit. However, Josephus's omission of the Spirit in contexts where miracles and special exploits are mentioned indicates that this is not the case. According to Judg. 14.6, the Spirit of the Lord came upon Samson and enabled him to tear apart a lion. Yet in *Ant.* 5.287 no mention is made of the activity of the Spirit. Again in Judg. 14.19 Samson, inspired by the Spirit, is said to have killed thirty Philistines; the record of this story in *Ant.* 5.294 omits any reference to the Spirit. According to Judg. 15.14-15, the Spirit of the Lord enabled Samson to break his bonds and kill a thousand Philistines with the jawbone of an ass. Yet in *Ant.* 5.301 the feat is attributed simply to 'the assistance of God' (θεοῦ συνεργίαν). Other exploits, such as the miraculous transportation of Elijah (*Ant.* 8.333 = 1 Kgs 18.12), the interpretation of dreams by Joseph (*Ant.* 2.87 = Gen. 41.38), and the special skills given to craftsmen (*Ant.* 3.200 = Exod. 28.3; 32.3; 35.31), although attributed to the Spirit in the LXX, are not explicitly connected with the divine πνεῦμα by Josephus.[1]

The omission of πνεῦμα in these texts indicates that Josephus viewed the Spirit exclusively as the source of esoteric wisdom and inspired speech. This perspective is consistent with the close association between the Spirit and prophecy we find elsewhere in Josephus' writings. For prophecy is the transmission of esoteric wisdom through inspired speech. Josephus's perspective also conforms to the general pattern of Jewish thought in the intertestamental period. The actions of the prophet were not limited to oracular prophecy by either Josephus (e.g. Samson, *Ant.* 5.285) or his contemporaries (*Ant.* 20.167-68; *War* 2.259). Indeed, Josephus ridicules leaders of revolutionary movements as 'false prophets' who promised to perform legitimating miracles (*Ant.* 20.168). Nevertheless, the Jewish authors of the period, like Josephus, exhibit a remarkable reluctance to attribute miraculous deeds to the Spirit.

---

1. See F. Manns, *Le symbole eau-esprit* (1983), p. 147 n. 33; and Best, 'Josephus', pp. 224-25.

4. *Wisdom of Solomon*

The author of Wisdom employs πνεῦμα with a variety of meanings. The term refers to breath or wind,[1] a permeating force which 'fills the world' and holds all things together (Wis. 1.7), the source of physical life, and the source of wisdom. The references to πνεῦμα which fall into the latter two categories shall form the basis of this analysis.

4.1. πνεῦμα *as the Source of Physical Life*

As the source of physical life, πνεῦμα refers to a permanent gift which God grants to every human at creation. The author of Wisdom states that God's 'immortal Spirit' (τὸ ἄφθαρτον πνεῦμα) is in everyone (12.1). Thus he chastizes the idol-maker, 'because he never came to know the God who shaped him, who inspired him with an active soul and breathed into him a living spirit' (πνεῦμα ζωτικόν; 15.11), and repudiates idolatry, for idols are made by a person 'who borrowed his spirit' (τὸ πνεῦμα δεδανεισμένος; 15.16).

4.2. πνεῦμα *as the Source of Wisdom*

The author of Wisdom also identifies the Spirit of God with the wisdom of God. He uses the terms πνεῦμα and σοφία interchangeably (Wis. 1.4-7; 9.17), refers to the 'spirit of wisdom' (πνεῦμα σοφίας; 7.7; cf. 7.22), and describes wisdom as 'a breath of God's power' (ἀτμὶς...τῆς τοῦ θεοῦ δυνάμεως; 7.25). He also transfers functions normally reserved for the Spirit to wisdom. The Spirit is frequently cited in the diaspora literature as the source of special insight granted to leaders (*Amtscharisma*).[2] Nevertheless, in Wisdom this role is taken over by wisdom; wisdom made Joseph the ruler of Egypt (10.14) and enabled Moses to stand up to Pharaoh (10.16). Prophecy, elsewhere in the literature attributed to the inspiration of the Spirit, is also associated with wisdom (7.27; 11.1). It is therefore difficult to distinguish between πνεῦμα and σοφία. However, as R. Scroggs notes, several texts suggest that 'σοφία is more the content of revelation, while πνεῦμα is the means by which this content is revealed'.[3] Thus it appears that the

---

1. For πνεῦμα as breath see Wis. 2.3; 5.3; and 11.20. For πνεῦμα as wind or air see Wis. 5.11, 23; 7.20; 13.2; 17.18.
2. See for example Josephus, *Ant.* 6.166 (1 Kgdms 16.13-14) and Philo, *Gig.* 24 (Num. 11.17).
3. R. Scroggs, 'Paul: ΣΟΦΟΣ and ΠΝΕΥΜΑΤΙΚΟΣ', *NTS* 14 (1967), p. 50.

identification of Spirit and wisdom in Wisdom should be seen principally in terms of function: wisdom is experienced through the Spirit.

The author of Wisdom clearly distinguishes the divine πνεῦμα, which all possess as the principle of life, from the Spirit of wisdom.[1] As the source of wisdom, the Spirit is granted only to those who humbly ask for it in prayer (7.7; cf. 8.20-21; 9.4). It is withheld from the impious (1.5). The character of this pneumatic gift is given clearest expression in Solomon's prayer:

> Who has learned your will, unless you gave him wisdom, and sent your Holy Spirit from on high (ἔπεμψας τὸ ἅγιόν σου πνεῦμα ἀπὸ ὑψίστων)? In this way people on earth have been set on the right path, have learned what pleases you, and have been saved by wisdom (καὶ τῇ σοφίᾳ ἐσώθησαν) (Wis. 9.17-18).

I have noted that the Spirit is frequently cited in diaspora texts as the source of esoteric wisdom.[2] The perspective of Wis. 9.17-18 is unique in that every level of sapiential achievement, from the lowest to the highest, is attributed to the gift of the Spirit. Indeed, apart from the illumination of the Spirit the will of God cannot be known. Thus the author of Wisdom views the gift of the Spirit as the essential source of moral and religious life. As such, it is necessary to possess the gift of the Spirit in order to attain salvation.[3] Although the σῴζω of v. 18 may refer principally to physical preservation,[4] elsewhere immortality and authority over the nations are promised to the righteous and wise (Wis. 3.1-9; cf. 5.1-23).[5]

J.C. Rylaarsdam correctly notes that the author of Wisdom, through the identification of wisdom with Spirit, has transformed the concept of wisdom.[6] The important corollary is that this identification has also transformed the concept of the Spirit.[7] In contrast to his contemporaries discussed below, the author of Wisdom does not view the gift of

---

Scroggs cites Wis. 1.4-7; 7.22-23; and particularly 9.17 in this regard.

1. G. Verbeke, *L'évolution de la doctrine du Pneuma* (1945), pp. 228-30.
2. See for example Sus. 45 (Theodotion); Eusebius, *Pr. Ev.* 8.10.4; and Josephus, *Ant.* 8.408.
3. J.S. Vos, *Traditionsgeschichtliche Untersuchungen zur paulinischen Pneumatologie* (1973), p. 64.
4. See Wis. 10.4; 14.4, 5; 16.7, 11; 18.5.
5. See also Wis. 6.18; 8.13, 17; 15.3.
6. J.C. Rylaarsdam, *Revelation in Jewish Literature* (1946), pp. 116-17.
7. G.T. Montague, *The Holy Spirit: Growth of a Biblical Tradition* (1976), p. 110.

the Spirit as a *donum superadditum* which enables prophets or sages to fulfill their divinely ordained task. Rather, the gift of the Spirit is the essential source of moral and religious life; and as such, it is a soteriological necessity.[1]

5. Philo

G. Verbeke notes that Philo, significantly influenced by Hellenistic philosophy, employs the term πνεῦμα in four distinct ways.[2] Philo uses the term with reference to one of the four elements, air (*Gig.* 22);[3] an immaterial force which links material elements together (*Deus Imm.* 35-36);[4] the rational aspect of the human soul (*Leg. All.* 1.32-33); and prophetic inspiration (*Gig.* 24). I shall confine my analysis to the latter two usages mentioned.

5.1. πνεῦμα *as the Rational Aspect of the Soul*

Philo states that the essence of the soul common to humans and animals is 'blood', but the essence of the 'intelligent and reasonable' (νοερᾶς καὶ λογικῆς) soul is πνεῦμα θεῖον (*Spec. Leg.* 4.123).[5] According to Philo, this divine πνεῦμα is breathed into every human soul at creation. It makes the mind (the νοῦς), which is the highest element of the soul, rational and capable of knowing God (*Leg. All.* 1.31-38).[6] Although the soul which allows the mind to be dominated by the desires of the body may, in some sense, die (*Leg. All.* 1.105-108),[7] the potential for immortality is resident in the divine gift of πνεῦμα, the mind or rational aspect of the soul, granted to every soul at creation.[8]

Philo, like the author of Wisdom, thus affirms that it is necessary to receive the gift of πνεῦμα in order to know the will of God and attain

---

1. Vos, *Untersuchungen*, p. 65.
2. Verbeke, *Pneuma*, pp. 237-51.
3. See also *Ebr.* 106; *Cher.* 111; and *Op. Mund.* 29–30.
4. See also *Rer. Div. Her.* 242; and *Op. Mund.* 131.
5. All citations of Philonic texts (Greek and English) are from F.H. Colson and G.H. Whitaker, *Philo* (10 vols. and 2 suppl. vols.; LCL, 1929–1962).
6. See also *Op. Mund.* 135; *Det. Pot. Ins.* 80–90; *Plant.* 18–22; and *Congr.* 97.
7. See also *Quaest. in Gen.* 1.16, 51; *Rer. Div. Her.* 52–57, 242–45.
8. See *Leg. All.* 1.31-38, the references cited above, and the following secondary literature: A. Wolfson, *Philo* (1948), I, pp. 393-413; Verbeke, *Pneuma*, p. 242; A. Laurentin, 'Le pneuma dans la doctrine de Philon', *ETL* 27 (1951), p. 411; D.T. Runia, *Philo of Alexandria and the Timaeus of Plato* (1986), pp. 336-38; B.A. Pearson, *The Pneumatikos-Psychikos Terminology* (1973), pp. 18-21.

immortality. However, in contrast to the author of Wisdom, Philo maintains that this gift has been given to all at creation.[1] This unique emphasis on the universality of the gift of the Spirit enables Philo to affirm the centrality of divine grace without forfeiting human responsibility.[2] Philo's perspective is given clear expression in *Leg. All.* 1.33-34, where he seeks to explain 'why God deemed the earthly and body-loving mind worthy of the divine breath'. In his initial response Philo emphasizes God's gracious character: God loves to give good things to all, 'even those who are not perfect' (καὶ τοῖς μὴ τελείοις), thus 'encouraging them to seek and participate in virtue' (προκαλούμενος αὐτοὺς εἰς μετουσίαν καὶ ζῆλον ἀρετῆς). Philo then points to the important corollary: since all have the capacity to seek virtue, none without virtue can claim that God punishes them unjustly.

5.2. πνεῦμα *as the Source of Prophetic Inspiration*

There is a sense in which the divine πνεῦμα is not the permanent possession of every human being. As the source of prophetic inspiration,[3] the gift of the Spirit is reserved for a select group and is temporary in nature.[4] The recipient of the gift is granted special insight and persuasiveness of speech.

According to Philo, there are three types of knowledge:[5] knowledge ascertained through the senses by observation, knowledge that is attained through philosophical reflection, and the highest form of knowledge, 'pure knowledge' (*Gig.* 22), which transcends reason.[6] 'Pure knowledge' is attained through an experience of Spirit-inspired prophetic ecstasy 'given only to a relatively few good and wise men'.[7] The ecstatic nature of this experience is frequently emphasized by Philo. He describes the prophetic state in terms of 'inspired frenzy' (θεοφορηθεῖσα; *Rer. Div. Her.* 69), 'divine intoxication' (θεία μέθη; *Leg. All.* 3.82) and 'ecstasy' (ἔκστασις; *Rer. Div. Her.* 249, 265-66).

Philo gives numerous examples of the revelatory power of the Spirit of prophecy. Moses, the prophet *par excellence*, is given special wisdom

---

1. Isaacs, *Spirit*, p. 42.
2. Verbeke, *Pneuma*, pp. 243-44.
3. For the term προφητικὸν πνεῦμα see *Fug.* 3 and *Vit. Mos.* 1.50, 277.
4. See *Gig.* 20-21; *Quaest. in Gen.* 1.90; *Rer. Div. Her.* 259; and *Deus Immut.* 2.
5. J. Davis, *Wisdom and Spirit* (1984), p. 52.
6. *Gig.* 13-14. Note also Wolfson, *Philo*, II, pp. 7-10.
7. Pearson, *Pneumatikos-Psychikos*, p. 45.

so that he can lead the nation (*Vit. Mos.* 2.40). When the children of Israel became despondent during their flight from the Egyptians, Moses gave them courage by prophesying their future deliverance (*Vit. Mos.* 2.246-52). Moses also issued prophetic words of guidance concerning the manna from heaven (*Vit. Mos.* 2.259-60) and the Sabbath (*Vit. Mos.* 2.263-64).

In *Gig.* 22 Philo declares that θεοῦ πνεῦμα is 'pure knowledge [ἀκήρατος ἐπιστήμη] which every wise man shares'. He supports the statement by citing two prooftexts from the Old Testament. A quotation from Exod. 31.2-3, 'God called up Bezaleel...and filled him with the divine spirit, with wisdom, understanding, and knowledge to devise in every work' (*Gig.* 23), is followed by an allusion to 'that spirit of perfect wisdom' (τοῦ πανσόφου πνεύματος ἐκείνου) which Moses imparted to the seventy elders (*Gig.* 24 = Num. 11.17).

The Spirit also enables the prophet to communicate the divine message with persuasive power. Philo describes how the Spirit came upon Abraham and gave his words special persuasiveness (*Virt.* 216-19). The close association between the Spirit of prophecy and inspired speech is consistent with Philo's emphasis on the ecstatic nature of prophecy. In *Spec. Leg.* 4.49 Philo describes the prophet as a passive vehicle through which the Spirit speaks:

> For no pronouncement of a prophet is ever his own; he is an interpreter prompted by Another in all his utterances, when knowing not what he does he is filled with inspiration, as the reason withdraws and surrenders the citadel of the soul to a new visitor and tenant, the Divine Spirit which plays upon the vocal organism and dictates words which clearly express its prophetic message.[1]

It is possible, as Marie Isaacs suggests, that Philo limited the inspiration of the prophetic Spirit to the prophets of the biblical periods.[2] Although Philo speaks of prophetic inspiration as a contemporary reality,[3] he, like Josephus, never links contemporary prophecy to the inspiration of the Spirit.

---

1. See also *Quaest. in Gen.* 3.9.
2. Isaacs, *Spirit*, p. 49. See also Wolfson, *Philo*, II, p. 54.
3. Philo claims that he has experienced prophetic inspiration (*Abr.* 35; *Migr. Abr.* 34-35; *Cher.* 27).

6. *Summary*

In the diaspora literature the Spirit of God almost always appears as the source of prophetic activity. As such, it inspires speech and grants esoteric wisdom. Sapiential achievement at a more fundamental level is attained through the study (unaided by the Spirit) of the Torah. The literature shows a general reluctance to associate the Spirit with miraculous deeds. Through the functional identification of Spirit and wisdom, the author of Wisdom breaks from his contemporaries and attaches soteriological significance to the pneumatic gift. He insists that the gift of the Spirit is the source of sapiential achievement at every level. Thus reception of the gift is necessary for one to know the will of God and attain immortality. Philo, with his conception of the Spirit as the rational element of the soul, offers the closest parallel to this perspective. However, in contrast to the author of Wisdom, Philo insists that this gift is granted to every human soul at creation. In Philo's perspective the pneumatic gift which is reserved for the pious is the Spirit of prophecy.

Chapter 3

THE PALESTINIAN LITERATURE*

1. *The Acquisition of Wisdom in Sirach*

For Ben Sira, the Law is the locus of wisdom.[1] The acquisition of wisdom is therefore inextricably linked to the study of the Law (6.37; 21.11; 15.1). However, Ben Sira can relate this nomistic wisdom to the inspiration of the Spirit:

> He who devotes himself to the study of the law of the Most High will seek out the wisdom of all the ancients, and will be concerned with prophecies; he will preserve the discourse of notable men and penetrate the subtleties of parables; he will seek out the hidden meanings of proverbs and be at home with the obscurities of parables. He will serve among great men and appear before rulers; he will travel through the lands of foreign nations, for he tests the good and the evil among men. He will set his heart to rise early

* The sources examined include the following Jewish writings written in Palestine between 190 BC and AD 100, most of which were written in a Semitic language: *Jubilees*; *1 Enoch*; *Pseudo-Philo*; 1 Baruch; *Psalms of Solomon*; 1 Esdras; *4 Ezra*; Sirach; Tobit; Judith; 1 and 2 Maccabees (although 2 Maccabees was originally written in Greek, I include it mong the Palestinian sources due to its close affinity to Palestinian Judaism; see R. Longenecker, *Paul: Apostle of Liberty* [1964], pp. 8, 12; and G. Stemberger, *Der Leib der Auferstehung* [1972], p. 8); *Testament of Moses*; *Life of Adam and Eve*; *The Lives of the Prophets*; *Eldad and Modad*; *More Psalms of David*; and *The Martyrdom of Isaiah*. I have excluded the *Testaments of the Twelve Patriarchs* from examination in this section because they reflect a high degree of Christian influence.

Subsections which focus on a single author are arranged in chronological order. These works may be dated as follows: (1) Sirach (c. 180 BC). See G. Nickelsburg, *Jewish Literature between the Bible and the Mishnah* (1981), p. 55; and E. Schürer, *The History of the Jewish People* (1986), III, 1, p. 202; (2) *1 Enoch* (second century BC–first century AD). *1 Enoch* is a composite work with many authors from a variety of periods. See E. Isaac, '1 (Ethiopic Apocalypse of) Enoch', in Charlesworth, *Pseudepigrapha*, I, pp. 6-7.

1. See Sir. 1.26; 3.22; 6.37; 15.1; 19.20; 21.11; 24.23; 33.3; 34.7-8.

to seek the Lord who made him, and will make supplication before the
Most High; he will open his mouth in prayer and make supplication for
his sins. If the great Lord is willing, he will be filled with the spirit of
understanding (πνεύματι συνέσεως ἐμπλησθήσεται); he will pour
forth words of wisdom and give thanks to the Lord in prayer. He will
reveal instruction in his teaching, and will glory in the law of the Lord's
covenant (Sir. 39.1-8).

The term πνεύματι συνέσεως (39.6) undoubtedly refers to the wisdom which comes from the Spirit of God. The anarthrous use of
πνεῦμα is consistent with this claim. For in Sir. 48.24 we read that
Isaiah looked into the future by means of a πνεύματι μεγάλῳ. Here the
anarthrous πνεῦμα is clearly 'a circumlocution for the Spirit of God,
the source of all true prophecy'.[1] Furthermore, the collocation of
πνεῦμα and σύνεσις is frequently found in the LXX with reference to
wisdom imparted by the Spirit of God (Exod. 31.3; Deut. 34.9; Isa.
11.2). My judgment is confirmed by the context, which indicates that
the Spirit of understanding is given in accordance with the will of the
Lord (39.6a).

James Davis notes that in Sir. 38.24–39.11 three levels of sapiential
achievement are delineated. The lowest level of sapiential achievement is
achieved by those who work with their hands, farmers and craftsmen
(38.25-34). A higher degree of wisdom is attained by the scribe who
studies the law (39.1-5). The highest level of wisdom is reserved for the
sage who receives the Spirit of understanding (39.6).[2] Therefore, while
Ben Sira attributes the highest level of sapiential achievement to the
inspiration of the Spirit, he affirms that sapiential achievement at a more
fundamental level is attained exclusively through the study of the Law.

The perspectives of Ben Sira and the author of *4 Maccabees* con-
verge at this point: both insist that wisdom can be attained by purely
rational means. This optimistic view of humanity's rational capacity is
reflected in Sir. 32.15: 'Study the Law and you will master it'. It is also
the presupposition upon which the call to responsible behavior is based:
'If you wish, you can keep the commandments' (ἐὰν θέλῃς,
συντηρήσεις ἐντολάς, 15.15).

Ben Sira also portrays the gift of the Spirit as the source of inspired
speech. The scribe who is filled with the spirit of understanding 'will
pour forth words of wisdom' (αὐτὸς ἀνομβρήσει ῥήματα σοφίας,

1. Davis, *Wisdom*, p. 164 n. 53.
2. Davis, *Wisdom*, pp. 16-21.

39.6) and 'reveal instruction in his teaching' (αὐτὸς ἐκφανεῖ παιδείαν διδασκαλίας αὐτοῦ, 39.8). Enabled to see into the future by means of Spirit-inspiration, Isaiah is said to have revealed the hidden things to come (48.25). Thus, according to Ben Sira, the Spirit endows the sage or prophet with esoteric wisdom so that he can communicate it to others.

2. *The Spirit in* 1 Enoch *and Jewish Apocalyptic*

2.1. *The Spirit and Divine Revelation*
References to the activity of the Spirit of God in *1 Enoch* are relatively rare. Only three references to the divine Spirit are found in the entire work (49.3; 62.2; 91.1), excluding the unusual passage in 99.16: 'He [God] will arouse the anger of his Spirit'.[1] Although the Ethiopic texts refer to the Spirit in 99.16, the only extant Greek text of this passage, the *Chester Beatty* papryus (*1 En.* 97.6-104, 106-107), simply refers to 'his anger' (τὸν θυμὸν αὐτοῦ).[2] In 91.1 the Spirit of God appears as the source of prophetic activity: Enoch declares to his son, Methuselah, 'a voice calls me, and the spirit is poured over me so that I may show you everything that shall happen to you'.

In 68.2 the 'power of the spirit' provokes the anger of the angel Michael on account of the severity of the judgment of the angels. Rather than a reference to the Spirit of God, this phrase speaks of Michael's emotional state in terms of his spirit.[3] According to 70.2, Enoch was taken up in 'a wind (or spirit) chariot'. The phrase probably refers to a whirlwind rather than the Spirit of God. In 2 Kgs 2.11, a biblical passage which is quite similar to 70.2, Elijah is caught up 'in a whirlwind' (בסערה). However, a reference to the Spirit's activity cannot be ruled out entirely, for in 2 Kgs 2.16 the sons of the prophets speculate, 'perhaps the Spirit of the Lord has taken him up and cast him on some mountain'.

The revelation of esoteric wisdom is, of course, a prominent theme in *1 Enoch*. However, in *1 Enoch* (and in Jewish apocalyptic in general[4])

---

1.   All texts from *1 Enoch* which are cited in English are from Isaac, '1 Enoch'.
2.   For the Greek text, see M. Black, *Apocalypsis Henochi Graece* (1970), p. 40.
3.   R.H. Charles has suggested that the text originally read 'the power of my spirit' (*The Book of Enoch* [1912], p. 135).
4.   D.S. Russell, *The Method and Message of Jewish Apocalyptic* (1964), pp. 148, 158-64.

the Spirit is rarely cited as a revelatory agent.[1] Although the divine Spirit is occasionally cited as the source of special revelation (49.3; 62.2; 91.1), these few references stand in stark contrast to the numerous occasions where special revelation comes by means of angelic messengers or visionary experiences.

2.2. *The Spirit and the Messiah*

There are numerous references in *1 Enoch* to the Messiah as a supernatural figure. Various names are given to the Messiah: 'the Elect One' (e.g. 49.2), 'the Son of Man' (e.g. 62.3), 'the Righteous One' (e.g. 53.6), and 'the Anointed One' (e.g. 52.4). In two passages (49.3; 62.2) the Messiah is said to be anointed with the Spirit. *1 En.* 49.3 describes 'The Elect One':

> In him dwells the spirit of wisdom, the spirit which gives thoughtfulness, the spirit of knowledge and strength, and the spirit of those who have fallen asleep in righteousness.

This text 'reproduces practically verbatim' Isa. 11.2;[2] a verse in which the referent is clearly 'the Spirit of the Lord'. There can be little doubt that the author of *1 Enoch* consciously borrows from Isa. 11.2 and thus depicts the Messiah as one endowed with the Spirit of God. In *1 En.* 49.3, as in Isa. 11.2, the Spirit provides the wisdom necessary to rule and exercise judgment (49.4; cf. 51.3). *1 En.* 62.2 picks up Isa. 11.4 and continues to extol the power of 'the Elect One' to judge and rule:

> The Lord of the Spirits has sat down on the throne of his glory, and the spirit of righteousness has been poured out upon him [the Elect One]. The word of his mouth will do the sinners in; and all the oppressors shall be eliminated from before his face.

In another Jewish writing with apocalyptic features, *Psalms of Solomon*, the gift of the Spirit is again depicted as the means by which the Messiah shall be endowed with special wisdom to rule (*Amtscharisma*).[3] The Messiah will be 'powerful in the holy spirit (δυνατὸν ἐν πνεύματι ἁγίῳ) and wise in the counsel of understanding, with strength and righteousness' (17.37). The connection between the

---

1.   Russell, *Jewish Apocalyptic*, p. 160.
2.   M. Black, *The Book of Enoch* (1985), p. 212.
3.   All texts from *Psalms of Solomon* which are cited in English are from R.B. Wright, 'Psalms of Solomon', in Charlesworth, *Pseudepigrapha*, II. Greek text from A. Rahlfs, *Septuaginta* (1979).

Messiah's wisdom and the gift of the Spirit is explicitly stated in *Pss. Sol.* 18.7. The coming Messiah will act 'in the fear of his God, in wisdom of spirit (ἐν σοφίᾳ πνεύματος), and of righteousness and of strength, to direct people in righteous acts, in the fear of God' (18.7). *1 Enoch* and the *Psalms of Solomon* thus state that the Messiah will be endowed with wisdom by the Spirit of God so that he may rule effectively. Nowhere in Jewish intertestamental literature is it recorded that the Messiah will bestow the Spirit of God upon his followers.

2.3. *The Spirit and the Resurrection of the Dead*
In apocalyptic thought the resurrection, viewed in a variety of ways, becomes an important aspect of God's future salvation.[1] Although the Spirit of God is associated with the resurrection in Ezek. 37.14, one of the few Old Testament texts in which a future resurrection is described, this association of Spirit and resurrection is strikingly absent in Jewish apocalyptic and the Jewish literature of the intertestamental period as a whole.[2]

Even though the exact nature of the resurrection depicted in the various parts of *1 Enoch* may be debated, it is clear that the resurrection of the body represents a prominent motif.[3] Resurrection also appears as a significant theme in *Psalms of Solomon*, 2 Maccabees, *4 Ezra*, Pseudo-Philo and *Life of Adam and Eve*.[4] Yet, as indicated above, the connection between resurrection and the Spirit of God, so prominent in Ezekiel 37, is not found in these writings.

3. *The Spirit and Prophetic Inspiration: Various Texts*

We have seen that the Spirit of God, when mentioned in Sirach and apocalyptic texts such as *1 Enoch*, is consistently portrayed as the source of esoteric wisdom and inspired speech. This tendency to identify

1. Montague, *Spirit*, p. 90.
2. See D. Müller, 'Geisterfahrung und Totenauferweckung' (1980), pp. 111-32. Müller argues that *2 Bar.* 23.5 is the only text from the OT pseudepigrapha which (along with several rabbinic citations) portrays the Spirit of God as the agent of the resurrection. However *2 Bar.* 23.5 has been excluded from my analysis due to its late origin (second century AD).
3. Important passages in *1 Enoch* concerning the resurrection include: 22.13; 51.1; 61.5; 90.33; 100.5.
4. See for example *Pss. Sol.* 3.12; 14.10; 2 Macc. 7.8, 13, 23, 29; 14.46; *4 Ezra* 7.32; *Ps.-Philo* 3.10; 19.12; 25.7; 51.5; 64.7; *LAE* 28.4; 41.3.

the Spirit of God with prophetic inspiration is also characteristic of other Palestinian texts from the intertestamental period. References to the Spirit of God occur frequently in Pseudo-Philo.[1] In 9.10 we read that 'the Spirit of God came upon Miriam' and revealed to her in a dream that she would give birth to Moses. According to Ps.- Philo 18.10, although the prophet Balaam had been filled with the Spirit, when he prophesied for Balak it gradually departed from him. After 'a holy spirit came upon Kenaz and dwelled in him', he prophesied in a state of ecstasy (28.6). Barak declares that the oracle which foretold the death of Sisera came from 'the Lord, who sent his Spirit' (31.9). Deborah, in the midst of her hymn of rejoicing, attributes her praise to the Spirit: 'But you, Deborah, sing praises, and let the grace of the holy spirit awaken in you, and begin to praise the works of the Lord' (32.14). In this text the locus of the Spirit's activity is not the revelation of special insight, but inspired utterance.

The Spirit also appears as *Amtscharisma* in Ps.-Philo 60.1: 'And in that time the spirit of the Lord was taken away from Saul'. It is debatable whether 62.2 speaks of the activity of the Spirit of God. D.J. Harrington translates the verse with spirit as an anarthrous noun: 'and a spirit abided in Saul and he prophesied'. However in the Latin text 'spirit' can be interpreted either as a definite or indefinite noun. 1 Sam. 19.23, the biblical text upon which this passage is based, attributes Saul's prophecy to the Spirit of God. It is possible that Pseudo-Philo has tried to modify the text at this point in light of 60.1, deliberately avoiding a reference to the Spirit of God. Yet this is unlikely since the biblical text makes no such modification.

A number of other intertestamental writings depict the divine Spirit as the source of prophecy. Most of the manuscripts of *Jub.* 25.14, extant only in Ethiopic, record that Rebecca blessed Jacob after 'a spirit of truth descended upon her mouth'.[2] However manuscript C reads 'the Holy Spirit', indicating that this passage should be interpreted as a reference to the Spirit of God.[3] *Jub.* 31.12-13 records Isaac's Spirit-inspired blessing of Jacob's sons, Levi and Judah: 'The spirit of prophecy [*spiritus profetiae*] came down into his [Isaac's] mouth' (31.12). In *Jub.*

---

1. Texts of Pseudo-Philo, also known by the Latin title *Liber Antiquitatum Biblicarum*, are extant in Latin only. All English texts cited are from D.J. Harrington, 'Pseudo-Philo', in Charlesworth, *Pseudepigrapha*, II.

2. ET from O.S. Wintermute, 'Jubilees', in Charlesworth, *Pseudepigrapha*, II.

3. R.H. Charles, *The Book of Jubilees* (1902), p. 158.

40.5 Pharaoh attributes Joseph's wisdom to the Spirit of the Lord.
It is recorded in *4 Ezra* 5.22-23 that Ezra, having 'recovered the spirit
of understanding [*spiritum intellectus*]' (5.22),[1] was once again able to
speak to God. However, in light of 5.14, 'my [Ezra's] mind was
troubled, so that it fainted', this reference probably refers to a restoration of Ezra's mental faculties. Nevertheless, in *4 Ezra* 14.22 the Holy
Spirit is clearly depicted as the source of special insight. Ezra requests
that the Holy Spirit (*spiritum sanctum*) be sent to him so that he can
write all that has taken place in the world from the beginning (14.22).

The close association between the Spirit and prophetic activity is also
highlighted by the author of the *Martyrdom of Isaiah*. In 1.7 the
prophet Isaiah refers to 'the Spirit which speaks in me' (τὸ πνεῦμα τὸ
λαλοῦν ἐν ἐμοί).[2] Isaiah's remarkable fortitude in the face of persecution is recounted in 5.14, where Isaiah, inspired by the Holy Spirit,
prophesies until sawn in half.

The *Lives of the Prophets* attributes miracles to the biblical prophets
(Jeremiah, 2.3-4; Ezekiel, 3.8-9; Elijah, 21.6; Elisha, 22.4). Yet significantly
these miracles are not performed in the power of the Spirit. Thus, while
miracles are linked to prophets, the distinctive activity of the Spirit of
God in relation to the prophet is revelation of the divine message and
inspiration of its proclamation. Indeed, a survey of the Palestinian literature reveals that in only one instance is the Spirit described as the agent
of miraculous activity not related to revelatory or speech functions. Ps.-
Philo 27.9-10 describes how the Spirit of God transformed Kenaz into a
mighty warrior, enabling him to kill 45,000 Amorites (v. 10):

> And Kenaz arose, and the Spirit of God clothed him, and he drew his
> sword... he was clothed with the Spirit of power and was changed into
> another man, and he went down to the Amorite camp and began to strike
> them down.

4. *Summary*

In the Palestinian literature surveyed, the Spirit consistently functions as
the source of esoteric wisdom and inspired speech. The Spirit enables
the sage to attain the heights of sapiential achievement, equips the Messiah

---

1. Latin text from B. Violet, *Die Esra-Apokalypse (IV. Esra)* (1910).
2. ET from M.A. Knibb, 'Martyrdom and Ascension of Isaiah', in Charlesworth,
Pseudepigrapha, II. Greek text (1.8) is from Denis, *Fragmenta Pseudepigraphorum*,
p. 107.

with special knowledge to rule, and grants special insight to various servants of the Lord. The inspiration of the Spirit, whether it be in relation to the sage, Messiah or servant, is almost always related to inspired speech. It is therefore apparent that the Palestinian authors viewed the Spirit as a *donum superadditum* granted to various individuals so that they might fulfill a divinely appointed task. The gift of the Spirit is not presented as a soteriological necessity: one need not possess the gift in order to live in right relationship to God and attain eternal life through the resurrection. The Spirit is not associated with the resurrection of the dead or the performance of miracles and feats of strength.[1]

1.   As I have noted, the only exception is Ps.-Philo 27.9-10.

Chapter 4

THE QUMRAN LITERATURE*

The term רוח occurs frequently in the scrolls from Qumran and with diverse meanings.[1] It can refer to wind as in 1QH 1.10: 'Thou hast spread...the mighty winds (רוחות עוז) according to their laws'.[2] רוח is also used anthropologically, often with reference to the disposition or attitude of humankind. Thus in 1QM 11.10 we read that God 'will kindle the downcast of spirit (ונכאי רוח)' and make them mighty in battle.[3] However, רוח frequently refers to the totality of the human being. The author of 1QH 1.22 describes himself as 'a straying and perverted spirit (רוח התועה ונעוה)' of no understanding'.[4] The scrolls' affinity to Jewish apocalyptic can be seen in the abundant references to supernatural spirits, both good and evil, created by God and active in the world of men. The angelic army which will fight with the righteous in the final battle are called 'the host of His spirits (צבא רוחיו)' in 1QM 12.9. Their foes shall be 'the host of Satan' and 'the spirits of wickedness' (רוחי רשעה; 1QM 15.14).[5] In the present study my primary focus will be directed to yet another category, those passages where רוח designates the Spirit of God. However, due to the ambiguous way the term רוח is often employed, there is some disagreement as to which texts should be included in this

---

* The sources examined include those texts contained in the third edition of Geza Vermes's convenient collection, *The Dead Sea Scrolls in English* (1987). The literature from Qumran was produced between c. 170 BC and AD 68.

1. K.G. Kuhn lists close to 150 references of רוח in his *Konkordanz zu den Qumrantexten* (1960).

2. All English translations are from Vermes, *The Dead Sea Scrolls in English*. All Hebrew texts are from E. Lohse, *Die Texte aus Qumran* (1971) unless otherwise indicated. For רוח as 'wind' see also 1QH 6.23; 7.5, 23; CD 8.13; 19.25.

3. For further examples of this use of רוח see: 1QS 3.8; 8.3; 10.12, 18; 11.2; 1QH 2.15; 1QM 7.5; 11.10; 14.7.

4. Further examples include: 1QS 10.18; 1QH 3.21; 8.29; 13.13.

5. See also 1QH 7.29; 9.16; 10.8; 1QM 13.10.

category. Disagreement also exists concerning the origin of the scrolls' pneumatology, particularly that of 1QS. Thus I begin with a discussion of the 'two spirits' in 1QS 3–4, a passage of importance for both debates.

1. *The Two Spirits in 1QS 3–4*

1QS 3.13–4.26 describes the conflict between two spirits which rages in every human. The outworking of this conflict shapes the behavior of each individual. Although the two spirits are named by a number of titles, the various terms, if not synonymous, are closely related. The spirit of truth (רוח האמת; 1QS 3.19; 4.23), spirit of light (רוח אור; 1QS 3.25), prince of lights (שר אורים; 1QS 3.20) and the angel of [his] truth (מלאך אמתו; 1QS 3.24) rule the children of righteousness. The spirit of falsehood (רוח העול; 1QS 3.19; 4.9, 20, 23), spirit of darkness (רוח חושך; 1QS 3.25) and angel of darkness (מלאך חושך; 1QS 3.21) rule the children of darkness. The battle in the heart of every human rages until the final age, when God will destroy falsehood forever (1QS 4.18-22).

1.1. *Dualism, Determinism and the Two Spirits*
There has been considerable disagreement as to the exact nature and function of these spirits. M. Burrows and K.G. Kuhn have emphasized the supernatural and cosmic character of the two spirits, and thus attributed a cosmic dualism of Persian origin to the scrolls.[1] In response, P. Wernberg-Møller has argued convincingly that the two spirits are human dispositions which are present equally in every person rather than opposing supernatural forces. Central to Wernberg-Møller's thesis is his observation that both spirits dwell in humans as created by God.[2] Likening the two spirits to the rabbinic good and evil impulses, Wernberg-Møller asserts that according to 1QS 3–4 each individual must choose which spirit to follow. Thus he rejects the notion that the scrolls are characterized by cosmic dualism and show evidence of direct dependency on Persian sources.[3]

---

1.   M. Burrows, *More Light on the Dead Sea Scrolls* (1958), p. 279; K.G. Kuhn, 'πειρασμός-ἁμαρτία-σάρξ im Neuen Testament und die damit zusammen-hängenden Vorstellungen', *ZTK* 49 (1952), p. 206.
2.   P. Wernberg-Møller, 'A Reconsideration of the Two Spirits in the Rule of the Community', *RevQ* 3 (1961), p. 442.
3.   Wernberg-Møller, 'Two Spirits', pp. 422-23.

Wernberg-Møller is supported in his conclusions by M. Treves, who also views the two spirits as 'simply tendencies or propensities which are implanted in every man's heart'.[1] Noting that each individual is influenced by both spirits (1QS 3.24; 4.23) and that sin is voluntary (1QS 5.1, 8-10, 12), Treves states that the predestinarianism of the author of 1QS 'has been somewhat exaggerated...he does not appear to have diverged widely from the traditional Jewish views'.[2]

Although considerable disagreement still exists concerning the extent to which predestinarianism is present in 1QS, the conclusions reached by P. Wernberg-Møller and M. Treves regarding the nature of the two spirits have received general acceptance. Their influence is reflected in the note of caution concerning the cosmic and supernatural character of the two spirits in subsequent studies by A. Anderson, D. Hill and H.W. Kuhn.[3] Representative is Kuhn, who speaks of רוח in 1QS 3–4 as 'the predestined essence or "self" of humans'.[4] As a result, caution has also been exercised in attributing the pneumatology of 1QS directly to Persian influences. It has been increasingly recognized that the pneumatology of the scrolls is not so different from that of the Judaism of its day.[5]

In view of the arguments presented by Wernberg-Møller and Treves, I conclude that the two spirits in 1QS are human dispositions. The doctrine of the two spirits was an attempt to reconcile the omnipotence of God with the mixed character of humanity. As the creator of all things, God has implanted in the heart of every human being the impulse (spirit) to do good and to do evil. Each individual must choose between the two impulses or spirits. The extent to which this choice is predetermined at creation by the allotment of the spirits is a point of continuing debate. Nevertheless, it is apparent that caution should be exercised in attributing to the scrolls on the basis of 1QS a rigid cosmic dualism and dependency on Persian (or gnostic) sources. The pneumatology of the scrolls is essentially Jewish.

1. M. Treves, 'The Two Spirits of the Rule of the Community', *RevQ* 3 (1961), p. 449.
2. Treves, 'Two Spirits', p. 451.
3. A. Anderson, 'The Use of "Ruah" in 1QS, 1QH, and 1QM', *JSS* 7 (1962), p. 299; H.W. Kuhn, *Enderwartung und gegenwärtiges Heil* (1966), pp. 121-22; and Hill, *Greek Words*, p. 236.
4. Kuhn, *Enderwartung*, p. 122.
5. See F. Nötscher, 'Heiligkeit in den Qumranschriften', *RevQ* 2 (1960), pp. 343-44; Hill, *Greek Words*, p. 236; and Anderson, '"Ruah"', p. 303.

1.2. *The Two Spirits and 1QH*

Having defined the two spirits as impulses within every human being,
we must now examine the arguments put forward by W. Foerster that
the spirit of truth in 1QS is identical to the Holy Spirit of 1QH.[1] Foerster
cites numerous parallels between the functions attributed to the spirit of
truth in 1QS and to the Holy Spirit in 1QH: the spirit of truth and the
Holy Spirit 'enlighten the heart of humans' (1QS 4.2; 1QH 1.21; 12.11-
12), instill fear into the hearts of men concerning the righteous deeds of
God (1QS 4.2; 1QH 1.23; 9.23), bestow insight and understanding (1QS
4.3, 6; 1QH 6.35-37), and grant steadfastness (1QS 4.4; 1QH 2.7-8, 25)
and purity (1QS 4.5; 1QH 3.21; 6.8) of heart.

Several factors speak against Foerster's identification. First, it should
be noted that none of the passages Foerster cites from 1QS explicitly
names the spirit of truth as the subject of the action. On the contrary, all
of the citations come from 1QS 4 and refer to the various spirits which
make up the counsel of the spirit of truth. Secondly, the parallels which
Foerster cites are often superficial, exhibiting only a general conceptual
correspondence. One would expect such similarities to exist between the
activity of the Spirit of God and that of the good impulse in every
human being. Thirdly, in contrast to the Holy Spirit in 1QH, the two
spirits in 1QS are created by God (3.13-14; 4.25). Fourthly, the dualistic
conflict between the two spirits in 1QS stands in sharp contrast to the
sovereign action of the Holy Spirit in 1QH.

More problematic are the references to רוח in association with אמת
('truth') and קודש ('holy') in 1QS 3.6-7 and 4.21. F. Nötscher has
argued that in these texts, the Holy Spirit and spirit of truth are identical
and they describe a power granted by God which becomes active in
humans for salvation.[2] This judgment is undoubtedly correct. But is this
salvific power granted by God identified with the Spirit of God in each
instance? And in light of Foerster's thesis we may ask: are the references to רוח קודש and רוח אמת in 1QS 3.6-7 and 4.20-21 to be equated
with the רוח קודש of 1QH? I suggest that the spirits cited in 1QS 3.6-7
and 4.20-21 should not be identified with the Spirit of God; and that
these spirits should therefore be distinguished from the רוח קודש of 1QH.

---

1. W. Foerster, 'Der Heilige Geist im Spätjudentum', *NTS* 8 (1961–62),
pp. 129-31.
2. Nötscher, 'Heiligkeit', pp. 340-41.

For it is through the spirit of true counsel (רוח עצת אמת) concerning the ways of man that all his sins shall be expiated that he may contemplate the light of life. He shall be cleansed from all his sins by the spirit of holiness (וברוח קדושה) uniting him to His truth, and his iniquity shall be expiated by the spirit of uprightness and humility (וברוח יושר ועניה). And when his flesh is sprinkled with purifying water and sanctified by cleansing water, it shall be made clean by the humble submission of his soul (נפשו) to all the precepts of God (1QS 3.6-8).

The terms 'spirit of true counsel', 'spirit of holiness', and 'spirit of uprightness and humility' (1QS 3.6-8) all refer to the disposition of the individual:[1] in this instance, the inclination to adhere to the ordinances of the community. Thus, although רוח may emphasize the divine origin of this inclination or impulse, it does not refer to the Spirit of God. This judgment is suggested by the larger context, which, as I have noted, discusses the conflict between the two spirits or impulses which rages within every human. It is supported further by the way in which the references to רוח cited above, all of which are related to the individual's cleansing from sin, are paralleled with the disposition of the soul: 'it [his flesh] shall be made clean by the humble submission of his soul (נפשו) to all the precepts of God'. This conclusion is confirmed by the use of רוח קודש in 1QS 9.3,[2] a passage which refers to the readmission into the community of those who, due to inadvertent sin, have undergone two years of penance:

> When these become members of the Community in Israel according to all these rules, they shall establish the spirit of holiness (רוח קודש) according to everlasting truth. They shall atone for guilty rebellion and for sins of unfaithfulness that they may obtain loving kindness for the Land without the flesh of holocausts and the fat of sacrifice (1QS 9.3-4).

Here רוח קודש refers to the inclination to adhere faithfully to the ordinances of the community. This inner disposition rather than sacrifices shall effect atonement.[3]

> Then God will purify by his truth all the deeds of man and will refine for himself the frame of man, removing all spirit of injustice (רוח עולה) from within his flesh, and purifying him by the spirit of holiness (ברוח קודש) from every wicked action. And he will sprinkle upon him the spirit of truth (רוח אמת) like waters for purification (to remove) all the abominations of

---

1. M.A. Knibb, *The Qumran Community* (1987), pp. 92-93.
2. See also the way in which רוח קודש is employed in CD 5.11; 7.4.
3. Knibb, *The Qumran Community*, p. 138.

falsehood (in which) he has defiled himself through the spirit of impurity (ברוח נדה), so that the upright may have understanding in the knowledge of the Most High and the perfect of way insight into the wisdom of the sons of heaven (1QS 4.20-22).[1]

Again the context is instructive. This passage forms the climax of the entire 'two spirits' discussion. The 'spirit of holiness' and 'spirit of truth' are contrasted with the 'spirit of injustice' and 'spirit of impurity' which in the endtime will be rooted out of humankind. Thus, the time of conflict between the two spirits will come to an end, and the spirit of holiness and truth will dominate. Although the phrase 'sprinkle upon him' implies that the spirit of truth will be bestowed upon the faithful at the end, this imagery is metaphorical and merely describes the culmination of a battle which has been raging since creation: the complete victory of the spirit of truth over the spirit of falsehood, of the good impulse over the evil impulse.[2] This conclusion is confirmed by 1QS 4.26: 'He [God] has allotted them [the two spirits] to the children of men...that the destiny of all the living may be according to the spirit within [them at the time] of the visitation'. The parallels between 1QS 4.20-22 and the numerous rabbinic texts which speak of the endtime removal of the evil יצר lend further support to the thesis that the two spirits are impulses placed within every individual at creation.[3]

The contrast between the רוח קודש of 1QS 3–4 and that of 1QH becomes clear when it is recognized that in 1QH the term is never simply רוח קודש, but always רוח קודשך (your [God's] Holy Spirit). Furthermore, it should also be noted that 1QS 4.20-22 represents the only eschatological use of רוח in all of the Qumran literature. On the basis of my rejection of Foerster's parallels, my examination of 1QS 3.6-8 and 4.20-22, and the considerations cited above, I conclude that the spirit of truth in 1QS 3–4 is not to be equated with the Holy Spirit of 1QH, the Spirit of God.[4]

---

1. ET from Knibb, *The Qumran Community*, p. 101.
2. Wernberg-Møller, 'Two Spirits', p. 423.
3. See *Exod. R.* 15.6; 41.7; *Num. R.* 14.4; *Deut. R.* 6.14; *Midr. Ps.* 14.6; *Cant. R.* 1.2.4; *Eccl. R.* 2.1; 9.15.
4. Unambiguous references to the Spirit of God are found in 1QH 7.6-7; 9.32; 12.12; 14.13; 16.2, 3, 7, 12; 17.26 (elsewhere in the scrolls: 1QS 8.16; CD 2.12; 4Q504 2 [frag. 4], 5; 1Q34bis 2.6-7). Other probable references to the Spirit of God include 1QH 12.11; 13.19; 16.9, 11.

2. *The Spirit and Wisdom*

The scrolls are the literary deposit of a 'wisdom community'.[1] Like Ben Sira, the authors of the scrolls identify wisdom with the law.[2] Nevertheless, they maintain that the wisdom of God remains inaccessible to those outside of the community (1QS 11.5-6). Wisdom is the exclusive possession of the community (CD 3.12-16; 1QS 5.11-12), for it cannot be apprehended by study alone. Divine illumination is required in order to attain wisdom,[3] and this revelatory gift is reserved for those within the community.

This pessimistic attitude toward humanity's ability to acquire wisdom apart from divine illumination is given clear expression in 1QH. God's ways and deeds are incomprehensible to humans (1QH 7.32), who are dust and creatures of clay (1QH 11.3). As spirits of flesh, they cannot understand God's wisdom (1QH 13.13, also 15.21). However, the hymns of 1QH also declare that the members of the community have overcome this deficiency through reception of the Spirit.

> And I know through the understanding
>   which comes from Thee,
> that in Thy goodwill towards [ashes
>   Thou hast shed] Thy Holy Spirit [upon me]
> and thus drawn me near to understanding thee (1QH 14.12b-13).

H.W. Kuhn has argued persuasively that 1QH 14.13 refers to the gift of the Spirit which is granted to every member upon entrance into the community.[4] The parallels between 14.12b-16 and 14.17-21a, particularly the repetition of ואני ידעתי ('I know') and the verb נגש ('draw near'), demonstrate that these passages are closely related. Therefore, since the formula ובשבועה הקימותי על נפשי (literally, 'an oath I have placed on my soul') in 14.17 undoubtedly refers to a pledge made upon entrance into the community,[5] we may assume that this setting is also in view in 1QH 14.13. This judgment is confirmed by the fact that נגש is a *terminus*

---

1. J.E. Worrell, 'Concepts of Wisdom in the Dead Sea Scrolls' (1968), pp. 120-54.

2. E. Schnabel, *Law and Wisdom from Ben Sira to Paul* (1985), pp. 206-26.

3. S. Holm-Nielsen, *Hodayot: Psalms from Qumran* (1960), p. 328.

4. Kuhn, *Enderwartung*, pp. 131-32. See also Holm-Nielsen, *Hodayot*, p. 221.

5. Kuhn, *Enderwartung*, p. 131. Cf. 1QS 5.7-11; CD 15.5-16.

technicus for entrance into the community.[1] Thus, according to 1QH
14.12b-13, the gift of the Spirit enables every member of the community
to draw near 'to the understanding of thee [God]' (לבינתך).

> And I know that man is not righteous
>   except through Thee,
> and therefore I implore Thee
>   by the spirit which Thou hast given [me]
>   to perfect Thy [favours] to Thy servant [for ever],
> purifying me by Thy Holy Spirit,
>   and drawing me near to Thee by Thy grace
>   according to the abundance of Thy mercies (1QH 16.11b-12).

1QH 16.11b-12 also refers to initiation into the community. The verb
נגש is employed in 16.12. Furthermore, the formula [ברוח אשר נתתה [בי
('by the Spirit which thou hast given me') occurs frequently with
reference to the Spirit as a gift given (suffix conjugation) upon entrance
into the community.[2] Although wisdom terms are absent in this passage,
the term ולהגישני ('to draw me near') implies the revelation of God's
hidden wisdom (cf. 1QH 14.13).

> I, the Master (משכיל), know Thee (ידעתיכה), O my God,
>   by the spirit which Thou hast given to me,
> and by Thy Holy Spirit I have faithfully hearkened
>   to Thy marvelous counsel (לסוד פלאכה).
> In the mystery of Thy wisdom (ברז שכלכה)
>   Thou has opened knowledge (דעת) to me,
> and in Thy mercies
>   [Thou hast unlocked for me] the fountain of Thy might
>   (1QH 12.11-13).

> And I, Thy servant (עבדך),
>   I know (ידעתי) by the spirit which Thou hast given to me
>   [that Thy words are truth],
> and that all Thy works are righteousness,
>   and that Thou wilt not take back Thy word (1QH 13.18-19).

1QH 12.11-13 and 13.18-19 are also instructive. The formula ברוח אשר
נתתה בי ('by the Spirit which thou hast given me') is found in both texts
and sapiential terms abound. According to these hymns, wisdom
is attained through reception of the Spirit upon entrance into the
community.

---

1. See 1QH 12.23; 14.13, 18, 19; 1QS 9.16; 11.13.
2. See Kuhn, *Enderwartung*, p. 130; and 1QH 12.11-12; 13.19.

In accordance with the previous passages cited, the author of 1QH 9.32 places the reception of the Spirit in the past and parallels it with the revelation of 'certain truth' (אמת נכון):

> Thou hast upheld me with certain truth;
> Thou hast delighted me with Thy Holy Spirit
> and [hast opened my heart] till this day.

1QH 7.6-7 and 1QH 17.26 also place the reception of the Spirit in the past, although their contexts are imprecise and fragmentary, respectively. 1QH 16.2 and 3 are also fragmentary, but 16.6-7 is more revealing:

> Bowing down and [confessing all] my transgressions,
> I will seek [Thy] spirit [of knowledge];
> cleaving to Thy spirit of [holiness];
> I will hold fast to the truth of Thy Covenant,
> that [I may serve] Thee in truth and wholeness of heart,
> and that I may love [Thy Name].

Although infinitives rather than finite verbs are found in 16.6-7, this is undoubtedly due to the declarative nature of the passage and does not contradict a past reception of the Spirit. This judgment is substantiated by the use of suffix conjugations in the verses prior to 16.6-7 and in 16.9, where discussion of the past event is again picked up: 'Thou... hast graced me with Thy spirit of mercy'. The revelation of God's truth is again linked to the gift of the Spirit received upon entrance into the community.

The texts cited above indicate that the hymns from 1QH associate reception of the Spirit with entrance into the community. As an essential element of initiation into the community, the gift of the Spirit reveals the previously hidden wisdom of God to the recipient. Sapiential achievement at every level is dependent upon the reception of this gift. Indeed, reception of the gift enables one to know God and live within the community. Thus the hymns of 1QH attribute soteriological significance to the gift of the Spirit.

It is possible that the hymns of 1QH which attribute soteriological functions to the Spirit represent a late stage in the development of the community's pneumatology.[1] The pneumatological perspective of 1QH is decidedly different from 1QS, where the two spirits, in a manner analogous to the rabbinic good and evil יצר, appear as impulses placed

---

1. A similar hypothesis of development, albeit for different reasons, is tentatively put forward by Davies, 'Flesh and Spirit', p. 165.

within every individual at creation. The fact that the soteriological pneumatology so prominent in 1QH is virtually absent from the other Qumran writings lends further support to this hypothesis.[1] This evidence suggests that the pneumatology of Qumran underwent a process of development not unlike that which occurred within the Jewish wisdom tradition as a whole. The wisdom tradition displays an increasing pessimism toward humanity's ability to attain wisdom by purely rational means (study of the law unaided by the Spirit). The relatively optimistic anthropology of Sirach is replaced by more pessimistic appraisals of humans in 1QH and Wisdom. Similar developments can be traced within the scrolls. According to 1QS, the spirit of truth and the spirit of falsehood reside within each individual. Thus the individual appears to have some capacity, however small, to know God's will and respond accordingly. In contrast, 1QH presents humans as utterly incapable of attaining wisdom apart from the illumination of the Spirit. Thus the gift of the Spirit, previously viewed as the source of esoteric wisdom and inspired speech, becomes the source of sapiential achievement at every level. The process of development, both within the Qumran community and Jewish sapiential thought as a whole, culminates in the attribution of soteriological significance to the gift of the Spirit (Wisdom; 1QH).

3. *The Spirit and Prophetic Inspiration*

Consistent with their Jewish contemporaries, the authors of the scrolls portray the Spirit as the source of prophetic inspiration. The link between the Spirit and prophecy is made explicit in 1QS 8.16 and CD 2.12:

> This [path] is the study of the Law which He commanded by the hand of Moses, that they may do according to all that has been revealed from age to age, and the Prophets have revealed by His Holy Spirit (1QS 8.15-16).

> And in all of them He raised for Himself men called by name, that a remnant might be left to the Land, and that the face of the earth might be filled with their seed. And He made known His Holy Spirit to them by the hand of His anointed ones, and He proclaimed the truth [to them]. But those whom He hated He led astray (CD 2.11-13).

Although the text is badly damaged, it is likely that 1Q34bis 2.6-7 also associates the Spirit with divine revelation:

---

1.   4Q504 2 (frag. 4), 5 and 1Q34bis 2.6-7 also attribute soteriological functions to the Spirit.

And Thou didst renew for them Thy covenant [founded] on a glorious vision and on the words of Thy Holy [Spirit], on the works of Thy hands and the writing of Thy right hand, that they might know the foundations of glory and the steps towards eternity.

These texts are, of course, descriptions of the Spirit's activity in the distant past.[1] However, the inspiration of the Spirit is not limited to the prophets of the past. The title 'prophet' is never ascribed to the Teacher of Righteousness or other members of the community, yet the scrolls suggest that the Spirit continued to grant esoteric wisdom to the wise in the community for the purpose of instruction.

These sages are most frequently designated by the term משׂכיל.[2] The various duties of the משׂכיל are set forth in 1QS 3.13-15, 4.22 and 9.12-20. Above all, the משׂכיל must 'instruct the upright in the knowledge of the Most High' (1QS 4.22). This knowledge is derived from an inspired interpretation of the law (1QS 9.17; 1QH 5.11). That the Spirit is the source of this inspiration is clear from 1QH 12.11, where, as we have seen, the משׂכיל attributes his wisdom to the Spirit of God. Several texts allude to divinely inspired speech, although without explicit reference to the Spirit (1QH 1.27-29; 3.6-18; 7.11; 8.36; 11.12).

The inspiration of the Spirit, initially experienced upon entrance into the community, continued to be active in the member as he increased in purity and holiness. Holiness was closely associated with study and observance of the law. Thus the community distinguished between various levels of sapiential achievement. All members of the community were ranked 'according to their understanding and deeds' (1QS 5.23-24).[3] The leaders of the community were to be perfect in holiness and wisdom (1QS 8.1-2).[4] Both attributes are associated with the inspiration of the Spirit throughout 1QH. The wise then, by definition, were those who experienced the Spirit in a particularly profound way. From their Spirit-inspired wisdom they were to instruct the community.

---

1.   There are also references in the scrolls to a messianic figure endowed with the Spirit (1QSb 5.25; 11QMelch). These texts are similar in character to the texts from *1 Enoch* and *Psalms of Solomon* previously discussed (see Chapter 3 §2.2 above).

2.   The title חכמי does occur (1QSa 1.28; 2.16), but it is less frequent and probably synonymous with משׂכיל.

3.   Davis, *Wisdom*, p. 42; and D. Flusser, 'The Dead Sea Scrolls and Pre-Pauline Christianity', in *Aspects of the Dead Sea Scrolls* (1967), p. 247.

4.   See also 1QH 10.27.

4. *Summary*

Although the Qumran community reserved the term 'prophet' for the biblical figures of the past, they clearly viewed the Spirit as active in their midst. The scrolls present the Spirit as the dynamic of the religious life of the community. The Spirit grants esoteric wisdom to the משכיל for the purpose of instruction and, according to 1QH, enables every member of the community to draw near to God. The pneumatological perspective of 1QH is, however, decidedly different from that of 1QS, where the two spirits, in a manner analogous to the rabbinic good and evil יצר, appear as impulses placed within every individual at creation. The hymns of 1QH may represent a later stage in the community's reflection on the Spirit. They declare that the gift of the Spirit is the source of sapiential achievement at every level. For this reason, reception of the gift of the Spirit is necessary for one to know God and live within the community of salvation. Thus the hymns of 1QH, like Wisdom, attribute soteriological significance to the gift of the Spirit.

Chapter 5

THE RABBINIC LITERATURE*

1. The Spirit and Prophetic Inspiration

The rabbis equated experience of the Spirit with prophetic inspiration.
The Spirit is consistently portrayed as the source of special insight and
inspired speech throughout the rabbinic literature. Numerous rabbinic
citations refer to various individuals 'seeing' or 'speaking in the Spirit'.[1]
However, an important question must be addressed before the significance of this material for our inquiry can be properly assessed. Do these
texts provide us with material valuable for reconstructing first-century
Jewish perspectives on the Spirit? I shall seek to answer this question in
the affirmative by demonstrating that rabbinic traditions which identify
the Spirit with prophetic inspiration can be traced back to the pre-
Christian era.

The Targum tradition also represents a rich source of information
concerning Jewish perspectives on the Spirit. After some preliminary
comments concerning the antiquity of the Targum tradition, I shall
examine relevant texts from the various Targums.

1.1. Early Rabbinic Tradition

Although the rabbinic writings were compiled between AD 200 and 500,
it is generally recognized that they contain traditions from the pre-
Christian era. However, these early traditions must be distinguished from
those of a later era.[2] A methodology which will help us meet this

---

* The rabbinic literature examined includes portions from the Mishnah, the
Tosefta, the Babylonian Talmud, the Jerusalem Talmud, the Tannaitic Midrashim, the
Homiletic Midrashim, the *Midrash Rabbah*, *Midrash on Psalms*, *PRE*, *ARN* and the
Targums.
    1. See the numerous texts cited by P. Schäfer, *Die Vorstellung vom heiligen
Geist in der rabbinischen Literatur* (1972), pp. 151-57, 161.
    2. New Testament scholars have been criticized for 'massive and sustained

objective has been proposed by Renée Bloch.[1] Bloch suggests that the antiquity of a tradition may be determined through a process of 'internal' and 'external comparison'. 'Internal comparison' involves tracing the development of a rabbinic tradition through the various stages which the documents containing the tradition represent. It is important to distinguish the primitive elements of the tradition from later additions or revisions. Jacob Neusner has offered some helpful guidelines for engaging in internal comparison.[2] Particularly noteworthy is Neusner's suggestion that related traditions be arranged into a logical sequence of development. 'External comparison' involves comparing rabbinic traditions, which are largely undated or dated inaccurately, with texts external to rabbinic Judaism 'which have at least an approximate date and in which the same traditions are found'.[3] With these methodological considerations in view, we turn to the rabbinic texts.

1.1.1. T. Soṭ. 13.2. A rabbinic lament over the cessation of prophecy is found in *t. Soṭ.* 13.2:

> When the latter prophets died, that is, Haggai, Zechariah, and Malachi, then the Holy Spirit came to an end in Israel. But even so, they made them hear [Heavenly messages] through an echo.[4]

The text clearly equates prophecy with the inspiration of the Spirit: the cessation of prophecy is the cessation of pneumatic experience. Furthermore, there are indications that *t. Soṭ.* 13.2 represents early tradition. As a Tannaitic document edited in the late third or early fourth century AD, the Tosefta comes from the earliest period of rabbinic redaction.[5] Internal criteria confirm the antiquity of the tradition contained in the text. External criteria suggest that the tradition originated in the pre-Christian era.

---

anachronism in their use of Rabbinic sources' (P.S. Alexander, 'Rabbinic Judaism and the New Testament', *ZNW* 74 [1983], p. 244).

1. R. Bloch, 'Methodological Note for the Study of Rabbinic Literature', in *Approaches to Ancient Judaism: Theory and Practice* (1978), pp. 56-61.

2. J. Neusner, 'The Teaching of the Rabbis: Approaches Old and New', *JJS* 27 (1976), pp. 231-33.

3. Bloch, 'Methodological Note', p. 56.

4. ET by J. Neusner, *Sota* 13.3 (Heb. text: 13.2), in *Nashim* (1979), *The Tosefta*, III. The more literal rendering below is my own.

5. Schürer, *History*, I, p. 77.

Internal Criteria

t. Sot. 13.2

When Haggai, Zechariah, and Malachi, the latter prophets, died, then the Holy Spirit departed from Israel (פסקה רוח הקודש מישראל). But even so, they made them hear [Heavenly messages] through an echo.

The passages which parallel *t. Sot.* 13.2 include:[1]

y. Sot. 9.13/14

When the latter prophets died, that is, Haggai, Zechariah, and Malachi, then the Holy Spirit departed from them (פסקה מהן רוח הקודש). But even so, they made them hear [Heavenly messages] through an echo.

b. Sot. 48b

When Haggai, Zechariah, and Malachi died; then the Holy Spirit went out from Israel (נסתלקה רוח הקודש מישראל:). But even so, they made them hear [Heavenly messages] through an echo.

b. Sanh. 11a

When the latter prophets died, that is, Haggai, Zechariah, and Malachi, then the Holy Spirit went out from Israel (נסתלקה רוח הקודש מישראל:). But even so, they made them hear [Heavenly messages] through an echo.

b. Yom. 9b

When the latter prophets died, that is, Haggai, Zechariah, and Malachi, then the Holy Spirit went out from Israel (נסתלקה רוח הקודש מישראל:). But even so, they made them hear [Heavenly messages] through an echo.

The striking similarities between these texts indicate that they are dependent upon related traditions. However, the texts differ at significant points and a comparison of these differences is revealing. While *t. Sot.* 13.2 and *y. Sot.* 9.13/14 employ פסקה with reference to the departure of the Holy Spirit from Israel/them respectively, the three texts from the Babylonian Talmud employ נסתלקה. However, all three citations from the Babylonian Talmud agree with *t. Sot.* 13.2 against the Jerusalem Talmud in their use of רוח הקודש מישראל ('Holy Spirit from Israel') rather than מהן רוח הקודש ('Holy Spirit from them'). Thus, at significant points of disagreement, the texts of the Jerusalem (*y. Sot.* 9.13/14) and Babylonian Talmuds (*b. Sot.* 48b; *b. Sanh.* 11a; *b. Yom.*

---

1. The Hebrew text of *t. Sot.* 13.2 is from M.S. Zuckermandel, *Tosefta* (1882). The Hebrew text of *y. Sot.* 9.13/14 is from תלמוד ירושלמי (Wilna: Romm, 1926). Texts for *b. Sot.* 48b, *b. Sanh.* 11a and *b. Yom.* 9b are from L. Goldschmidt, *Der Babylonische Talmud*. ETs are my own.

9b) agree with *t. Soṭ.* 13.2. This fact suggests that the Jerusalem and Babylonian Talmuds are dependent upon the earlier tradition contained in *t. Soṭ.* 13.2.[1] This judgment receives further support from an analysis of the immediate context of *t. Soṭ.* 13.2 and the parallel texts. Each of the passages cited above, with the exception of *b. Yom.* 9b,[2] record a message uttered by the בת קול ('echo') in the midst of a gathering of the wise in Jericho:

> 'There is among you a man who is worthy to receive the Holy Spirit
> (יש כאן אדם שראוי כרוח הקודש), but the generation is unworthy of such an
> honor'. They all set their eyes upon Samuel the Small. At the time of his
> death what did they say? 'Woe for the humble man, woe for the pious
> man, the disciple of Hillel the Elder!' (*t. Soṭ.* 13.4).[3]

The parallel texts in the Babylonian Talmud (*b. Soṭ.* 48b; *b. Sanh.* 11a) replace the רוח הקודש ('Holy Spirit') of *t. Soṭ.* 13.4 with שכינה ('divine presence'). The use of שכינה rather than רוח הקודש is characteristic of the Babylonian Talmud and probably represents a later redaction.[4] This suggests that the Babylonian Talmud has altered the early tradition preserved in *t. Soṭ.* 13.4.

The rabbinic discussion concerning the dating of the withdrawal of the Holy Spirit and the cessation of prophecy follows a logical progression of thought. By placing *t. Soṭ.* 13.2 within this logical sequence, it is possible to uncover further evidence for the relative antiquity of the tradition underlying this text. *T. Soṭ.* 13.2 dates the withdrawal of the Holy Spirit from the death of Haggai, Zechariah and Malachi. This statement contradicts another strand of rabbinic tradition which associates the withdrawal of the Holy Spirit with the destruction of the first temple,[5] for Haggai, Zechariah and Malachi lived in the post-exilic period after the destruction of the first temple.

---

1.   Schäfer, *Die Vorstellung*, p. 95.

2.   *B. Yom.* 9b does not follow the other parallel passages at this point and represents an independent redaction of several traditions.

3.   Samuel the Small is from the second generation Tannaim (AD 90–130; H.L. Strack, *Introduction to the Talmud and Midrash* [1931], p. 112).

4.   See Schäfer, *Die Vorstellung*, pp. 93, 97, 142; A.M. Goldberg, *Untersuchungen über die Vorstellung von der Schekhinah in der frühen rabbinischen Literatur* (1969), pp. 219-24.

5.   Rabbinic citations which link the withdrawal of the Holy Spirit with the first temple include: *Lam. R. Proem* 23; *Eccl. R.* 12.7.1; *Num. R.* 15.10.

Two attempts to resolve this apparent contradiction are recorded in
Pes. K. 13,14:

As Benjamin was the last of the tribes, so was Jeremiah the last of all the
prophets. Did Haggai, Zechariah, and Malachi not prophesy after him?
Rabbi Eleazar and Rabbi Samuel bar Nachman: R. Eleazar said: They
shortened (קיצרי) his [Jeremiah's] prophecy. R. Samuel bar Nachman
said: The commission to prophesy to them was already laid in the hands,
the hands of Haggai, Zechariah, and Malachi.[1]

With the term קיצר ('shortened'), Rabbi Eleazar states that Haggai,
Zechariah and Malachi were dependent on the prophecy of Jeremiah.
Rabbi Eleazar is thus able to associate the post-exilic prophets with the
period before the destruction of the first temple and reconcile the two
apparently contradictory traditions concerning the withdrawal of the
Holy Spirit and the cessation of prophecy. Rabbi Samuel bar Nachman
resolves the problem in a different manner. He argues that the post-exilic
prophets had already received their prophecies or prophetic commissions in the time of Jeremiah, that is before the destruction of the first
temple: they *only proclaimed* their prophecies after the first temple was
destroyed.[2] These attempts at reconciliation indicate that the two
conflicting views were already firmly established at a relatively early
date.[3] Thus, in light of *Pes. K.* 13,14, *t. Soṭ.* 13.2 must be placed in the
earliest period of the development of rabbinic thought on this matter.

External Criteria. Outside the rabbinic literature we search in vain for
exact parallels to *t. Soṭ.* 13.2. Nevertheless, 1 Macc. 4.46, 9.27 and
14.41 reflect the conviction that the age of prophecy had ceased.[4] These
texts bear witness to the existence of a tradition concerning the cessation
of prophecy in the early part of the first century BC.[5] This external

1.   The Hebrew text of *Pes. K.* 13,14 is from B. Mandelbaum, *Pesikta de Rab
Kahana* (1962), p. 238. ET is my own.
2.   Schäfer, *Die Vorstellung*, p. 96.
3.   R. Samuel bar Nachman and R. Eleazar (ben Pedath) may be placed in the
early part of the fourth century AD (see J. Bowker, *The Targums and Rabbinic
Literature* (1969), p. 369; Strack, *Introduction*, pp. 124-25).
4.   Thus Marmorstein asserts that the author of 1 Maccabees must have been
familiar with the view that the Holy Spirit vanished with the last prophets (*Studies in
Jewish Theology* [1950], pp. 123-24). See also Ps. 74.9; Zech. 13.2-6; Josephus,
Apion 1.41; *2 Bar.* 85.1-3.
5.   Nickelsburg dates 1 Maccabees between 104 and 63 BC (*Jewish Literature,*

witness, coupled with the internal criteria detailed above, suggests that *t. Soṭ.* 13.2 represents a tradition which originated in the pre-Christian era.

1.1.2. ARN A.34. A commentary on the mishnaic tractate *Pirke Aboth*, *Aboth de Rabbi Nathan (ARN)* offers important insight into rabbinic perspectives on the Spirit:

> By ten names was the Holy Spirit called, to wit: parable, metaphor, riddle, speech, saying, glory, command, burden, prophecy, vision (*ARN* A.34).[1]

There is a striking coherence in the ten names given for the Holy Spirit in *ARN* A.34: virtually all of the names are related to phenomena characteristic of prophetic inspiration. The majority of the names are directly related to aspects of speech. The Spirit is also associated with special revelation (vision), and explicitly cited as the source of prophecy.

In several of the texts which parallel *ARN* A.34 the term 'Holy Spirit' is replaced with 'Prophecy' (e.g. *ARN* B.37; *Gen. R.* 44.6; *Cant. R.* 3.4).[2] These texts do not refer to the Holy Spirit. *Cant. R.* 3.4 serves as an example of this variation in the tradition:

> There are ten expressions denoting prophecy: vision, prophecy, preaching, speaking, saying, commanding, burden, poetry, riddle.[3]

A third variation in the tradition is found in *MHG* Gen. 242:

> With ten names prophecy is named: 'seeing' as it is said 'is the Seer here?' (1 Sam. 9.11); 'watching' as it is said 'I have appointed you a watchman' (Ezek. 3.17 and 33.7); 'proverb' as it is said 'the proverbs of Solomon' (Prov. 1.1); 'interpretation' as it is said 'my interpreters are my friends' (Job 16.20); 'the Holy Spirit' as it is said 'take not your Holy Spirit from me' (Ps. 51.13);[4] 'prophecy' as it is said 'I will raise up a prophet for them' (Deut. 18.18); 'vision' as it is said 'the vision of Isaiah the son of Amoz' (Isa. 1.1); 'oracle' as it is said 'the oracle which Habakkuk saw' (Hab. 1.1); 'sermon' as it is said 'do not preach against the house of Isaac' (Amos 7.16); 'riddle' as it is said 'son of man speak a riddle' (Ezek. 17.2).[5]

p. 117); see also Schürer, *History*, III, p. 181.

1.   ET from J. Goldin, *The Fathers according to Rabbi Nathan* (1955).
2.   For a more comprehensive list of texts see Schäfer, *Die Vorstellung*, p. 19.
3.   ET is from M. Simon, 'Song of Songs', *The Midrash Rabbah* (1977), IV.
4.   MT Ps. 51.13; ET Ps. 51.11.
5.   Hebrew text is from M. Margulies, *Midrash Haggadol on the Pentateuch: Genesis* (1947), p. רמב (242). ET is my own.

Reversing the roles of the terms 'Holy Spirit' and 'prophecy' found in *ARN* A.34, *MHG* Gen. 242 lists רוח הקדש as a name for נבואה. The biblical text which *MHG* Gen. 242 cites as support for the identification of the Spirit with prophecy, Ps. 51.11 (MT Ps. 51.13), is particularly striking. This text is frequently interpreted by modern exegetes with reference to the Spirit as the source of the moral-religious life. Yet, according to *MHG* Gen. 242, the Spirit of Ps. 51.11 is the Spirit of prophecy. Thus *MHG* Gen. 242 gives us valuable insight into how extensively the gift of the Spirit was identified with prophetic inspiration by the rabbis.

Internal Criteria. The tradition of the 'ten names' has been preserved in three variant forms represented by *ARN* A.34, Song 3.4 and *MHG* Gen. 242. How are we to assess the development of this tradition? In terms of final redaction, *ARN* A is to be dated earlier than *Midrash Rabbah* and *Midrash Haggadol*.[1] Although *ARN* A, in its present form, belongs to the post-Talmudic period, all of the rabbis whom it cites belong to the age of the Mishnah and it 'may be considered as Tannaitic in substance'.[2] The question of the relationship between *ARN* A and *ARN* B is relevant, in that they represent two of the variant forms of this tradition. Although this question has not yet received a definitive answer, some feel that *ARN* A represents an earlier (if less faithful) version of a lost proto-*ARN*.[3] If we are allowed to borrow a criterion from textual criticism in our analysis of the literary relationship of these texts, 'the harder reading is to be preferred', *ARN* A.34 would undoubtedly be selected as the more primitive version. We can visualize later redactors altering the text to read 'prophecy' rather than 'Holy Spirit' for contextual reasons. However, it is more difficult to speculate why a redactor would do the reverse, particularly in light of the fact that *ARN* A.34 is the only text which preserves the tradition in this way. It is also possible that the inclusion of 'Holy Spirit' as one of the names for prophecy in *MHG* Gen. 242 is an accommodation to the early tradition preserved in *ARN* A.34 and its alteration by later redactors. Therefore, it is most probable

---

1.   Schürer places *Midrash Haggadol* in the thirteenth century AD and *Cant. R.* in the seventh or eighth century AD (*History*, I, pp. 93, 95).

2.   Schürer, *History*, I, p. 80. See also Goldin, *The Fathers* (1955), p. xi; and Bowker, *The Targums*, p. 88.

3.   See Goldin, *The Fathers*, p. xxii.

that *ARN* A.34 represents an early tradition, one upon which the other parallel texts are dependent.[1]

External Criteria. There are no texts outside the rabbinic literature which parallel *ARN* A.34. Nevertheless, as we have seen, numerous texts throughout the intertestamental period associate the Spirit with prophetic inspiration in a manner similar to *ARN* A.34. It is therefore quite probable that this tradition cited by the rabbis of the Tannaitic period originated in the pre-Christian era.

1.2. *The Targums*

It is generally recognized that the Targums 'embody ancient exegetical traditions'.[2] Thus, although the nature of the development of the Targum tradition remains a matter of dispute, most scholars agree that the Targums constitute an invaluable source for reconstructing first-century Jewish thought.[3] I shall therefore assess the significance of the Targums for this inquiry into Jewish perspectives on the Spirit.

1.2.1. *The Targums of the Pentateuch*

Codex Neofiti. In *CN*, apart from the references to the Spirit in connection with creation,[4] the Spirit of God is almost always designated by the term רוח קודשה.[5] The only occurrence of רוח נבואה is found in the margin of Exod. 2.12. *CN* Exod. 31.3 also contains a reference to רוח דנבי ('spirit of a prophet') which may be a corruption of רוח נבואה ('Spirit of prophecy'). In each of these occurrences רוח קודשה appears as the source of prophetic inspiration.

---

1.   Schäfer, *Die Vorstellung*, p. 20.

2.   G. Vermes, *Scripture and Tradition in Judaism: Haggadic Studies* (1973), p. 177.

3.   I refer to the Targums of the Pentateuch (*CN, TO, Targ. Ps.-J., Frag. Targ.*) and *Targum Jonathan* (*TJ*) to the Prophets. The Targums on the Writings are, on the whole, considered to be of later origin (Aramaic fragments of Job have, however, been discovered at Qumran). For this reason I shall limit the inquiry to the Targums of the Pentateuch and Prophets. For a survey of recent trends see M. McNamara, *Palestinian Judaism and the New Testament* (1983), pp. 211-17.

4.   See *CN* Gen. 1.2; 2.7.

5.   Or similar expressions (ברוח קודשא; רוח דקדש). See Gen. 31.21 (M); 41.38; 42.1; Exod. 2.12 (M2); 35.31; Num. 11.17, 25 (2×), 26, 28, 29; 14.24; 24.2; 27.18. This list includes the marginal readings in Gen. 31.21 and Exod. 2.12. Exod. 2.12 has two marginal readings (M1: ברוח נבואה; M2: ברוח קודשא).

The pneumatological perspective of *CN* is particularly apparent in those texts where the MT text has been significantly modified. Jacob's flight from Laban to the hill country of Gilead is described in Gen. 31.21. *CN* adds in the margin this explanatory note: 'because he had seen in the holy spirit (ברוח קודשא) that liberation would be effected there for Israel in the days of Jephthah of Gilead'.[1] According to *CN* Gen. 42.1, Jacob saw 'in the holy spirit' (ברוח קודשא) that corn was being sold in Egypt. The margin of *CN* Exod. 2.12 gives justification for Moses' murder of the Egyptian: '[Moses saw] in the holy spirit (ברוח קודשא) the two worlds and behold, there was no proselyte destined to arise from that Egyptian; and he smote the Egyptian and buried him in the sand'.[2] *CN* Num. 11.28 records that Joshua, in response to the prophesying of Eldad and Medad, asked Moses to 'withhold the holy spirit from them' (מנע מנהון רוח קודשה). In each of these additions to the MT by *CN*, the Spirit is the source of special revelation or inspired speech.

Targum Onqelos. This Targum explicitly states what is implied in the redaction of *CN*: the Spirit of God is 'the Spirit of prophecy' (רוח נבואה).[3] The only exception is a reference to רוח קודשא in *TO* Gen. 45.27. J.P. Schäfer has questioned the authenticity of this reading.[4] Regardless of which reading is to be preferred, in *TO* Gen. 45.27 the Spirit functions as the Spirit of prophecy, revealing to Jacob the veracity of the message brought to him that Joseph lives. The *TO* frequently translates the רוח אלהים of the MT with רוח נבואה. Two examples are listed below.

Gen. 41.38:

MT ...a man in whom is the Spirit of God (רוח אלהים).

TO ...a man in whom is the Spirit of prophecy (רוח נבואה) from before the Lord.

---

1. The Aramaic text of *CN* is from Diez Macho, *Neophyti I* (6 vols.; 1968). An ET is provided by M. McNamara and M. Maher in the same work.

2. This is the reading of M2. M1 reads, '[Moses looked] in a spirit of prophecy in this world and in the world to come and he saw and behold, there was no innocent man to go forth from him and he smote the Egyptian and buried him in the sand'.

3. See *TO* on Gen. 41.38; Exod. 31.3; 35.31; Num. 11.25, 26, 29; 24.2; 27.18. Aramaic texts are from A. Sperber, *The Bible in Aramaic*. I. *The Pentateuch according to Targum Onkelos* (1959). ETs cited below are my own.

4. P. Schäfer, 'Die Termini "Heiliger Geist" und "Geist der Prophetie" in den Targumim und das Verhältnis der Targumim zueinander', *VT* 20 (1970), p. 307.

Num. 27.18:

MT 　　　...a man in whom is the Spirit (רוח).

TO 　　　...a man in whom is the Spirit of prophecy (דרוח נבואה).

These redactions in *TO* represent further evidence of the tendency in the Targum tradition to equate the activity of the Spirit with prophetic inspiration.

Targum Pseudo-Jonathan. This Targum reflects the terminology characteristic of both *CN* and *TO*, using the term רוח קודשא 15 times and the term רוח נבואה 11 times.[1] For *Targ. Ps.-J.*, like *CN*, רוח קודשא is the source of prophetic inspiration. Particularly noteworthy are the numerous texts into which *Targ. Ps.-J.* inserts the term רוח קודשא which do not parallel *CN*. One example is *Targ. Ps.-J.* Gen. 27.5, which states that Rebecca was enabled by the Holy Spirit to hear the words Isaac spoke to Esau:

MT 　　　　　Rebekah listened as Isaac spoke to Esau.

CN 　　　　　Rebekah listened as Isaac spoke to Esau.

Targ. Ps.-J. 　Rebekah listened through the Holy Spirit (ברוח קודשא) as Isaac spoke to Esau.[2]

The Fragmentary Targum. As in *CN*, the *Frag. Targ.* generally uses the term רוח קודשה rather than רוח נבואה. However, רוח נבואה does appear in *Frag. Targ.* Num. 11.28:

> And Joshua son of Nun, Moses' attendant, from among the youths, spoke up and said: 'My master, Moses, stop the prophetic spirit from them (פסוק מנהון רוח נבואה)'.[3]

Furthermore, only five occurrences of רוח קודשה can be found in *Frag. Targ.*,[4] and of these five occurrences, two are unique to *Frag. Targ.* in relation to *CN*: Gen. 27.1 and Gen. 37.33. According to *Frag. Targ.* Gen. 27.1, Isaac was capable of being deceived by Jacob because 'he

---

1. רוח קודשא: Gen. 6.3; 27.5, 42; 30.25; 31.21 (= *CN*); 35.22; 37.33; 43.14; Exod. 31.3 (= *CN*); 33.16; Deut. 5.21; 18.15, 18; 28.59; 32.26. רוח נבואה: Gen. 41.38 (= *TO*); 45.27; Exod. 33.16; 35.31 (= *TO*); Num. 11.17, 25 (= *TO*), 26 (= *TO*), 28, 29 (= *TO*); 24.2 (= *TO*); 27.18 (= *TO*).

2. The Aramaic text of *Targ. Ps.-J.* is from M. Ginsburger, *Pseudo-Jonathan* (1903). ETs are my own.

3. The Aramaic text and ET are from M.L. Klein, *The Fragment-Targums of the Pentateuch according to their Extant Sources* (2 vols.; 1980).

4. Gen. 27.1; 37.33; 42.1 (= *CN*); Exod. 2.12 (= *CN*); Num. 11.26 (= *CN*).

was old and his eyes were too dim to see' (with the MT) and furthermore, because 'the holy spirit departed from him'. In *Frag. Targ.* Gen.
37.33 the entire sense of the biblical passage is changed. Upon seeing
Joseph's torn tunic, rather than assuming the worst (as in the MT), Jacob
responds:

> It is my son's garment; a wild beast has not devoured him nor has my son
> been killed at all; however, I see through the holy spirit that an evil woman
> stands opposite him, the wife of Potiphar (*Frag. Targ.* Gen. 37.33).

In the texts unique to *Frag. Targ.* there is no change from *CN* in the
way the activity of the Holy Spirit is perceived: the Spirit is the source
of special revelation and inspiration. Although the Targums of the
Pentateuch refer to the Spirit of God with different terms and in different contexts, they all agree on a fundamental point: the Spirit of God is
the Spirit of prophecy.

1.2.2. *Targum Jonathan to the Prophets*. *Targum Jonathan* modifies the
Spirit-terminology of the MT in a variety of ways.[1] References to the
Spirit of God in the MT are often translated רוח נבואה in *Targum
Jonathan*.[2] According to *TJ* 1 Sam 10.10, 'the Spirit of prophecy (רוח
נבואה) from before the Lord resided upon [Saul] and he sang praise in
their midst'. So also *TJ* Isa. 61.1 reads: 'The Spirit of prophecy (רוח
נבואה) from before the Lord Elohim is upon me'.

The prophetic character of pneumatic experience is presupposed in
three other texts from the Targum of Isaiah. Compare the following
texts from *TJ* Isaiah with their counterparts in the MT:

MT Isa. 40.13   Who has understood the spirit of the Lord (רוח־יהוה)?

TJ Isa. 40.13   Who hath directed the holy spirit (רוח קודשא) in the mouth
                   of all the prophets (בפום כל נבייא)?

MT Isa. 63.11   Where is he who set his Holy Spirit (רוח קדשו) among them?[3]

---

1.   Aramaic texts are from A. Sperber, *The Bible in Aramaic*. II. *The Former
Prophets according to Targum Jonathan* (1959); and *The Bible in Aramaic*. III. *The
Latter Prophets according to Targum Jonathan* (1962). ETs are from: S.H. Levey,
The Targum of Ezekiel (1987); D.J. Harrington and A.J. Saldarini, *Targum Jonathan
of the Former Prophets* (1987); J.F. Stenning, *The Targum of Isaiah* (2nd edn, 1953).
2.   See for example *TJ* Judg. 3.10; 1 Sam. 10.6, 10; 19.20, 23; 2 Sam. 23.2;
1 Kgs 22.24; 2 Kgs 2.9; Isa. 61.1; Ezek. 11.5.
3.   A similar alteration occurs in *TJ* Isa. 63.10. רוח is frequently translated with
מימר in the Targum of Isaiah: see *TJ* Isa. 4.4; 28.6; 30.28; 34.6; 48.16; 59.19; 63.10,
11, 14.

TJ Isa. 63.11	Where is he who caused the word of his holy prophets (מימר נבי קודשׁיה) to dwell among them?
MT Isa. 59.21	This is my covenant with them, says the Lord, My Spirit (רוחי), who is on you, and my words (דברי) that I have put in your mouth will not depart from you.
TJ Isa. 59.21	This is my covenant with them, saith the Lord; my holy spirit (רוח קדשׁי) which is upon thee, and the words of prophecy (ופתגמי נבואתי) which I have put in thy mouth, shall not depart from thy mouth.

In the Targum of Ezekiel the phrase 'the hand of the Lord' (MT: יד-יהוה) is frequently altered to 'the Spirit of prophecy' (רוח נבואה).[1] Compare, for example, TJ Ezek. 1.3, 'the Spirit of prophecy (רוח נבואה) from before the Lord rested upon (Ezekiel)', with the biblical text: 'the hand of the Lord (יד-יהוה) was upon (Ezekiel)'. In texts where prophetic inspiration is not in view, references to the Lord's hand, 'my hand' (MT: ידי), are rendered 'my power' (גבורתי).[2] In texts from the former prophets which speak of miraculous (non-prophetic) deeds, such as Samson's exploits, 'the Spirit of the Lord' (MT: רוח יהוה) is often rendered 'Spirit of power' (רוח גבורא).[3] However, רוח נבואה is occasionally found in texts where we would expect to find רוח גבורא (e.g. TJ Judg. 3.10; 2 Kgs 2.9). These texts, along with the modifications of TJ Ezekiel and TJ Isaiah cited above, indicate that the redactors of TJ tended to associate the Spirit exclusively with prophetic inspiration.

2. The Spirit and the Age to Come

Several passages in the Hebrew Scriptures anticipate a universal outpouring of the Spirit over the house of Israel in 'the last days'.[4] In the following section I shall examine how these biblical passages were interpreted by the rabbis and discuss the relevance of the rabbinic evidence for reconstructing eschatological expectations in first-century Judaism.

---

1. See TJ Ezek. 1.3; 3.22; 8.1; 40.1. Compare also TJ Ezek. 3.14, 'and a prophecy from before the Lord overwhelmed me', with the biblical text: 'and the strong hand of the Lord upon me'.
2. See TJ Ezek. 6.14; 13.9; 14.9, 13; 25.7, 13, 16; 39.21. This practice is not limited to TJ Ezekiel: see for example TJ Josh. 4.24; Jer. 6.12; 15.6; 16.21; 51.25.
3. See for example TJ Judg. 11.29; 13.25; 14.6, 19; 15.14; 1 Sam. 16.13, 14. See also 1 Sam. 11.6, where 'the Spirit of God' is rendered 'Spirit of power'.
4. Num. 11.29; Joel 3.1-2; Ezek. 36.27; 37.14; 39.29; Isa. 44.3; Zech. 12.10.

2.1. *The Eschatological Bestowal of the Spirit*

The expectation of an endtime outpouring of the Spirit is found in a number of rabbinic texts. Although the rabbis maintained that the Spirit had departed from Israel due to her sin,[1] they looked forward to the day when the Spirit would once again come upon her people. This eschatological outpouring of the Spirit is generally interpreted in light of Joel 3.1-2 (MT) as a restoration of the Spirit of prophecy.[2] *MHG* Gen. 140 and *Num. R.* 15.25 are representative of this perspective:

> The Holy Spirit, as in Scripture: 'I will raise up prophets from your sons' (Amos 2.11). But because they sinned, he departed from them, as it is written: 'Also, her prophets find no vision from the Lord' (Lam. 2.9). But one day the Holy One will bring him back to Israel, as it is written: 'And afterward, I will pour out my Spirit on all flesh, and your sons and daughters will prophesy' (Joel 3.1) (*MHG* Gen. 140).

> The Holy One, blessed be He, said: 'In this world only a few individuals have prophesied, but in the World to come all Israel will be made prophets', as it says: 'And it shall come to pass afterward, that I will pour out my spirit upon all flesh, and your sons and your daughters shall prophesy, your old men', etc. (Joel 3.1). Such is the exposition given by R. Tanhuma, son of R. Abba (*Num. R.* 15.25).[3]

Ezek. 36.26 is frequently cited with reference to the age to come. However, it is usually interpreted as a prophecy concerning the endtime removal of the evil יצר (impulse), and, in this regard, almost always without reference to the activity of the Spirit.[4] A notable exception is *Tan. add.* to חקת:

> Concerning this the Wise say: The one who does not look at another's wife, the evil impulse (יצר הרע) has no power over him. In the World to come the Holy One, blessed be He, will take the evil impulse from us and

---

1. See *MHG* Gen. 135, 139-40; *MHG* Exod. 438; *Ruth R. Proem* 2; *Sif. Deut.* §173.

2. See *MHG* Gen. 139-40; *Num. R.* 15.25; *Deut. R.* 6.14; *Lam. R.* 4.14; *Midr. Ps.* 14.6, 138.2. *Ag. Ber.* §23.2 clearly refers to a restoration of the Spirit of prophecy, but without reference to Joel 3.1.

3. Hebrew text of *MHG* Gen. 140 is from M. Margulies, *Midrash Haggadol on the Pentateuch, Genesis*, p. 140. ET is my own. ET of *Num. R.* 15.25 is from J.J. Slotki, 'Numbers', in *The Midrash Rabbah*, III.

4. *Exod. R.* 15.6; 41.7; *Num. R.* 14.4; *Deut. R.* 6.14; *Cant. R.* 1.2.4; *Eccl. R.* 9.15; *Midr. Ps.* 14.6. Jer. 31.33 is also cited in conjunction with the hope that the evil יצר would be removed in the age to come: *Cant. R.* 1.2.4; *Eccl. R.* 2.1.

place in us his Holy Spirit (רוח קדשו), as it is written: 'I will remove the heart of stone from your flesh and I will put my Spirit in you' (Ezek. 36.26-27).[1]

Numerous texts cite Ezek. 36.26 independent of any reference to the evil יצר. These texts are also remarkably silent concerning the activity of the Spirit: they usually refer to the endtime transformation of the heart without alluding to the Spirit.[2]

My judgment that the rabbis generally interpreted the eschatological outpouring of the Spirit as a restoration of the Spirit of prophecy (Joel 3.1-2) is confirmed by *Deut. R.* 6.14 and *Midr. Ps.* 14.6. These texts speak of the age to come with reference to both Ezek. 36.26 and Joel 3.1. In each instance, the transformation of the heart alluded to in Ezek. 36.26 is presented as a prerequisite for the eschatological bestowal of the Spirit, which is interpreted in light of Joel 3.1 as an outpouring of the Spirit of prophecy.

In *Deut. R.* 6.14 the future eradication of the evil יצר is linked to Ezek. 36.26 and cited as a precondition for the endtime restoration of the divine presence (שכינה). The rabbis commonly believed that experience of the Spirit was dependent upon the immanence of the שכינה.[3] Therefore, Joel 3.1 is offered as scriptural proof that in the age to come the שכינה shall be restored to Israel.

> God said: 'In this world, because there are amongst you slanderers, I have withdrawn My divine Presence (שכינתי) from amongst you', as it is said, 'Be Thou exalted, O God, above the heavens' (Ps. 52.12). 'But in the time to come, when I will uproot the Evil Inclination from amongst you', as it is said, 'And I will take away the stony heart out of your flesh' (Ezek. 36.26), 'I will restore My Divine Presence (שכינתי) amongst you'. Whence this? For it is said, 'And it shall come to pass afterward, that I will pour out My Spirit upon all flesh', etc. (Joel 3.1); 'and because I will cause My Divine Presence (שכינתי) to rest upon you, all of you will merit the Torah,

---

1. Hebrew text is from S. Buber, *Midrasch Tanchuma* (1885). ET is my own. *Num. R.* 17.6 also refers to the Spirit by quoting from Ezek. 36.27 as does *Tan. add.* to חקת. However Num. 17.6 lacks the editorial comment, ויתן בקרבנו רוח קדשו, which is unique to *Tan. add.* to חקת.
2. See *b. Suk.* 52a; *Gen. R.* 34.15; *Num. R.* 15.16; *Cant. R.* 6.11.1; *Eccl. R.* 1.16. By way of contrast, the following texts refer to the activity of the Spirit with reference to Ezek. 36.26-27: *b. Ber.* 31b; *b. Suk.* 52b; *Num. R.* 9.49; *Midr. Ps.* 73.4.
3. See *b. Yom.* 9b, *Ag. Ber.* §23.2, and Schäfer, *Die Vorstellung*, pp. 140-43.

and you will dwell in peace in the world', as it is said, 'And all children shall be taught of the Lord; and great shall be the peace of thy children' (Isa. 44.13) (*Deut. R.* 6.14).[1]

Midr. Ps. 14.6 also refers to the transformation of Israel's heart (Ezek. 36.26) as a precondition for the eschatological bestowal of the Spirit of prophecy (Joel 3.1-2).

Another comment: David spoke the first time in behalf of the Master, the Holy One, blessed be He, who said: 'Oh that they had such a heart as this always, to fear Me, and keep My commandments' (Deut. 5.25); and he spoke the second time in behalf of the disciple Moses who said: 'Would that all the Lord's people were prophets' (Num. 11.29). Neither the words of the Master nor the words of the disciple are to be fulfilled in this world, but the words of both will be fulfilled in the world-to-come: The words of the Master, 'A new heart also will I give you and ye shall keep Mine ordinances' (Ezek. 36.26), will be fulfilled; and the words of the disciple, 'I will pour out My spirit upon all flesh; and your sons and daughters shall prophesy' (Joel 3.1), will also be fulfilled (*Midr. Ps.* 14.6).[2]

A large group of texts refer to the eschatological bestowal of the Spirit in general terms.[3] These texts offer little information concerning the Spirit's future function. However, in view of the evidence cited above and the general tendency of the rabbis to identify the Spirit with prophetic inspiration, one may assume that these texts are harmonious with the perspective of *MHG* Gen. 140 and *Num. R.* 15.25: the eschatological outpouring of the Spirit signifies the restoration of the prophetic gift.

Although many of the texts cited above were edited at a relatively late date,[4] the following factors suggest that they bear witness to traditions which accurately reflect aspects of the hope of first-century Judaism.[5] First, 1QS 3.13–4.26 offers an early parallel to the rabbinic texts which speak of the end-time eradication of the evil יצר in light of Ezek. 36.26. The conceptual similarities between 1QS 3–4 and the relevant rabbinic texts are apparent; and the term יצר appears in 1QS 4.5.[6] Secondly, in

1. ET is from J. Rabinowitz, 'Deuteronomy', in *The Midrash Rabbah*. Hebrew text is from S. Liebermann, *Midrash Debarim Rabbah* (1940).
2. ET is from W.G. Braude, *The Midrash on Psalms* (1959).
3. *MHG* Gen. 135; *Num. R.* 15.10; *Cant. R.* 1.1.11; *Pes. R.* 1b; *Lam. R.* 3.138.
4. For example, *Midrash Haggadol* was compiled in the thirteenth century AD (Schürer, *History*, I, p. 93).
5. So also Davies, *Paul*, p. 216.
6. On the relationship between the יצר in the scrolls and the rabbinic יצר see B. Otzen, 'יצר', *ThWAT*, III, p. 839. Cf. *Jub.* 1.20-25.

view of the antiquity of the tradition concerning the withdrawal of the
Spirit and biblical texts such as Num. 11.29 and Joel 3.1-2, it is highly
probable that traditions similar to those found in *MHG* Gen. 140 and
Num. R. 15.25 were current in the first century. Indeed, although it is
quite likely that these traditions were often suppressed in the post-
Christian era for polemical reasons,[1] it is difficult to imagine why rabbis
of this later period would create such traditions in light of Christian
claims. However, the silence of the non-rabbinic intertestamental literature concerning a universal outpouring of the Spirit of prophecy may
indicate that this expectation was a peripheral element in the hope of
first-century Judaism.[2]

2.2. *The Spirit and the Resurrection*

The rabbis occasionally associate the Holy Spirit with the resurrection in
the age to come. These citations generally fall into one of two categories:
texts which refer to the 'chain' saying of R. Phineas b. Jair,[3] and texts
which cite Ezek. 37.14.[4]

The 'chain' of R. Phineas b. Jair is found in the earliest strata of the
rabbinic literature, the Mishnah:

> R. Phineas b. Jair says: Heedfulness leads to cleanliness, and cleanliness
> leads to purity, and purity leads to abstinence, and abstinence leads to
> holiness, and holiness leads to humility, and humility leads to the shunning
> of sin, and the shunning of sin leads to saintliness, and saintliness leads to
> [the gift of] the Holy Spirit, and the Holy Spirit leads to the resurrection of
> the dead. And the resurrection of the dead shall come through Elijah of
> blessed memory. Amen (*m. Soṭ* 9.15).[5]

The initial part of the 'chain' (up to and including 'saintliness leads to
[the gift of] the Holy Spirit') portrays the Spirit as a gift presently
available to the pious individual. The latter part of the 'chain' ('the Holy
Spirit leads to the resurrection of the dead') describes the Spirit as an

1. See Kremer, *Pfingstbericht*, pp. 81-82.
2. See D. Hill, *New Testament Prophecy* (1979), pp. 35-36 and M.A. Chevallier,
L'Esprit et le Messie (1958), p. 105.
3. See *m. Sota* 9.15; *b. 'Abod. Zar.* 20b; *Yalq. Isa.* §503; *y. Sheq.* 3.4; *Cant.
R.* 1.1.9 and the various other texts cited by Schäfer, *Die Vorstellung*, pp. 118-19.
4. *Gen. R.* 14.8; 96 (*MSV*); 96.5; *Exod. R.* 48.4; *Cant. R.* 1.1.9; *Midr. Ps.* 85.3;
Pes. R. 1.6. In the 'chain' of *Cant. R.* 1.1.9, Ezek. 37.14 is cited as the prooftext for
the statement, 'the Holy Spirit leads to the resurrection of the dead'.
5. Strack places R. Phineas b. Jair in the fourth generation of the Tannaim
(c. 180 AD) (*Introduction*, p. 117). ET is from H. Danby, *The Mishnah* (1933).

eschatological gift granted to the nation. How can these disparate conceptions of the Spirit (contemporary–individual/eschatological–national) be reconciled? P. Schäfer suggests a possible solution.[1] He postulates that the initial part of the 'chain' represents the original form of a tradition which originated in mystical circles outside of orthodox Judaism. The latter part of the 'chain' was inserted later to accommodate the 'chain' to the orthodox perspective (withdrawal of the Spirit in the past/ return in the age to come).

Schäfer's hypothesis is not entirely convincing. Although there is some textual support for his suggestion that the reference to Elijah is secondary,[2] the crucial phrase which links the Spirit to the resurrection is found in all of the parallel texts. Furthermore, a number of other texts refer to the Spirit as a reward for piety.[3] Since these texts were not expunged or altered by the rabbis, I am hesitant to view *m. Soṭ* 9.15 as the product of such activity.

There is an alternative solution, one that is not dependent on hypothetical redactional activity. F. Büchsel argued that when the rabbis spoke of the Spirit as a reward for pious living, they did not imply that contemporary experience of the Spirit was possible.[4] Rather, they were using language descriptive of the age to come for the purpose of moral exhortation in the present. Thus Büchsel interprets the Spirit references in the 'chain' as descriptions of the ideal future.[5] In this way Büchsel provides a satisfying solution to the problem posed by the text. The temporal contradiction is resolved, for both statements concerning the Spirit refer to that which will be experienced in the age to come. The individual and national dimensions of the text are also reconciled, for the purpose of the text is to provide moral exhortation: the text affirms that the piety of the individual leads to the future redemption of the nation. This redemption is described in terms of the future resurrection, which is associated with the eschatological gift of the Spirit.

The second group of texts relate the Spirit to the resurrection by

1.   Schäfer, *Die Vorstellung*, pp. 120-21.
2.   '*Abod. Zar.* 20b and *Yalq. Isa.* §503 omit the part which speaks of Elijah.
3.   The Holy Spirit is cited as a reward for: 'obedience to the law' (*Mech.* 113-14); 'learning and doing [the law]' (e.g. *Lev. R.* 35.7; *b. Ber.* 17a); 'good works' (*Num. R.* 10.5; *Ruth R.* 4.3); 'the proclamation of the Torah' (*Cant. R.* 1.1.8-9); 'devotion to Israel' (*Num. R.* 15.20); 'study of the Torah' (*Eccl. R.* 2.8.1).
4.   Büchsel, *Der Geist Gottes*, pp. 128-29.
5.   Büchsel, *Der Geist Gottes*, p. 131.

drawing upon Ezek. 37.14.[1] Several of these texts repeat a tradition dealing with the fate of the righteous who die outside of Israel.[2] Ezek. 37.12-13 is a crucial element in the tradition because it associates the resurrection with 'the land of Israel' (Ezek. 37.12). The phrase בכם רוחי ונתתי ('and I will put my Spirit in you', Ezek. 37.14), however, plays a relatively minor role. This is particularly apparent in *Pes. R.* 1.6, where the phrase is interpreted in light of Isa. 42.5 as a reference to the restoration of the 'breath' (נשמה) of life.

> 'And His land shall make expiation for His people' (Deut. 32.43). Does this statement mean that the righteous outside the Land will lose out? No! Why not? Because, as R. Eleazar, citing R. Simai, went on to say, God will make underground passages for the righteous who, rolling through them like skin bottles, will get to the Land of Israel, and when they get to the Land of Israel, God will restore their breath to them, as is said, 'He that giveth breath unto the people upon it, and spirit to them that go through it' (Isa. 42.5). As a matter of fact, in Ezekiel there is an explicit verse on this point: 'You shall know that I am the Lord when I open your graves' (Ezek. 37.13), 'and bring you into the Land of Israel' (Ezek. 37.12). In that hour, 'I will put My spirit in you, and ye shall live' (Ezek. 37.14). You thus learn that in the days of the Messiah the dead of the Land of Israel are to be [at once] among the living; and that the righteous [dead] outside the Land are to get to it and come to life upon it (*Pes. R.* 1.6).[3]

Ezek. 37.14 does not appear to have exerted significant influence on rabbinic eschatological expectations. The texts which refer to Ezek. 37.14 are few and relatively late. Furthermore, when Ezek. 37.14 is cited in the literature, it is often ancillary to Ezek. 37.12. The 'chain' of R. Phineas b. Jair (*m. Soṭ* 9.15) indicates that the Spirit was, in some quarters, associated with the resurrection at a relatively early date. However, in view of the virtual silence on this matter in the non-rabbinic sources of the intertestamental period,[4] one must conclude that the Spirit of God was generally not associated with the resurrection in first-century Judaism.

---

1. *Gen. R.* 14.8; 96 (*MSV*); 96.5; *Exod. R.* 48.4; *Midr. Ps.* 85.3; *Pes. R.* 1.6.
2. *Pes. R.* 1.6; *Gen. R.* 96.5; cf. *Gen. R.* 96 (*MSV*).
3. ET of *Pes. R.* 1.6 is from W.G. Braude, *Pesikta Rabbati: Discourses for Feasts, Fasts, and Special Sabbaths* (1968).
4. See Chapter 3 §2.3 above.

3. *Summary*

We have seen that early rabbinic tradition identifies the Spirit as the source of prophetic inspiration. The ancient exegetical traditions contained in the Targums also tend to associate the Spirit exclusively with prophetic inspiration. This pneumatological perspective is reflected in the eschatological expectation of the rabbis. According to the rabbis, the Spirit had departed from Israel due to her sin; however, in the age to come the Spirit would once again come upon her people. This eschatological outpouring of the Spirit is generally interpreted in light of Joel 3.1-2 as a restoration of the Spirit of prophecy. By way of contrast, Ezek. 36.26-27 is usually interpreted as a prophecy concerning the endtime removal of the evil יצר, and most frequently without reference to the activity of the Spirit. Indeed, the eradication of the evil יצר is presented as a prerequisite for the end-time bestowal of the Spirit of prophecy. These expectations are probably rooted in early tradition, although they may represent a peripheral element in the hopes of first-century Judaism. Ezek. 37.14 did not exert much influence on rabbinic conceptions of the age to come. Thus, one may conclude with some confidence that the Spirit of God was generally not associated with the resurrection in first-century Judaism.

CONCLUSION

The literature of intertestamental Judaism consistently identifies experience of the Spirit with prophetic inspiration. The Spirit enables the sage to attain the heights of sapiential achievement, equips the Messiah with special knowledge to rule, and grants insight to the prophet of the Lord. The inspiration of the Spirit, whether it be in relation to the sage, Messiah, or prophet, is almost always related to inspired speech. However, the literature shows a general reluctance to associate the Spirit with miraculous deeds. The man or woman endowed with the Spirit may perform miracles, but these works of wonder are usually not attributed to the Spirit. Furthermore, contemporary experience of the Spirit was deemed either an impossibility or less profound in nature than that of the past. The outlook for the future was more positive. Although Jewish expectations centered on the appearance of a prophetic or messianic figure endowed with the Spirit, an eschatological bestowal of the Spirit of prophecy probably constituted an aspect of the Jewish hope. Thus I conclude that the Jews of the pre-Christian era generally regarded the gift of the Spirit as a *donum superadditum* granted to various individuals so that they might fulfill a divinely appointed task. The gift of the Spirit was not viewed as a soteriological necessity: one need not possess the gift in order to live in right relationship to God and attain eternal life through the resurrection. Indeed, the gift of the Spirit was generally not associated with the resurrection of the dead.

The only exceptions to the perspective outlined above are found in sapiential writings. The wisdom tradition displays an increasing pessimism toward humanity's ability to attain wisdom by purely rational means (study of the law unaided by the Spirit). The relatively optimistic anthropology of Sirach is replaced by more pessimistic appraisals of humanity in Wisdom and 1QH. In these texts, the gift of the Spirit, previously viewed as the source of esoteric wisdom and inspired speech, is presented as the source of sapiential achievement at every level. Thus the developments within the sapiential tradition culminate in the attribution of soteriological significance to the gift of the Spirit.

Part II
THE PROPHETIC PNEUMATOLOGY OF LUKE

INTRODUCTION

My goal in the following section is to uncover Luke's distinctive pneumatology. The method of analysis employed is redaction critical. I shall examine relevant passages in Luke–Acts in an effort to detect Luke's 'creative contribution in all its aspects' to the tradition concerning the work of the Spirit which he transmits.[1] I shall not assume Luke's theological perspective is revealed only in his modification of received sources; thus my concern will include Luke's selection, as well as his arrangement and modification of received material.

I accept the two-document hypothesis as axiomatic. Therefore, I have assumed that Luke knew Mark and a written source Q. Although Markan priority has been subjected to severe criticism of late, it still remains, in my opinion, the best solution to a complex problem. Similarly, while recognizing that questions related to Q are equally complex, I have concluded that it represents (at least partially) a written source utilized by both Matthew and Luke.

The separation of tradition from redaction is more difficult in Acts than in Luke's Gospel since we are unable to reconstruct with the same degree of certainty any of the sources employed by the author.[2] I reject, however, the notion that due to a lack of source material Luke produced Acts in a manner entirely different from his Gospel. In spite of notable claims to the contrary,[3] the conditions for the formation of tradition were not unfavorable in apostolic times. In the formation of Acts, like his Gospel, Luke used a variety of written (and perhaps oral) sources. It is, however, generally impossible to determine to what extent Luke's narrative is based on traditional material. Nevertheless, since Luke 'is not satisfied with transcribing his sources' but 'rewrites the text by putting

1. S.S. Smalley, 'Redaction Criticism', in *New Testament Interpretation* (1977), p. 181.
2. J. Dupont, *The Sources of Acts: The Present Position* (1964), pp. 166-67.
3. M. Dibelius, *Studies in the Acts of the Apostles* (1956), pp. 2-3 and E. Haenchen, *The Acts of the Apostles* (1971), pp. 81-90.

the imprint of his vocabulary and style everywhere',[1] Acts remains an invaluable source for determining Luke's distinctive pneumatological perspective.

1.   Dupont, *Sources*, p. 166.

Chapter 6

PROPHECY RENEWED:
THE INFANCY NARRATIVES (LUKE 1.5–2.52)

1. *Source Criticism*

Attempts at reconstructing the sources behind the initial chapters of Luke's Gospel have produced limited and rather varied conclusions. Raymond Brown has emphasized Luke's creative hand,[1] while others, such as Stephen Farris have argued for a more substantial core of traditional material behind Luke's account.[2] The issue is a complicated one: does Luke 1–2 reflect the 'translation Greek' of originally Semitic sources or a skillful imitation of Septuagint style on the part of the author? Brown despaired of reaching a conclusion on stylistic grounds, and therefore his conclusions were reached purely on the basis of content and thought pattern.[3] Farris, however, utilizing criteria developed by Raymond Martin for distinguishing between translation Greek and original Greek, has argued persuasively on the basis of style that Luke 1 and 2 are based largely on Semitic sources.[4] Attempts to reconstruct these sources have not produced any assured results.[5] Indeed, the problem at this point in time appears unsolvable. Since my primary concern is with isolated portions of the non-hymnic sections of Luke 1–2, it will be sufficient to note the following points. First, the linguistic

1. R.E. Brown, 'Luke's Method in the Annunciation Narratives of Chapter One', in *Perspectives on Luke–Acts* (1978), pp. 126-38, and *The Birth of the Messiah: A Commentary on the Infancy Narratives in Matthew and Luke* (1977), esp. pp. 247-48.

2. See S.C. Farris, 'On Discerning Semitic Sources in Luke 1–2', in *Gospel Perspectives* (1981), II, pp. 201-38 and Farris, *The Hymns of Luke's Infancy Narratives: Their Origin, Meaning and Significance* (1985).

3. Brown, *The Birth of the Messiah*, p. 246.

4. See Farris, 'Sources', pp. 201-38, and *Hymns*, pp. 50-66.

5. H. Schürmann, *Das Lukasevangelium* (1969), I, pp. 143-44.

evidence, as Farris has shown, indicates that in all probability Luke's use of traditional material reaches beyond the hymnic material.[1] Secondly, although Luke probably drew upon traditional material for the narrative portions of Luke 1-2, these sections, in their final forms, have been significantly shaped by Luke. Luke has selected, organized, and modified the traditional material at his disposal. By comparing the text of Luke 1-2 with Luke's literary style and theological perspective reflected throughout his two-volume work, I believe it is possible, at least with regard to those sections which refer to the activity of the Spirit, to distinguish between tradition and Lukan redaction. In light of these considerations I conclude that we have in chs. 1 and 2 material which provides important insight into Luke's unique perspective on the Spirit.

2. *Various Texts*

The theme of fulfillment is central to the infancy narratives of Luke. Providing commentary on the narrative portions of the text, the canticles proclaim that the promises of God find their fulfillment in the events of Luke 1-2. Indeed, from the beginning a sense of anticipation is created as the reader enters into the world of pietistic Judaism. We are introduced to a host of righteous characters: Zechariah and Elizabeth are 'upright (δίκαιοι) in the sight of God' (1.6), Mary is 'highly favored' (κεχαριτωμένη, 1.28), Simeon is 'righteous and devout' (δίκαιος καὶ εὐλαβής, 2.25), Anna is a 'prophetess' (2.36).[2] These devout figures are dedicated to the law (1.59; 2.21-22) and the Temple cult (1.9; 2.27, 37). The atmosphere is permeated with a sense of joy (χαρά, 1.14; 2.10; χαίρω, 1.14, 28, 58; ἀγαλλίασις, 1.14, 44; ἀγαλλιάω, 1.47; σκιρτάω, 1.41). These twin themes of piety and joy highlight the sense of expectation which is generated by angelic visitations and prophecy and which culminates in the births of the precursor and the Messiah.

A leading role in this drama of fulfillment is played by the Spirit. The silence of spirit-inspired prophetic activity to which the intertestamental literature attests is shattered at the very outset of the narrative, and pneumatic inspiration constitutes a recurring motif. In 1.13-14 the angel Gabriel announces to Zechariah that his wife Elizabeth will bear a son, John. Of John it is written: 'he will be filled with the Holy Spirit

---

1.   See also I.H. Marshall, *The Gospel of Luke: A Commentary on the Greek Text* (1978), pp. 46-49.

2.   All English biblical citations are from the *NIV* unless otherwise noted.

(πνεύματος ἁγίου πλησθήσεται) while yet in his mother's womb'
(1.15).[1] Here the Spirit is depicted as the impetus of John's prophetic
ministry. This judgment is confirmed by the immediate context: John
will go before the Lord 'in the spirit and power of Elijah' (ἐν πνεύματι
καὶ δυνάμει Ἠλίου, 1.17). John's unique reception of the Spirit while
still in the womb points to John's special status and role: he is 'more
than a prophet' (7.26, 28) and 'shall go before the Lord' (1.17).
The use of πίμπλημι in conjunction with the anarthrous usage of
πνεῦμα ἅγιον in v. 15 and the collocation of πνεῦμα and δύναμις in
v. 17 indicate that these phrases are to be attributed to Luke. The use of
πίμπλημι with the Spirit is characteristic of Luke (Lk. 1.41, 67; Acts
2.4; 4.8, 31; 9.17; 13.9, 52). Although πίμπλημι is also found in
conjunction with the Spirit in the LXX (Exod. 28.3; 31.3; 35.31; Deut.
34.9; Wis. 1.7; A of Sir. 48.12), the frequency is rather low when compared with Luke. The anarthrous usage of πνεῦμα ἅγιον in v. 15 is
clearly Lukan.[2] Similarly, the combination of πνεῦμα and δύναμις is
also common to Luke (Lk. 1.35; 4.14; Acts 1.8; 10.38; cf. Lk. 24.49;
Acts 6.3-8), although again this usage is not entirely unique (1QH 7.6-7).
It is significant that the phrases 'he will be filled with the Holy Spirit
while yet in his mother's womb' in v. 15 and 'in the spirit and power of
Elijah' in v. 17 can be omitted from the text without significantly
altering the flow of thought. On the whole, the evidence suggests that
these phrases are to be attributed to Luke. Although it is quite possible,
indeed I suggest likely, that Luke had access to traditional material
concerning John's miraculous birth by the aged Elizabeth, I conclude
that Luke has placed the references to the Spirit (1.15, 17) in the narrative in order to emphasize the pneumatic and prophetic character of
John's ministry and to strengthen the links between John and Jesus.
    Luke 1.41 states that upon meeting Mary, Elizabeth 'was filled with
the Holy Spirit' (ἐπλήσθη πνεύματος ἁγίου) and pronounced an
inspired blessing upon her and the child she would bear. The phrase
ἐπλήσθη πνεύματος ἁγίου occurs again in Lk. 1.67 with reference to
Zechariah. The close association between the activity of the Spirit and
prophecy is made explicit in this introductory formula: 'Zechariah was
filled with the Holy Spirit and prophesied (ἐπροφήτευσεν)'. This usage

---

1.   ET is my own.
2.   G. Schneider, 'Jesu geistgewirkte Empfängnis (Lk 1,34f)', *TPQ* 119 (1971),
p. 109. The anarthrous usage occurs with the following frequency: Matthew, 3×;
Mark, 1×; Luke, 8×; John, 2×; Acts, 16×.

of προφητεύω in 1.67 parallels that of ἀνεφώνησεν κραυγῇ μεγάλῃ ('in a loud voice she exclaimed') in 1.42. Thus in Lk. 1.41 and 1.67 the Spirit acts as the Spirit of prophecy, inspiring prophetic speech. Luke's penchant for using πίμπλημι with the Spirit, the parallels between 1.41 and 1.67, and the introductory role of the phrases lead us to conclude that Luke is responsible for at least the phrase ἐπλήσθη πνεύματος ἁγίου in v. 41 and v. 67.[1] Luke highlights the Spirit's role in the prophetic activity of Elizabeth and Zechariah, as well as John.

A cluster of references to the Spirit appear in Lk. 2.25-27 with reference to Simeon. After a description of Simeon's piety we read: 'and the Holy Spirit was upon him' (καὶ πνεῦμα ἦν ἅγιον ἐπ' αὐτόν, 2.25). The following verses define more precisely how the Spirit functioned in the life of Simeon. In v. 26 the Spirit is cited as the source of special revelation: 'it had been revealed to him by the Holy Spirit' (ὑπὸ τοῦ πνεύματος τοῦ ἁγίου) that he would live to see the Messiah. The phrase 'he went in the Spirit into the temple' (ἦλθεν ἐν τῷ πνεύματι εἰς τὸ ἱερόν, v. 27)[2] refers to the state of inspiration which not only led Simeon into the temple, but which also led to his spontaneous outburst of praise. Thus in 2.25-27 the Spirit functions as the Spirit of prophecy, granting special revelation, guidance, and inspiring speech.

The separation of source material from Lukan redaction is exceedingly difficult in these verses. The issue is irrelevant if Luke created the story in its entirety, but as I have suggested, this is unlikely. If vv. 25-27 reflect traditional material as I suspect, it is quite possible that Luke has influenced its present form. Even if a written source forms the basis of vv. 25-27, it would not have been difficult for Luke to have altered this source by inserting the three references to the Spirit. The phrase 'and the Holy Spirit was upon him' is not integral to the flow of thought and could easily have been added to the end of v. 25. Similarly, 'by the Holy Spirit' (v. 26) and 'in the Spirit' (v. 27) can be deleted (and thus added) without the sense of the verses being altered. This of course does not constitute proof that Luke added these phrases to an existing source. However, in light of Luke's interest in the Spirit elsewhere in the infancy narratives and throughout Luke–Acts I suggest this as a plausible hypothesis. Although the linguistic evidence by itself is unconvincing, it does lend credibility to my hypothesis of Lukan redaction in v. 25 and

---

1. Fitzmyer concludes that Lk. 1.67 is 'undoubtedly redactional' (*The Gospel According to Luke I–IX* [1981], p. 382).
2. ET is my own.

v. 27. The unusual construction of πνεῦμα-verb-ἅγιον (2.25) is found in Acts 1.15, and ἐπί with πνεῦμα is frequently employed by Luke (Lk. 4.18; Acts 1.8; 2.17; 10.44, 45; 11.15; 16.6).[1] The verb of motion with ἐν τῷ πνεύματι (2.27) finds parallels in Lk. 4.1 and 4.14, material which is clearly Lukan.

In a manner similar to Simeon, the prophetess Anna speaks over the child in the Temple (2.36-37). There is no allusion to the activity of the Spirit here. This silence concerning the Spirit may be the result of two factors. First, whether it be due to a lack of source material or his own literary purpose, Luke does not record the content of Anna's inspired message. This contrasts sharply with the experience of Elizabeth, Mary, Zechariah and Simeon.[2] Secondly, the activity of the Spirit is implicit in the reference to Anna as a 'prophetess'. I suggest that since Luke did not record Anna's inspired words, he refrained from alluding to the Spirit's activity in a direct way, choosing simply to name her as a prophetess. Although this is conjecture, it fits the general pattern of the infancy narratives where the Spirit inspires oracles transcribed by Luke.

From this analysis of the passages cited above it is evident that Luke not only has a special interest in the Holy Spirit, but also that his understanding of the Spirit is inextricably related to prophetic phenomena. This conclusion is not dependent on any specific source theory. Those who argue for a minimal amount of traditional material behind Luke's infancy narratives will have no difficulty in accepting my conclusions. However, I have attempted to demonstrate that this conclusion is also compatible with the view that Luke did have access to a considerable amount of traditional material, largely in the form of written sources. Indeed, we can go a step further. Although my case is advanced if these hypotheses regarding Luke's modification of source material in the infancy narratives are accepted, the conclusion stated above is not dependent upon them. Regardless of whether Luke is responsible for the Spirit references in the infancy narratives or whether they are to be attributed to his sources, the fact that he has chosen this material is in itself an indication of his theological *Tendenz*. Clearly, in each of the passages cited above the Spirit functions as the source of prophecy.

---

1. Lk. 4.18 and Acts 2.17 are quotations from the OT.
2. The reference to John the Baptist in 1.15 is in the future tense. However, it would appear that his filling is accompanied by the prophecy of Elizabeth (1.41-42) and his leaping in the womb.

However, there is one exception to this otherwise uniform pattern. To this exception I now turn.

3. *Birth by the Spirit (Luke 1.35)*

Lk. 1.35 records Gabriel's explanation to Mary concerning how the miraculous birth is to take place:

πνεῦμα ἅγιον ἐπελεύσεται ἐπὶ σέ,
    καὶ δύναμις ὑψίστου ἐπισκιάσει σοι.
The Holy Spirit will come upon you,
    and the power of the Most High will overshadow you.

The passage poses a problem. If Luke, consistent with the Judaism of his day, understands the Spirit as the Spirit of prophecy, how can he attribute creative functions to the Spirit? Not only is this description of the Spirit's activity unique to Luke, but it is also quite uncommon to the Jewish thought world of Luke's day.[1] In light of these considerations the question cannot be overlooked: what does this passage tell us of Luke's understanding of the activity of the Spirit? By way of response I shall examine the traditional basis of the passage, the role this passage plays in the Jesus–John parallels which are so central to the structure of Luke's narrative, and the significance of the parallelism in v. 35.

In his 'Jesu geistgewirkte Empfängnis (Lk. 1,34f)', G. Schneider has argued persuasively on the basis of style that Luke has substantially shaped Lk. 1.34-35.[2] It is equally clear that, although the infancy narratives of Luke and Matthew represent independent accounts, they are both based upon a tradition that connected Jesus' miraculous conception to the activity of the Spirit (Mt. 1.18, 20). This tradition then forms the basis of Luke's reference to the Spirit in 1.35, which in its present form reflects Luke's hand.[3]

Luke's decision to include in his Gospel the tradition concerning the Spirit's creative role in Jesus' conception was probably influenced by his desire to draw parallels between John and Jesus. Indeed, the Jesus–John parallels form the basis of the structure of Luke's narrative: John is

---

1. See Davies, *Paul*, pp. 189-90 and L. Legrand, 'L'arrière-plan néotestamentaire de Lc. 1,35', *RB* 70 (1963), p. 177.

2. Schneider, 'Jesu geistgewirkte Empfängnis', p. 110, see pp. 109-10 for his discussion of the Lukan characteristics of Lk. 1.34-35.

3. Schneider sees an oral tradition behind the two accounts ('Jesu geistgewirkte Empfängnis', p. 110).

the precursor, Jesus the Messiah. As we have seen, John was 'filled with the Spirit' while yet in his mother's womb. It would only be natural for Luke to include traditional material which shows the superiority of Jesus.[1] There is also evidence that, through his formulation of v. 35, Luke has attempted to minimize the contrast between the creative role of the Spirit in the tradition and his own prophetic understanding of the Spirit. First, G. Schneider notes that Luke does not connect the Spirit to the conception process as explicitly as Matthew. Whereas Matthew directly relates the Spirit's activity to the one who has been conceived (τὸ γεννηθέν, aorist passive, Mt. 1.20) in Mary's womb, Luke simply refers to the one who is born (τὸ γεννώμενον, present passive, Lk. 1.35).[2] Secondly, Luke does not attribute the birth of Jesus exclusively to the activity of the Spirit. With the phrase καὶ δύναμις ὑψίστου ἐπισκιάσει σοι Luke adds another dimension to the tradition. Although this phrase is often ignored as a redundant piece of synonymous parallelism,[3] Luke's usage of δύναμις elsewhere suggests this addition is theologically motivated.

E. Schweizer has pointed out that Luke nowhere attributes exorcisms or miracles of healings to the work of the Spirit. Certainly Schweizer is right when he notes that according to Lk. 12.10 'the Spirit is no longer the power of God manifested in exorcisms' (Mk 3.29), but 'the power of God manifested in the inspired utterance of the witnesses of Jesus'.[4] Luke's insertion of 'by the finger of God' (Lk. 11.20) in lieu of Q's 'by the Spirit of God' (Mt. 12.28),[5] despite his interest in the Spirit, is striking and points in a similar direction. This makes Luke's omission of 'to heal the broken hearted' (ἰάσασθαι τοὺς συντετριμμένους τῇ καρδίᾳ) in Lk. 4.18-19 (Isa. 61.1, LXX) all the more significant.[6] It is to be noted that although Luke describes Stephen as 'a man full of the Holy Spirit' (Acts 6.3), he prefaces the comment that Stephen 'did great wonders and miraculous signs' with the appellation, 'a man full of God's grace and δύναμις' (Acts 6.8). It can also be argued that Luke attributes

1. Schweizer, 'The Spirit of Power', p. 263.
2. Schneider, 'Jesu geistgewirkte Empfängnis', p. 112.
3. See for example C.K. Barrett, *The Holy Spirit and the Gospel Tradition* (1947), p. 76.
4. Schweizer, 'πνεῦμα', p. 407. See also Haya-Prats, *Force*, pp. 37-44.
5. See Chapter 9 §3 below for an analysis of this text.
6. ET is my own.

the blinding of Elymas in Acts 13.11 to the 'hand of the Lord' so that the action of the Spirit on Paul described in Acts 13.9 has an exclusively prophetic sense. Similarly, in light of this Lukan tendency I would argue that the longer reading of Acts 8.39 is the more original: 'the Holy Spirit fell upon the eunuch, but the angel of the Lord caught up Philip'.[1] If this is the case, Philip is snatched away by an angel of the Lord, not by the Holy Spirit. Consistent with the general tendency in the writings of intertestamental Judaism, Luke takes great care not to associate the Spirit directly with the broader dimensions of the miraculous, such as healings and exorcisms; rather he limits reference regarding the direct agency of the Spirit to prophetic activity: the Spirit is the source of special revelation and inspired speech.

Luke does, however, attribute healings and exorcisms to the δύναμις of God (Lk. 4.36; 5.17; 6.19; 8.46; 9.1; Acts 4.7; 6.8).[2] Luke's redactional employment of δύναμις in Lk. 9.1 (cf. Mk 6.7) is particularly instructive, for here the disciples are granted δύναμις to expel demons and heal the sick even though they have not yet received the Spirit. This would appear to indicate an important distinction between Luke's use of δύναμις and πνεῦμα. The question becomes more complicated, however, when it is recognized that Luke can use the two terms together with little apparent distinction, as is the case in Lk. 1.35 (Lk. 1.17; 4.14; 24.49; Acts 1.8; 10.38). Are the terms synonyms for Luke or is a distinction intended? Certainly the evidence cited above would point to a nuanced usage of these terms on the part of Luke, but what of the passages where the terms occur together?

John's ministry, in Lk. 1.17, is described in terms of Elijah's: 'and he will go on before the Lord, in the Spirit and power of Elijah' (ἐν πνεύματι καὶ δυνάμει Ἠλίου). In 4.14 of his Gospel Luke writes that Jesus returned to Galilee 'in the power of the Spirit' (ἐν τῇ δυνάμει τοῦ πνεύματος), clearly a redactional addition of Luke. In Lk. 24.49 the disciples are told to wait in Jerusalem until they are clothed with 'power from on high' (ἐξ ὕψους δύναμιν), a reference to the gift of the Spirit. This is made explicit by Acts 1.8: 'But you will receive power

---

1. As I.H. Marshall notes, 'This [the shorter ending] is an abrupt ending to the story, and it is considerably eased by a longer form of the text... Although the ms evidence for the longer text is weak, it could be original' (*The Acts of the Apostles* [1980], p. 165).

2. Note that the references to δύναμις in Lk. 4.36, 6.19, 9.1 and probably Acts 10.38 are redactional.

(δύναμιν) when the Holy Spirit comes upon you'. Finally, in Acts 10.38 Peter declares of Jesus: 'God anointed [him] with the Holy Spirit and power' (πνεύματι ἁγίῳ καὶ δυνάμει). These passages indicate that for Luke the Holy Spirit is the source of 'power'. However, they do *not* indicate that the two terms are merely synonyms.[1] Close examination reveals that Luke uses these terms in a highly nuanced way. In each of the cases cited above Luke uses δύναμις in relation to πνεῦμα in order to describe the source of both prophetic activity and miracles of healing or exorcisms. That is to say that when Luke uses the terms δύναμις and πνεῦμα together he has in mind a combination of prophetic speech *and* miracles of healing and exorcisms, rather than the separate activities which are normally associated with πνεῦμα and δύναμις respectively. In Lk. 1.17 Luke likens John's ministry to that of Elijah, an Old Testament figure known for 'power of miracles *and* his gift of the prophetic spirit, both of which were passed on to Elisha' (2 Kgs 2.15).[2] Lk. 4.14 is a redactional insertion on the part of Luke describing the means by which Jesus proclaimed the good news (4.15-32) *and* performed exorcisms (4.33-36) and miracles of healing (4.40) in Galilee. Lk. 24.49 and Acts 1.8 are Lukan descriptions of the means by which the disciples became witnesses, a role which included proclaiming the gospel (Peter, Acts 2.14) *and* healing the sick (Peter, Acts 3.1). In these passages it is by virtue of its relationship to πνεῦμα that δύναμις can refer to a broad range of activities including prophetic speech as well as exorcisms and miracles of healing. Each of these passages is programmatic and refer to the means by which God enables a broad range of activities to take place. Similarly, Acts 10.38 is a panoramic description in retrospect: Peter summarizes the entire earthly ministry of Jesus (who 'went around doing good and healing all') and the means by which it was accomplished. Therefore, I conclude that although Luke can speak of πνεῦμα as the source of δύναμις, the two terms are not synonymous. Each produces a specific nexus of activities and, when Luke refers to both, a broader range of activities is envisioned.[3]

---

1. Schweizer, 'πνεῦμα', p. 407; Haya-Prats, *Force*, pp. 37-44; A. George, 'L'Esprit Saint dans l'œuvre de Luc', *RB* 85 (1978), p. 516.

2. Brown, *The Birth of the Messiah*, p. 261. The italics are mine.

3. See M. Turner's critique of this position and my response: Turner, 'The Spirit and the Power of Jesus' Miracles in the Lukan Conception', *NovT* 33 (1991), pp. 124-52; R.P. Menzies, 'Spirit and Power in Luke-Acts: A Response to Max Turner', *JSNT* 49 (1993), pp. 11-20.

It may at first appear strange that Luke can speak of the Spirit as the source of 'power' and yet take great care not to associate the Spirit directly with healings and exorcisms. However, this is remarkably consistent with what we have found in the intertestamental literature: the prophet is a person of the Spirit and may work miracles, but these miracles are not attributed directly to the Spirit.[1] For Luke, as for intertestamental Judaism, the Spirit inspires prophetic activity. For this reason, although miracle-working power may find its origin in the Spirit of God, miracles are carefully distanced from the Spirit (e.g. Lk. 11.20). Luke frequently maintains this distance through his nuanced use of δύναμις.

Luke's use of πνεῦμα and δύναμις can be shown as follows:

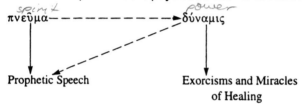

Luke's highly nuanced usage of πνεῦμα and δύναμις supports my contention that he has crafted the parallel statements in v. 35 in order to accomodate the traditional account of the Spirit's creative role in the birth of Jesus with his own prophetic understanding of the Spirit. Consistent with his usage elsewhere, in v. 35 Luke associates δύναμις with the πνεῦμα of the tradition because he has in mind a broad range of activities. The divine intervention alluded to in v. 35 is the source of Mary's miraculous pregnancy and her inspired proclamation in 1.46-47.

The connection between the promise of the Spirit's presence in v. 35 and Mary's utterance in vv. 46-55 can hardly be questioned. All three of the canticles attributed to men or women are proclaimed under the influence of the Spirit's activity (Zechariah—the Benedictus; Elizabeth and Mary—the Magnificat; Simeon—the Nunc Dimittis), and the only major adult character who is not brought into direct relationship with the Spirit, Anna, does not utter an oracle. Furthermore, references to the appellation ἅγιον link v. 35 with the Magnificat (v. 49).

The wording of the parallel stichs in v. 35 coincides nicely with the

---

1.   Josephus is particularly close to Luke at this point. Josephus alters his sources in order to distance the Spirit from non-prophetic miraculous activity (see Chapter 2 §3.2 above) and he corrolates δύναμις with πνεῦμα in a manner analogous to Luke (*Ant.* 8.408).

thesis that Luke emphasizes here the prophetic role of the Spirit and the creative role of δύναμις. The ἐπέρχομαι[1] + ἐπί construction with πνεῦμα ἅγιον in the first stich parallels the reference to the Pentecostal outpouring of the Spirit in Acts 1.8. This would suggest prophetic phenomena, not supernatural creation. A verb more likely to speak of divine creation for Luke, ἐπισκιάζω, appears in the second stich in relation to δύναμις ὑψίστου. Although there is no evidence that would suggest ἐπισκιάζω is descriptive of procreation, it does refer to the presence of God in a very personal and immediate way (Exod. 40.35).

In short, I have argued that Luke attributes the miraculous birth of Jesus to the the activity of the Spirit because this accurately reflected early Christian tradition and it suited his structural scheme of paralleling John with Jesus. However, Luke sought to minimize the contrast between the creative role of the Spirit in the tradition and his own prophetic understanding of the Spirit. He accomplished this task by modifying the tradition, which associated the Spirit with biological conception in an explicit manner (cf. Mt. 1.20). Luke's principal alteration involved the insertion of a reference to δύναμις paralleling πνεῦμα into the narrative. Consistent with his usage elsewhere, this association of δύναμις with πνεῦμα enabled Luke to relate the activity of the Spirit to Mary's prophetic proclamation and in a less direct way to the miraculous birth.

4. *The Pneumatology of the Pre-Lukan Tradition*

This analysis of Lk. 1.35 has confirmed my findings in the other portions of the infancy narratives: Luke's understanding of the Spirit is inextricably related to prophetic activity. However, it has also shed light on the pneumatology reflected in the pre-Lukan tradition. The tradition reflected in Lk. 1.35 indicates that the primitive church spoke of the activity of the Spirit in broader terms than Luke. It was not reluctant to attribute miraculous events, such as the virgin birth of Jesus, exorcisms or healings directly to the intervention of the Spirit. This judgment is confirmed by Mt. 12.28 = Lk. 11.20 and Mk 3.29 = Lk. 12.10. While the pneumatology of the primitive church may be designated charismatic, that of Luke is more specifically prophetic.

The distinction between the charismatic pneumatology of the primitive

---

1. ἐπέρχομαι is Lukan (Lk. 11.22; 21.26; Acts 1.8; 8.24; 13.40; 14.19). It occurs only twice elsewhere in the NT (Eph. 2.7 and Jas 5.1).

church and the prophetic pneumatology of Luke is due on the one hand to the influence that Jesus exerted on the primitive church.¹ The experience and teaching of Jesus shaped the primitive church's understanding of the Spirit of God as the source of miracle-working power. I have already noted how infrequently miraculous events are attributed to the Spirit of God in intertestamental Judaism. The difference between the perspective of Jesus and that of Judaism is illustrated with reference to exorcism. While Jesus claimed to cast out demons by 'the Spirit of God',² there is not a single text in the Old Testament or in the Jewish literature of the intertestamental period which attributes the exorcism of demons to the agency of the Spirit.³ One of the many strengths of James Dunn's *Jesus and the Spirit* is the stress which it places on the uniqueness of Jesus' consciousness of the Spirit.⁴ This uniqueness is most evident in Jesus' claim to perform exorcisms and miracles by the Spirit of God.

On the other hand, the distinction results from the way in which Luke has appropriated and yet kept distinct (as outlined above) two spheres of thought: the traditional Jewish understanding of πνεῦμα θεοῦ as the source of prophetic inspiration and the Hellenistic understanding of δύναμις as miracle-working power. Whereas Jesus and the primitive church viewed the divine πνεῦμα as the direct agent of prophetic inspiration and miracle-working power,⁵ Luke, as we have seen, described the former in terms of πνεῦμα and the latter in terms of δύναμις. In short, the primitive church, following in the footsteps of Jesus, broadened the perceived functions of the Spirit of God so that it was viewed not only in traditional Jewish terms as the source of prophetic power, but also as miracle-working power. Luke, on the other hand, retained the traditional Jewish understanding of the Spirit as the Spirit of prophecy and, with the term δύναμις, incorporated a Hellenistic mode of expression to speak of miracle-working power. While δύναμις may be mediated through the Spirit (thus the phrase ἐν τῇ δυνάμει τοῦ πνεύματος, Lk. 4.14), the former rather than the latter is understood to be the divine potency by which miracles are wrought.

1. See Chapter 9 §3 and § 4 below.
2. On πνεύματι θεοῦ of Mt. 12.28 (= Lk. 11.20) as the original reading of Q see Chapter 9 §3 below. Note also Mt. 12.31-32; Mk 3.28-30; and Lk. 12.10.
3. See Chapter 9 §4.3 below.
4. Dunn, *Jesus and the Spirit*, p. 53.
5. See Chapter 9 §4.3 below.

The antiquity of the tradition reflected in Lk. 1.35, and thus its significance for the primitive church, has been questioned. Two arguments
against the antiquity of this tradition have been put forth; both view it as
reflecting a late stage in the development of the early church's
Christology. First, H. Schürmann insists this tradition must be late since
it is not found in Mark or the Pauline epistles.[1] However, this argument
from silence is not compelling, particularly when the purposes of Mark
or Paul may have precluded their incorporation of this material.[2]
Secondly, there is the commonly held theory that the early church progressively 'read back' the christological moment (the moment at which
Jesus became the Son of God indicated by formulations centering on the
terms 'Spirit', 'power' and 'Son of God') originally associated with
Jesus' resurrection into his earthly ministry (transfiguration and baptism)
and then into the account of his birth.[3] A key weakness in this theory is
that there is little evidence that the pre-Pauline church viewed the Spirit
as the source or power of Jesus' resurrection. Thus, the initial link in the
chain is broken. Romans 1.3-4 is often cited in support of this notion,
but the actual wording of the pre-Pauline formula is disputed. H. Schlier,
for example, does not place the Holy Spirit in the original formula,
although he does view it as pre-Pauline.[4] The latter judgment I shall
question. This theory has also been criticized on other grounds: the
exegetical evidence does not support the contention that the primitive
church understood the resurrection of Jesus as the moment at which
Jesus became the Son of God.[5] In light of these considerations the view
of I.H. Marshall is to be preferred:

> May it not be the case that the early church regarded the resurrection as
> confirmation of an already-existent status rather than as the conferring of a
> new status? We would suggest that this is a more accurate exegesis of the
> relevant texts.[6]

1.   Schürmann, 'Die geistgewirkte Lebensentstehung Jesu', in *Einheit in Vielfalt*
(1974), p. 158.
2.   See D. Guthrie, *New Testament Theology* (1981), pp. 368-69.
3.   For a good summary of this position see Brown, *The Birth of the Messiah*,
pp. 29-32, 135-37.
4.   H. Schlier, 'Zu Röm 1,3f ', in *Neues Testament und Geschichte* (1972),
pp. 207-18.
5.   Marshall, *The Origins of New Testament Christology* (1976), pp. 119-20. See
also R. Laurentin, *Les évangiles de l'enfance du Christ* (1982), pp. 52-54.
6.   Marshall, *Christology*, p. 120.

The affirmation of Jesus' miraculous birth by the Spirit reflected in Lk. 1.35 is undoubtedly pre-Lukan and there is no convincing reason for rejecting it as an early tradition of the primitive church.

5. *The Theological Homogeneity of Luke–Acts*

Having reached these conclusions concerning the nature of Luke's pneumatology as reflected in the infancy narratives, the question must now be asked how significant this material is for understanding Luke's pneumatology as a whole. Certainly Hans Conzelmann's outright dismissal of the significance of the infancy material for ascertaining Luke's theological perspective is to be rejected.[1] Yet what are we to make of his *heilsgeschichtlich* scheme with three distinct epochs? Can the infancy material be fitted into this scheme, or does it represent an insurmountable challenge to the validity of Conzelmann's approach?

Representatives of the former position include H.H. Oliver, who used the infancy material to support Conzelmann's conclusions with only minor modifications,[2] and W.B. Tatum, who arrived at similar conclusions by attempting to contrast the work of the Spirit in Luke 1–2 with the operation of the Holy Spirit elsewhere in Luke–Acts.[3] Tatum's article merits special attention since it centers on the work of the Spirit.

According to Tatum, Luke 'uses the birth narratives to characterize that period in salvation history before the ministry of Jesus as the Epoch of Israel'.[4] In support of this claim Tatum attempts to distinguish between the work of the Spirit in the three epochs of *Heilsgeschichte*: the epoch of Israel, the epoch of Jesus' ministry, and the epoch of the church. In spite of these divisions Tatum notes that the Spirit functions as the Spirit of prophecy in Luke 1–2 (epoch of Israel) *and* in Acts 2–28 (epoch of the church). The only distinction is that what was formerly limited to a few chosen individuals in the epoch of Israel is universally available in the epoch of the church.[5] This leads Tatum to conclude that

---

1.   C.H. Talbert, 'Shifting Sands: The Recent Study of the Gospel of Luke', in *Interpreting the Gospels* (1981), p. 202.

2.   H.H. Oliver, ' The Lucan Birth Stories and the Purpose of Luke–Acts', *NTS* 10 (1964), pp. 202-26.

3.   W.B. Tatum, ' The Epoch of Israel: Luke I–II and the Theological Plan of Luke–Acts', *NTS* 13 (1966–67), pp. 184-95.

4.   Tatum, ' The Epoch of Israel', p. 190.

5.   'The Epoch of Israel', p. 191.

'the prophetic Spirit in the nativity stories recalls the role of the Spirit in the past history of Israel'.[1] Although this may be true, Tatum ignores the fact that the renewed activity of the prophetic Spirit, once prominent in the past history of Israel, is itself an indicator of the dawning of the messianic age.[2] Far from designating the events of Luke 1–2 as a 'period of preparation',[3] the activity of the prophetic Spirit marks the decisive transition in God's plan for the restoration of his people. Indeed, the profusion of prophetic activity inspired by the Spirit characterizes Luke 1–2 as a drama of fulfillment. The content of the prophets' proclamation reveals the true significance of the events related in the narrative. Thus, both the *form* and the *content* of prophecy herald the message: God is *now* fulfilling his promises of old. Only by ignoring the eschatological significance of the restoration of the gift of Spirit and the prophecy which it produces can Tatum attempt to separate Luke 1–2 from the rest of Luke–Acts.

Tatum also argues that the Spirit motif in Luke 1–2 sets John apart from Jesus and places the former in the epoch of Israel.[4] Tatum's argument rests on his attempt to distinguish between the prophetic function of the Spirit in Luke 1–2 and the messianic function of the Spirit in the epoch of Jesus' ministry. This distinction is based on three observations: first, during his ministry Jesus is the sole bearer of the Spirit, this is in striking contrast to the profusion of the Spirit's activity elsewhere; secondly, while the passive forms of πληρόω (frequently used in Luke 1–2) suggest intermittent association, Jesus' relation to the Spirit (πλήρης, Lk. 4.1) intimates a more permanent connection; thirdly, following Schweizer, Tatum suggests that Jesus is no longer a Man of the Spirit, but is now Lord of the Spirit. It should be noted, however, that Tatum's initial point does not further his argument. The limitation of the Spirit to Jesus during his ministry does not indicate that the function of the Spirit has changed. Indeed, I shall argue that the Spirit in relation to Jesus continues to function as the source of special revelation and inspired speech. Tatum's second point is mitigated by the fact that πλήρης πνεύματος ἁγίου is not applied exclusively to Jesus (Lk. 4.1), but is also a description used of various disciples in the epoch of the

---

1.   'The Epoch of Israel', p. 191.
2.   E. Ellis, *The Gospel of Luke* (1974), pp. 28-29.
3.   Ellis, *Luke*, p. 193.
4.   The fact that the births of both John and Jesus are announced as 'good news' (εὐαγγελίζομαι, 1.19; 2.10) should call for caution at this point.

church (Acts 6.3, 5; 7.55; 11.24), an epoch in which by Tatum's own admission the Spirit functions as the Spirit of prophecy. The contrast Tatum attempts to draw between the intermittent or temporary character of the experiences of the Spirit recorded in Luke 1–2 and the permanent character of Jesus' experience of the Spirit breaks down when it is recognized that for John the gift of the Spirit of prophecy was permanent (Lk. 1.15, 76; 20.6) and, although the references to Jesus are less conclusive, in Acts the gift of the Spirit was clearly repetitive for the disciples (Acts 2.4; 4.8, 31).[1] Tatum's third point is also dubious. Lk. 4.1, 14 will not support the claim that Jesus is 'no longer a Man of the Spirit, but is now Lord of the Spirit',[2] and, in any event, what is at issue here is not the function of the Spirit, but the status of Jesus and his relationship to the Spirit.

In short, Tatum does point to superficial differences in the activity of the Spirit in various stages of Luke's work: reference to the Spirit's activity is limited to Jesus during the period of his earthly ministry and the Spirit, as never before, is universally available in Acts. However, Tatum fails to demonstrate that these epochs mark a transformation in the *function* of the Spirit. In each epoch the Spirit functions as the Spirit of prophecy. This fact and the eschatological significance of the Spirit's return suggest that Luke's pneumatology does not support a rigid three-epoch interpretation of Luke's scheme of *Heilsgeschichte*; on the contrary, Luke's pneumatology emphasizes the fundamental continuity which unites his story of fulfillment.

Recent trends in Lukan scholarship have confirmed this judgment by demonstrating the theological homogeneity of Luke–Acts. P. Minear has argued persuasively that it is only by ignoring the infancy narratives that Conzelmann can put forth his thesis.[3] According to W.C. Robinson, a theme that unites the ministry of Jesus with that of the church is Luke's depiction of both in terms of 'a journey'. Both Jesus and the early church travel 'the way of the Lord'.[4] I.H. Marshall has emphasized the continuity which exists between Luke and Acts with regard to christological,

---

1. R. Stronstad, *The Charismatic Theology of St. Luke* (1984), p. 4; Haya-Prats, *Force*, p. 198.

2. See Chapter 8 §2 below. Note also Bovon, *Luc le théologien*, p. 226.

3. P.S. Minear, 'Luke's Use of the Birth Stories', in *Studies in Luke–Acts* (3rd edn, 1978), p. 121. See also Tannehill, *The Narrative Unity of Luke–Acts: A Literary Interpretation* (1986), I, pp. 21-22.

4. W.C. Robinson, *Der Weg des Herrn* (1964).

soteriological and eschatological themes.[1] G. Braumann views persecution as a theme which unites Luke's two-volume work.[2] E. Lohse has presented 'promise and fulfillment' as a connecting thread which runs throughout Luke–Acts.[3] Therefore, it would appear that Martin Hengel gives voice to a consensus in Lukan scholarship when he writes:

> The argument introduced by H. Conzelmann and often repeated since then, that Luke divides history up into three periods, was certainly attractive, but nevertheless misleading... In reality, the whole double work covers the one history of Jesus Christ, which also includes the interval between resurrection and parousia as the time of his proclamation in the 'last days' (Acts 2.17), and which Luke clearly distinguishes from the epoch of the old covenant as the time of the messianic fulfilment of the prophetic promises.[4]

This conclusion confirms my conviction that the Spirit material in Luke 1–2 is of vital importance for understanding Luke's pneumatology as a whole. Since Luke–Acts is 'one history of Jesus Christ', the material in the infancy narratives cannot be seen in isolation from the rest of Luke's two-volume work. Distinctions between the pneumatology of Luke 1–2 and the rest of Luke–Acts based on a rigid three-epoch scheme of Luke's *Heilsgeschichte* must be rejected.

1. I.H. Marshall, *Luke: Historian and Theologian* (1970); see also Marshall, 'Luke and his "Gospel" ', in *Das Evangelium und die Evangelien* (1983), esp. pp. 300-301.
2. G. Braumann, 'Das Mittel der Zeit', *ZNW* 54 (1963), pp. 117-45.
3. E. Lohse, 'Lukas als Theologe der Heilsgeschichte' (1953), in *Die Einheit des Neuen Testaments* (1973).
4. M. Hengel, *Acts and the History of Earliest Christianity* (1979), p. 59.

Chapter 7

THE BAPTIST'S PROPHECY (LUKE 3.16)

1. The Original Form of the Prophecy

John's prophecy concerning the coming Spirit-baptizer is presented in variant forms in Mark and Q:

Mk 1.8: αὐτὸς δὲ βαπτίσει ὑμᾶς ἐν πνεύματι ἁγίῳ.

Q–Lk. 3.16-17 = Mt. 3.11-12: αὐτὸς ὑμᾶς βαπτίσει ἐν πνεύματι ἁγίῳ καὶ πυρί. οὗ τὸ πτύον ἐν τῇ χειρὶ αὐτοῦ διακαθᾶραι τὴν ἅλωνα αὐτοῦ καὶ συναγαγεῖν τὸν σῖτον εἰς τὴν ἀποθήκην αὐτοῦ, τὸ δὲ ἄχυρον κατακαύσει πυρὶ ἀσβέστῳ.

Mk 1.8: but he will baptize you with the Holy Spirit.

Q–Lk. 3.16-17 = Mt. 3.11-12: He will baptize you with the Holy Spirit and fire. His winnowing fork is in his hand to clear his threshing floor and to gather the wheat into his barn, but he will burn up the chaff with unquenchable fire.

Although the history of interpretation has produced a variety of views concerning the original form of John's prophecy, several factors indicate that the tradition presented in Q faithfully represents the Baptist's original words. First, the Q version is to be preferred over that of Mark. Mark's omission of καὶ πυρί ('and fire') and the winnowing metaphor (Lk. 3.17 = Mt. 3.12) can be easily reconciled with his intent to present the 'gospel of Jesus' (εὐαγγελίου Ἰησοῦ, Mk 1.1). However, it is unlikely that this aspect of the prophecy would have been inserted into Q had it not originated from John, for the prophesied judgment does not find its fulfillment in the narratives of the Gospels or Acts. The argument that καὶ πυρί represents a 'Christian pesher-ing to the Pentecostal

124   *Empowered for Witness*

fulfillment'[1] cannot be sustained in view of the note of judgment already present in the context of Q (Mt. 3.7-10, 12; Lk. 3.7-9, 17).[2] Secondly, attempts to reduce the original scope of the Baptist's prophecy to a 'baptism of fire'[3] must be rejected: there is no textual evidence for this view and it necessitates 'a considerable degree of development of the tradition within a comparatively short period'.[4] Thirdly, there are no convincing reasons to reject the Q version as an authentic witness to the Baptist's prophecy.[5] Although the purported parallels to the Baptist's prophecy which J. Dunn has adduced from the Qumran scrolls cannot be accepted,[6] the Baptist should be allowed a certain degree of creativity. We would expect as much from a prophet. Nevertheless, the extent of his creativity need not be overstated. I shall argue that when the Baptist's prophecy, as faithfully represented in Q, is correctly interpreted, it is harmonious with messianic and pneumatological views current in the Judaism of John's day.

2. *The Original Meaning of the Prophecy*

Just as there have been a variety of views regarding the original form of the prophecy, so also have interpretations of the prophecy been numerous and varied. Yet acceptance of the authenticity of the Q form of the prophecy narrows the field considerably. One of the most widely accepted interpretations of the prophecy has been put forth by Dunn, an advocate of the authenticity of the Q version.[7] Dunn asserts that the phrase βαπτίσει ἐν πνεύματι ἁγίῳ καὶ πυρί refers to a single baptism which, from the perspective of the Baptist, was to be experienced by all.[8] In this 'one purgative act of messianic judgment' the Spirit and fire

1. Ellis, *Luke*, p. 89.
2. Fitzmyer also affirms there is no evidence of Christian peshering here (*Luke I–IX*, p. 473).
3. Leisegang, *Pneuma Hagion*, pp. 72-80; von Baer, *Der heilige Geist*, pp. 161-63; R. Bultmann, *The History of the Synoptic Tradition* (1968), p. 246.
4. E. Best, 'Spirit-Baptism', *NovT* 4 (1960), p. 239.
5. See the arguments by Marshall, *Commentary on Luke*, pp. 145-48 and Dunn, 'Spirit-and-Fire Baptism', *NovT* 14 (1972), pp. 86-92 and *Holy Spirit*, pp. 9-10.
6. Dunn, *Holy Spirit*, pp. 9-10 and 'Spirit-and-Fire Baptism', pp. 89-92. My own study of the scrolls has confirmed the objections to this view offered by Best, 'Spirit-Baptism', p. 237. See my comments on this subject in Chapter 7 §2 below.
7. Dunn, *Holy Spirit*, pp. 8-22 and 'Spirit-and-Fire Baptism', pp. 81-92.
8. *Holy Spirit*, pp. 11-13.

function together as agents of both cleansing and destruction. Of particular importance for this study is Dunn's claim that the Spirit is 'purgative and refining for those who had repented, destructive...for those who remained impenitent'.[1] This leads Dunn to conclude that 'for the repentant it (the Spirit-and-fire baptism) would mean a refining and purging away of all evil and sin which would result in salvation and qualify to enjoy the blessings of the messianic kingdom'.[2]

Dunn's thesis has a number of attractive features. Unlike several other theories, Dunn's interpretation is not dependent on a hypothetical reconstruction of the text. He accepts as original and accounts for a baptism ἐν πνεύματι ἁγίῳ καὶ πυρί. Dunn's interpretation also attributes both positive and negative dimensions to the baptism. This dual understanding of the prophecy is necessary if one is to account for its positive treatment by Mark and Luke, and its negative portrayal by Matthew.[3] However, as attractive as Dunn's thesis is and as skillfully as it is presented, it must be rejected in light of *religionsgeschichtlich* and contextual considerations.

First, let us address the *religionsgeschichtlich* question. Dunn portrays the Spirit as an agent which cleanses the repentant (individuals) of Israel and in this way initiates them into the messianic kingdom. Dunn adduces parallels for this understanding of the Spirit from the Qumran scrolls (1QS 3.7-9; 4.21; 1QH 16.12; 7.6; 17.26; frag. 2.9, 13) and from various Old Testament passages. He attaches particular importance to Isa. 4.4, which may well have been 'in the Baptist's mind'.[4] However, neither the Qumran literature nor Isa. 4.4 supports Dunn's case.

Several factors speak against the appropriateness of reading John's prophecy against the background provided by the scrolls of Qumran. I have already suggested that the references to 'spirit' in 1QS 3–4 refer to a disposition of man, not to the Spirit of God. And, although the hymns do contain references to the cleansing work of the Spirit of God, these references are not related to judgment, as is clearly the case in Q. On the contrary, they refer to a gift of the Spirit which is given upon entrance into the covenant community. There is no hint of a dual aspect of the Spirit's work, encompassing both purification and destruction, in these

---

1. *Holy Spirit*, p. 13.
2. *Holy Spirit*, p. 14.
3. See Chapter 7 §3 below.
4. J. Dunn, *Holy Spirit*, p. 12. For Dunn's comments on the Qumran references see pp. 9-10.

passages. Furthermore, while the hymns speak of the cleansing of the individual, I shall argue that the Baptist's prophecy refers to the cleansing of Israel *by the separation of the righteous from the wicked*.[1] As we have seen, in Dunn's reading of the prophecy the Spirit functions to purify the individual and initiate him into the messianic kingdom. This aspect of his interpretation may fit well with the hymns of Qumran, but it does not coincide with the Baptist's prophecy, as contextual considerations discussed below indicate.

Isa. 4.4 cannot be adduced in support of Dunn's thesis, for this text does not refer to the inner renewal or moral transformation of the individual. Rather, the text refers to the cleansing of the nation through the removal of the wicked.[2] Isa. 4.3 names the 'holy' as 'those who are left in Zion'. Thus the reference in Isa. 4.4 to cleansing by means of 'a spirit of judgment and a spirit of fire' refers to the cleansing of the righteous remnant by means of separation from the wicked: while the former are established in Jerusalem, the latter are driven out. My analysis is supported by the Targum to Isa. 4.3-4:

> And it shall come to pass that he that shall be left shall return to Zion, and he that hath kept the law shall be established in Jerusalem, holy shall he be called; everyone that is written down for eternal life shall see the consolation of Jerusalem: when the Lord shall have removed the pollution of the daughters of Zion, *and carried off from the midst of her the spillers of innocent blood that are in Jerusalem*, by the word of judgment and by the word of his final decree.[3]

Contextual considerations confirm that the future baptism of which John prophesied involved a sifting of Israel, not the inner purification of the individual. This is the thrust of the winnowing metaphor of Q (Lk. 3.17 = Mt. 3.12), with its vivid threshing imagery. Threshing involved tossing the grain into the air with the aid of a wheat shovel (πτύον). This was done so that the wind might separate the grain from the chaff.[4] The double meaning of רוח/πνεῦμα as 'Spirit' and 'wind' may well have been in the mind of the Baptist and later picked up by the synoptists,[5] although this is not essential for my interpretation. According to the Q metaphor, after its separation from the grain, the chaff was to

1. Best, 'Spirit-Baptism', p. 237.
2. M.A. Chevallier, *Souffle de dieu* (1978), pp. 100-101.
3. ET from J.F. Stenning, *The Targum of Isaiah* (italics are mine).
4. See Isa. 41.16; Jer. 4.11; Marshall, *Commentary on Luke*, p. 148.
5. F.J. Foakes-Jackson and K. Lake, *The Beginnings of Christianity*, IV, p. 238.

be consumed by fire. The metaphor then clearly suggests that the future baptism would include aspects of cleansing and destruction. Yet we can go further: the metaphor also specifies what kind of cleansing the baptism would effect. The cleansing envisioned is not the purification or moral transformation of the individual, as Dunn suggests; rather, it involves a cleansing of Israel by means of separation: the righteous (grain) shall be separated from the unrighteous (chaff). This then is the work of the Spirit prophesied by the Baptist: separation. The 'fire' is the destructive wrath of God which will consume the unrighteous. Thus the baptism ἐν πνεύματι ἁγίῳ καὶ πυρί which John prophesied was to be a deluge of messianic judgment which all would experience.[1] All would be sifted and separated by a powerful blast of the Spirit of God: the unrighteous would be consumed in fire, and in this way the righteous remnant would be gathered together and the nation purified.[2]

This reading of the text not only does justice to the immediate context, it also has a number of other attractive features.

First, it solves the *religionsgeschichtlich* problem mentioned above. The functions attributed to the Spirit in this interpretation of the Baptist's prophecy are entirely consistent with messianic and pneumatological views current in Judaism. Isa. 4.4 refers to the Spirit of God as the means by which Israel shall be sifted and cleansed;[3] and, as I have already noted, a number of intertestamental texts describe the Messiah as charismatically endowed with the Spirit of God so that he may rule and judge (e.g. *1 En.* 49.3; 62.2). Several texts tie these two concepts together. Perhaps most striking is *Pss. Sol.* 17.26-37, a passage which describes how the Messiah, 'powerful in the Holy Spirit' (17.37), shall purify Israel by ejecting all aliens and sinners from the nation. Isa. 11.2, 4, which is echoed in *1 En.* 62.2 and 1QSb 5.24-25, declares that the Spirit-empowered Messiah will slay the wicked 'with the breath of his lips' (רוח שפתיו)[4]. Against this background it is not difficult to envision

---

1. In 'The Meaning of the Verb "to Baptize"' (*EvQ* 45 [1973], pp. 130-40) Marshall argues persuasively that in Mk 1.8 and parallels βαπτίζω should be translated 'deluge', 'flood' or 'drench' with the Spirit.

2. The grammatical significance of the single ἐν governing two dative nouns connected by καί should not be overemphasized. The omission rather than repetition of a preposition before phrases connected by καί is common in the NT and is particularly characteristic of Luke and Matthew.

3. Note also Ps. 1.4-5 and Job 15.30.

4. Note how 1QSb 5.24-25 and *1 En.* 62.2 compress and bring together the language of Isa. 11.2 and 11.4.

the Spirit of God as an instrument employed by the Messiah to sift and cleanse Israel. Indeed, the texts cited above suggest that when John referred in metaphorical language to the messianic deluge of the Spirit, he had in mind Spirit-inspired oracles of judgment uttered by the Messiah (cf. Isa. 11.4), blasts of the Spirit which would separate the wheat from the chaff. However, we search in vain for a reference to a messianic bestowal of the Spirit which purifies and morally transforms the individual. I have already noted that references to the soteriological activity of the Spirit during the intertestamental period are exceedingly rare and limited to a minor strand within the wisdom tradition.

Secondly, this interpretation renders attempts to read John's prophecy as a baptism in 'wind and fire' superfluous.[1] John likens the activity of the Spirit to the sifting force of a powerful wind, but this in itself is an insufficient reason to deny him a direct reference to the Holy Spirit. Textual evidence for the omission of ἅγιος is lacking,[2] and thus proponents of the 'wind and fire' view are forced to speculate that John's words were reinterpreted by the church at a very early stage.

Thirdly, this interpretation fits well with the subsequent and varied usage of the text by the synoptic writers. To this point I now turn.

3. *The Use and Interpretation of the Prophecy in the Early Church*

The omission of καὶ πυρί, coupled with the τοῦ εὐαγγελίου Ἰησοῦ Χριστοῦ of Mk 1.1 and the absence of any mention of judgment or wrath, indicates that Mark interpreted John's preaching and prophecy largely in positive terms. The form of Mark's account (Mk 1.8), so similar to Acts 1.5 and 11.16, probably reflects the conviction that the prophecy was fulfilled, at least in part, at Pentecost. However, Mark's purpose in relating the Baptist's prophecy is essentially christological: the prophecy serves to point to the unique status of Jesus as the Spirit-baptizer. Therefore, Mark fails to elaborate further on the nature of the prophecy's fulfillment. For more specific information we shall have to turn elsewhere.

---

1. Proponents of this view include R. Eisler, *The Messiah Jesus and John the Baptist* (1931), pp. 274-79; Barrett, *Gospel Tradition*, p. 126; Schweizer, 'πνεῦμα', p. 399 and *The Holy Spirit* (1980), pp. 52-53.
2. The evidence for the omission of ἅγιος is exceedingly weak (MSS 63, 64; Tert.; Aug.; Clem. Alex.).

Matthew's account of the Baptist's preaching in Mt. 3.7-12 corresponds more closely to Q than to that of Luke in Lk. 3.7-18.[1] Although Lk. 3.10-15 cannot be attributed to Luke on stylistic grounds and is likely to represent traditional material, it probably came from a source other than Q.[2] This judgment is supported by Luke's summary of John's preaching recorded in Lk. 3.18, a verse which is clearly from Luke's hand.[3] The εὐηγγελίζετο τὸν λαόν ('he preached good news to the people') of Lk. 3.18 indicates that Luke interpreted John's preaching, particularly his prophecy concerning the coming baptizer, in a predominantly positive way. Thus it is probable that Luke inserted Lk. 3.10-15, traditional material from another source which emphasized and illustrated the concept of repentance, into the narrative of Q (Mt. 3.7-12 = Lk. 3.7-9, 16-17) in order to separate the negative pronouncement of judgment in Lk. 3.7-9 = Mt. 3.7-10 from John's prophecy of the coming baptizer. In this way Luke created a context appropriate for his positive appraisal of the Baptist's prophecy. Matthew, on the other hand, following the Q version more closely, retains and possibly heightens[4] the emphasis on the negative and judgmental aspect of John's preaching. Addressed to the 'Pharisees and Sadducees', the prophecy serves as a warning against the rejection of Jesus: to reject Jesus is to reject the Messiah and future judge; it will inevitably result in the judgment of God and destruction. Therefore, Matthew (following Q) frames the Baptist's prophecy in largely negative terms, featuring destructive judgment, Luke emphasizes its positive elements: the sifting and purification of the righteous remnant.

Yet this raises an interesting question: If Luke interpreted the Baptist's prophecy in a predominantly positive way and thus sought to emphasize this aspect of the prophecy in his account, why did he follow the Q version with its reference to καὶ πυρί (Lk. 3.16 = Mt. 3.11) and the 'unquenchable fire' of the winnowing metaphor? Presuming that Luke had the Markan and Q versions before him, it is indeed striking that

1. T.W. Manson, *The Sayings of Jesus* (1949), pp. 253-54.

2. Luke has clearly edited his source, as the ὄχλοι of 3.10 corresponds to the ὄχλοις of 3.7.

3. Verses 18-20 are 'strongly Lucan in language' (Marshall, *Commentary on Luke*, p. 149).

4. The phrase πολλοὺς τῶν Φαρισαίων καὶ Σαδδουκαίων (Mt. 3.7) is likely redactional, it probably reflects a reference to 'Pharisees' in Q. In Mt. 16.1/ Mk 8.11 and Mt. 16.6/Lk. 12.1 Matthew inserts 'Pharisees and Sadducees' for 'Pharisees'.

Luke follows Q in Lk. 3.16-17. The question becomes even more pressing when we remember that Luke refers only to a Spirit-baptism in Acts 1.5 and 11.16. What was so significant about the Q account that, in spite of these incongruities with his own view, Luke chose to follow it? The answer to this question is found in the importance Luke attached to the winnowing metaphor of Q. For Luke, the winnowing metaphor was essential if the true significance of the future Spirit-baptism was to be recognized. The winnowing metaphor specified that the deluge of Spirit, initiated by the Messiah, would *sift* the people of Israel. This thought of *sifting* is vital to Luke's interpretation of the bestowal of the Spirit on the disciples at Pentecost: 'John baptized with water, but in a few days, you will be baptized with the Holy Spirit…But you will receive power when the Holy Spirit comes on you; and you will be my witnesses' (Acts 1.5, 8). Just as John prophesied that the Spirit would sift and separate, so also Luke understood the Pentecostal bestowal of the Spirit to be the means by which the righteous remnant would be separated from the chaff (cf. Lk. 2.34-35). John did not specify how this sifting would occur, alluding to the Spirit's role in the coming apocalypse only in very general terms; however, in light of Pentecost, Luke interprets the Spirit-empowered mission and preaching of the disciples to be the means by which this sifting occurs. For this reason the Q version, with its winnowing metaphor, was of vital importance to Luke. It pointed to the decisive role which the Spirit would play in the early church: as the source of the supernatural guidance of the mission of the church and its inspired proclamation of the gospel, the Spirit was the catalyst of the Christian mission and, as such, an instrument of *sifting*.

Thus, in Luke's perspective, John's prophecy finds initial fulfillment at Pentecost and continuing fulfillment in the Spirit-empowered mission of the church. However, the final act of separation, the destruction of the unrighteous in the fire of messianic judgment, still awaits its fulfillment. While it is likely that John viewed the sifting activity of the Spirit and the consuming activity of the fire as different aspects of one apocalyptic event, Luke has separated these aspects chronologically in view of the ongoing mission of the church.

I am now in a position to summarize these conclusions and assess their implications for my argument. John declared that a deluge of messianic judgment was coming: the righteous would be separated from the wicked by a powerful blast of the Spirit of God, and the latter would be consumed by fire. In this way the righteous remnant would be gathered together and the nation purified.

Mark and Luke, in their respective accounts, emphasize the positive aspect of the prophecy: the sifting out of the righteous remnant. Therefore, they do not hesitate to associate John with the εὐαγγέλιον (Mk 1.1; Lk. 3.18). Luke clearly interprets the sifting activity of the Spirit of which John prophesied to be accomplished in the Spirit-directed mission of the church and its Spirit-inspired proclamation of the gospel (Acts 1.5, 8; 11.16). Thus the mission of the church anticipates the final act of messianic judgment. Although Mark does not elaborate on the nature of the prophecy's fulfillment, he probably interpreted the prophecy in a similar manner.

Matthew emphasizes the negative and judgmental aspect of John's preaching. Matthew, like Mark, is not interested in pointing to the future fulfillment of the prophecy in the mission of the church, although he undoubtedly was aware of this perspective. Rather his interest centers on the christological significance of the prophecy and the didactic purpose it serves.

Of particular importance for this study is the light that John's prophecy, and its subsequent use in the synoptic Gospels, sheds on the pneumatological perspective of John the Baptist, the primitive church and Luke. According to John, the Spirit of God was the means by which the Messiah would sift and judge Israel. If, as the parallels from the intertestamental literature suggest, John had Spirit-inspired oracles of judgment in mind at this point, then his perspective on the Spirit is not so different from that of Luke. For Luke, interpreting John's prophecy as a reference to the Spirit-empowered mission of the church highlights the prophetic aspects of the Spirit's activity: the Spirit, in guiding the mission of the church grants special insight, and, as the impetus behind the proclamation of the gospel, inspires speech. In view of the similarities between Mark's account and Acts 1.5 and 11.16, it would appear that the viewpoint of the primitive church is accurately reflected in Luke's interpretation. Thus 'Spirit and fire baptism', as prophesied by John and as interpreted by the early church, refers neither to the means by which the individual is purified nor to an event which initiates one into the the blessings of the messianic kingdom. John's prophecy, particularly as interpreted by Luke, attributes prophetic rather than soteriological functions to the Spirit.

Chapter 8

JESUS AND THE SPIRIT:
THE PNEUMATIC ANOINTING (LUKE 3–4)

Luke not only affirms that Jesus was begotten by the Spirit, he also declares that the coming Spirit-baptizer was himself anointed with the Spirit (Lk. 3.22; 4.18; Acts 10.38). This leads us to a question of central importance: what significance does Luke attach to Jesus' pneumatic anointing? Can we affirm with F. Büchsel that Jesus became uniquely aware of God as Father through his reception of the Spirit at the Jordan? And, in light of the preceding discussion and the texts to be examined, how are we to evaluate Dunn's claim that the primary purpose of Jesus' anointing at the Jordan was not to empower him for his messianic ministry, but rather to initiate him into the new age and covenant? Certainly the positions of Büchsel and Dunn represent a direct challenge to my thesis that Luke understands and consistently portrays the activity of the Spirit in prophetic categories. These questions then provide the impetus for the analysis of the Spirit passages in Lk. 3.21-22, 4.1, 14, 16-30. While the description of Jesus' pneumatic anointing accounts for only one extended sentence in Luke's Gospel (3.21-22), the significance which Luke attaches to this event can be seen only in light of the context into which he has placed it.

1. *Jesus' Pneumatic Anointing (Luke 3.21-22)*

1.1. *Source Criticism*

I begin this analysis of the baptism pericope by addressing the pressing source-critical question: was Luke's account of Jesus' baptism influenced by another written source (Q) or are the features peculiar to Luke to be attributed simply to his alteration of Mark? A comparison of the synoptic accounts of Jesus' baptism reveals two minor agreements of Luke with Matthew against Mark: first, Matthew and Luke use forms of ἀνοίγω rather than Mark's σχιζομένους with reference to the opening of heaven; and secondly, while Mark has the Spirit descending εἰς αὐτόν, Matthew and Luke agree with ἐπ' αὐτόν. These minor agreements probably reflect coincidental redaction rather than traces of Q.[1] Matthew and Luke often tone down the forceful language of Mark[2] and on several occasions replace a Markan εἰς with ἐπί or ἐν.[3]

The strongest argument that Q did contain an account of Jesus' baptism is found in the structure of Q itself, not in the minor agreements of Matthew and Luke against Mark.[4] An account of Jesus' baptism would serve to link the ministry of John with that of Jesus and provide a suitable introduction to the temptation narrative, which presupposes the divine sonship of Jesus. However, if such an account did exist, it has not exerted much visible influence on Matthew or Luke. The deviations from the Markan text peculiar to Matthew and Luke reflect their respective interests and styles, not an underlying text.[5] In light of these considerations it appears unlikely that Luke's account of Jesus' baptism (Lk. 3.21-22) was influenced by a written source other than Mk 1.9-11.

1.2. *Lukan Redaction*

Luke has made a number of changes to the Markan text. However, several of these alterations reflect literary or stylistic motivations, rather than a particular theological *Tendenz*. We should not overemphasize the significance of Luke's movement of John's imprisonment forward in his narrative (Lk. 3.20; Mk 6.17), nor of his omission of any explicit reference to John the Baptist in the baptismal account. By concluding the story of John's ministry before beginning that of Jesus', Luke was able to bring out the parallels between John and Jesus more clearly, particularly the fate of the prophet, which they would share.[6] Moreover, while the addition of σωματικῷ εἴδει ('in bodily form') emphasizes the objective character of the descent of the Spirit, this merely heightens

---

1. So also Fitzmyer, *Luke I–IX*, p. 479.
2. See for example Mk 1.43 and the alterations in Mt. 8.4 and Lk. 5.14. However, this kind of alteration may also reflect the influence of Q, as in the case of Mk 1.12 (ἐκβάλλω); Mt. 4.1 (ἀνάγω) = Lk. 4.1 (ἄγω).
3. See Mk 4.7, 18; 11.8 and parallels.
4. L.E. Keck, 'The Spirit and the Dove', *NTS* 17 (1970), pp. 58-59.
5. For example note the language characteristic of Matthew in Mt. 3.15 (πληρῶσαι πᾶσαν δικαιοσύνην) and the clearly Lukan addition of προσευχομένου in Lk. 3.21.
6. G. Braumann, 'Das Mittel der Zeit', *ZNW* 54 (1963), p. 125.

what was already present or, if L.E. Keck is correct,[1] what Luke believed to have been present in the Markan text. The replacement of Mark's εἶδεν ('he saw') by the ἐγένετο (literally, 'it happened') construction may also be due to Luke's desire to emphasize the objective character of the event, but it probably simply reflects stylistic concerns, as with Luke's addition of τὸ ἅγιον ('Holy') to the Markan τὸ πνεῦμα ('Spirit').

More significant are Luke's alterations of the events surrounding Jesus' reception of the Spirit: unlike Mark, Luke has Jesus receive the Spirit after his baptism,[2] while praying. Luke is not concerned to draw connections between Jesus' water baptism and his reception of the Spirit.[3] Indeed, what was of central importance to Luke was not Jesus' baptism, rather, his reception of the Spirit, occasioned by prayer. For this reason Luke has transformed an account of Jesus' baptism into an account of Jesus' reception of the Spirit.

These changes, as striking as they may be, represent a shift in emphasis rather than specific content.[4] The elements which provide the interpretative clues necessary for uncovering the significance of Jesus' pneumatic anointing are essentially the same in Mark as in Luke. I refer to the phenomena which accompany Jesus' reception of the Spirit: the dove metaphor and, more significantly, the declaration of the heavenly voice.

1.3. *The Significance of Jesus' Pneumatic Anointing*
The Enigmatic Dove. A number of interpretations regarding the significance of the dove have emerged, but none is entirely satisfactory.[5]

---

1. Keck maintains that Mark's ambiguous rendering of an original adverbial phrase was later misinterpreted and given an adjectival meaning ('The Spirit and the Dove', pp. 41-67, esp. pp. 63-67).

2. In view of the change in the tenses of the participles (aorist participle: βαπτισθέντος; present participle: προσευχομένου), my translation reads: 'After all the people and Jesus had been baptized, while he was praying...'

3. The reception of the Spirit is associated with prayer, not water baptism (see also Lk. 11.13; Acts 1.14; 4.31; 8.15).

4. The key exception is the emphasis on prayer, a motif which runs throughout Luke's Gospel (5.16; 6.12; 9.18, 28-29; 11.1; 22.41; 23.46) and Acts as well (see the preceding note).

5. For a survey and critique of the various options, see F. Lentzen-Deis, *Die Taufe Jesu nach den Synoptikern* (1970), pp. 170-83; Keck, 'The Spirit and the Dove', pp. 41-57.

Some have sought to link the symbol of the dove with the establishment of the new covenant by relating the περιστερά ('dove') of the baptismal account with Noah's dove.[1] Yet these attempts prove unconvincing, for Noah's dove is nowhere connected to the Spirit.[2] Others, linking the baptismal dove to the creative activity of God in Gen. 1.2, have interpreted the symbol as pointing to a new creation.[3] Rabbinic tradition seemingly supports this viewpoint when it speaks of the movement of the Spirit over the primaeval chaos in terms of the fluttering of a dove.[4] However, the chief and fatal weakness of this theory is that in the rabbinic sources cited the dove is not a symbol of the Spirit, rather the point of comparison 'is the motion of the Spirit and the movement of a dove'.[5] For this reason the dove is not integral to the comparison; as the text from *Gen. R.* 2.4 indicates, the comparison can be made with any bird.[6]

Perhaps the most convincing view has been put forth by L.E. Keck,[7] who maintains that Mark's ὡς περιστεράν reflects an original adverbial reference to the descent of the Spirit which, due to its ambiguity,[8] was later misinterpreted and given adjectival significance. While this interpretation does justice to the rabbinic parallels which compare the movement of the Spirit to that of a dove, it is questionable whether a natural reading of Mk 1.10 supports such an interpretation. Given the enigmatic nature of the reference to the dove, we shall be on firmer ground if we look to the declaration of the heavenly voice for a basis from which to interpret the Spirit's role at Jordan.

---

1. Von Baer, *Der heilige Geist*, p. 58; suggested as a possibility by G.W.H. Lampe, *The Seal of the Spirit* (1951), p. 36.
2. Keck, 'The Spirit and the Dove', p. 49.
3. Barrett, *Gospel Tradition*, pp. 38-39; Dunn, *Holy Spirit*, p. 27.
4. While the Ben Zoma tradition of *Gen. R.* 2.4 refers simply to a bird, an allusion to a dove is found in the Babylonian Talmud's version of the Ben Zoma story (*b. Hag.* 15a).
5. Keck, 'The Spirit and the Dove', p. 52.
6. See also Marshall, *Commentary on Luke*, p. 153.
7. Keck, 'The Spirit and the Dove', pp. 41-67, esp. pp. 63-67.
8. According to Keck, this was the result of translating the phrase from Aramaic to Greek.

The Heavenly Declaration. The declaration of the heavenly voice consists of two stichs: the first reminiscent of Ps. 2.7, the second of Isa. 42.1.[1]

σὺ εἶ ὁ υἱός μου ὁ ἀγαπητός,
ἐν σοὶ εὐδόκησα.

You are my beloved Son,
with you I am well pleased.

In view of the royal character of Psalm 2 and the reference to messianic judgment (Mk 1.7-8) in the immediate context, it is virtually certain that Mark understood σὺ εἶ ὁ υἱός μου ὁ ἀγαπητός as a reference to Jesus as the Messiah-King.[2] However, it is possible that in this instance υἱός ('Son') signifies more: that Jesus was the Messiah because he stood in unique filial relationship to God.[3] Since few would deny that during his earthly ministry Jesus related to God as Father in a relatively unique way,[4] it is quite possible that the reference to υἱός would have been understood in this way. In view of Lk. 1.35 and 2.49, this is almost certainly the case for Luke. Whether or not on the basis of this passage we can attribute Jesus' messianic status to his filial relation to God, it is clear that the declaration identifies Jesus as the Messiah-King. The addition of the second stich, drawn from Isa. 42.1, is significant in that it brings the concept of the Servant of Israel together with that of the royal Messiah. Jesus is thus identified by the heavenly voice as the Servant-Messiah. It is noteworthy that both figures, the Servant of Isa. 42.1 and the Davidic Messiah of Ps. 2.7, are enabled by the Spirit to carry out their respective tasks.[5]

Of course the Christology presented by the heavenly voice is not the primary concern here; we are chiefly concerned with the implications the divine declaration holds for the relationship between Christology and pneumatology. The pressing question remains: what light does the heavenly declaration shed on the significance of Jesus' pneumatic anointing?

The reference to υἱός has encouraged F. Büchsel to speak of Jesus'

1. ET is my own.
2. D.L. Bock, *Proclamation from Prophecy and Pattern* (1987), p. 104.
3. Marshall, *Christology*, p. 117.
4. J. Jeremias, *The Prayers of Jesus* (1967), pp. 11-67.
5. See Isa. 11.1-2; Isa. 42.1. G.R. Beasley-Murray, 'Jesus and the Spirit', in *Mélanges Bibliques* (1970), p. 474.

pneumatic anointing in adoptionistic terms: 'For Jesus, possession of the Spirit is divine Sonship'.[1] Although Büchsel acknowledged that 'Jesus is God's Son from his birth',[2] he asserted that through his pneumatic anointing at Jordan Jesus' sonship is perfected and completed.[3] According to Büchsel, Jesus' experience at Jordan marked the beginning of a new and deeper existential awareness of God as Father. Similarly, J. Dunn, while acknowledging that Jesus is Messiah and Son from birth, declares that 'there is also a sense in which he only becomes Messiah and Son at Jordan'.[4] For Dunn this means that at the River Jordan the Spirit initiates Jesus into the new age and covenant.

How are we to evaluate such claims? Does Jesus in some sense become Son and Messiah at the Jordan? Does the Spirit provide Jesus with a new awareness of God as Father and/or initiate him into the new age and covenant? I suggest that the evidence points in a different direction. The divine declaration does not designate Jesus' reception of the Spirit as the beginning, in any sense, of his sonship or messiahship. On the contrary, through his reception of the Spirit Jesus is equipped for his messianic task. We may speak of the Jordan event as signalling the beginning of Jesus' messianic ministry, but not of his messiahship.

This judgment is supported by the form of the citation from Ps. 2.7. The word order of the Septuagintal reading, Υἱός μου εἶ σύ, has been altered in the Markan tradition to σὺ εἶ ὁ υἱός μου. The shift in word order suggests that the declaration was understood as the identification of Jesus as the υἱός of God, rather than as confirming the bestowal of the status of sonship upon Jesus.[5] If the tradition had intended to signify Jesus' adoption or his entrance into a new dimension of sonship by quoting from Ps. 2.7, it would have been natural to include the latter part of the verse as well: ἐγὼ σήμερον γεγέννηκά σε ('Today I have begotten you').[6] That the voice merely identifies an already existing status is also suggested by the repetition of the declaration ('This is my Son') on the mount of transfiguration (Mk 9.7 and par.).

Further support for my rejection of an adoptionistic reading of the text is found in the messianic conceptions which form the background to

1. Büchsel, *Der Geist Gottes*, p. 165. ET is my own.
2. *Der Geist Gottes*, p. 166. ET is my own.
3. *Der Geist Gottes*, p. 167.
4. Dunn, *Holy Spirit*, p. 28.
5. E. Lohmeyer, *Das Evangelium des Markus* (1959), p. 23.
6. ET is my own.

the heavenly declaration. As noted above, the Spirit equips both the
Servant of Israel (Isa. 42.1) and the Davidic Messiah (Isa. 11.1) for their
respective tasks. Reference to the Spirit as the source of the Servant-
Messiah's special status or unique standing before God is conspicuously
absent in these texts. The correlation of the messianic concepts associated with the Servant of the Lord and the Davidic Messiah together
with the anointing of the Spirit suggests divine empowering, not divine
adoption.[1]

If it is unlikely that Mark interpreted the Jordan event as Jesus'
adoption, in light of the infancy narratives (Lk. 1.35; 2.49), it is virtually
certain that Luke did not. Not only is a divine begetting precluded by
Lk. 1.35, but Jesus is well aware of his unique relationship to God as
Father long before the Jordan event (Lk. 2.49). Moreover, when the
eschatological nature of Luke 1–2 is recognized and Conzelmann's rigid
heilsgeschichtlich scheme is discarded, it cannot be maintained that
Jesus' baptism is the *pivot* of salvation history—the point at which Jesus
enters into the new age.[2] The evidence suggests that neither Büchsel nor
Dunn has adequately explained the significance of Jesus' pneumatic
anointing at the Jordan.

This is not to deny that the Jordan event represents a significant event
in salvation history; indeed, this is suggested by the heavenly declaration
and the events which accompany it. Furthermore, it is equally clear that
Jesus' experience at the Jordan represents a new beginning. However, in
view of the discussion above, I conclude that the Jordan event represents
the inauguration of Jesus' messianic task, not the beginning of his sonship or messiahship. Similarly, the heavenly declaration, as a confirmation of Jesus' existing status, constitutes Jesus' call to begin his messianic
mission.[3] The important corollary for this study is that Jesus' pneumatic
anointing, rather than being the source of his unique filial relationship to
God or his initiation into the new age, is the means by which Jesus is
equipped for his messianic task.[4] That this is indeed how Luke interprets

---

1.   Hill, *Greek Words*, p. 244; G.R. Beasley-Murray, *Baptism in the New
Testament* (1962), p. 61; and I. de la Potterie, 'L'onction du Christ: Etude de
théologie biblique', *NRT* 80 (1958), p. 235.
2.   *Contra* Dunn, *Holy Spirit*, pp. 24-32.
3.   So also Hill, *New Testament Prophecy*, p. 48.
4.   See also J. Jeremias, *New Testament Theology* (1971), p. 52; Hill, *New
Testament Prophecy*, p. 48; C.H. Talbert, *Literary Patterns, Theological Themes,
and the Genre of Luke–Acts* (1974), pp. 117-18.

Jesus' pneumatic anointing is confirmed by his redactional activity in Lk. 4.1, 14, 16-30, to which I shall now turn.

2. The Redactional Bridge: Luke 4.1, 14

2.1. Luke 4.1

Each of the synoptic authors preface their accounts of Jesus' temptation with reference to the Spirit:

Mt. 4.1:   Τότε ὁ Ἰησοῦς ἀνήχθη εἰς τὴν ἔρημον ὑπὸ τοῦ πνεύματος.
Mk 1.12:   Καὶ εὐθὺς τὸ πνεῦμα αὐτὸν ἐκβάλλει εἰς τὴν ἔρημον.
Lk. 4.1:   Ἰησοῦς δὲ πλήρης πνεύματος ἁγίου ὑπέστρεψεν ἀπὸ τοῦ Ἰορδάνου, καὶ ἤγετο ἐν τῷ πνεύματι ἐν τῇ ἐρήμῳ.

Mt. 4.1:   Then Jesus was led by the Spirit into the desert.
Mk 1.12:   At once the Spirit sent him out into the desert.
Lk. 4.1:   Jesus, full of the Holy Spirit, returned from the Jordan and was led by the Spirit in the desert.

Luke probably had access to two written sources at this point, Mark and Q. The fundamental function of the verse, for which the reference to the Spirit is of particular importance, is the same in each of the synoptic Gospels: it serves to link the account of Jesus' temptation with that of his baptism. While Luke retains the essential content of his sources, he significantly alters the form in which it is presented. Two alterations are particularly striking: first, Luke has inserted the phrase Ἰησοῦς δὲ πλήρης πνεύματος ἁγίου ('[and] Jesus, full of the Holy Spirit');[1] and secondly, rather than following the constructions of Mark or Q (Matthew), Luke states that Jesus ἤγετο ἐν τῷ πνεύματι ἐν τῇ ἐρήμῳ ('was led by the Spirit in the desert').[2]

E. Schweizer has made much of Luke's redaction here. On the basis of these two alterations he concludes:

> Luke, then, avoids the idea that the Spirit stands over Jesus. The OT view of the power of God coming upon men does not satisfy him. Jesus becomes the subject of an action in the Holy Spirit. He is not a pneumatic, but the Lord of the πνεῦμα.[3]

1.   The use of πλήρης is common to Luke (Lk. 5.12; Acts 6.3, 5, 8; 7.55; 9.36; 11.24; 13.10; 19.28), and the use of πλήρης with πνεῦμα undoubtedly reflects Luke's hand (Acts 6.3, 5; 7.55; 11.24). Note also Luke's use of πνεῦμα with πίμπλημι (Lk. 1.15, 41, 67; Acts 2.4; 4.8, 31; 9.17; 13.9).
2.   In view of Lk. 2.27 and particularly 4.14 this alteration can be attributed to Luke with a high degree of confidence.
3.   Schweizer, 'πνεῦμα', pp. 404-405.

However, Schweizer has surely exaggerated the significance of these alterations. The similarities between the description of Jesus in 4.1 and that of John in 1.15, 17 and Simeon in 2.25, 27 should warn us against reading too much into the wording here. While it is true that πλήρης πνεύματος ἁγίου ('full of the Holy Spirit') is not found prior to Lk. 4.1, the phrase is used of disciples in Acts[1] and therefore is not unique to Jesus.

This is all the more significant when it is realized that Luke uses ἐπλήσθη/σαν πνεύματος ἁγίου ('filled with the Holy Spirit') to describe the experience of the disciples in Acts, as well as that of John, Elizabeth and Zechariah in the infancy narratives.[2] Certainly the distinction between πλήρης πνεύματος ἁγίου and ἐπλήσθη/σαν πνεύματος ἁγίου should not be overemphasized. Although the latter, as the aorist tense dictates, describes a momentary experience, the effects can be long lasting (e.g. Lk. 1.15; Acts 4.31). And the former, as Acts 7.55 indicates, can refer to a special and momentary state of inspiration.[3] The only real distinction that can be made is that πλήρης πνεύματος ἁγίου implies the prior experience designated by the phrase ἐπλήσθη πνεύματος ἁγίου. This explains why Luke describes only Jesus, Stephen and Barnabas as πλήρης πνεύματος ἁγίου: the phrase ἐπλήσθη πνεύματος ἁγίου, while used to describe the experience of most of the major characters in Luke–Acts, is never related to these three. In Lk. 4.1 the phrase signifies that Jesus, as one who has been filled with the Spirit at Jordan, has constant access to the Spirit of God who provides what is required (either special knowledge or the ability to communicate God's message effectively) at each moment of need. There is a remarkable consistency which runs throughout Luke's two-volume work: whether it be Simeon, Jesus, Stephen or Paul, the terms used to describe the Spirit's work and the action it inspires are similar. Therefore, it is highly improbable that the description of Jesus as πλήρης πνεύματος ἁγίου signifies any change in Luke's perspective concerning the way in which the Spirit functions.

The differences which exist between Luke's ἤγετο ἐν τῷ πνεύματι ἐν τῇ ἐρήμῳ ('was led by the Spirit in the desert') and the corresponding

---

1. See the general reference in Acts 6.3 and the references to Stephen (Acts 6.5; 7.55) and Barnabas (Acts 11.24).

2. John: 1.15 (future passive); Elizabeth: 1.41; Zechariah: 1.67.

3. *Contra* Schweizer, 'πνεῦμα', p. 405 n. 463. See Acts 19.28 for an example where πλήρης with a noun other than πνεῦμα (θυμός) designates a state of temporary duration.

phrases in Mk 1.12 and Mt. 4.1 can hardly bear the weight that Schweizer's conclusion demands. Although Schweizer contends that 'Jesus becomes the subject of an action in the Holy Spirit',[1] Luke's ἤγετο is a passive nonetheless, and whether ἐν τῷ πνεύματι is taken as a dative of agency or sphere, Luke's construction portrays Jesus as subordinate to the Spirit.[2] While Luke's construction certainly softens Mark's τὸ πνεῦμα αὐτὸν ἐκβάλλει εἰς τὴν ἔρημον ('the Spirit sent him out into the desert'), it is difficult to see how it differs significantly from Matthew's 'Ιησοῦς ἀνήχθη εἰς τὴν ἔρημον ὑπὸ τοῦ πνεύματος ('Jesus was led by the Spirit into the desert'). The distinctions become all the more blurred when it is recognized that Luke can use ὑπὸ τοῦ πνεύματος and ἐν τῷ πνεύματι as functional equivalents. According to Luke, Simeon was instructed by the Spirit (ὑπὸ τοῦ πνεύματος τοῦ ἁγίου, Lk. 2.26) and, in the immediate context, Luke states that Simeon entered into the temple 'by the Spirit' (ἦλθεν ἐν τῷ πνεύματι εἰς τὸ ἱερόν). This suggests that Luke's ἤγετο ἐν τῷ πνεύματι ἐν τῇ ἐρήμῳ is a slightly modified form of Q, and that the alterations were made by Luke for purely stylistic reasons.

While it is difficult to see any theological *Tendenz* in Luke's alteration of Q, his decision to follow Q over Mark may reflect his prophetic understanding of the Spirit. Mark's account, with its emphasis on compulsion (ἐκβάλλει), implies that the Spirit led Jesus in a physical way, rather than by special revelation. Q on the other hand avoids the more physical connotations of Mark. Thus Luke is quite content to follow Q, for there is nothing in Q's account incompatible with his prophetic understanding of the Spirit: the Spirit, by means of special revelation, provides special guidance.

If we reject Schweizer's thesis, how shall we account for Luke's insertion of 'Ιησοῦς δὲ πλήρης πνεύματος ἁγίου into the text? A single reference to the Spirit would have been sufficient to link the account of Jesus' baptism with that of his temptation. Luke appears to have something special in mind with this added or second reference to the Spirit. I suggest that with the insertion of this phrase Luke has consciously edited his source in order to emphasize the fact that Jesus' experience at Jordan was the moment at which he 'was filled with the Spirit'. In this way Luke was able to bring out the continuity between Jesus' experience of the Spirit and that of the early church. The insertion

1. Schweizer, 'πνεῦμα', p. 405.
2. Fitzmyer, *Luke I–IX*, p. 514.

of ἐπλήσθη πνεύματος ἁγίου at Lk. 3.21-22 would have necessitated a radical departure from his source and Luke, as the text indicates, was reluctant to do so. However, with the insertion of Ἰησοῦς δὲ πλήρης πνεύματος ἁγίου at 4.1, a more convenient place for such an insertion, Luke was able to make the same point: just as Jesus was empowered by the Spirit at the Jordan, so it was also for the early church at Pentecost and beyond; and so it must be for the church to which Luke writes. This hypothesis not only explains why Luke has inserted a phrase which otherwise appears awkward and redundant, but it also does justice to the remarkable continuity in Spirit-terminology which exists throughout Luke's two-volume work. In short, rather than pointing to the uniqueness of Jesus' experience of the Spirit, Luke's description of Jesus as πλήρης πνεύματος ἁγίου indicates that he regarded Jesus' experience at the Jordan as the moment at which 'he was filled with the Spirit'— the moment at which Jesus, like the early church, was empowered to carry out his divinely appointed task.

2.2. *Luke 4.14*

While Lk. 4.14-15 has customarily been viewed as the product of Luke's free redaction of Mk 1.14, H. Schürmann asserts that the tradition-history of this pericope is more complex.[1] Schürmann maintains that Lk. 3.1–4.44 is based on an account of the beginning of Jesus' ministry preserved in Q. This *Bericht vom Anfang* ('report of the beginning') contained two major sections: the first section undergirds Lk. 3.3-17, 4.1-13; the second section, analogous to, yet independent of, Mk 1.14-39 (6.1-6), lies behind Lk. 4.14-44. According to Schürmann, Lk. 4.14-16, which forms the *Eingangstor* ('gate of entry') of Luke's narrative, is a composite of the major structural elements of the second section of the *Bericht* ('report') and thus cannot be attributed solely to Lukan redaction of Mark.

Schürmann's thesis is vulnerable at a number of points. If Q did contain a *Bericht* such as this, we would expect to find more prominent traces of its influence in Matthew than actually exist. Would Matthew, with his interest in portraying Jesus as the fulfillment of Old Testament expectations, pass over an account of Jesus' self-referential *pesher* of

---

1. Schürmann, 'Der "Bericht vom Anfang"—Ein Rekonstruktionsversuch auf Grund von Lk 4,14-16', in *Untersuchungen* (1968), pp. 69-80; see also Schürmann's 'Zur Traditionsgeschichte der Nazareth-Perikope Lk 4,16-30', in *Mélanges Bibliques* (1970), pp. 187-205.

Isa. 61.1? It is possible, but highly improbable. Even more telling is J. Delobel's critique of the heart of Schürmann's hypothesis. On the basis of his detailed analysis of Lk. 4.14-16, Delobel concludes that the linguistic features of Lk. 4.14-16 can be most adequately explained as Lukan redaction of Mk 1.14-15.[1]

The weakness of Schürmann's hypothesis is clearly seen in his analysis of v. 14a.[2] Schürmann puts forth three arguments in support of a pre-Lukan source: first, the apparent agreement of Mt. 4.12 (ἀνεχώρησεν) with Luke (ὑπέστρεψεν) against Mk 1.14 (ἦλθεν); secondly, the transitional nature of v. 14a, which indicates that the verse originally served as both a conclusion to the temptation narrative and an introduction to a variant account of the exorcism at Capernaum (Mk 1.21-28; Lk. 4.31-37); and thirdly, the previous point is supported by the reference to δύναμις in Lk. 4.14, which points to the Capernaum account (Lk. 4.36: ἐξουσίᾳ καὶ δυνάμει). Regarding the first point, Delobel points out that ἀναχωρέω is common to Matthew and ὑποστρέφω is clearly a Lukanism.[3] When this linguistic evidence is coupled with the recognition that the two terms have different nuances, the apparent agreement between Matthew and Luke disappears. The second and third points also fail to convince. In view of Luke's usage of δύναμις with πνεῦμα elsewhere, it is almost certain that the occurrence of δύναμις in Lk. 4.14 is redactional. Similarly, since the term does not occur in Mark's account at 1.27, it is equally certain that its inclusion in Lk. 4.36 is the result of Lukan redaction. Luke inserts the reference to δύναμις in v. 14a in order to anticipate the account of Jesus' expulsion of the demon at Capernaum (4.31-37). Indeed, Luke's statement that Jesus returned to Galilee ἐν τῇ δυνάμει τοῦ πνεύματος ('in the power of the Spirit') points forward to the preaching of Jesus in Nazareth (4.15, 18-19) and to the exorcism in Capernaum. Consistent with his prophetic understanding of the Spirit, Luke refrains from introducing Jesus' ministry in Galilee with reference to the Spirit only, such as in 4.1 (πλήρης πνεύματος ἁγίου), for the ministry in Galilee includes both

---

1.   J. Delobel, 'La rédaction de Lc., IV, 14-16a et le "Bericht vom Anfang"', in *L'évangile de Luc* (1973), pp. 203-23.

2.   Schürmann, '"Bericht vom Anfang"', pp. 70-71.

3.   Delobel, 'La rédaction de Lc., IV, 14-16a', p. 210: ἀναχωρέω—Matthew, 10×; Mark, 1×; Luke–Acts, 2×; John, 1×; ὑποστρέφω—Luke–Acts, 32×; the rest of the NT, 3×.

inspired preaching (4.15, 18-19) and an exorcism (4.36).[1] Schürmann correctly emphasized the connection between Lk. 4.14 and 4.36; he was wrong, however, to attribute this connection to pre-Lukan tradition. The evidence suggests that the connection was made by Luke himself. Luke's redactional activity in 4.14 not only plays an important introductory role, as noted above, but it also concludes the temptation narrative and, as such, provides valuable insight into Luke's unique understanding of the temptation account. Luke's redaction in 4.14 complements his earlier insertion in 4.1 and together these alterations form a redactional bridge which enables Luke to highlight the unique pneumatic significance which he attaches to the temptation account. Luke alone tells us that Jesus entered the desert πλήρης πνεύματος ἁγίου (4.1), equipped by the Spirit for his messianic task, and that after the temptation he left as he had entered: ἐν τῇ δυνάμει τοῦ πνεύματος (4.14). This has encouraged some to conclude that, for Luke, the Spirit is the power by which Jesus overcomes the temptings of the devil.[2] However, this conclusion is improbable. Luke gives no indication that the Spirit enabled Jesus to overcome the temptation. As the repetition of γέγραπται ὅτι ('it is written') indicates,[3] Jesus was supported in his victory over the devil by his commitment to Scripture. Therefore, any connection to the Spirit must be inferred from the context. That this is not Luke's intention is indicated by his usage elsewhere: the Spirit is never portrayed as the direct cause of a decision to orient one's life toward God. The Spirit may provide guidance (as in 4.1) which ultimately leads to the fulfillment of God's plan, but the Spirit is never the direct source of one's obedience to God. I suggest that there is a more adequate interpretation of the data, consistent with Luke's overall theological scheme. Luke's redactional activity in 4.1, 14 indicates not that the Spirit is the source of Jesus' obedience, rather, that Jesus' obedience is the source of his continuing relationship with the Spirit. In Luke's perspective, when Jesus enters into the desert his commitment to his messianic task is tested and thus also his worthiness to be a man of the Spirit, for the purpose of the Spirit is to enable Jesus to carry out his

---

1.   For a more detailed discussion of Luke's use of πνεῦμα and δύναμις see Chapter 6 §3 above.

2.   See J. Dupont, *Les tentations de Jésus au désert* (1968), pp. 49-50; U. Busse, *Das Nazareth-Manifest Jesu: Eine Einführung in das lukanische Jesubild nach Lk 4,16-30* (1977), p. 19; Fitzmyer, *Luke I–IX*, p. 513.

3.   See Lk. 4.4, 10. Cf. v. 12: ὅτι εἴρηται.

messianic task. Because Jesus remained committed to his task, he returned to Galilee ἐν τῇ δυνάμει τοῦ πνεύματος.[1] Thus, Luke's perspective is not unlike that of the rabbis, who held that the gift of the Spirit was given only to the worthy and that the Spirit departed from those who failed to remain worthy.[2] For Luke, the Spirit gives significance to Jesus' temptation.

The redactional bridge also enables Luke to maintain the pneumatic thrust of his narrative and emphasize the connections between Jesus' pneumatic anointing and his sermon at Nazareth. That Luke intends to draw parallels between the two accounts is substantiated by his movement of the Nazareth pericope (Lk. 4.16-30) forward in his narrative (cf. Mk 6.1-6)[3] and by his use of ἐπί in 3.22 and 4.18. The significance of these connections will be explored in the next section.

3. *The Sermon at Nazareth (Luke 4.16-30)*

The Nazareth pericope (4.16-30) not only sheds light on Luke's understanding of Jesus' pneumatic anointing, but it stands as the cornerstone of Luke's entire theological program. This conclusion is universally accepted and stems from two observations: first, Luke alters Mark's chronology in order to place this pericope at the outset of Jesus' ministry; secondly, the pericope combines the major theological themes of Luke–Acts: the work of the Spirit, the universality of the gospel, the grace of God, and the rejection of Jesus. For this reason the passage is invaluable for this inquiry into Luke's pneumatology, and more specifically, into the significance Luke attaches to Jesus' pneumatic anointing.

3.1. *Tradition and Redaction in Luke 4.18-19*
While I have rejected Schürmann's hypothesis that a pre-Lukan *Bericht vom Anfang*, preserved in Q, forms the basis of Lk. 4.14-44, this does not necessarily lead to the conclusion that Lk. 4.16-30 is the product of Luke's redaction of Mk 6.1-6. On the contrary, it is highly probable that

---

1.   Note the contrast with Saul, who as the King of Israel was endowed with the Spirit of God (1 Sam. 10.6, 10; 11.6), yet as a result of his disobedience, the Spirit departed from him (1 Sam. 16.14).

2.   See Chapter 5 §1.1.1 and §2.1 above for relevant rabbinic citations.

3.   Lk. 4.23, which presupposes prior miracles in Capernaum, indicates that the position of the account has been altered by Luke.

Luke, in writing the account, has drawn upon traditional material other than Mk 6.1-6. Jesus undoubtedly taught in the synagogue at Nazareth; while we have no other record of the content of his preaching at Nazareth, the general thrust of the passage accords well with what we know of his teaching elsewhere (Lk. 7.22 = Mt. 11.5).[1] It is not improbable that an account of such an event circulated among the early Christians and, indeed, there are numerous linguistic features which indicate that Luke's account is based on traditional material other than Mk 6.1-6.[2] However, when one attempts to move beyond these general conclusions, the questions of tradition and history become numerous and exceedingly complex.[3] Fortunately, since our concern centers on the quotation from Isaiah in Lk. 4.18-19, we can justifiably narrow the initial discussion to the following source-critical question: to what extent does the quotation from Isaiah in Lk. 4.18-19 represent traditional material?

The question is a difficult one, for since the text is taken almost verbatim from the LXX, we cannot rely on linguistic evidence for indications of Lukan redaction. However, since the citation in Lk. 4.18-19 diverges from Isa. 61.1-2 (LXX) at several points, it may be possible to determine whether these alterations point to a particular theological *Tendenz* and, if so, whether the *Tendenz* corresponds to distinctive aspects of Luke's theological program expressed elsewhere.

An analysis of Lk. 4.18-19 reveals close adherence to the Septuagint text of Isa. 61.1-2, with a number of striking divergences:[4]

Luke 4.18-19	*Isaiah 61.1-2 (LXX)*
πνεῦμα κυρίου ἐπ' ἐμὲ	Πνεῦμα κυρίου ἐπ' ἐμέ,
οὗ εἵνεκεν ἔχρισέν με	οὗ εἵνεκεν ἔχρισέν με·
εὐαγγελίσασθαι πτωχοῖς,	εὐαγγελίσασθαι πτωχοῖς
ἀπέσταλκέν με,	ἀπέσταλκέν με·
	ἰάσασθαι τοὺς συντετριμμένους
	τῇ καρδίᾳ,

1. In light of 11QMelch, Jesus' application of Isa. 61.1 to himself is not at all surprising.
2. Chilton argues that ἐν ταῖς συναγωγαῖς αὐτῶν (4.15) and Ναζαρά (4.16) reflect traditional material ('Announcement in Nazara: An Analysis of Luke 4.16-21', in *Gospel Perspectives* [1981], pp. 161-62) and Jeremias suggests the βιβλίον of 4.17, 20 is one among many traditional words in the account (*Die Sprache des Lukasevangeliums* [1980], pp. 121-28).
3. For a summary of these issues see Marshall, *Commentary on Luke*, pp. 177-80.
4. ET is my own.

κηρύξαι αἰχμαλώτοις ἄφεσιν
καὶ τυφλοῖς ἀνάβλεψιν,
ἀποστεῖλαι τεθραυσμένους ἐν
ἀφέσει,
κηρύξαι ἐνιαυτὸν κυρίου δεκτόν.

The Spirit of the Lord is upon me
because he has anointed me
to preach good news to the poor
He has sent me

to proclaim freedom for the prisoners
and recovery of sight for the blind
to set free the oppressed,
to proclaim the year of the Lord's favor.

κηρύξαι αἰχμαλώτοις ἄφεσιν
καὶ τυφλοῖς ἀνάβλεψιν...
ἀπόστελλε τεθραυσμένους ἐν
ἀφέσει...[Isa. 58.6]
καλέσαι ἐνιαυτὸν κυρίου δεκτὸν
καὶ ἡμέραν ἀνταποδόσεως.

The Spirit of the Lord is upon me
because he has anointed me
to preach good news to the poor
He has sent me
to heal the brokenhearted

to proclaim freedom for the prisoners
and recovery of sight for the blind
to set free the oppressed...[Isa. 58.6]
to *announce* the year of the Lord's favor
and the day of vengeance.

As the comparison above indicates, the citation in Lk. 4.18-19 deviates from the text of Isa. 61.1-2 (LXX) at four points: the phrase ἰάσασθαι τοὺς συντετριμμένους τῇ καρδίᾳ ('to heal the brokenhearted') has been omitted; an excerpt from Isa. 58.6 (LXX), ἀπόστελλε τεθραυσμένους ἐν ἀφέσει ('to set free the oppressed'), has been inserted in the quotation; the καλέσαι ('announce') of the LXX has been altered to κηρύξαι ('proclaim'); the final phrase of the LXX (καὶ ἡμέραν ἀνταποδόσεως), which refers to divine retribution, has been omitted.

It has already been indicated that the historicity of the general outline of Luke's account need not be doubted:[1] Jesus entered into the synagogue in Nazareth, read from the scroll of Isaiah (61.1-2), applied the passage to himself, and encountered resistance. Luke's account is generally consistent with the format of the ancient synagogue service. After the recitation of the *Shema* (Deut. 6.4-9; 11.13-21) and prayers, including the *Shemoneh Esreh*, a passage from the Pentateuch was read (*seder*), and this was followed by a reading from the Prophets (*haphtara*).[2] The *seder* and *haphtara* were followed by the singing of a psalm, and then came the sermon, introduced by an introductory reading (*petitha*) chosen from the Prophets or Writings.[3] The choice of

1. So also D. Hill, 'The Rejection of Jesus at Nazareth (Lk 4.16-30)', *NovT* 13 (1971), pp. 161-80, esp. p. 179.

2. While the *seder* was usually at least twenty-one verses, the *haphtara* was often around ten verses. The Targum was read after the completion of three verses.

3. P. Billerbeck, 'Ein Synagogengottesdienst in Jesu Tagen', *ZNW* 55 (1965),

the *haphtara* was somewhat flexible, with verbal and thematic links to the *seder* usually guiding the choice.[1] Although a fixed lectionary was developed for the *haphtara*, it is generally accepted that the lectionary system was not operative before the destruction of the temple.[2] This would have allowed Jesus to read from the text of his choosing, as Luke's account suggests. It is quite possible then that Lk. 4.18-19 represents a condensed form of the *haphtara*, which would have extended to at least Isa. 61.9.[3]

However, the historicity of the event notwithstanding, it is unlikely that the variant form of Isa. 61.1-2 found in Lk. 4.18-19 stems from Jesus himself. It is difficult to imagine a synagogue reader taking such liberties with the text.[4] Particularly striking is the insertion of the phrase from Isa. 58.6 into the text of Isa. 61.1-2, for, although skipping verses was permissable in the *haphtara*, it is unlikely that such a rearrangement of the text would have been tolerated (*m. Meg.* 4.4; *t. Meg.* 4.19).[5] I am, therefore, justified in concluding that it is improbable that Jesus, during the course of the *haphtara* in a synagogue service, inserted Isa. 58.6c into the text of Isa. 61.1-2 and made the other alterations to Isa. 61.1-2 recorded in Lk. 4.18-19. The question which remains is, of course, whether the interpretative reproduction of the *haphtara*, in the form in which it is presented in Lk. 4.18-19, stems from Luke or is carried over from pre-Lukan tradition. As I have indicated, this question can only be answered on the basis of an analysis of the alterations of the text from Isaiah and the theological motivations which have produced them. To this task we now turn.

The Omission of ἰάσασθαι τοὺς συντετριμμένους τῇ καρδίᾳ. It is often suggested that Isa. 61.1d has been omitted in order to make room

---

pp. 143-61.

1. C. Perrot, 'Luc 4, 16-30 et la lecture biblique de l'ancienne Synagogue', *RSR* 47 (1973), pp. 331-32. Perrot also notes that the *haphtara* usually started from a point within the section that was opened.

2. L. Morris, *The New Testament and Jewish Lectionaries* (1964), pp. 11-34; L. Crockett, 'Luke IV. 16-30 and the Jewish Lectionary Cycle: A Word of Caution', *JJS* 17 (1966), pp. 13-14.

3. Perrot, 'Synagogue', p. 327.

4. Perrot, 'Synagogue', p. 327.

5. On the strength of *t. Meg.* 4.19, P. Billerbeck argues that it was forbidden to jump backwards in the *haphtara* (Strack–Billerbeck, *Kommentar*, IV, p. 167).

for the insertion of Isa. 58.6c.[1] If structural concerns motivated the omission, it is of little use in determining whether the quotation stems from pre-Lukan tradition or Luke's final redaction, for such concerns could have influenced the text at either stage. However, the weakness of this hypothesis becomes evident when it is recognized that the structural elements of the passage have been used to explain why Isa. 61.1d has been omitted *and* why the phrase must have been included in the original reading of the text.[2] In view of the ambiguous nature of the arguments from structure and the varied conclusions they have produced, it is unlikely that structural elements played a significant role in the omission of Isa. 61.1d.

Much more probable is the view put forth by M. Rese that Luke omits Isa. 61.1d because of his prophetic understanding of the Spirit: 'Through the omission Luke insures that the Spirit of the Lord will be understood as the Spirit of prophecy and not as wonder-working power'.[3] This conclusion accords well with my analysis of Luke's redactional activity elsewhere and offers a plausible explanation of an omission which is otherwise extremely difficult to explain. However, Rese's conclusion has been criticized by M. Turner, who offers three objections.[4]

First, noting that the reference to healing in Isa. 61.1d is metaphorical, Turner argues that Luke's 'alleged predilection for the concept of the Spirit of prophecy' does not provide a motive for its omission.[5] However, the force of this objection is mitigated by the special significance which Luke attaches to ἰάομαι. The metaphorical usage of the term in Isa. 61.1d notwithstanding, ἰάομαι is used frequently by Luke (Luke, 11×; Acts, 4×; cf. Matthew, 4×; Mark, 1×; John, 3×) and as a *terminus technicus* for the miraculous healings of Jesus.[6]

Secondly, Turner claims that the insertion of Isa. 58.6c adds a new

1.   Busse, *Das Nazareth-Manifest Jesu*, p. 34; R. Morgenthaler, *Die lukanische Geschichtsschreibung als Zeugnis: Gestalt und Gehalt der Kunst des Lukas* (1949), I, pp. 84-85; Turner, 'Luke and the Spirit', p. 70.

2.   For the former view see Busse and Turner cited above; for the latter view see B. Reicke, 'Jesus in Nazareth—Lk 4,14-30', in *Das Wort und die Wörter* (1973), pp. 48-49.

3.   M. Rese, *Alttestamentliche Motive in der Christologie des Lukas* (1969), p. 214. ET is my own. See also pp. 144-45, 151-52.

4.   Turner, 'Luke and the Spirit', pp. 60-67.

5.   'Luke and the Spirit', p. 61. See also C. Tuckett, 'Luke 4,16-30, Isaiah and Q', in *Logia* (1982), p. 348 n. 28.

6.   Lentzen-Deis, *Die Taufe Jesu*, p. 147 n. 206.

element to the quotation, one that is incompatible with Luke's purported prophetic understanding of the Spirit. According to Isa. 58.6c, Jesus not only proclaims ἄφεσις, but effects it through acts of power, such as healing and exorcisms: 'This broader concept of "setting the afflicted at liberty" has nothing to do with the activities of the Spirit of prophecy'.[1] However, it is by no means certain that this is how Luke interpreted Isa. 58.6c. Indeed, each of the other three infinitival phrases in 4.18-19 refer to preaching, a point which is emphasized through the alteration of καλέσαι (LXX) to κηρύξαι:

a. εὐαγγελίσασθαι πτωχοῖς
b. κηρύξαι αἰχμαλώτοις ἄφεσιν καὶ τυφλοῖς ἀνάβλεψιν
c. ἀποστεῖλαι τεθραυσμένους ἐν ἀφέσει
d. κηρύξαι ἐνιαυτὸν κυρίου δεκτόν.

The passage as it stands undeniably emphasizes preaching as the most prominent dimension of Jesus' mission.[2] That this motif is characteristic of Luke is evident in Lk. 4.44, where he retains Mark's reference to preaching, but omits his reference to exorcisms. This indicates that Luke probably understood ἀποστεῖλαι τεθραυσμένους ἐν ἀφέσει as the effect of Jesus' preaching ministry. It is quite likely that the insertion of Isa. 58.6d was made as a result of the verbal linkage which ἄφεσις provides with the preceding phrase (see b. above) and that these stichs (b. and c.) were viewed as presenting a unified message: Jesus effects salvation through his Spirit-inspired proclamation. The fact that Luke elsewhere portrays miracles of healings and exorcisms as a vital part of Jesus' ministry of liberation is irrelevant to the present discussion. The point is that Luke, in 4.18-19 and throughout his two-volume work, does not relate these activities directly to the work of the Spirit. As I have noted, this theological *Tendenz* is unique to Luke.

Thirdly, and perhaps most significantly, Turner challenges the basis upon which Rese's conclusion rests: Schweizer's claim that 'Luke adopts the typically Jewish idea that the Spirit is the Spirit of prophecy'.[3] Turner maintains that, as the source of Jesus' inspired preaching, the Spirit 'bears little relationship to any "typical Jewish idea" of the Spirit

---

1. Turner, 'Luke and the Spirit', p. 62.
2. The specific elements of the preaching named in Isa. 61.1-2, such as 'release of the captives' and 'recovery of sight to the blind', are employed by Luke as metaphors which speak of the eschatological liberation effected by Jesus' proclamation, of which a primary element is 'forgiveness of sins'.
3. Turner, 'Luke and the Spirit', pp. 62-67.

of prophecy'.[1] Turner argues that, according to the Old Testament and the writings of intertestamental Judaism, the role of the Spirit in relation to prophet was not to impart power and authority in the delivery of the message; rather, prior to and independent of the proclamation of the message, the Spirit revealed the content of the message which was to be delivered. In short, Turner asserts that the Jews viewed the Spirit of prophecy as the organ of revelation rather than the source of inspired speech.

It is extremely doubtful, however, whether the distinction Turner makes between the Spirit's role as the agent of revelation and as the source of inspired speech would have been recognized by the Jews of antiquity. Undoubtedly this distinction was alien to rabbis, who commonly described the prophet simply as one who 'speaks in the Holy Spirit' (מדבר ברוח הקודש). Indeed, by definition the prophet was not simply a man who received revelation; he was the mouthpiece of God. Revelation and proclamation go hand in hand, and both are attributed to the Spirit.[2] While some passages focus on the Spirit's role in the revelatory act, others, such as Isa. 61.1, focus on the prophet's Spirit-inspired utterance.[3] Generally, to emphasize one aspect of the prophetic event is to imply the other.[4]

Numerous other texts indicate that the distinction proposed by Turner was not maintained. Ecstatic prophecy, such as that recorded in Num. 11.25-26, is a case in point.[5] In light of passages such as Num. 24.2-3,[6] 1 Sam. 10.10 and Joel 3.1-2 (LXX), it cannot be maintained that other, less enthusiastic forms of prophetic speech, were deemed uninspired by the Spirit of God. Indeed, Philo declares the very thing that Turner

1. Turner, 'Luke and the Spirit', p. 65.
2. This is stated with particular clarity in the 'ten names given to the Holy Spirit' recorded in *ARN* A.34 and alternatively in the variant traditions, the 'ten names given to prophecy'. See Chapter 5 §1.1.2.
3. See for example: Num. 23.7 (LXX); *Frag. 2* of Aristobulus, Eusebius, *Prae. Ev.* 8.10.4; *Ps.-Philo* 62.2; Josephus, *Ant.* 6.166; and the alterations which Josephus makes to the LXX (*Ant.* 4.165 = Num. 27.18; *Ant.* 8.295 = 2 Chron. 15.1; *Ant.* 9.168 = 2 Chron. 24.20; *Ant.* 9.10 = 2 Chron. 20.14).
4. Note the close relationship between revealed wisdom and inspired speech in Sir. 39.6 and *1 En.* 62.2.
5. See also Philo, *Spec. Leg.* 4.49; *Leg. All.* 3.82; *Rer. Div. Her.* 249, 265-66; *Ps.-Philo* 28.6.
6. See also Josephus on Num. 22.15-16 (*Ant.* 4.108) and on Num. 23.12 (*Ant.* 4.119-20).

denies: the Spirit endowed Abraham's words with special persuasive power (*Virt.* 217).[1]

A decisive objection to Turner's criticism is that Luke himself made the connection. He explicitly describes Spirit-inspired speech as prophetic activity in the infancy narratives and Acts 2.17 (cf. 2.4-5); and the idea is implicit in Lk. 4.18-19 (Isa. 61.1).[2] Indeed, where else could these notions have come from if Luke's conception of the Spirit as the source of inspired speech was not influenced by Judaism? Turner's response that Luke owes much more to 'such messianic ideas as are found in Isa. 11.4, or to relatively characteristic christian concepts' than to the Jewish concept of the Spirit of prophecy is no alternative.[3] We have already noted how messianic and prophetic functions merge in intertestamental Judaism,[4] and there can be little doubt that these 'Christian concepts' were shaped by Judaism.

If, on the one hand, Turner incorrectly exaggerates the Jewish emphasis on the Spirit as the source of revelation to the exclusion of the Spirit's role in the inspiration of the prophetic message, Schweizer, on the other hand, heightens the apparent difference between the Jewish understanding of the Spirit and that of Luke by failing to emphasize that, according to Luke, the Spirit is the source of both inspired speech and special revelation, and that often the two functions merge. This is true for Jesus (Lk. 10.21), as well as the early church (Lk. 12.12). Indeed, it is difficult to make rigid distinctions at this point.

In short, it is inaccurate to distinguish sharply between the purported Jewish view of the Spirit as the source of revelation and Luke's understanding of the Spirit as the means by which a previously understood message is powerfully proclaimed, for both descriptions are caricatures.

Having reviewed the evidence, I have found Turner's criticisms of Rese's position to be untenable at each point. Perhaps the weakest link in Turner's argument against Rese is his inability to present a plausible

---

1. See Chapter 2 §5.2, Note also *t. Job* 43.2, 48.3, *Ps.-Philo* 32.14 and *Jub.* 25.14, 31.12-13, where the Spirit is cited as the source of inspired praise or blessing, and *Mart. Isa.* 5.14, which states that Isaiah, inspired by the Spirit, prophesied until sawn in half.

2. The connection is explicitly expressed in the Targum of Isaiah, which reads: ' The spirit of prophecy [רוח נבואה] from before the Lord Elohim is upon me' (text of Isa. 61.1 from J.F. Stenning, *The Targum of Isaiah* [1953]).

3. Turner, 'Luke and the Spirit', p. 66.

4. Indeed, Isa. 11.4 speaks of inspired speech. This point is emphasized in the Targum to Isa. 11.4.

alternative. I have already noted the inadequacy of arguments based on structure. On this basis I conclude that Luke was responsible for the omission of Isa. 61.1d in Lk. 4.18 and that the motivation for this alteration came from Luke's prophetic understanding of the Spirit. This conclusion accords well with Luke's redactional activity elsewhere and offers a plausible explanation of an omission which is otherwise extremely difficult to explain.

The Insertion of Isaiah 58.6c (LXX): ἀποστεῖλαι τεθραυσμένους ἐν ἀφέσει. We noted above that the insertion of Isa. 58.6c was probably made as a result of the verbal linkage which ἄφεσις provides with the preceding phrase. M. Rese suggests that the linkage was made by Luke because he interpreted ἄφεσις to refer to the forgiveness of sins which Jesus, inspired by the Spirit, proclaimed.[1] On the other hand, M. Turner, building on the work of R. Sloan, asserts that the linkage was motivated by jubilary concerns.[2] In contrast to Sloan, Turner argues that Luke does not develop jubilary themes elsewhere and therefore concludes that the linkage of Isa. 61.1-2 with 58.6 points to the traditional origin of the quotation.[3] While Turner's hypothesis is plausible, several factors indicate that the insertion is to be attributed to Luke. First, although Luke does not develop jubilary themes elsewhere, he does display special interest in the term ἄφεσις (Luke, 5×; Acts, 5×; cf. Matthew, 1×; Mark, 2×), generally understood as 'release from sins'.[4] Secondly, Turner's suggestion that Isa. 58.6 was linked with Isa. 61.1-2 in order to heighten a distinctive jubilee emphasis is unconvincing.[5] There is no evidence of such a linkage in the literature of intertestamental Judaism and, although Isa. 61.1-2 employs the picture of the jubilee as a 'metaphorical expression of the eschatological salvation of God',[6] it is by no means certain that the jubilary motif is emphasized in other parts of Luke's narrative (4.16-30), whether traditional or redactional. This indicates that the linkage of Isa. 61.1-2 with Isa. 58.6 was made by Luke,

---

1. Rese, *Alttestamentliche Motive*, p. 146.
2. 'Luke and the Spirit', p. 70; R.B. Sloan, *The Favorable Year of the Lord* (1977), pp. 39-40.
3. 'Luke and the Spirit', pp. 67-71.
4. Of the ten occurrences of ἄφεσις in Luke–Acts, excluding the two occurrences in Lk. 4.18-19, all are related to 'sins' (e.g. ἄφεσις ἁμαρτιῶν).
5. Turner, 'Luke and the Spirit', p. 70. See also Sloan, *The Favorable Year*, pp. 39-40.
6. Sloan, *The Favorable Year*, pp. 162-63.

and not in order to heighten a distinctive jubilary emphasis, but rather as a result of his interest in ἄφεσις as a description of the liberating power of Jesus' preaching, of which an important aspect was forgiveness of sins. Thirdly, this conclusion is confirmed by the text's correlation with another motif of Luke: the duplication of a word in Old Testament quotations, such as ἄφεσις and ἀποστέλλω in 4.18, is characteristic of Lukan style.[1]

The Alteration of καλέσαι *(LXX) to* κηρύξαι. Since Luke never uses καλέω in reference to preaching, it is quite probable that this alteration reflects his emphasis on preaching as the pre-eminent activity inspired by the Spirit.[2] However, noting that the preference for κηρύσσω is not unique to Luke, D. Bock maintains that 'the change points as firmly to a traditional source as it does to Luke'.[3] Nevertheless, the force of Bock's point is lessened by Luke's frequent duplication of words in quotations from the Old Testament. Thus the alteration of καλέσαι (LXX) to κηρύξαι corresponds to Luke's handling of Old Testament citations elsewhere and strongly suggests that the alteration reflects Luke's hand.[4]

The Omission of καὶ ἡμέραν ἀνταποδόσεως *(LXX)*. It is debatable whether any particular theological interest should be attached to this omission for, strictly speaking, it does not represent an alteration of the LXX. Nevertheless, the quotation is broken off abruptly in the middle of a sentence. Thus, while a number of factors may have influenced the length of the quotation, it is quite likely that the phrase was omitted from the citation in order to stress the grace of God.[5] While this emphasis on the salvific dimension of Jesus' work may have been taken over from tradition, it is equally compatible with Luke's perspective,[6]

---

1.   Note the repetition of κηρύξαι (Lk. 4.18, 19 = Isa. 61.1-2); ἐν ταῖς... ἡμέραις (Acts 2.17, 18 = Joel 3.1-2); καὶ προφητεύσουσιν (Acts 2.17, 18 = Joel 3.1-2); ἔργον (Acts 13.41, 2× = Hab. 1.5); σου (Lk. 7.27 = Mal. 3.1).
2.   So also Rese, *Alttestamentliche Motive*, p. 146.
3.   Bock, *Proclamation*, p. 106. None of the evangelists uses καλέω with reference to preaching, and κηρύσσω is used frequently by the other evangelists as well: Luke, 8×; Matthew, 9×; Mark, 12×.
4.   So also T. Holtz, *Untersuchungen über die alttestamentlichen Zitate bei Lukas* (1968), p. 40.
5.   W. Grundmann, *Das Evangelium nach Lukas* (1961), p. 121; K. Giles, 'Salvation in Lukan Theology (1)', *RTR* 42 (1983), p. 12.
6.   Rese, *Alttestamentliche Motive*, pp. 152-53.

and therefore indecisive in determining whether the quotation stems from a traditional source or Luke's hand. However, in view of the conclusions cited above, it is most probable that the entire quotation, as it stands in Lk. 4.18-19, reflects Luke's redactional stamp.

3.2. Conclusion: The Significance of Luke's Redaction in Luke 4.18-19

Having examined the alterations of Isa. 61.1-2 (LXX) in Lk. 4.18-19, I am now in a position to summarize my conclusions and assess their significance for Luke's pneumatology and, more specifically, his understanding of Jesus' pneumatic anointing.

The historicity of the general outline of events in Luke's account (4.16-30) need not be questioned for the linguistic data indicate that the account is based on traditional material other than Mk 6.1-6. Nonetheless, it is evident that Luke has made at least two decisive alterations to the traditional material available to him. First, he has moved the account forward in the chronology of his Gospel. Secondly, he has altered the wording of the quotation from Isa. 61.1-2. While the pre-Lukan tradition in all probability portrayed Jesus' preaching at Nazareth as centering on Isa. 61.1-2, it is highly unlikely that the quotation as it stands in Lk. 4.18-19 is traditional. As a result of my analysis of the text I have concluded that it is highly probable that: the phrase ἰάσασθαι τοὺς συντετριμμένους τῇ καρδίᾳ was omitted by Luke due to his distinctive prophetic pneumatology; due to the verbal linkage which ἄφεσις provides with the preceding phrase, Luke inserted Isa. 58.6c (ἀποστεῖλαι τεθραυσμένους ἐν ἀφέσει) into the text of Isa. 61.1-2 in order to emphasize the liberating power of Jesus' Spirit-inspired preaching; Luke is responsible for the alteration of καλέσαι (LXX) to κηρύξαι—this change, while reflecting Luke's emphasis on preaching as the pre-eminent activity inspired by the Spirit, is due principally to stylistic concerns. I have also concluded that it is quite likely that Luke omitted the final phrase of Isa. 61.2a (καὶ ἡμέραν ἀνταποδόσεως) in order to emphasize the salvific dimension of Jesus' work.

The profound implications which these conclusions have for this inquiry into Luke's understanding of Jesus' pneumatic anointing cannot be missed. First, by moving the Nazareth pericope forward in the chronology of his Gospel, Luke links the account with that of Jesus' reception of the Spirit at the Jordan and, as a result, highlights the significance of Jesus' pneumatic anointing for his entire ministry. The quotation from Isaiah, which plays such a prominent role in the narrative, defines with precision the significance which Luke attaches to Jesus' pneumatic anointing: Jesus' reception of the Spirit at the Jordan was the means by which he was equipped to carry out his messianic mission. Secondly, by altering the text of Isa. 61.1-2 (LXX), Luke brings the quotation into conformity with his distinctive prophetic pneumatology and thus highlights preaching as the primary product of Jesus' anointing and the pre-eminent aspect of his mission. While the activity of the Spirit is generally portrayed in prophetic terms in Isa. 61.1-2 (i.e. as the source of inspired speech), through his redactional activity Luke has heightened this aspect of the text. Indeed, according to Luke, the Spirit-inspired preaching of Jesus effects salvation. This assessment of Luke's pneumatology is entirely consistent with his Christology—Luke, more than any of the other synoptic evangelists, views Jesus' entire ministry,[1] as well as his 'anointing' (as Lk. 4.18-19 indicates),[2] in prophetic terms. In short, my analysis of Lk. 4.18-19 has confirmed the conclusions from the previous analysis of Lk. 3.21-22 and 4.1, 14: according to Luke, Jesus' pneumatic anointing, rather than the source of his unique filial relationship to God or his initiation into the new age, was the means by which Jesus was equipped to carry out his divinely appointed task. Thus Luke's portrayal of Jesus' pneumatic anointing, which anticipates the experience of the early church,[3] is consistent with his prophetic pneumatology.

---

1.   Luke often depicts people reacting to Jesus as a prophet (Lk. 7.16, 39; 9.8, 19; 24.19; Acts 2.30). Jesus refers to himself as a prophet (Lk. 4.24) and he accepts the fate of a prophet (Lk. 11.49-50; 13.33). Jesus is explicitly identified as the prophet-like-Moses in Acts 3.22 and 7.37; and perhaps this identification is also suggested in Luke's portrayal of Jesus' childhood (Isaacs notes the parallels to Philo's depiction of Moses' childhood [*Spirit*, p. 130]) in Lk. 9.35 (Deut. 18.15: αὐτοῦ ἀκούετε), in Lk. 10.1 (Num. 11.25: commissioning of the 70), in 11.20 (Exod. 8.19: δάκτυλος) and in the attribution of τέρατα καὶ σημεῖα to Jesus in Acts 2.22; 4.30 (cf. Acts 7.36).

2.   This conclusion is also supported by Lk. 4.23-24.

3.   See Chapter 8 §2.1 above.

Chapter 9

JESUS AND THE SPIRIT: THE PNEUMATIC SAYINGS

Several texts in Luke–Acts, apart from Lk. 4.18-19, relate sayings of Jesus pertaining to the Holy Spirit. In the following chapter I shall examine these texts as they occur in Luke–Acts and assess their significance for Luke's pneumatology.

1. The Spirit-Inspired Exultation (Luke 10.21)

Luke follows his account of the return of the seventy (two) with material drawn from Q (10.21-24).[1] The pericope records Jesus' joyful expression of thanksgiving to the Father, who, through Jesus, has revealed 'things hidden from the wise' to the disciples. This inspired exultation is followed by a pronouncement to the disciples: they are indeed 'blessed', for they are the favored recipients of God's revelation. Of particular importance for this study is the way in which Luke introduces Jesus' initial words of praise in Lk. 10.21b:[2]

Mt. 11.25b: ἀποκριθεὶς ὁ Ἰησοῦς εἶπεν
Lk. 10.21b: ἠγαλλιάσατο ἐν τῷ πνεύματι τῷ ἁγίῳ καὶ εἶπεν

Mt. 11.25b: Jesus answering, said
Lk. 10.21b: He rejoiced in the Holy Spirit and said

A comparison of Lk. 10.21b with Mt. 11.25b reveals that Matthew preserves the original introductory phrase of Q, which Luke has decisively altered. The verb ἀγαλλιάω ('be glad, rejoice') and its cognate noun, ἀγαλλίασις ('joy'), are characteristic of Luke;[3] and, as I have already established, Luke frequently alters his sources in accordance with his pneumatological interests. Thus it is clear that Luke has replaced

1.   The two passages are linked by the temporal phrase in v. 21a: Ἐν αὐτῇ τῇ ὥρᾳ.
2.   ET is my own.
3.   Seven out of the sixteen occurrences in the NT of ἀγαλλιάω (NT, 11×; Luke–Acts, 4×) and ἀγαλλίασις (NT, 5×; Luke–Acts, 3×) are found in Luke–Acts.

the ἀποκριθείς of Q with a phrase more to his liking: ἠγαλλιάσατο ἐν τῷ πνεύματι τῷ ἁγίῳ. In assessing the significance of Luke's redaction it is important to define with precision the action signified by the verb ἀγαλλιάω. In the LXX ἀγαλλιάω, which is usually found in Psalms and the poetic portions of the Prophets, denotes spiritual exultation which issues forth in praise to God for his mighty acts. The subject of the verb is not simply ushered into a state of sacred rapture; the subject also 'declares the acts of God'.[1] The close association between ἀγαλλιάω and the utterance of inspired words of praise is illustrated in the phrase, καὶ ἠγαλλιάσατο ἡ γλῶσσά μου ('my tongue rejoices', Ps. 15.9, LXX; quoted in Acts 2.26),[2] and in Ps. 94.1 (LXX), where the verbs ἀγαλλιασώμεθα and ἀλαλάξωμεν are employed as synonyms:[3]

Δεῦτε ἀγαλλιασώμεθα τῷ κυρίῳ,
ἀλαλάξωμεν τῷ θεῷ τῷ σωτῆρι ἡμῶν.

Come, let us sing for joy to the Lord,
`let us shout aloud to God, our saviour.

In the New Testament the verb is used in a similar manner.[4] The linkage between ἀγαλλιάω and the declaration of the mighty acts of God is particularly striking in Luke–Acts.[5] The verb describes the joyful praise of Mary (Lk. 1.47), Jesus (Lk. 10.21) and David (Acts 2.25) in response to God's salvific activity in Jesus. That ἀγαλλιάω in Lk. 10.21b refers to the declaration of words of praise is confirmed by the Semitic structure of the verse, which parallels ἀγαλλιάω with εἶπεν. Luke's addition of the instrumental phrase, ἐν τῷ πνεύματι τῷ ἁγίῳ, in Lk. 10.21b is consistent with the usage of ἀγαλλιάω cited above: the praise of Mary and Jesus is uttered under the inspiration of the Spirit (Lk. 1.35; 10.21), and David is described as a prophet (Acts 2.30). Indeed, Jesus' experience of the Spirit in 10.21b parallels that of the leading figures in the infancy narratives and the disciples in Acts. In short, for Luke the phrase ἠγαλλιάσατο ἐν τῷ πνεύματι τῷ ἁγίῳ καὶ

1.   R. Bultmann, 'ἀγαλλιάομαι', p. 20.
2.   Note also Ps. 125.2 (LXX) where a similar expression is used.
3.   See also (LXX): Pss. 5.12; 9.2-3; 34.27; 91.5; 95.11; 96.1; Isa. 12.6; 25.9; 61.10. ET is my own.
4.   R. Bultmann, 'ἀγαλλιάομαι', p. 20; W.G. Morrice, *Joy in the New Testament* [1984], p. 21.
5.   The linkage is made explicit in three out of four occurrences of the verb (Lk. 1.47; 10.21; Acts 2.25). The only exception is Acts 16.34.

εἶπεν was an appropriate way of describing prophetic activity:[1] it signified the Spirit-inspired declaration of the acts of God. Thus Luke's alteration of Q in Lk. 10.21b, which emphasized the pneumatic and prophetic character of Jesus' declaration, reflects Luke's unique interpretation of the event and his distinctive prophetic pneumatology.

2. Encouragement to Pray for the Spirit (Luke 11.13)

Luke 11.1-13 forms a section devoted to Jesus' teaching on prayer. The section begins with a disciple's request for instruction on how to pray (11.1), which Jesus answers in the form of a model prayer (11.2-4)[2] and parabolic teaching concerning the willingness and certainty of God's response (11.5-13). The section concludes by comparing the heavenly Father with an earthly counterpart: 'If you then, who are evil, know how to give good gifts to your children, how much more will the heavenly Father give the Holy Spirit to those who ask him!' (11.13). This concluding comparison, with its reference to the Holy Spirit, warrants examination.

The similarities in wording between Lk. 11.9-13 and Mt. 7.7-11 indicate that the passage stems from Q. However, there is a crucial difference: Mt. 7.11b has ἀγαθά ('good [gifts]') rather than the πνεῦμα ἅγιον of Lk. 11.13b.[3] There can be little doubt that Matthew's ἀγαθά represents the original wording of Q. Matthew follows his sources closely with reference to the Spirit: he never omits a reference to the Spirit which is contained in his sources and he never inserts πνεῦμα into Markan or Q material. Luke, on the other hand, inserts πνεῦμα into Q material on three occasions (Lk. 4.1; 10.21; 11.13) and into Markan material once (Lk. 4.14).[4] These data suggest that Luke, rather

---

1. Strack–Billerbeck, *Kommentar*, II, p. 176: 'ἠγαλλιάσατο ἐν τῷ πνεύματι τῷ ἁγίῳ = im Geist prophetischer Rede'. See also Barrett, *Gospel Tradition*, pp. 101-102.

2. The variant reading in 11.2, ἐλθέτω τὸ πνεῦμα σου τὸ ἅγιον ἐφ' ἡμᾶς καὶ καθαρισάτω ἡμᾶς, is undoubtedly secondary. See G. Schneider, 'Die Bitte um das Kommen des Geistes im lukanischen Vaterunser (Lk 11,2 v.l)', in *Studien zum Text und zur Ethik des Neuen Testaments* (1986), pp. 370-71.

3. There are several variant readings, but the external evidence for πνεῦμα ἅγιον is strong (𝔓75 ℵ C L X Θ Ψ) and the other variant readings can be explained as assimilation with Matthew (B. Metzger, *A Textual Commentary on the Greek New Testament* [1975], p. 158).

4. See C.S. Rodd, 'Spirit or Finger', *ExpTim* 72 (1960–61), pp. 157-58.

than Matthew, has altered Q. This conclusion is confirmed by the awkwardness of Luke's construction: the insertion of πνεῦμα ἅγιον breaks the parallelism of the *a minore ad maius* argument which links the δόματα ἀγαθά ('good gifts') given by earthly fathers (Lk. 11.13a = Mt. 7.11a) with the ἀγαθά ('good [gifts]') given by the heavenly Father (Lk. 11.13b = Mt. 7.11b).

Having established that the πνεῦμα ἅγιον of Lk. 11.13b is redactional, the significance of this alteration for Luke's pneumatology must now be assessed. Three observations will be made.

First, Luke's alteration of the Q form of the saying anticipates the post-resurrection experience of the church.[1] This is evident from the fact that the promise that the Father will give πνεῦμα ἅγιον to those who ask begins to be realized only at Pentecost. By contemporizing the text in this way, Luke stresses the relevance of the saying for the post-Pentecostal community to which he writes.

Secondly, the context indicates that the promise is made to disciples (Lk. 11.1).[2] Thus Luke's contemporized version of the saying is directed to the members of the Christian community. Since it is addressed to Christians, the promise cannot refer to an initiatory or soteriological gift.[3] This judgment is confirmed by the repetitive character of the exhortation to pray:[4] prayer for the Spirit (and, in light of the promise, we may presume this includes the reception of the Spirit) is to be an ongoing practice. The gift of πνεῦμα ἅγιον to which Luke refers neither initiates one into the new age, nor is it to be received only once; rather, πνεῦμα ἅγιον is given to disciples and is to be experienced on an ongoing basis.

Thirdly, Luke's usage elsewhere indicates that he viewed the gift of πνεῦμα ἅγιον in 11.13b as an endowment of prophetic power. On two occasions in Luke–Acts the Spirit is given to those praying;[5] in both the Spirit is portrayed as the source of prophetic activity. Luke alters the

---

1. Fitzmyer, *Luke X–XXIV*, p. 916; Ellis, *Luke*, p. 164; Stronstad, *Charismatic Theology*, p. 46.
2. Beasley-Murray, *Baptism*, p. 119.
3. Montague, *Spirit*, pp. 259-60.
4. Note for example the repetitive force of ὅταν προσεύχησθε, λέγετε (11.2) and the continuous action implicit in the present indicative active verbs in 11.10: λαμβάνω, εὑρίσκω.
5. Prayer is implicitly associated with the reception of the Spirit at Pentecost (Acts 1.14; 2.4). Here also the gift of the Spirit is presented as a prophetic endowment (see Chapter 10 below).

Markan account of Jesus' baptism so that Jesus receives the Spirit after his baptism while praying (Lk. 3.21). As I have noted, this gift of the Spirit, portrayed principally as the source of Jesus' proclamation (Lk. 4.18-19), equipped Jesus for his messianic task. Later, in Acts 4.31, the disciples after having prayed 'were all filled with the Holy Spirit and spoke the word of God boldly'. Again the Spirit given in response to prayer is the impetus behind the proclamation of the word of God. To sum up, through his redactional activity in Lk. 11.13b, Luke encourages post-Pentecostal disciples to ask for the gift of the Spirit which, for Luke, meant open access to the divine πνεῦμα—the source of power which would enable them to be effective witnesses for Christ (Lk. 12.12; Acts 1.8) by providing what was required in time of need, whether it be special knowledge or the ability to powerfully proclaim the gospel in the face of persecution.

3. ἐν δακτύλῳ θεοῦ *(Luke 11.20)*

Luke's account of the Beelzebub Controversy stems from Q, as the close correspondence with Matthew's text indicates (Lk. 11.14-23 = Mt. 12.22-30). However, in Lk. 11.20 there is a significant deviation from its Matthean counterpart:

Lk. 11.20: εἰ δὲ ἐν **δακτύλῳ θεοῦ** [ἐγὼ] ἐκβάλλω τὰ δαιμόνια,
ἄρα ἔφθασεν ἐφ' ὑμᾶς ἡ βασιλεία τοῦ θεοῦ.

Mt. 12.28: εἰ δὲ ἐν **πνεύματι θεοῦ** ἐγὼ ἐκβάλλω τὰ δαιμόνια
ἄρα ἔφθασεν ἐφ' ὑμᾶς ἡ βασιλεία τοῦ θεοῦ.

Lk. 11.20: But if I drive out demons by the *finger of God*,
then the kingdom of God has come upon you.

Mt. 12.28: But if I drive out demons by the *Spirit of God*,
then the kingdom of God has come upon you.

The question as to which evangelist preserves the original reading of Q has been much discussed. While it has been customary to view Luke's δακτύλῳ θεοῦ ('finger of God') as original,[1] a number of more recent works suggest that this judgment should be reassessed[2] and, as the

1. T.W. Manson, *The Teaching of Jesus* (1952), p. 82, and *Sayings*, p. 86; Barrett, *Gospel Tradition*, p. 63.
2. Rodd, 'Spirit or Finger', pp. 157-58; J.E. Yates, 'Luke's Pneumatology and Luke 11.20', in *Studia Evangelica II* (1964), pp. 295-99; R.G. Hamerton-Kelly, 'A Note on Matthew XII.28 Par. Luke XI. 20', *NTS* 11 (1964–65), pp. 167-69; Dunn, *Jesus and the Spirit*, pp. 45-46; Turner, 'Luke and the Spirit', p. 88.

following points indicate, an analysis of the evidence supports this claim.

1. In view of their use of πνεῦμα elsewhere, it is more likely that Luke deleted the reference contained in Q than that Matthew added the term to the tradition. As I have noted, Matthew follows his sources closely with reference to the Spirit, never omitting a reference to πνεῦμα which is contained in Mark and/or Q. Luke, on the other hand, feels free to alter his sources: not only does he add πνεῦμα to his sources; he is also willing, when inclined, to omit the term (Lk. 20.42 = Mk 12.36).[1]

2. The fact that Matthew's version includes the phrase ἡ βασιλεία τοῦ θεοῦ ('kingdom of God') rather than his customary ἡ βασιλεία τῶν οὐρανῶν ('kingdom of heaven') suggests 'that Matthew has hurried over the Q version of Mt. 12.28 without stopping to modify it as he normally would have done'.[2] When the phrase ἡ βασιλεία τοῦ θεοῦ appears in his source material, Matthew normally alters it to ἡ βασιλεία τῶν οὐρανῶν.[3]

3. In the Q account of the Beelzebub Controversy the saying (Lk. 11.20 = Mt. 12.28) is followed by Jesus' statement concerning blasphemy against the Holy Spirit (Mt. 12.32 = Lk. 12.10).[4] This suggests that Matthew's πνεύματι θεοῦ formed part of the text of Q; for, as the editorial comment in Mk 3.30 indicates, the 'blasphemy saying' is unintelligible apart from this prior reference to πνεῦμα.[5]

4. A plausible motive for Matthew's alteration of the text is lacking. Although it has been suggested that Matthew altered the text in order to avoid an anthropomorphism,[6] C.S. Rodd points out that Matthew had no special aversion to anthropomorphic expressions.[7] Indeed, as J. Dunn

---

1. Note also Lk. 21.15 = Mk 13.11; however, Luke includes a variant of this tradition which does refer to the Holy Spirit (Lk. 12.12). See Rodd, 'Spirit or Finger', pp. 157-58 and Yates, 'Luke's Pneumatology and Luke 11.20', pp. 295-99.

2. Dunn, *Jesus and the Spirit*, p. 45. See also Rodd, 'Spirit or Finger', p. 158.

3. Note for example Mt. 4.17; 5.3; 8.11; 10.7; 11.11-12; 13.11, 31, 33; 19.14, 23. The only exception to this practice, other than Mt. 12.28, is Mt. 19.24.

4. See §4.1 below for evidence supporting the claim that Mt. 12.12-32 reflects the original order of Q.

5. Note also how in Lk. 12.10, Luke alters the meaning of the blasphemy saying by changing the context. This is possible because the meaning of the blasphemy saying is dependent on the way in which πνεῦμα is employed in the context.

6. Manson, *Teaching of Jesus*, p. 82.

7. In support of his judgment, Rodd cites Mt. 5.34 and 6.4, two anthropomorphisms found only in Matthew ('Spirit or Finger', p. 158).

notes, it is improbable that Matthew would have altered 'finger of God' to 'Spirit of God' in view of the fact that his interest in drawing parallels between Moses and Jesus is much more prominent than his interest in the Spirit.[1]

5. We need not search long for a plausible motive for Luke's alteration of 'Spirit of God' to 'finger of God': the alteration is consistent with and motivated by his distinctive prophetic pneumatology. I have already noted Luke's reluctance to associate the Spirit directly with activities which do not correspond to strictly prophetic categories (e.g. exorcisms and miracles of healing) and his willingness to alter his sources accordingly, whether by adding (1.35; 4.14) or deleting material (4.18). That Luke's alteration in Lk. 11.20 was indeed motivated by pneumatological concerns is confirmed by Luke's movement of the blasphemy saying from its original context in Q (Mt. 12.32) to Lk. 12.10. To this modification of Q we now turn.

4. *'Blasphemy against the Spirit' and Fearless Witness (Luke 12.10, 12)*

4.1. *The Context of the Saying in Q*
Jesus' saying concerning blasphemy against the Holy Spirit circulated in two variant forms preserved by Mark and Q. A comparison of the synoptic accounts reveals that Matthew records both traditions, inserting the Q saying into the one preserved by Mark (Mt. 12.31-32),[2] while Luke, predominantly following Q, conflates the two accounts:[3]

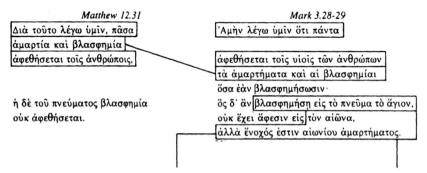

Matthew 12.31	Mark 3.28-29
Διὰ τοῦτο λέγω ὑμῖν, πᾶσα ἁμαρτία καὶ βλασφημία ἀφεθήσεται τοῖς ἀνθρώποις,	Ἀμὴν λέγω ὑμῖν ὅτι πάντα ἀφεθήσεται τοῖς υἱοῖς τῶν ἀνθρώπων τὰ ἁμαρτήματα καὶ αἱ βλασφημίαι ὅσα ἐὰν βλασφημήσωσιν·
ἡ δὲ τοῦ πνεύματος βλασφημία οὐκ ἀφεθήσεται.	ὃς δ' ἂν βλασφημήσῃ εἰς τὸ πνεῦμα τὸ ἅγιον, οὐκ ἔχει ἄφεσιν εἰς τὸν αἰῶνα, ἀλλὰ ἔνοχός ἐστιν αἰωνίου ἁμαρτήματος.

1. Dunn, *Jesus and the Spirit*, p. 45.
2. The comparison follows that of R. Holst, 'Re-examining Mk 3.28f. and its Parallels', *ZNW* 63 (1972), pp. 122-24.
3. While Lk. 12.10 is primarily drawn from Q, the εἰς τὸ ἅγιον πνεῦμα βλασφημήσαντι is influenced by Mark. So also T. Schramm, *Der Markus-Stoff bei Lukas* (1971), p. 46. ET is my own.

Matthew 12.32	Luke 12.10
καὶ ὃς ἐὰν εἴπῃ λόγον κατὰ τοῦ υἱοῦ τοῦ ἀνθρώπου, ἀφεθήσεται αὐτῷ· ὃς δ' ἂν εἴπῃ κατὰ τοῦ πνεύματος τοῦ ἁγίου, οὐκ ἀφεθήσεται αὐτῷ οὔτε ἐν τούτῳ τῷ αἰῶνι οὔτε ἐν τῷ μέλλοντι.	Καὶ πᾶς ὃς ἐρεῖ λόγον εἰς τὸν υἱὸν τοῦ ἀνθρώπου, ἀφεθήσεται αὐτῷ· τῷ δὲ εἰς τὸ ἅγιον πνεῦμα βλασφημήσαντι οὐκ ἀφεθήσεται.

Matthew 12.31	Mark 3.28-29
And this I say to you, every sin and blasphemy will be forgiven men, but the blasphemy against the Spirit will not be forgiven.	I tell you the truth, all shall be forgiven the sons of men the sins and blasphemies whatever they might blaspheme, but whoever blasphemes against the Holy Spirit, will never be forgiven, but is guilty of an eternal sin.

Matthew 12.32	Luke 12.10
Anyone who speaks a word against the Son of Man, will be forgiven, but anyone who speaks against the Holy Spirit, will not be forgiven, either in this age or in the age to come	And everyone who speaks a word against the Son of Man, will be forgiven, but those blaspheming against the Holy Spirit, will not be forgiven.

The important corollary for this study is that the Q form of the blasphemy saying is preserved, at least in part, by Matthew and Luke; yet in different contexts. In Matthew's Gospel the saying forms part of the Beelzebub Controversy (Mt. 12.22-32), while in Luke the saying is sandwiched between an exhortation to confess Christ fearlessly before people (Lk. 12.2-9) and a promise of the Spirit's assistance in the face of persecution (Lk. 12.11-12). This raises a crucial question: which evangelist has preserved the original context of the Q saying? Three points are relevant.

1. The blasphemy saying in Lk. 12.10 fits awkwardly into the Lukan context. While the statement in v. 9, 'he who denies me [the Son of Man] before men will be denied before the angels of God', stands in sharp contrast to v. 10, 'everyone who speaks a word against the Son of man will be forgiven', the thematic links between vv. 2-9 and vv. 11-12 are strong.

2. The context which Matthew provides for the saying is appropriate from a historical and literary perspective: the saying is a fitting response to the charge that Jesus cast out demons by the prince of demons

(Mt. 12.24) and there is no reason to doubt its historicity.[1] That Matthew does indeed provide the correct historical context for the saying is confirmed by Mark (Mk 3.22-30).[2] I have already noted that the reference to the Spirit in Mt. 12.28 links the blasphemy saying to that which precedes and makes the passage intelligible.[3] The context is essential for the interpretation of the saying. Indeed, as the analysis of Lk. 12.10 will reveal, if the context of the saying is altered, the meaning is changed. This leads to the third point.

3. It is unlikely that Q would have preserved the saying in the Lukan context, since this would have altered the original meaning of the saying.

The evidence thus suggests that Luke has taken the blasphemy saying (Lk. 12.10 = Mt. 12.32) from its original context in Q (and Mark) and placed it in another block of Q material (Lk. 12.2-9, 11-12).[4] In order to evaluate the significance of this alteration we must examine the meaning of the saying as it occurs in the context of Q/Mark and Luke.

4.2. The Meaning of the Saying in the Contexts of Q/Mark and Luke
In both Q and Mark the saying forms part of the Beelzebub Controversy (Mt. 12.22-30, 32; Mk 3.20-33). It is recorded as Jesus' response to the charge that he casts out demons by the prince of demons (Mt. 12.24; Mk 3.22). In this context the meaning is clear: to 'blaspheme against the Holy Spirit' is to attribute to the agency of Satan the exorcisms which Jesus performs by the Holy Spirit.[5] The Spirit is thus the means by which Jesus casts out demons.

The saying in its Lukan context has been subject to a variety of interpretations; but scholarly opinion is generally divided between two options, both of which view the saying as directed to the early church. One views 'blasphemy against the Spirit' as an offense committed by the opponents of the Christian mission. The saying is thus a word of comfort to the disciples: those who reject their message will not be

---

1.   Dunn, *Jesus and the Spirit*, p. 52.
2.   Note C.E.B. Cranfield, who argues that Mark presents the saying in its proper historical context (*The Gospel according to Saint Mark* [5th edn, 1977], p. 139).
3.   See Chapter 9 §3, point 3 above.
4.   Lk. 12.11-12 represents a saying from Q (Schulz, *Q*, p. 442; Schürmann, 'Mt 10,23', pp. 150-55) which has been heavily reworked by Luke and conflated with Mk 13.11 by Matthew. Luke probably preserves the original context of Q at this point since the thematic link with 12.2-9 is strong.
5.   Cranfield, *Mark*, p. 141.

forgiven.[1] The other interpretation sees in 'blasphemy against the Spirit' an offense committed by Christians: it is their failure to heed the voice of the Spirit and bear witness to Christ in the face of persecution.[2] The second interpretation is to be preferred: Lk. 12.8-9 indicates that the saying should be viewed as a warning to disciples;[3] and the first view fails to account adequately for the Son of Man/Spirit distinction in 12.10.[4] Although it is possible to argue, as does G. Bornkamm, that 'blasphemy against the Son of Man' refers to the pre-Pentecostal denial of Jesus, which, in contrast with 'blasphemy against the Spirit', is forgivable since it is only after Pentecost that the true identity of Jesus is made known,[5] as Marshall notes, there is no distinction of tenses in v. 10 to support this suggestion.[6] The Son of Man/Spirit distinction is easily accounted for by the second interpretation: 'blasphemy against the Son of Man' refers to the unbeliever's rejection of Jesus; 'blasphemy against the Spirit' is committed by the believer who rejects the inspiration of the Spirit and denies Christ in the face of persecution.[7]

This examination of the blasphemy saying has revealed that in Luke's version the Spirit functions in an altogether different manner than in that of Q and Mark. No longer the power to exorcise demons, the Spirit is the means by which the disciples bear witness to Jesus in the face of persecution.[8]

4.3. *The Significance of Luke's Alteration of Q*

I am now in a position to summarize these findings and assess their significance for Luke's pneumatology. Luke has decisively altered the account of the Beelzebub Controversy in Q (Mt. 12.22-30, 32 =

---

1.   K.H. Rengstorf, *Das Evangelium nach Lukas* (1937), p. 155; Chevallier, *Souffle*, p. 131.
2.   Von Baer, *Der heilige Geist*, p. 138; Schweizer, 'πνεῦμα', p. 407 n. 483; Lampe, 'The Holy Spirit', pp. 190-91; and A.A. Trites, *The New Testament Concept of Witness* (1977), p. 182.
3.   See Schweizer, who notes that vv. 8-9 are 'undoubtedly addressed to disciples' as is the βλασφημεῖν of Acts 26.11 ('πνεῦμα', p. 407).
4.   I.H. Marshall, 'Hard Sayings—VII. Lk 12.10', *Theology* 67 (1964), p. 65.
5.   G. Bornkamm, *Jesus of Nazareth* (1960), p. 212 (n. 1 of ch. 8).
6.   Marshall, 'Hard Sayings', p. 66.
7.   For Luke, 'the denial of the Son of Man before men' in v. 9 corresponds to 'the blasphemy against the Spirit' in v. 10.
8.   Schweizer, 'The Spirit of Power', p. 266; George, 'L'Esprit Saint', p. 519; Leisegang, *Pneuma Hagion*, p. 108.

Lk. 11.14-23; 12.10) at two points. He has (1) replaced πνεύματι θεοῦ (Mt. 12.28) with δακτύλῳ θεοῦ (Lk. 11.20) and (2) taken the blasphemy saying (Lk. 12.10 = Mt. 12.32) from its original setting and inserted it into a block of Q material (Lk. 12.2-9, 11-12) containing exhortations to bear witness to the Son of Man. Both alterations are consistent with and motivated by Luke's distinctive prophetic pneumatology. By replacing πνεύματι θεοῦ with δακτύλῳ θεοῦ Luke eliminated a reference which attributed Jesus' exorcisms to the agency of the Spirit. By altering the context of the blasphemy saying Luke was able to alter the function which it ascribed to the Spirit: no longer the power to exorcise demons, in its Lukan context the Spirit is the means by which the disciples courageously bear witness to Jesus in the face of persecution.[1] In short, while the redactors of Q, Mark and Matthew attribute Jesus' exorcisms to the agency of the Spirit, Luke avoids the concept by modifying the tradition.

Luke's modification of the Q account of the Beelzebub Controversy highlights the distinctiveness of his prophetic pneumatology in relation to the charismatic pneumatology of the primitive church, and it reveals how closely Luke's understanding of the Spirit conforms to pneumatological perspectives current in Judaism. There is not a single text in the Old Testament or in the Jewish literature of the intertestamental period which attributes the exorcism of demons to the agency of the Spirit.[2] Exorcisms are wrought by God in response to prayer. While a prominent feature of such prayers is the evocation of the divine name,[3] reference to the Spirit of God is strikingly absent.

I have suggested that the reasons for the difference in outlook at this point between the early church on the one hand and that of Judaism and Luke on the other are twofold:[4] (1) the primitive church, following in the footsteps of Jesus, broadened the perceived functions of the Spirit of God so that it was viewed not only in traditional Jewish terms as the

1. E. Schweizer, 'πνεῦμα', p. 405.
2. Leisegang, *Pneuma Hagion*, p. 101. Notice also that miracles of healing are not directly associated with the Spirit in the OT (thus the healings performed by Elijah [1 Kgs 17.19-24] and Elisha [2 Kgs 4.33-35; 5.10-15; 6.18-20] are attributed to the intervention of God in response to prayer and various complementary acts, but never to the agency of the Spirit [see also Gen. 20.17; Num. 12.13-15; 2 Kgs 20.5; Kee, *Medicine*, pp. 9-20]) or in intertestamental Judaism.
3. See for example PGM 4.1180-81, 1220-21, 1230-31, 3015-16, 3070-71; 5.115-16, 475-76.
4. See Chapter 6 §4 above.

source of prophetic power, but also as miracle-working power. Thus the
Spirit was envisioned as the agent of exorcism. (2) Luke, on the other
hand, retained the traditional Jewish understanding of the Spirit as the
Spirit of prophecy and, with the term δύναμις, incorporated a Hellenistic
mode of expression to speak of miracle-working power. Therefore, while
δύναμις may be mediated through πνεῦμα (as in Lk. 4.14), the former
rather than the latter is the divine agent by which exorcisms are
wrought.[1]

5. The Pre-Ascension Promise (Luke 24.49; Acts 1.4-5, 8)

Luke 24.47-49 and Acts 1.4-8 present parallel accounts of Jesus'
preascension commission to the disciples. Both accounts are decidedly
Lukan in style, and together they provide an important thematic link
which unites Luke's two-volume work.[2] These facts indicate that Luke
has carefully crafted both accounts in order to further his literary and
theological aims. Nevertheless, the extent of Luke's literary activity at
this point should not be overestimated. A comparison with Mt. 28.16-30
and Jn 20.21-23 suggests that these Lukan pericopes are based on a
core of traditional material.[3] The specific content of this traditional
material and the extent to which it has influenced Luke's account is
exceedingly difficult, if not impossible, to ascertain. For my purposes it
will be sufficient to point out the significance of these parallel accounts
for Luke's literary and theological program.

5.1. The Renewal of 'Israel's' Prophetic Calling to the World
Jesus' commission to the disciples recorded in Lk. 24.47-49 is set in the
broader context of his explication of Scripture (24.44-49). After a preliminary statement concerning the necessary fulfillment of all scriptural
prophecies pertaining to himself (24.44), Jesus explains to the disciples
that his passion and resurrection were prophesied in Scripture and were

---

1.   See Lk. 4.33-37 = Mk 1.23-28; Lk. 6.17-20a = Mk 3.7-13a; Lk. 9.1 = Mk
6.7; Acts 10.38. It is significant that the references to δύναμις in Lk. 4.36, 6.19, 9.1
(and I suspect Acts 10.38) are redactional.
2.   Jesus' pre-ascension commission to the disciples forms the end of Luke's
Gospel and the beginning of Acts. This literary overlapping is clearly intended to
emphasize the continuity between the Gospel and Acts. See Talbert, *Literary Patterns*,
p. 60.
3.   Marshall, *Commentary on Luke*, pp. 903-904; V. Taylor, *The Passion
Narrative of St Luke: A Critical and Historical Investigation* (1972), pp. 112-14.

thus essential elements of the divine plan (24.46). In v. 47 Jesus indicates that the mandate of scriptural prophecy includes the future mission of the church: 'and repentance and forgiveness of sins will be preached in his name to all nations, beginning at Jerusalem' (24.47). The scriptural basis for this assertion is probably Isa. 49.6, which is cited in Paul's sermon in Pisidian Antioch (Acts 13.47) and alluded to elsewhere in Luke–Acts (Lk. 2.32; Acts 1.8; 26.23; perhaps 28.28).[1] By accepting the vocation of Israel to be a prophet commissioned to bring 'light to the nations' and 'salvation to the ends of the earth' (Isa. 49.6), the disciples actively participate in the fulfillment of Old Testament prophecy.

The conceptual background of Isa. 49.6 is also prominent in the parallel version of the commission recorded in Acts 1.4-8. Jesus' commission is again set in the context of instruction (Acts 1.2-3), although the instruction is not explicitly tied to Scripture as in Lk. 24.44-45. His command to wait in Jerusalem for ἡ ἐπαγγελία τοῦ πατρός ('the promise of the Father', Acts 1.4) is followed by a question from the disciples: 'Lord, are you at this time going to restore the Kingdom to Israel?' The question is a literary device which anticipates possible misconceptions and thus calls for further clarification.[2] Jesus' response is intended to challenge the disciples' narrow expectation of a restoration limited to the faithful of Israel: 'you will be my witnesses... to the ends of the earth' (ἕως ἐσχάτου τῆς γῆς, Acts 1.8; cf. Isa. 49.6). Echoing the words and concepts of Isa. 49.6,[3] Jesus declares that God's promises are indeed being fulfilled; however, 'the promise of God's reign is not simply the restoration of the preserved of Israel, but the renewal of the vocation of Israel to be a light to the nations to the ends of the earth'.[4]

5.2. ἡ ἐπαγγελία τοῦ πατρός *(Luke 24.49; Acts 1.4)*

The disciples are able to assume this collective prophetic vocation to which they have been called only after they have received ἡ ἐπαγγελία

---

1.   See D.L. Tiede, 'The Exaltation of Jesus and the Restoration of Israel in Acts 1', *HTR* 79 (1986), pp. 285-86.

2.   As D. Hill notes ('The Spirit and the Church's Witness: Observations on Acts 1:6-8', *IBS* 6 [1984], pp. 16-17), this literary device is found frequently in Luke–Acts: Lk. 1.34; 7.23; 22.24; Acts 2.37; 7.1; 17.19.

3.   The phrase ἕως ἐσχάτου τῆς γῆς occurs in Isa. 8.9; 48.20; 49.6; 62.11; cf. 45.22 (LXX). The link between Acts 1.8 and Isa. 49.6 is affirmed by D. Seccombe, 'Luke and Isaiah', *NTS* 27 (1981), pp. 258-59, and Tiede, *Prophecy and History in Luke–Acts* (1980), pp. 59-60, 'The Exaltation of Jesus', p. 285.

4.   Tiede, 'The Exaltation of Jesus', p. 286.

τοῦ πατρός. Luke makes the point in both pre-ascension accounts by recording Jesus' command to the disciples to remain in Jerusalem until they have received ἡ ἐπαγγελία τοῦ πατρός (Lk. 24.49; Acts 1.4). The reason for the delay is made explicit: the reception of 'the promise' will result in the disciples being 'clothed with power from on high' and thus enable them to become effective 'witnesses' (Lk. 24.48-49; Acts 1.8).

Luke identifies this source of prophetic power, ἡ ἐπαγγελία τοῦ πατρός, with the gift of the Spirit which was initially bestowed upon the disciples at Pentecost. (1) A comparison of Lk. 24.48-49 with Acts 1.8 reveals that ἡ ἐπαγγελία τοῦ πατρός (Lk. 24.49) and ἅγιον πνεῦμα (Acts 1.8) are used interchangeably to describe the source of power which would enable the disciples to fulfill their role as 'witnesses' (μάρτυρες). (2) In Acts 1.4-5 ἡ ἐπαγγελία τοῦ πατρός is presented as the fulfillment of John's prophecy concerning the messianic deluge of the Spirit. I have already noted that, according to Luke, John's prophecy of a messianic deluge of the Spirit which would sift and separate the just from the unjust found its initial fulfillment in the Pentecostal bestowal of the Spirit and the proclamation which it inspired.[1] That Luke views Pentecost (Acts 2.4) as the fulfillment of the Baptist's prophecy follows from the temporal phrase in Acts 1.5 ('but in a few days'). (3) Acts 2.33 states what is implicit in the narrative: at Pentecost (Acts 2.4) Jesus poured out on the disciples the ἐπαγγελίαν τοῦ πνεύματος τοῦ ἁγίου ('promise of the Holy Spirit') which he received from the Father.

Does Luke provide any clues concerning why he chooses to speak of the gift of the Spirit as ἡ ἐπαγγελία τοῦ πατρός? I have noted that Luke views the gift of the Spirit given to the disciples at Pentecost as a fulfillment of John's prophecy concerning the messianic deluge of the Spirit, but it is unlikely that this prophecy would have prompted Luke to speak of the gift as 'the promise of the Father'.

In Acts 1.4 Jesus indicates that he has spoken of 'the promise of the Father' to the disciples on a prior occasion, but this ambiguous reference offers little by way of explanation concerning the origin of the term. Since Lk. 24.49 and Acts 1.4 record the same address from different perspectives,[2] Jesus' remark must refer to one of two prior statements regarding the Spirit (if recorded by Luke): Lk. 11.13 or 12.12. Neither passage connects the promise of the Spirit to an Old Testament text,

---

1. See Chapter 7 §3 above.
2. I.H. Marshall, 'The Significance of Pentecost', *SJT* 30 (1977), p. 350.

although Lk. 11.13 affirms that the gift of the Spirit is given by the Father.

The only Old Testament text cited by Luke which adequately accounts for his use of the term 'the promise of the Father' with reference to the gift of the Spirit is Joel 3.1-5a (LXX; Acts 2.17-21).[1] Several factors suggest that this passage has indeed motivated Luke's usage of the term. First, I have noted that according to Luke 'the promise of the Father' was received by the disciples at Pentecost (Acts 2.4, 33). Luke interprets this event in light of Joel 3.1-2 (Acts 2.17-21). Secondly, Luke's desire to emphasize that the promise comes from the Father explains his insertion of λέγει ὁ θεός ('God says') into the Joel text in Acts 2.17. Thirdly, Peter's speech in Acts 2 concludes with a call to repent, be baptized and receive the gift of the Spirit (Acts 2.38). In his closing words, Peter affirms that 'the promise (ἡ ἐπαγγελία) is for you and... for all whom the Lord our God will call' (Acts 2.39). The final refrain echoes the words of Joel 3.5a (quoted in Acts 2.21), thus the promise is tied linguistically and contextually to the Joel citation. Although the ἐπαγγελία of Acts 2.39 includes both the Spirit of prophecy (Joel 3.1; Acts 2.17) and salvation (Joel 3.5a; Acts 2.21), whereas ἡ ἐπαγγελία τοῦ πατρός in Lk. 24.49 and Acts 1.4, 2.33 refers exclusively to the gift of the Spirit of prophecy, the connection to the Joel citation is clear. In Acts 2.39 Luke extends the range of the promise envisioned to include the promise of salvation offered in Joel 3.5 (as well as the promise of the Spirit of prophecy in Joel 3.1) because the audience addressed are not disciples. Consistent with Lk. 24.49, Acts 1.4 and 2.33, the promised gift of the Spirit in Acts 2.38 refers to the promise of Joel 3.1, and thus it is a promise of prophetic enabling granted to the repentant.[2] The promise of Acts 2.39, like the promise of Jesus in Acts 1.8, points beyond 'the restoration of the preserved of Israel': salvation is offered (Joel 3.5), but the promise includes the renewal of Israel's prophetic vocation (Joel 3.1).

This brief summary of the relevant passages has revealed that ἡ ἐπαγγελία τοῦ πατρός (Lk. 24.49, Acts 1.4; cf. 2.33) and ἡ ἐπαγγελία with reference to the Spirit (Acts 2.38-39) find their origin in Joel 3.1

---

1.   E. Lohse, 'Die Bedeutung des Pfingstberichtes im Rahmen des lukanischen Geschichtswerkes', in *Die Einheit des Neuen Testaments* (1973), p. 188.

2.   Lake and Cadbury, *The Beginnings of Christianity*, IV, p. 26; P. Tachau, 'Die Pfingstgeschichte nach Lukas. Exegetische Überlegungen zu Apg. 2,1-13', *EE* 29 (1977), p. 101.

(LXX): ἐκχεῶ ἀπὸ τοῦ πνεύματός μου ἐπὶ πᾶσαν σάρκα, καὶ προφητεύσουσιν ('I will pour out my Spirit on all people, and they shall prophesy'). J. Dunn's attempt to interpret the Lukan promise of the Spirit (Lk. 24.49; Acts 1.4; 2.33, 38-39) against the backdrop of Gen. 17.7-10, Ezek. 36.25-27 and Jer. 31.33-34 ignores the evidence from Luke's own hand, and thus his description of the gift of the Spirit as 'the means whereby men enter into the blessings of Abraham' and 'the essence and embodiment of the new covenant' must be questioned.[1] For Luke the promise with reference to the Spirit refers to the gift of the Spirit of prophecy promised in Joel 3.1. This promise, which is initially fulfilled at Pentecost (Acts 2.4), mediates the δύναμις necessary for the disciples to take up their prophetic vocation. It is important to note that Luke's use of δύναμις in Lk. 24.49 and Acts 1.8 is consistent with my description of his usage elsewhere: δύναμις is mediated by the Spirit but not equivalent to it; and, in conjunction with the Spirit, δύναμις designates the ability to perform a broad range of activities (inspired speech and miracles of healing/exorcisms).[2]

---

1. Dunn, *Holy Spirit*, pp. 47-48.
2. L. O'Reilly, *Word and Sign in the Acts of the Apostles* (1987), pp. 16-17. See also Chapter 6 §3 above.

Chapter 10

THE DISCIPLES AND THE SPIRIT: THE PROPHETIC GIFT (ACTS 2)

The importance of Pentecost for this inquiry into Luke's distinctive pneumatology can hardly be exaggerated. Strategically placed at the outset of his second volume, Luke's account of the Pentecostal bestowal of the Spirit occupies a central place in his theological plan and thus serves as an interpretative key to Luke's understanding of the Spirit's work in the church.

In spite of its obvious importance for Luke's pneumatology and numerous studies on the topic, considerable disagreement continues to exist concerning the significance which Luke attaches to the Pentecostal gift. In the introductory survey I noted two particularly significant interpretations of the Pentecostal gift. First, J. Dunn speaks for many when he asserts that the Pentecostal bestowal of the Spirit is the means by which the disciples enter into the new age and experience the blessings of the new covenant.[1] Thus Dunn insists that the disciples' reception of the Spirit at Pentecost 'is primarily initiatory, and only secondarily an empowering'.[2] Secondly, while denying that the Pentecostal gift of the Spirit mediates the blessings of the new covenant *in toto*, G. Haya-Prats and M. Turner, albeit in different ways, also argue that the gift of the Spirit is not primarily an endowment of power for mission.[3] According to Haya-Prats the Spirit is received by the disciples at Pentecost principally as an anticipation of the fullness of salvation.[4] For Turner the

---

1. See Dunn, *Holy Spirit*, pp. 38-54; G.W.H. Lampe, 'The Holy Spirit in the Writings of St. Luke', in *Studies in the Gospels* (1957), p. 162; cf. *God as Spirit*, p. 65; Büchsel, *Der Geist Gottes*, pp. 234-35; F.F. Bruce, 'The Holy Spirit in the Acts of the Apostles', *Int* 27 (1973), pp. 170-72; F.D. Bruner, *A Theology of the Holy Spirit: The Pentecostal Experience and the New Testament Witness* (1970), p. 214.
2. Dunn, *Holy Spirit*, p. 54.
3. See Chapter 1 §2.3.2 and §2.3.3 above.
4. Haya-Prats, *Force*, pp. 173-76, 185-89.

Pentecostal gift is, above all, the organ of revelation to each disciple and, as such, it is the *sine qua non* of Christian existence.[1] Whereas Jesus received the Spirit for others, at Pentecost the disciples receive the Spirit largely for themselves.[2]

My own research points to conclusions which are decidedly different from those presented above. In attempting to put forth the thesis that Luke consistently portrays the Spirit as the source of prophetic activity (inspiring speech and granting special insight), I have thus far analysed several passages which are crucial for an accurate assessment of Luke's understanding of the Pentecostal bestowal of the Spirit. I have argued that Luke interprets the sifting and separating activity of the Spirit of which John prophesied (Lk. 3.16) to be accomplished in the Spirit-directed and Spirit-empowered mission of the church. Thus John's prophecy finds its initial fulfillment in the Pentecostal bestowal of the Spirit. I have also asserted that the Spirit came upon Jesus at the Jordan in order to equip him for his messianic task (Lk. 3.22; 4.18-19). The striking parallels between Jesus' pneumatic anointing at the Jordan and that of the disciples at Pentecost suggest that Luke interpreted the latter event in light of the former: Pentecost was for the disciples what the Jordan was for Jesus.[3] The logical corollary is that at Pentecost the Spirit came upon the disciples in order to enable them to be effective witnesses. Finally, I have affirmed that for Luke the 'promise' with reference to the Spirit (Lk. 24.49; Acts 1.4, 2.33, 38-39) refers to the gift of the Spirit of prophecy promised by Joel. This 'promise', initially fulfilled at Pentecost, enables the disciples to take up the prophetic vocation to the nations to which they have been called.

The picture which emerges from my conclusions outlined above is remarkably clear: according to Luke, the Spirit, understood to be the source of prophetic activity, came upon the disciples at Pentecost in order to equip them for their prophetic vocation (i.e. for their role as 'witnesses'). The disciples receive the Spirit, not as the source of

1. Turner, 'Luke and the Spirit', pp. 159, and 'Spiritual Gifts', pp. 40-41.
2. 'Luke and the Spirit', pp. 182-84.
3. Talbert lists four literary features which Luke duplicates in order to tie Jesus' anointing at the Jordan with that of the disciples at Pentecost: (1) both Jesus and the disciples are praying; (2) both accounts place the descent of the Spirit after prayer; (3) both accounts record a physical manifestation of the Spirit; (4) in both accounts the respective ministries of Jesus and the disciples begin with a sermon which is thematic of what follows, appeals to the fulfillment of prophecy, and speaks of the rejection of Jesus (*Literary Patterns*, p. 16).

cleansing and a new ability to keep the law, not as a foretaste of the salvation to come, nor as the essential bond by which they (each individual) are linked to God; indeed, not primarily for themselves. Rather, as the driving force behind their witness to Christ, the disciples receive the Spirit for others.[1] If my exegesis is correct, the gift of the Spirit is principally an endowment of power for mission, and thus the interpretations put forth by Dunn, Haya-Prats and Turner need modification. In the following chapter I shall seek to demonstrate that these conclusions are harmonious with Luke's account of that first Christian Pentecost recorded in Acts 2.

1. *Pentecost: The Event Described (Acts 2.1-13)*

Luke's account of the Pentecostal outpouring of the Spirit recorded in Acts 2.1-13 is undoubtedly based on traditional material[2] and, in spite of numerous difficulties in the text, the historicity of the event which it describes need not be doubted.[3] The account has been subjected to detailed source analysis.[4] Although the numerous attempts to reproduce the sources underlying Luke's account have failed to produce any conclusive results, they have shown that the account reflects Luke's literary style and therefore has been significantly shaped by Luke himself.[5] As such, the Pentecost account is a good example of Luke's literary method: he is both a historian who utilizes traditional material and a theologian who skillfully shapes and interprets it.

---

1. I. Broer, 'Der Geist und die Gemeinde: Zur Auslegung der lukanischen Pfingstgeschichte (Apg 2,1-13)', *BibLeb* 13 (1972), p. 282.

2. Broer, 'Der Geist', pp. 276-77; Tachau, 'Pfingstgeschichte', pp. 92-93; Kremer, *Pfingstbericht*, pp. 259-67; A.T. Lincoln, 'Theology and History in the Interpretation of Luke's Pentecost', *ExpT* 96 (1984–85), p. 209. *Contra* Haenchen, *Acts*, pp. 172-75.

3. See Dunn, *Jesus and the Spirit*, pp. 135-56; Marshall, 'Pentecost', pp. 360-65. Haenchen's contention that the account is a fictitious literary production created by Luke (*Acts*, pp. 172-75) is extreme.

4. See Tachau, 'Pfingstgeschichte', pp. 88-92 for a summary and evaluation of the source-critical issues. Broer, 'Der Geist', pp. 267-69, 271-73 and G. Schneider, *Die Apostelgeschichte* (1980), I, pp. 243-47, survey the various attempts to reconstruct the sources behind the pericope.

5. Broer, 'Der Geist', p. 270; Lohse, 'Die Bedeutung', p. 183, 190; N. Adler, *Das erste christliche Pfingstfest: Sinn und Bedeutung des Pfingstberichtes Apg. 2,1-13* (1938), pp. 32-33.

The account itself poses numerous problems for the interpreter, but the main points of the narrative may be reconstructed as follows. A band of disciples numbering about 120 (Acts 1.15)[1] gathered together in 'the upper room' of a house (Acts 2.1-2; cf. 1.13).[2] Here the disciples were 'all filled with the Holy Spirit' (ἐπλήσθησαν πάντες πνεύματος ἁγίου), an experience which was accompanied by heavenly signs (ἦχος ὥσπερ φερομένης πνοῆς βιαίας and γλῶσσαι ὡσεὶ πυρός) and produced inspired speech (Acts 2.3-4). A crowd composed of diaspora Jews (and thus ἀπὸ παντὸς ἔθνους τῶν ὑπὸ τὸν οὐρανόν) currently residing in Jerusalem[3] assembled[4] in amazement, for they heard the disciples miraculously declaring 'the mighty acts of God' (τὰ μεγαλεῖα τοῦ θεοῦ) in each of their own native languages (Acts 2.5-12).[5] The diversity of the nationalities represented by the crowd, and so also the miraculous character of the disciples' speech, is highlighted by the *Völkerliste* of Acts 2.9-11a. The crowds' mixed response to this dramatic event (Acts 2.12-13) sets the stage for Peter's speech.

Several features of the narrative have important implications for this inquiry.

1. Consistent with his usage elsewhere, in his Pentecost account Luke

1. The πάντες of 2.1 refers to the 120 mentioned in Acts 1.15 and not simply the apostles: (1) this is the most natural reading of πάντες, since the 120 are present in the preceding verses; (2) this conclusion is supported by the repetition of ἐπὶ τὸ αὐτὸ in 1.15 and 2.1; (3) the potentially universal character of the gift is stressed in 2.17 and 2.39; therefore it would be strange if any of the disciples present were excluded from the gift at Pentecost; (4) more than twelve languages are recorded to have been heard, implying more than twelve were present.

2. The upper room (Acts 1.13) is to be preferred over the temple (Lk. 24.53) as the referent of οἶκον in Acts 2.2: (1) Luke almost always calls the temple τὸ ἱερόν; (2) Luke uses οἶκος with reference to the temple (Acts 7.47) only when the context makes its meaning clear.

3. The phrase εἰς Ἰερουσαλὴμ κατοικοῦντες Ἰουδαῖοι (2.5, 14) suggests that the crowd of Jews consisted of residents of Jerusalem and not pilgrims temporarily staying in Jerusalem in order to observe the Feast of Pentecost. The apparent contradiction with 2.9 (οἱ κατοικοῦντες τὴν Μεσοποταμίαν) and 2.10 (οἱ ἐπιδημοῦντες Ῥωμαῖοι) is resolved when it is understood that the list refers to the various Jews of the Diaspora now living in Jerusalem by reference to their country of origin (Kremer, *Pfingstbericht*, pp. 148-49).

4. That the disciples left the house to meet the crowd is implicit in the narrative.

5. Luke's description of the event makes it clear that in this instance λαλεῖν ἑτέραις γλώσσαις refers to intelligible human languages and not unintelligible glossolalia found elsewhere in Acts (10.46; 19.6) and 1 Corinthians (12–14).

portrays the gift of the Spirit as the source of prophetic inspiration. The immediate result of the Spirit's activity is inspired speech. As I noted, the disciples miraculously declare 'the mighty acts of God' (τὰ μεγαλεῖα τοῦ θεοῦ) in the various languages spoken by the representatives of the *Völkerliste* (Acts 2.9-11). A comparison of 2.4b (καθὼς τὸ πνεῦμα ἐδίδου ἀποφθέγγεσθαι αὐτοῖς) with 2.14a (καὶ ἀπεφθέγξατο αὐτοῖς) indicates that Luke also understood Peter's sermon to be inspired by the Spirit.

2. Luke's account highlights the missiological significance of the Pentecostal gift. By skillfully integrating the *Völkerliste* into his narrative, Luke stresses what is central in the narrative: the gift of the Spirit enables the disciples to communicate with people 'from every nation under heaven' (Acts 2.5). The product of this divine gift should not be understood simply as praise directed to God. It is, above all, proclamation. This is suggested by the language miracle and confirmed by the content of the inspired speech, τὰ μεγαλεῖα τοῦ θεοῦ (Acts 2.11).[1] In the LXX τὰ μεγαλεῖα is usually connected with verbs of proclamation and, as such, is addressed to people.[2] One may thus affirm with H. von Baer that 'the Spirit of Pentecost is the Spirit of Missions'.[3]

3. Luke's use of the phrase ἐπλήσθησαν πάντες πνεύματος ἁγίου (Acts 2.4) with reference to the disciples at Pentecost indicates that their experience was not unlike that of John, Elizabeth, Zechariah or Jesus. Whether it be John in his mother's womb, Jesus at the Jordan, or the disciples at Pentecost, the Spirit comes upon them all as the source of prophetic inspiration, and as such empowers them to carry out their divinely appointed tasks. Although the phrase ἐπλήσθη/σαν πνεύματος ἁγίου is descriptive of an experience which produces an inspired state of rather short duration (resulting in inspired speech) and which is clearly repetitive,[4] the experience so designated also has a more permanent dimension.[5] This is most evident from the experiences of John (1.15), Jesus and Paul (9.17), each of whom received the Spirit when

1. Kremer, *Pfingstbericht*, pp. 143-44.
2. Kremer (*Pfingstbericht*, p. 144) cites Tob. 11.15 (A, B); Pss. 104/105.1 (S); Sir. 17.8, 10; 33 [36].8; 2 Macc. 3.34. Note also that the inspired utterances in the infancy narratives are generally given in the third person (Lk. 1.46-55, 67-75; 2.33-35) and, if given in the second person are usually directed to people, not to God himself (Lk. 1.42-45, 76-79).
3. Von Baer, *Der heilige Geist*, p. 103. ET is my own.
4. See Acts 4.8, 31; 13.9 (cf. 9.17); note also 13.52.
5. Marshall, *Luke: Historian and Theologian*, p. 201.

they were 'filled with the Spirit' as an initial and lasting endowment which equipped them for their respective ministries. Luke's usage suggests that the divine activity designated by the phrase ἐπλήσθη/σαν πνεύματος ἁγίου[1] involves a permanent promise of pneumatic assistance (either special knowledge or power of speech) for each moment of need.[2] The momentary and repetitive instances of inspiration linked to the phrase represent specific and concrete realizations of this promise. It is therefore appropriate to speak of the disciples' pneumatic anointing at Pentecost as the moment at which they, like Jesus at the Jordan, were equipped with prophetic power for the mission which lay ahead (Lk. 24.49; Acts 1.8).

2. Pentecost: The Event Interpreted (Acts 2.14-21)

Luke's narrative continues with an account of Peter's interpretation of the Pentecostal event (2.14-21). Responding to those from the crowd who charged that the inspired disciples 'had drunk too much wine', Peter declares that, far from the antics of inebriated men, the dramatic event of which they are witnesses is, in reality, a fulfillment of Joel 3.1-5a: ἀλλὰ τοῦτό ἐστιν τὸ εἰρημένον διὰ τυῦ προφήτου Ἰωήλ ('this is what was spoken by the prophet Joel', Acts 2.16). The text of Joel 3.1-5a is then cited with a few modifications:

Acts 2.17-21/Joel 3.15a

Καὶ ἔσται ἐν ταῖς ἐσχάταις ἡμέραις, λέγει ὁ θεός,———— μετὰ ταῦτα καὶ
  ἐκχεῶ ἀπὸ τοῦ πνεύματός μου ἐπὶ πᾶσαν σάρκα,
    καὶ προφητεύσουσιν οἱ υἱοὶ ὑμῶν καὶ αἱ θυγατέρες ὑμῶν,
    καὶ οἱ νεανίσκοι ὑμῶν ὁράσεις ὄψονται,————————————Inverted
    καὶ οἱ πρεσβύτεροι ὑμῶν ἐνυπνίοις ἐνυπνιασθήσονται· ══ ἐνύπνια
  καί γε ἐπὶ τοὺς δούλους μου καὶ ἐπὶ τὰς δούλας μου ἐν ταῖς ἡμέραις ἐκείναις┐
  ἐκχεῶ ἀπὸ τοῦ πνεύματός μου,
    καὶ προφητεύσουσιν.
    καὶ δώσω τέρατα ἐν τῷ οὐρανῷ **ἄνω** καὶ σημεῖα ἐπὶ τῆς γῆς **κάτω**,
    αἷμα καὶ πῦρ καὶ ἀτμίδα καπνοῦ· ┘ Insertions

---

1. Luke can speak of the Pentecostal outpouring of the Spirit in a variety of ways, all of which designate the same experience (e.g. Acts 1.4—τὴν ἐπαγγελίαν τοῦ πατρός; 1.8—ἐπελθόντος τοῦ ἁγίου πνεύματος ἐφ' ὑμᾶς; 2.4—ἐπλήσθησαν ... πνεύματος ἁγίου; 2.17—ἐκχεῶ ... πνεύματός μου; 2.38—τὴν δωρεὰν τοῦ ἁγίου πνεύματος; 10.47—τὸ πνεῦμα τὸ ἅγιον ἔλαβον; 11.15— ἐπέπεσεν τὸ πνεῦμα τὸ ἅγιον ἐπ' αὐτούς; 11.17—τὴν ... δωρεὰν ἔδωκεν αὐτοῖς. See Dunn, *Holy Spirit*, pp. 70-72.

2. Haya-Prats, *Force*, p. 198.

ὁ ἥλιος μεταστραφήσεται εἰς σκότος καὶ ἡ σελήνη εἰς αἷμα
πρὶν ἐλθεῖν ἡμέραν κυρίου τὴν μεγάλην ὑκαὶ ἐπιφανῆρ.
καὶ ἔσται πᾶς ὃς ἂν ἐπικαλέσηται τὸ ὄνομα κυρίου σωθήσεται.

Acts 2.17-21/Joel 3.15a

In the last days, God says,————————————————after these things
I will pour out my Spirit on all people.
Your sons and daughters will prophesy,
Your young men will see visions,————————————————Inverted
and your old men will dream **dreams.**————————————dreams (acc. pl.)
[Indeed,] on my servants, both men and women, in those days
I will pour out my Spirit,
and they will prophesy.   Insertions
I will show wonders in the heaven **above** and **signs** on the earth **below,**
blood and fire and billows of smoke.
The sun will be turned to darkness and the moon to blood
before the coming of the great and glorious day of the Lord.
And everyone who calls on the name of the Lord will be saved.

The tradition-history of the passage, as with the speeches in Acts generally, is problematic. However, whether one follows M. Dibelius in viewing the speeches in Acts as 'inventions of the author'[1] or, under the influence of F.F. Bruce, insists that the speeches are 'condensed accounts of speeches actually made',[2] the significance of Peter's *pesher*[3] of the Joel citation for Luke's pneumatology cannot be missed. For, whether by creation or selection, modification and arrangement of received tradition, Luke has placed his unique stamp on the text. One is therefore justified in assuming that Peter's *pesher* of Joel 3.1-5a was central for, though not necessarily the result of, Luke's understanding of the Pentecostal bestowal of the Spirit.

1. M. Dibelius, *A Fresh Approach to the New Testament and Early Christian Literature* (1936), p. xv; see also 'The Speeches in Acts and Ancient Historiography', in *Studies in the Acts of the Apostles* (1956), pp. 138-85.
2. F.F. Bruce, 'The Speeches in Acts: Thirty Years After', in *Reconciliation and Hope* (1974), p. 53, see also pp. 53-68. Note also W.W. Gasque, 'The Speeches of Acts: Dibelius Reconsidered', in *New Dimensions in New Testament Study* (1974), pp. 232-50.
3. In *pesher* interpretation the author brings out the contemporary relevance of a particular text by pointing to its fulfillment in current events. As a method of biblical exegesis common in certain sectors of first-century Judaism—most notably in the Qumran community—*pesher* took the form of 'this is that' (or 'that is this', where the OT quotation is followed by its interpretation). Note the 'this is that' form of Acts 2.16: τοῦτό ἐστιν τὸ εἰρημένον διὰ τοῦ προφήτου Ἰωήλ.

The judgment stated above encourages us to move beyond the broader and more complex questions of tradition and history pertaining to Peter's speech in Acts 2 and to focus attention on the source-critical question immediately relevant to this study: are the various modifications to Joel 3.1-5a (LXX) which are reflected in Acts 2.17-21 to be attributed to Lukan redaction or early Christian tradition? In an effort to answer this question I shall examine Acts 2.17-21 seeking to determine what theological concerns (if any) have motivated modifications to the Joel text and whether these modifications reflect any literary and/or theological tendencies which suggest that they are the product of Lukan redaction.

1. *The alteration of* μετὰ ταῦτα *to* ἐν ταῖς ἐσχάταις ἡμέραις *in v. 17.* E. Haenchen has argued that the ἐν ταῖς ἐσχάταις ἡμέραις of v. 17 conflicts with Luke's perspective.[1] According to Haenchen Luke was not of the opinion that the *Endzeit* had broken in with Pentecost and the church, therefore the phrase must be judged as a secondary emendation. But, as F. Mussner has demonstrated, neither μετὰ ταῦτα nor ἐν ταῖς ἐσχάταις ἡμέραις stands in tension with Luke's eschatology, for both readings place Pentecost in 'the last days' *before* the Day of the Lord.[2]

Haenchen is not alone in exaggerating the eschatological import of this alteration. Pointing to the ἐν ταῖς ἐσχάταις ἡμέραις of v. 17, J. Dunn asserts that for the disciples Pentecost represents the decisive pivot of the aeons, the point at which they enter into 'the last days'.[3] However, as I have already established, Luke considered the time of messianic fulfillment to have begun with Jesus' miraculous birth and the other events chronicled in the infancy narratives.[4] It follows that the entire ministry of Jesus is carried out in 'the last days'.[5] Therefore, although the Pentecostal bestowal of the Spirit, as an event of the prophesied *Endzeit*, constitutes irrefutable proof that 'the last days' have arrived, it is one in a series of such events and does not mark the beginning of 'the last days'.

1. E. Haenchen, 'Schriftzitate und Textüberlieferung in der Apostelgeschichte', *ZTK* 51 (1954), p. 162.
2. F. Mussner, 'In den letzen Tagen (Apg 2,17a)', *BZ* 5 (1965), pp. 263-65.
3. Dunn, *Holy Spirit*, pp. 46-47; see also von Baer, *Der heilige Geist*, p. 92.
4. See Chapter 6 above.
5. A. Weiser, *Die Apostelgeschichte. Kapitel 1–12* (1981), p. 92.

The phrase ἐν ταῖς ἐσχάταις ἡμέραις does not alter the eschatological perspective of the Joel text nor does it signify that Pentecost ushers in the new age; rather, it clarifies what with μετὰ ταῦτα could only be gleaned from the broader context of Joel: the Pentecostal bestowal of the Spirit is an event of the *Endzeit*, that period of God's deliverance which precedes the Day of the Lord. Thus, while the alteration highlights the eschatological significance of the Joel prophecy and its Pentecostal fulfillment, it does not represent a significant contribution to or departure from the original text of Joel. I have noted that the eschatological perspective of the text is harmonious with the theology of Luke. However, since the alteration merely reflects a perspective already present in the text of Joel, it cannot be termed distinctively Lukan. For this reason theological considerations do not provide an adequate basis on which to make a judgment concerning the traditional or Lukan origin of the alteration.

I turn now to arguments of style. Noting that ἐν ταῖς ἐσχάταις ἡμέραις appears nowhere else in Luke's two-volume work, D. Bock suggests that the phrase stems from tradition.[1] However, although the phrase is indeed unique to Luke, a close parallel occurs in the following verse: ἐν ταῖς ἡμέραις ἐκείναις (Acts 2.18 = Joel 3.2). I have already noted Luke's penchant for duplicating words and phrases in quotations from the Old Testament.[2] Thus ἐν ταῖς ἐσχάταις ἡμέραις (Acts 2.17), as a slightly modified duplicate of ἐν ταῖς ἡμέραις ἐκείναις (Acts 2.18), corresponds to Lukan style and is to be attributed to his hand.

2. *The insertion of* λέγει ὁ θεός *in v. 17.* The original sense of the Joel citation remains unaltered by the insertion of λέγει ὁ θεός. As with the alteration discussed above, λέγει ὁ θεός merely clarifies what is evident from the broader context of Joel:[3] the promise of Joel 3.1-5a originates with God himself.[4] While insertions of this type are not uncommon in Old Testament quotations cited by New Testament

---

1. Bock, *Proclamation*, p. 161.
2. See Chapter 8 §3.1 above. Note the repetition of κηρύξαι (Lk. 4.18, 19 = Isa. 61.1-2); ἐν ταῖς... ἡμέραις (Acts 2.17-18 = Joel 3.1-2); καὶ προφητεύσουσιν (Acts 2.17-18 = Joel 3.1-2); ἔργον (Acts 13.41, 2× = Hab. 1.5); σου (Lk. 7.27 = Mal. 3.1).
3. Note the ἐγὼ κύριος ὁ θεὸς ὑμῶν of Joel 2.27 and the εἶπεν κύριος of Joel 3.5b.
4. Holtz points out that such clarification is necessary because of the introduction in Acts 2.16 which attributes the saying to Joel (*Untersuchungen*, p. 6).

authors,[1] we may presume the redactor deemed it important that the promise of Joel be attributed directly to God. A motive for the insertion may be found in Luke's previous reference to the Pentecostal gift of the Spirit as ἡ ἐπαγγελία τοῦ πατρός (Lk. 24.49, Acts 1.4). Through the insertion of λέγει ὁ θεός the redactor, now identified as Luke, was able to emphasize that the promise of Joel 3.1-5a was indeed ἡ ἐπαγγελία τοῦ πατρός.

3. *Stylistic modifications in v. 17.* Two alterations have been motivated by stylistic concerns and as such they are of little consequence for this study. The transposition of the lines which begin with καὶ οἱ νεανίσκοι ὑμῶν and καὶ οἱ πρεσβύτεροι ὑμῶν was perhaps motivated by the desire to place 'young men' (rather than 'old men') directly after the reference to 'sons' and 'daughters'.[2] The use of the dative ἐνυπνίοις rather than the accusative ἐνύπνια of the LXX defies explanation since the verb ἐνυπνιάζομαι normally takes the accusative.[3] Presumably the dative was preferred by the redactor.

4. *The insertion of* γε *and* μου *(2×) in v. 18.* It is generally recognized that the double insertion of μου in v. 18 alters the original meaning of Joel 3.2.[4] The δοῦλοι and δοῦλαι of Joel 3.2 represent yet another segment of Jewish society to whom the Spirit will be given and thereby add to the series of examples which illustrate the promise of Joel 3.1: ἐκχεῶ ἀπὸ τοῦ πνεύματός μου ἐπὶ πᾶσαν σάρκα.[5] However, with the insertion of μου in Acts 2.18 these terms no longer refer to literal slaves nor to an additional group which will receive the Spirit. In Acts 2.18 the terms become religious metaphors which include and give further definition to the groups previously mentioned. The transformation of 'slaves' into 'servants of God' highlights what is implicit in the text of Joel: the gift of the Spirit is given only to those who are members of the eschatological community of salvation. The motive for such redactional activity was undoubtedly a desire to emphasize that the disciples of Jesus, as recipients of the Spirit of prophecy, are indeed members of

---

1. See Acts 7.6, 49; Rom. 12.19; 1 Cor. 14.21; 2 Cor. 6.17.
2. Schneider, *Die Apostelgeschichte*, I, p. 268.
3. Holtz, *Untersuchungen*, p. 9.
4. See for example Haenchen, *Acts*, p. 179, and 'Schriftzitate', p. 161; Schneider, *Die Apostelgeschichte*, I, p. 268; H. Conzelmann, *Acts of the Apostles* (1987), p. 20; Kremer, *Pfingstbericht*, p. 172; J. Roloff, *Die Apostelgeschichte* (1981), p. 53.
5. L.C. Allen, *The Books of Joel, Obadiah, Jonah and Micah* (1976), p. 99; H.W. Wolff, *Joel and Amos* (1977), p. 67.

this community. The insertions also highlight the pneumatological perspective of the redactor: membership in the community of salvation is not dependent on the gift of the Spirit; rather, the former is a presupposition for the latter. The Spirit of prophecy is given to those who already are the servants of God. This perspective accords well with the pneumatology of early Judaism, the primitive church and Luke. As such, it does not provide sufficient criteria on which to judge the ultimate origin of the insertions.

T. Holtz has argued that the γε and double μου of v. 18 are not redactional, for they do not represent alterations to the text of Joel. Holtz suggests that the text of the LXX which Luke employed was, at this point, similar to Codex Alexandrinus and thus the terms were simply carried over by Luke from the LXX.[1] Central to Holtz's argument is his contention that the phrase καί γε is conceptually incompatible with the change in perspective occasioned by the double insertion of μου. According to Holtz the intensive καί γε, rendered as 'sogar' ('even'), fits well with the unexpected promise directed specifically to slaves in Joel 3.2; but it is irreconcilable with the less exceptional and broader prophecy concerning servants of God in Acts 2.18.[2]

Holtz's thesis is, however, vulnerable at several points. First, καί γε is characteristic of Luke. Luke uses γε more frequently than any other Gospel writer[3] and the two—possibly three—occurrences of καί γε in the New Testament are found in Luke–Acts.[4] Secondly, in Acts 2.18 καί γε should be rendered 'indeed' rather than 'sogar' ('even') as Holtz suggests. In Acts 17.27 καί γε simply confirms the statement which follows (that God is near) and is most accurately translated in English as 'indeed'.[5] Therefore in Acts 2.18 καί γε need not imply, as the translation 'even' suggests, that the prophecy which follows is distinct from and more exceptional than those which precede.[6] If, as in Acts 17.27,

1. Holtz, *Untersuchungen*, pp. 10-11.
2. Holtz, *Untersuchungen*, p. 10.
3. Matthew, 4×; Mark, 0×; Luke, 8×; John, 1×; Acts, 4×.
4. The phrase occurs in Acts 2.18, 17.27 and variant readings of Lk. 19.42. The omission of the phrase in Lk. 19.42 is supported by א B D Θ L 579. Witnesses supporting the inclusion of the phrase are: A Ψ K W Δ Π f¹ f¹³. The UBS text supports the omission of the phrase, but gives its preferred reading a C rating.
5. Haenchen, *Acts*, pp. 524, 515.
6. Note the translation of Acts 2.18 offered by Lake and Cadbury, *The Acts of the Apostles* (1933; *The Beginnings of Christianity*, IV), pp. 21-22, 'Yes, and on my slaves and on my handmaids in those days I will pour out my spirit' (see also the RV).

the phrase simply confirms the statement which follows and is rendered 'indeed', then Holtz's purported contradiction disappears. Even if Holtz is right and the verse does contain a genuine contradiction, he is left with the problem of explaining its occurrence in the LXX. Thirdly, the critical editions of the LXX agree that the γε and double μου readings of the Alexandrian text group represent late additions.[1] The Alexandrian text has a tendency to adopt readings from citations in the New Testament[2] and thus the occurrence of γε and double μου in the Alexandrian text group may be attributed to assimilation with Acts 2.18. I conclude therefore that the insertions in Joel 3.2 are redactional and, on the basis of style, that they stem from Luke.

5. *The insertion of* καὶ προφητεύσουσιν *in v. 18*. Although Holtz and Haenchen have suggested that the καὶ προφητεύσουσιν of v. 18, reduplicated from v. 17, crept into the text of the LXX through scribal error,[3] stylistic and theological considerations provide conclusive evidence that the insertion is the result of Lukan redaction.[4] The insertion, as a reduplication of καὶ προφητεύσουσιν in v. 17, is consistent with Luke's penchant for duplicating words and phrases in quotations from the Old Testament noted above. Theologically the insertion is also significant. It serves to emphasize that the gift of the Spirit produces prophetic inspiration. The corollary is that the disciples, as recipients of the gift, are not inebriated men—they are eschatological prophets proclaiming the word of God. This emphasis on the gift of the Spirit as the source of prophetic inspiration is characteristic of Luke.

6. *The insertion of* ἄνω, σημεῖα *and* κάτω *in v. 19*. The collocation of σημεῖα and τέρατα formed by the insertion is characteristic of Luke[5] and thus confirms the Lukan origin of the alteration. The precise

1. See J. Ziegler (ed.), *Duodecim prophetae: Septuaginta Vetus Testamentum Graecum* (Göttingen, 1967), III, pp. 41, 43, 235 (Joel 3.2); A. Rahlfs (ed.), *Septuaginta*, p. 522 (Joel 3.2); see also Wolff, *Joel and Amos*, p. 56.

2. Ziegler (ed.), *Duodecim prophetae*, XIII, p. 43. By way of example Ziegler cites the Alexandrian text of Hos. 10.8 which follows Lk. 23.30 against the other principal manuscripts.

3. Holtz, *Untersuchungen*, pp. 11-12 and (more tentatively) Haenchen, *Acts*, p. 179 n. 4.

4. Schneider (*Die Apostelgeschichte*, I, pp. 268-69), Kremer (*Pfingstbericht*, p. 172), and Schweizer ('πνεῦμα', p. 408) all recognize the Lukan character of the insertion.

5. The collocation of σημεῖα and τέρατα occurs in the NT as follows:

referent of the τέρατα ἐν τῷ οὐρανῷ ἄνω and σημεῖα ἐπὶ τῆς γῆς κάτω is difficult to determine. The miracles of Jesus,[1] the cosmic signs accompanying the crucifixion,[2] the phenomena which accompanied the Pentecostal outpouring of the Spirit,[3] the miracles of the disciples,[4] and the cosmic portents associated with the Day of the Lord[5] are all viable possibilities. Luke probably had a combination of these events in mind when he penned the verse.

I.H. Marshall suggests that τέρατα designates the cosmic portents which shall herald the end of the world, while σημεῖα alludes to the gift of tongues and healing miracles recorded throughout Acts.[6] This proposal accounts for the ἄνω and κάτω of v. 19 and accords well with the immediate context of the citation (vv. 19b, 20), but it is incompatible with the numerous occasions in Acts where the disciples are cited as performing both σημεῖα and τέρατα.[7] Luke's usage of τέρατα καὶ σημεῖα as a technical term for charismatic activity suggests that the distinctions between τέρατα ἐν τῷ οὐρανῷ ἄνω and σημεῖα ἐπὶ τῆς γῆς κάτω should not be pressed too far. For Luke the principal purpose of ἄνω and κάτω is not to distinguish between two spheres of divine intervention (heaven and earth), but rather to emphasize the universal character of the 'signs and wonders'—they are portents that cannot be overlooked. So also τέρατα and σημεῖα do not refer to two specific and distinctive types of miraculous acts; rather, together they refer to a single series of divine acts—events such as the miracle of Pentecost, the healings recorded in Acts, and the cosmic portents to come—which anticipate the near arrival of the Day of the Lord. In view of the reference to τέρασι καὶ σημείοις in v. 22, it is virtually certain that the semantic range of the collocation in v. 19 also includes the miracles of

Matthew, 1×; Mark, 1×; John, 1×; Acts, 9× (Acts 2.19, 22, 43; 4.30; 5.12; 6.8; 7.36; 14.3; 15.12); the rest of the NT, 4×.

1.   G. Stählin, *Die Apostelgeschichte* (1936), pp. 42, 44–45; U. Wilckens, *Die Missionsreden der Apostelgeschichte* (1974), p. 33; G. Lüdemann, *Das frühe Christentum nach den Traditionen der Apostelgeschichte* (1987), p. 51.

2.   F.F. Bruce, *The Acts of the Apostles* (1951), p. 90; Rese, *Alttestamentliche Motive*, p. 54.

3.   Roloff, *Die Apostelgeschichte*, p. 53; Montague, *Spirit*, pp. 285-86.

4.   Weiser, *Die Apostelgeschichte. Kapitel 1–12*, p. 92.

5.   Schneider, *Die Apostelgeschichte*, I, p. 269; Bock, *Proclamation*, p. 167; Kremer, *Pfingstbericht*, pp. 172-74.

6.   Marshall, *Acts*, p. 74.

7.   See Acts 2.43; 4.30; 5.12; 6.8; 14.3; 15.12.

Jesus, and it may embrace the miraculous events accompanying Jesus' supernatural birth as well.[1] The theological significance of the insertions is now evident. Through his redactional activity in v. 19 Luke was able to link the miraculous events associated with Jesus (v. 22) and his disciples (vv. 3-11, 43) together with the cosmic portents listed by Joel (vv. 19b-20) as 'signs and wonders' which mark the end of the age. In this way Luke stresses the imminence of the Day of the Lord: the miracles in Luke–Acts are precursors of those cosmic signs which shall signal the Day of the Lord.

Having examined the various alterations and determined their Lukan origin, we are now in a position to assess the significance of the modified quotation of Joel 3.1-5a for Luke's understanding of the Pentecostal bestowal of the Spirit. Three points emerge.

1. *The Spirit of Pentecost is the Spirit of prophecy.* Luke's insertion of καὶ προφητεύσουσιν in v. 18 emphasizes what is otherwise evident from his use of Joel 3.1-5a as the hermeneutical key for the miracle of Pentecost: the Spirit comes upon the disciples as the source of prophetic inspiration. Indeed, the Joel passage explicitly declares what can be deduced from a survey of Luke–Acts: the Spirit, as the Spirit of prophecy, produces inspired speech—intelligible and unintelligible (10.46; 19.6)[2]—and grants special insight, often through visions and revelatory dreams. While the Pentecost event centers on inspired speech, visions and dreams are cited as manifestations of the prophetic gift (2.17) and they appear regularly throughout the narrative in Acts. This indicates that for Luke the value of the Joel passage as an interpretative key is not limited to the manifestation of the Spirit on the day of Pentecost, but extends to those pneumatic events described in the subsequent sections of Acts.[3]

For Luke, the Spirit of prophecy is a gift given exclusively to the people of God. The gift does not produce faith, it is given to faith. Nor can it be said that the gift is the means by which one is justified before God, for a heart for God is the precondition rather than the result of the prophetic gift. This is the clear implication of Luke's use of the Joel text

---

1. For a discussion of the eschatological significance of Lk. 1–2 see Chapter 6 above. Note also Lk. 2.12, καὶ τοῦτο ὑμῖν τὸ σημεῖον, although here σημεῖον refers to the lowly and unspectacular circumstances of Jesus' birth.

2. Luke, unlike Paul, regards 'tongues' as a special type of prophecy (Turner, 'Luke and the Spirit', p. 132; D. Carson, *Showing the Spirit* [1987], p. 141).

3. Kremer, *Pfingstbericht*, p. 172.

and particularly his insertion of γε and μου (2×) in v. 18. Attempts to interpret the gift of the Spirit prophesied by Joel in light of Ezekiel's promise of cleansing from moral defilement and a new heart for God (Ezek. 36.25-27) have no basis in either the text of Luke–Acts or in prevailing Jewish expectations concerning the eschatological bestowal of the Spirit. My survey of relevant passages from the Jewish literature[1] revealed that the promise of Ezekiel was generally not related to the eschatological bestowal of the Spirit. Rather, Ezek. 36.26 was usually interpreted as a prophecy concerning the endtime removal of the evil יצר (impulse), and most frequently without any reference to the activity of the Spirit.[2] The eschatological bestowal of the Spirit, when it appears in the literature, is generally interpreted in connection with Joel 3.1-2 as a restoration of the Spirit of prophecy.[3] The hope is frequently expressed that the Spirit of prophecy, withdrawn from Israel due to past sin, will be restored in greater measure in the age to come. Righteousness remains the precondition for the restoration of the prophetic gift. On the two occasions when the promises of Ezekiel and Joel are brought together (*Deut. R.* 6.14; *Midr. Ps.* 14.6), the transformation of Israel's heart (Ezek. 36.26) is cited as a prerequisite for the eschatological bestowal of the Spirit, which is interpreted in light of Joel 3.1-2 as an outpouring of the Spirit of prophecy.

The purpose of the prophetic gift, explicitly stated in Lk. 24.49 and Acts 1.8, is to equip the disciples with power for the mission which lay ahead. This judgment finds confirmation in Luke's citation of Joel, which equates the proclamation of the word of God with prophetic speech. Indeed, the fruit of the prophetic gift is consistently portrayed throughout Acts as the driving force behind the ongoing mission of the church.[4] The Spirit gives the disciples boldness and persuasive power in

---

1. For my discussion on the various texts see Chapter 5 §2.1 above.

2. See for example *Exod. R.* 15.6, 41.7; *Num. R.* 14.4; *Deut. R.* 6.14; *Midr. Ps.* 14.6; *Cant. R.* 1.2.4; *Eccl. R.* 9.15.

3. See for example *MHG* Gen. 139-40; *Num. R.* 15.25; *Deut. R.* 6.14; *Lam. R.* 4.14; *Midr. Ps.* 14.6, 138.2.

4. Acts 9.31 demonstrates that the words of παράκλησις delivered by Spirit-inspired προφῆται to members of the Christian community cannot be separated from the Christian mission to the world: καὶ τῇ παρακλήσει τοῦ ἁγίου πνεύματος ἐπληθύνετο (on Acts 9.31 see Hill, *New Testament Prophecy*, pp. 102-103). Prophetic inspiration in Acts is always given principally for the benefit of others (not the recipient of the Spirit) and ultimately for the expansion of the church.

their proclamation of the word of God[1] and provides direction, frequently through visions and dreams, for the expanding mission.[2]

2. *The Spirit of Pentecost is universally available to the people of God.* By applying Joel 3.1-5 to Pentecost, Luke asserts that Moses' wish for a bestowal of the Spirit of prophecy upon 'all the Lord's people' (Num. 11.29)—reaffirmed as a hope for the age to come in later Jewish tradition—had found initial fulfillment in the Pentecostal gift. Although the πᾶσαν σάρκα of Joel 3.1 refers to '"everybody" in Israel'[3] and Luke probably intended Peter's words to be understood initially along similar lines, it is evident that Luke understood the promise to extend ultimately to the Gentiles who were incorporated into the people of God (Acts 10.44-45; 11.15-16). According to Luke the community of faith is, at least potentially, a community of prophets; and, it was his expectation that this potential would be realized in the church of his day (Lk. 11.13; 12.10-12; Acts 2.38-39) as it had been in the past (e.g. Acts 2.4; 19.6). Once the exclusive possession of an elite group within the covenant community, the Spirit of prophecy is now, in the last days, universally available to the people of God.

The view advocated above has not received universal acceptance from the scholarly community. Pointing to Luke's description of a special group within the church as προφῆται, many have rejected the notion that Luke viewed the church as a community of prophets.[4] However, this objection fails to account for the flexibility with which the terms προφῆται and προφητεύειν were used in the early church. Paul, for example, refers to a special group of προφῆται (1 Cor. 12.29), yet 'clearly expected that other members of the assembly other than the prophets would be inspired to prophesy (cf. 14.5, 24, perhaps 31)'.[5] And

---

1. See Acts 4.13, 31; 5.32; 6.10; 9.31; 13.9, 52. Note Hill's observation that miracle-working is distinguished from prophecy in Acts (2.17-18, 43; 5.12-16; 10.34, 40; 19.11-12; *New Testament Prophecy*, p. 108).

2. See Acts 7.56; 9.10-11; 10.3-23; 16.9-10; 18.9-10; 22.17-18; 23.11. Stephen's vision in Acts 7.55-56 (cf. 16.9-10) is explicitly linked to the Spirit. Guidance is often attributed directly to the Spirit: Acts 8.29; 10.19; 11.12, 28; 13.2, 4; 15.28; 16.6, 7; 19.21; 20.22, 23, 28; 21.4.

3. Wolff, *Joel and Amos*, p. 67; see also Allen, *Joel, Obadiah, Jonah and Micah*, p. 98.

4. R.N. Flew, *Jesus and his Church* (1960), p. 105; Lampe, *God as Spirit*, pp. 66-69; J. Jervell, *The Unknown Paul* (1984), pp. 103-104.

5. Dunn, *Jesus and the Spirit*, p. 281. See also Carson, *Showing the Spirit*, pp. 117-18, and G. Fee, *The First Epistle to the Corinthians* (1987), pp. 685, 695.

Luke's usage is considerably more flexible than Paul's. Thus, it appears that Luke's designation of various individuals as προφῆται, while implying that these individuals exercise the prophetic gift in a more regular and perhaps profound way than others in the community,[1] does not invalidate the claim that Luke expected each member of the church to receive the Spirit as the Spirit of prophecy and, as such, to become prophets.[2]

3. *The Spirit of Pentecost is an eschatological sign.* Luke's application of the Joel text to Pentecost—and particularly his alteration of μετὰ ταῦτα to ἐν ταῖς ἐσχάταις ἡμέραις (Acts 2.17)—highlights the eschatological significance of the Pentecostal gift. The Pentecostal deluge of the Spirit, as an event of the *Endzeit*, is proof that the period immediately preceding the Day of the Lord ('the last days') has indeed arrived. The miracle of Pentecost does not, however, mark the beginning of the *Endzeit*. Rather, it is one in a series of 'signs and wonders' (Acts 2.19) which extends from the miraculous events associated with the birth and ministry of Jesus to the cosmic portents yet to come and heralds the imminent arrival of the Day of the Lord.

3. *Pentecost: A New Sinai?*

Jacques Dupont gives voice to a perception held by many when he describes Pentecost as 'a new Sinai'.[3] According to this popular line of interpretation, striking points of correspondence between the Pentecost account and Jewish Sinai traditions suggest that Luke and the early Christians viewed the Pentecostal outpouring of the Spirit as the promulgation of a new law and the establishment of a new covenant.[4] Three interrelated arguments are generally offered in support of this conclusion. It is asserted that: (1) by the time Luke penned Acts, Pentecost was regarded as a feast commemorating the giving of the law on Sinai; (2) the Pentecost account contains numerous literary allusions

---

1. Hill, *New Testament Prophecy*, pp. 99, 108.
2. So also Turner, 'Luke and the Spirit', pp. 130-34 and C.M. Robeck, 'The Gift of Prophecy in Acts and Paul, Part I', *StBT* 5 (1975), pp. 29-30, 35.
3. J. Dupont, 'La nouvelle Pentecôte (Ac 2, 1-11)', in *Nouvelles études sur les Actes des Apôtres* (1984), p. 193. ET is my own.
4. Dupont, 'La nouvelle Pentecôte', pp. 193-95. See also Dunn, *Holy Spirit*, pp. 48-49; Hull, *Acts*, pp. 53-55; Lampe, *God as Spirit*, p. 68; W.L. Knox, *The Acts of the Apostles* (1948), p. 86; O'Reilly, *Word and Sign*, pp. 18-29; R. Le Déaut, 'Pentecost and Jewish Tradition', *DL* 20 (1970), pp. 250-67.

to Sinai traditions and therefore was shaped with this event in mind; (3) Acts 2.33 is based on Ps. 67.19 (LXX) and should be interpreted in light of the psalm. Whereas the rabbis interpreted Ps. 67.19 with reference to Moses who, at Sinai, ascended into heaven to receive the Torah in order that he might give it to humanity, in Acts 2.33 the psalm is applied to Jesus who ascended to the right hand of God, received the Spirit, and poured it out on the disciples. Thus the gift of the Spirit is viewed as the essence of the new covenant and the new law—an interior law, written on the heart (Jer. 31.33; cf. Ezek. 36.26).

This line of interpretation is admittedly incompatible with my assessment of Luke's understanding of the Pentecostal gift. Yet how strong are the arguments adduced in support of the position outlined above? Did Luke really intend to present Pentecost as a new Sinai?

3.1. *Pentecost as a Feast Commemorating the Giving of the Law at Sinai*

The term 'feast of Weeks' (חג שבעות) referred to the period of seven weeks during which the grain was harvested (Deut. 16.9-10)[1] and, more specifically, to the festival day culminating this period on which the firstfruits of the wheat harvest (i.e. the cereal offering, Lev. 23.17-21) were offered by the people to the Lord.[2] The date of this festival day was established as the fiftieth day (seven weeks and a day) after the sheaf offering (Lev. 23.9-10) was presented by the priest to God on behalf of the people. Thus the festival became known among Greek speaking Jews as 'the day of Pentecost' (ἡ ἡμέρα τῆς πεντηκοστῆς).[3] As such, Pentecost was a festival of harvest.

The feast ultimately became associated with the giving of the law at Sinai. This is implied by R. Jose b. Chalaphta (c. AD 150)[4] and R. Eleazar (c. AD 270),[5] who place the giving of the law on the day of Pentecost, and confirmed by the lectionary (triennial) cycle which normally called

1.   See also Exod. 34.22; Num. 28.26; 2 Chron. 8.13.
2.   Thus the feast was also known as the 'feast of harvest' (Exod. 23.16) and the 'day of firstfruits' (Num. 28.26).
3.   See Tob. 2.1; 2 Macc. 12.32; Philo, *Dec.* 160; *Spec. Leg.* 2.176; Josephus, *Ant.* 3.252; 13.252; 14.337; 17.254; *War* 1.253; 2.42; 6.299; Acts 2.1; 20.16; 1 Cor. 16.8.
4.   *S. 'Ol. R.* 5: 'The Israelites immolated the Passover lamb in Egypt on the fourteenth of Nisan and it was a Thursday . . . The third month, the sixth day of the month, the Ten Commandments were given to them, and it was a sabbath day' (cited from Le Déaut, 'Jewish Tradition', pp. 256-57).
5.   *B. Pes.* 68b: 'It [the feast of Weeks] is the day on which the Torah was given'.

for the Decalogue to be read on Pentecost. However, this evidence is late and of little value for reconstructing Jewish attitudes toward the feast before the destruction of the temple.[1] The transformation of the feast from a harvest festival to a festival commemorating the law was undoubtedly given impetus through the destruction of the temple.[2] Without the temple the rituals of sacrifice so central to the harvest feast could no longer be performed. New practices and emphases would have emerged out of necessity; and, in view of the Pharisees' emphasis on the law, it is only natural that the reading of the Decalogue and the commemoration of its revelation at Sinai became prominent features of the feast.

What evidence is there that Pentecost had been transformed into a festival commemorating the giving of the law at Sinai by the time of Luke's writing? *Jubilees* portrays the feast as a harvest festival (22.1; 6.21-22) and, more significantly, as a ceremony for the renewal of the covenant made to Noah (6.1-20). However, the connections between the feast and the giving of the law at Sinai are minor (1.1; 6.19) and based on the perception of Sinai as a renewal of the Noahic covenant.[3] Indeed, while the feast is emphatically linked to the covenants made with Noah (6.1-20) and Abraham (15.1-24), a similar emphasis with regard to the giving of the law at Sinai is lacking.

The liturgical practice of the Qumran community included an annual ceremony of covenant renewal (1QS 1.8–2.18), but associations with the feast of Pentecost remain obscure. On the basis of the community's use of *Jubilees* and 'oath terminology'[4] in the *Damascus Document* and the *Community Rule*, Roger Le Déaut concludes that the feast of שבעות was celebrated by the community as a feast of the covenant.[5] Although this suggestion is supported by the community's probable adoption of the solar calendar of *Jubilees*,[6] it has not been substantiated by evidence from the scrolls.

---

1.   The lectionary system was not operative until after the destruction of the temple.

2.   E. Lohse, 'πεντηκοστή', *TDNT*, VI, pp. 48-49, and 'Die Bedeutung', p. 186; J.C. Rylaarsdam, 'Feast of Weeks', *IDB*, IV, p. 827; Kremer, *Pfingstbericht*, pp. 18-19; B. Noack, 'The Day of Pentecost in Jubilees, Qumran, and Acts', *ASTI* 1 (1962), p. 80.

3.   J. Potin, *La fête juive de la Pentecôte* (1971), pp. 128, 135.

4.   The unpointed שבעות can be read as either 'weeks' or 'oaths'.

5.   Le Déaut, 'Jewish Tradition', pp. 254-56.

6.   See S. Talmon, 'The Calendar Reckoning of the Sect from the Judaean

The evidence from *Jubilees* and the scrolls of Qumran establishes that in some sectarian circles the feast of Pentecost was, by the mid-second century BC, celebrated as a harvest festival *and* a feast of covenant renewal. However, this evidence does not indicate that the feast of Pentecost was viewed more specifically as a festival commemorating the giving of the law at Sinai. While it is possible that the linkage of the feast with a ceremony for covenant renewal led to the later associations with Sinai, such a linkage does not demonstrate that these later associations occurred prior to the destruction of the temple.[1] And, even more significantly, several factors indicate that the sectarian observance of Pentecost as a feast of covenant renewal was not indicative of general practice in first-century Judaism.[2] Josephus and Philo know nothing of the feast as either a festival of covenant renewal or a celebration of the Torah.[3] In fact, Philo connects the giving of the law with the feast of Trumpets.[4] Similarly, the New Testament shows no awareness of the feast as a remembrance of the covenant or Sinai. The allusions to the feast in the New Testament consistently draw upon imagery taken from the harvest festival.[5] And the rabbis offer decisive proof that at least as late as the early second century AD the association of the law with Pentecost was open to dispute.[6]

My conclusions may be summarized as follows: (1) Pentecost was not

Desert', in *Scripta Hierosolymitana*. IV. *Aspects of the Dead Sea Scrolls* (1967), pp. 177-79.

1.   See Rylaarsdam, 'Feast of Weeks', p. 827.

2.   The unique and sectarian nature of the Qumran community's celebration of the feast of Weeks is illustrated in the peculiar liturgical calendar of the Temple Scroll (11QT). The feast of First-fruits or Weeks is divided into three different feasts (the feasts of New Wheat, New Wine, and Oil), each separated by an interval of fifty days (cf. 11QT cols. 18-24). See Y. Yadin, *The Temple Scroll: The Hidden Law of the Dead Sea Sect* (1985), pp. 91-96.

3.   For texts that indicate the feast was viewed as a harvest festival see Philo, *Spec. Leg.* 2.176-87, *Dec.* 160 and Josephus, *Ant.* 3.252-57. Note also Tob. 2.1: ἐν τῇ πεντηκοστῇ τῇ ἑορτῇ, ἥ ἐστιν ἁγία ἑπτὰ ἑβδομάδων.

4.   *Spec. Leg.* 2.188.

5.   As Rylaarsdam ('Feast of Weeks', p. 828) notes, the NT allusions are 'in terms of the symbolic meaning of the sacrificial loaves as first fruits (Rom. 8:23; 11:16; 1 Cor. 15:20, 23)'.

6.   In *b. Yom.* 4b R. Jose the Galilean and R. Akiba discuss whether or not the Torah was proclaimed on the day of the feast of Weeks. As Noack notes, 'this would seem to indicate that, at the time of Trajan or even Hadrian, this was still a matter for contention among the Rabbis' ('The Day of Pentecost', p. 81).

celebrated as a festival commemorating the giving of the law at Sinai at the time of Luke's writing; (2) While Pentecost was regarded as a feast of covenant renewal in some sectarian circles during the first century, the feast was generally celebrated simply as a harvest festival in the Judaism of this period; (3) It is therefore illegitimate to assume that the mere mention of τὴν ἡμέραν τῆς πεντηκοστῆς (Acts 2.1) would have evoked images of Moses, Sinai or the covenant renewal ceremony in the minds of Luke's readers.

3.2. Acts 2.1-13: Literary Allusions to Sinai Traditions?

Numerous passages have been cited in support of the contention that Luke was influenced by Sinai traditions when he penned the Pentecost account. The most prominent of these include texts from Philo (*Dec.* 32–36, 44–49; *Spec. Leg.* 2.188-89), *Targ. Ps.-J.* on Exod. 20.2, and several rabbinic legends (e.g. *b. Šab.* 88b).[1] The texts from Philo and *Targ. Ps.-J.* contain imagery similar to that employed by Luke in Acts 2.1-4, and the rabbinic legends refer to a language miracle at Sinai which is often paralleled with the miraculous speech of the disciples in Acts 2.5-13.

How significant are these parallels? Do they suggest that Luke has consciously shaped his Pentecost account in light of these or similar Sinai traditions? In assessing the significance of these texts for Luke's literary activity in Acts 2.1-13 one must be mindful of the cautions voiced by S. Sandmel in his helpful article, 'Parallelomania'.[2] Sandmel offers three comments which are particularly relevant for this inquiry. First, he notes that similarities may reflect a shared milieu rather than direct literary dependence. For this reason it is imperative not only to isolate the parallels between Acts 2.1-13 and the various Sinai traditions, but also to determine the parameters of the milieu in which these parallels are found. Indeed, a crucial yet often ignored question must be addressed: are the parallels between Acts 2.1-13 and the texts from Philo and *Targ. Ps.-J.* unique to Sinai traditions or are they representative of a broader milieu? Secondly, Sandmel notes that distinctions are often more important than similarities. As one compares Acts 2.1-13 with the various Sinai traditions, it is important to be alert to distinctions as well as to similarities. Thirdly, Sandmel warns against anachronistically

---

1. For a more complete listing of the rabbinic legends see Strack–Billerbeck, *Kommentar*, II, pp. 604-605.
2. S. Sandmel, 'Parallelomania', *JBL* 81 (1962), pp. 1-13.

reading late rabbinic citations as 'persuasive parallels' for the New Testament documents. This warning serves to remind us of the tenuous nature of the purported parallels between Acts 2.1-13 and the rabbinic legends. Is there any support for the assumption that these legends are based on first-century traditions? With these cautionary words and questions in mind, I shall examine the texts cited above and assess their significance for the tradition-history of Acts 2.1-13.

3.2.1. *Language/Imagery Parallels: Philo and Targum Pseudo-Jonathan*. In *Dec.*

33 Philo describes the declaration of God at Sinai as 'an invisible sound in the air' (ἦχον ἀόρατον ἐν ἀέρι) which changed into 'flaming fire' (πῦρ φλογοειδές) and sounded forth like 'breath through a trumpet' (πνεῦμα διὰ σάλπιγγος). Indeed, Philo indicates in *Dec.* 46 that the divine voice (φωνή) came out of the midst of this heavenly fire (ἀπ' οὐρανοῦ πυρός) for the flame was transformed into the language (φλογὸς εἰς διάλεκτον) of the people present. We read in *Spec. Leg.* 2.189 that this 'blast of the trumpet' reached to the 'ends of the earth' (ἐν ἐσχατιαῖς κατοικοῦντας).

The images of wind and fire are also associated with the word of God delivered at Sinai in *Targ. Ps.-J.* on Exod. 20.2:

> The first word (דבירא קדמאה), as it came forth from the mouth of the Holy One, whose Name be blessed, was like storms (כזיקין), and lightnings (כברקין), and flames of fire (כשלהוביין דינור), with a burning light on His right hand and on His left. It winged its way through the air of the heavens (באויר שמיא), and was made manifest unto the camp of Israel, and returned, and was engraven on the tables of the covenant that were given by the hand of Mosheh.[1]

These descriptions of the word of God in terms of wind and fire from heaven are quite similar to aspects of Luke's Pentecost account. At Pentecost the Spirit's coming is associated with the sound of wind from heaven (ἐκ τοῦ οὐρανοῦ ἦχος ὥσπερ φερομένης πνοῆς βιαίας) and the imagery of fire (γλῶσσαι ὡσεὶ πυρός). The immediate result is inspired speech (λαλεῖν ἑτέραις γλώσσαις) in the languages (διαλέκτῳ) of those present. Indeed, a number of the terms utilized by Philo with reference to the Sinai event are also found in Acts 2.1-13: ἦχον, πῦρ, πυρός, πνεῦμα, φωνή, οὐρανοῦ, διάλεκτον, κατοικοῦντας.

These similarities should not obscure the significant differences which

---

1. ET from J.W. Etheridge, *The Targums of Onkelos and Jonathan Ben Uzziel on the Pentateuch* (1968); Aramaic text from M. Ginsburger, *Pseudo-Jonathan*.

exist between the Lukan account and the Sinai traditions of Philo and
Targ. Ps.-J.[1] In contrast to the Sinai traditions, Luke associates the
Spirit rather than the voice of God with the wind and fire imagery. In
Luke's account these metaphors are not directly related to the language
miracle. It is particularly significant that neither Philo nor *Targ. Ps.-J.*
refers to the voice of God at Sinai being transformed into *different* languages as in the miracle of Pentecost. Indeed, according to Philo the
words are not so much heard as they are seen (*Dec.* 46-47). The lightning
motif present in the accounts of Philo and *Targ. Ps.-J.* is entirely absent
in Acts 2.1-13. Similarly, the trumpet blast metaphor so prominent in
Philo's description of the Sinai event (cf. Heb. 12.18-19) is without
parallel in Luke's account. Philo of course connected the giving of the
law with the feast of Trumpets (*Spec. Leg.* 2.188-89), not Pentecost.

In spite of these important differences the collocation of terms such
as 'wind', 'fire', 'heaven', 'language', 'word' or 'voice' in each of the
texts suggests that they stem from a similar milieu. However, as I noted
above, it is important to determine the parameters of this shared milieu.
It is often assumed that these parallels indicate Luke's account has been
influenced by Sinai traditions. Yet this assumption is valid only if the
collocation of terms outlined above is unique to Sinai traditions.
Evidence from numerous Jewish texts reveals that this is not the case.
The following texts are unrelated to the giving of the law at Sinai, yet
they contain the terms and imagery common to Acts 2.1-13 and the
Sinai traditions.[2]

1. In the sixth vision of *4 Ezra* (13.1-10) Ezra sees a divine figure
whom he likens to 'wind' (*ventus*) and associates with 'clouds from
heaven' (*nubibus caeli*; 13.3). The figure's 'voice' (*vox*) is compared to
'fire' (*ignem*; 13.4). From his mouth issue forth 'streams of fire' (*fluctum
ignis*), from his lips 'flaming breath' (*spiritum flammae*), and from his
tongue (*lingua*) 'a storm of sparks' (*scintillas tempestatis*; 13.10).[3]

2. In ch. 14 of *1 Enoch* the author describes his visionary transport by

---

1. Kremer, *Pfingstbericht*, pp. 245-48.

2. See also the imagery employed in Exod. 3.2 (fire/voice); Exod. 13.21; 14.24;
Num. 14.14 (cloud/fire); 1 Kgs 19.11-12 (fire/wind); Job 37.2-5 (thunder/lightning/
voice); Ezek. 1.25-28 (voice/fire); Dan. 7.9-14 (fire/ cloud/languages); 1 Thess. 1.7
(heaven/fire).

3. ET from Metzger, 'The Fourth Book of Ezra', in Charlesworth, *The Old
Testament Pseudepigrapha*, I, p. 551; Latin text from the edition of Violet, *Die Esra-
Apokalypse (IV. Esra)*, pp. 366-67.

the 'winds' (ἄνεμοι) into 'heaven' (οὐρανόν, 14.8-9). There he encountered a wall surrounded by 'tongues of fire' (γλῶσσαι τοῦ πυρός, 14.9, 10). Passing through the wall and a house of fire, Enoch entered into a second house built entirely of 'tongues of fire' (14.15). In this house of fire stood a fiery throne and upon this throne sat 'the Great Glory' (14.18-20). From this dazzling throne, engulfed with fire, came the voice of God: 'Come near to me, Enoch, and to my holy Word' (14.25).[1]

3. 2 Sam. 22.8-15 contains a graphic and visionary description of the Lord's intervention on David's behalf. With 'fire' (πῦρ) flaming from his mouth, the Lord 'parted the heavens' (ἔκλινεν οὐρανούς) and came down (22.9-10). Soaring on the 'wings of the wind' (πτερύγων ἀνέμου, 22.11), 'the voice [φωνήν] of the Most High resounded'. This divine declaration is likened to thunder (22.14) and the 'rebuke of the Lord' to a 'blast of the breath of his anger' (πνοῆς πνεύματος θυμοῦ αὐτοῦ, 22.16).

4. Isa. 66.15-16 records a prophecy of eschatological judgment and restoration: 'See, the Lord is coming with fire (πῦρ), and his chariots are like a whirlwind (ὡς καταιγίς); he will bring down his anger with fury, and his rebuke with flames of fire (φλογὶ πυρός; 66.15)'. Then the Lord will 'gather all nations and tongues' (πάντα τὰ ἔθνη καὶ τὰς γλώσσας) (66.18).

These texts indicate that the terms shared by Luke, Philo and Jonathan Ben Uzziel are not unique to Sinai traditions but characteristic of theophanic language in general.[2] This fact and the notable differences between Acts 2.1-13 and the texts of Philo and *Targ. Ps.-J.* suggest that Luke's Pentecost account was not influenced by these or similar Sinai traditions. The similarities between Luke's Pentecost account and the Sinai traditions of Philo and Jonathan Ben Uzziel are best explained by their common acquaintance with the language of Jewish theophany.

3.2.2. The Language Miracle Parallel: b. Šab. 88b. Representative of the rabbinic Sinai legends cited as parallels to Acts 2.5-13 are two

---

1. ET from E. Isaac, '1 Enoch', pp. 20-21; Greek text from the edition of Black, *Apocalypsis Henochi Graece*, pp. 28-29. In the final phrase cited ('my holy Word') Isaac's translation follows the Ethiopic text. The Greek text, however, reads: τὸν λόγον μου ἄκουσον.

2. Conzelmann, *Acts*, p. 16; Schneider, *Die Apostelgeschichte*, I, pp. 246-47; Kremer, *Pfingstbericht*, pp. 245, 248.

traditions recorded in the Babylonian Talmud (*b. Šab.* 88b).[1] With reference to the divine declaration at Sinai, Rabbi Jochanan (d. AD 279) is quoted as saying: 'Eveɩy single word that went forth from the Omnipotent was split up into seventy languages'. A similar tradition from the school of Rabbi Ishmael (d. AD 135) is also cited: 'Just as a hammer is divided into many sparks, so every single word that went forth from the Holy One, blessed be He, split up into seventy languages'.

These descriptions of the miraculous division of the divine word into seventy languages bear some resemblance to the language miracle of Acts 2.5-13. The key parallel is the communication of a divine oracle in different languages. Yet this similarity can hardly be cited as proof that Luke's account was influenced by these rabbinic traditions. Given the contexts of Sinai (divine oracle) and Pentecost (inspired speech) and the respective writers' interest in the universal significance of the events which they describe, it is not surprising that a parallel of this nature is found in these accounts.

Apart from the superficial parallel outlined above, these texts have little in common. In the rabbinic legends the oracle is delivered by God himself; in Luke's account it is transmitted by Spirit-inspired disciples. The rabbinic legends speak of individual words being divided into different languages, a concept completely foreign to Luke's account. And of course the number of language groups represented by Luke's *Völkerliste* is considerably less than the seventy cited in the rabbinic legends. These differences demonstrate the improbability of any direct link between Luke's account and the rabbinic Sinai legends.[2]

The theory that Luke was influenced by these rabbinic legends can also be questioned on the grounds that it anachronistically reads Acts 2 in light of rabbinic texts from a later era.[3] Although it is possible that these texts reflect traditions which stem from the first century, support for such an assumption is lacking. Indeed, an analysis of the Sinai accounts produced in the first century of our era[4] suggests that the tradition concerning the division of the divine voice into seventy

---

1. ET from H. Freedman, *Shabbath* (1938), II, in I. Epstein (ed.), *The Babylonian Talmud*, p. 420.

2. Strack-Billerbeck, *Kommentar*, II, p. 604; Kremer, *Pfingstbericht*, p. 251.

3. E. Lohse, 'πεντηκοστή', *TDNT*, VI, p. 49 n. 33 and 'Die Bedeutung', p. 185.

4. Philo, *Dec.* 32–36; 44–49; *Spec. Leg.* 2.188-189; Josephus, *Ant.* 3.79-80, 90; cf. Heb. 12.18-21.

languages was a later development. Neither Philo nor Josephus shows an awareness of this tradition. The tradition's absence from Philo's Sinai account is particularly striking since his emphasis on the universal dimension of the divine oracle (*Spec. Leg.* 2.189) points toward the necessity of such a view. It would appear that Philo represents a stage in the progressive development of the Sinai tradition which was a necessary antecedent to the tradition concerning the seventy languages. It is therefore unlikely that the tradition cited in *b. Šab.* 88b was widely known at the time of Luke's writing.

Having completed the examination of the relevant texts from Philo, *Targ. Ps.-J.* and the Babylonian Talmud, I am now in a position to summarize my findings. The similarities and differences between Acts 2.1-13 and the Sinai traditions of Philo and *Targ. Ps.-J.* suggest that these accounts represent two independent textual traditions produced by authors who were familiar with the language of Jewish theophany. The often cited parallels between Luke's account and the rabbinic legends are more apparent than real and, in all probability, these legends belong to a later era. The evidence thus indicates that Luke was not influenced by these or similar Sinai traditions when he penned his Pentecost account. This judgment precludes the more radical claim that Luke consciously shaped his account in order to present Pentecost as a 'new Sinai'.

3.3. *Acts 2.33: Moses Typology and Associations with Psalm 67.19 (LXX)?*

The assertion that Luke (or the tradition he utilized) portrays the gift of the Spirit in Acts 2.33 as the essence of the new covenant is founded on two suppositions: (1) Acts 2.33, as Eph. 4.8, is based on Ps. 67.19 (LXX); (2) Acts 2.33 represents a Christian counterpart to rabbinic exegesis of Psalm 67[1] and, as such, presents the bestowal of the Spirit as a gift which supersedes the Torah. In the following section I shall examine the validity of these suppositions.

Proponents of the view that Acts 2.33 is based on Ps. 67.19 (LXX)/ Eph. 4.8 generally analyse the verse in the following manner.[2] The

---

1.   The Targum of Ps. 68.19 (MT) reads: 'You have ascended to heaven, that is Moses the prophet. You have taken captivity captive, you have learned the words of the Torah, you have given them as gifts to men'. For the rabbinic exegesis of the Psalm see Strack–Billerbeck, *Kommentar*, III, pp. 596-98.
2.   See B. Lindars, *New Testament Apologetic* (1961), pp. 42-44, 51-59;

words τήν τε ἐπαγγελίαν ('the promise') and τοῦτο ὃ ὑμεῖς [καὶ] βλέπετε καὶ ἀκούετε ('what you now see and hear') are judged Lukan and therefore regarded as additions to the psalm citation. So also τοῦ πνεύματος τοῦ ἁγίου and ἐξέχεεν ('has poured out') are to be attributed to Lukan redaction since they have been imported from the Joel citation (2.17). Pointing to the version of Ps. 67.19 recorded in Eph. 4.8, Barnabas Lindars suggests that ἔδωκεν ('gave') originally stood in the place now taken by the redactional ἐξέχεεν.[1] The phrase τῇ δεξιᾷ οὖν τοῦ θεοῦ ('[therefore] to the right hand of God') can also be dismissed as redactional, for it anticipates Ps. 110.1 in Acts 2.35. We are therefore left with ὑψωθείς ('exalted') and λαβὼν παρὰ τοῦ πατρός ('received from the Father'). These words, taken in conjunction with the reconstructed ἔδωκεν and the ἀνέβη of v. 34, are thus offered as evidence that Ps. 67.19 forms the basis of the text (see diagram).

Eph. 4.8: διὸ λέγει,

| Ἀναβὰς εἰς ὕψος ᾐχμαλώτευσεν αἰχμαλωσίαν, | ἔδωκεν | δόματα | τοῖς | ἀνθρώποις. |

Ps. 67.19: ἀνέβης εἰς ὕψος ᾐχμαλώτευσας αἰχμαλωσίαν, ἔλαβες δόματα ἐν ἀνθρώπῳ,

Acts 2.33-34: τῇ δεξιᾷ οὖν τοῦ θεοῦ ὑψωθεὶς

τήν τε ἐπαγγελίαν τοῦ πνεύματος τοῦ ἁγίου λαβὼν παρὰ τοῦ πατρὸς

ἐξέχεεν τοῦτο ὃ ὑμεῖς [καὶ] βλέπετε καὶ ἀκούετε.

οὐ γὰρ Δαυὶδ ἀνέβη εἰς τοὺς οὐρανούς...

Eph. 4.8:   This is why it says,

When he ascended on high, he led captives in his train and gave gifts to men.

Ps. 67.19:   You ascended on high, you led captives in your train; you have received gifts for man,

Acts 2.33-34:   Exalted to the right hand of God,

he has received from the Father the promised Holy Spirit

and has poured out what you now see and hear.

For David did not ascend to heaven...

In spite of the obvious differences between Acts 2.33 and Ps. 67.19 (LXX)/Eph. 4.8, this ingenious proposal appears plausible at first sight. Yet after detailed examination, the tenuous nature of each of the proposed verbal links becomes apparent. First, ὑψωθείς ('exalted') hardly constitutes a genuine parallel to the phrase ἀνέβης εἰς ὕψος ('you

J. Dupont, 'Ascension du Christ et don de l'Esprit d'après Actes 2,33', in *Nouvelles études sur les Actes des Apôtres* (1984), pp. 199-209; and Turner, 'Christology', pp. 176-79.

1.   Lindars, *Apologetic*, p. 54.

ascended on high', Ps. 67.19).[1] And R. O'Toole argues persuasively that the covenant which underlies the Lukan Pentecost is not that of Sinai but the promise made to David in 2 Sam. 7.12-16. According to O'Toole, since Luke's entire argument in Acts 2.22-36 is based on the promises made to David, ὑψωθείς is best explained by the Davidic tradition in Psalm 88 (cf. Ps. 117.16; Isa. 52.13).[2] Secondly, as D. Bock correctly notes, when the method employed above to separate redactional elements from Luke's underlying source in Acts 2.33 is consistently applied to the entire verse, ἀνέβη and λαβὼν παρὰ τοῦ πατρός are also seen to be redactional. The term ἀναβαίνω appears frequently in Luke–Acts (27×) and in the general context (Acts 1.13). The promise of the Father (τοῦ πατρός) is alluded to in Lk. 24.49 and Acts 1.4. We are thus left with λαβών which occurs frequently in Luke–Acts (51×) and is 'naturally to describe the movement of the promise of the Spirit from the initiating sender...to the mediating dispenser'.[3] Thirdly, the suggestion that ἔδωκεν originally stood behind ἐξέχεεν is pure conjecture.

The evidence suggests that Acts 2.33 was not influenced by Psalm 67. All the elements of the verse 'are traceable within the Lucan narrative',[4] the key term from Psalm 67, δόματα ('gifts'), is lacking, and Luke's argument focuses on the promises made to David, not Moses.[5] The absence of any reference to Moses, the law or the covenant in Acts 2 speaks decisively against this proposal and the other two previously discussed. While Acts 2.33 clearly signifies that the Pentecostal outpouring of the Spirit constitutes irrefutable proof that Jesus has been exalted to the right hand of God, this proof does not consist of a powerful pneumatic transformation of the recipient's ethical life. Rather, the proof is an irruption of Spirit-inspired prophetic activity which is visible to all.

Even if the improbable hypothesis outlined above could be established, serious objections to the thesis that Acts 2.33 represents a Christian counterpart to rabbinic exegesis of Psalm 67 and, as such, presents the gift of the Spirit as the essence of the new covenant would remain. For even if this rabbinic exegetical tradition dates back to the first century, it

---

1. Wilckens, *Missionsreden*, p. 233.
2. R.F. O'Toole, 'Acts 2:30 and the Davidic Covenant of Pentecost', *JBL* 102 (1983), pp. 245-58.
3. Bock, *Proclamation*, p. 182.
4. Bock, *Proclamation*, p. 182.
5. O'Toole, 'Davidic Covenant', pp. 245-58.

is by no means evident that the Christian interpretation of the psalm is dependent upon it. Barnabas Lindars, for example, argues that the association of the psalm with Moses in the Targum tradition and the application of the psalm to Christ in the early church (Eph. 4.8) represent independent developments.[1] Furthermore, in the one clear reference to Ps. 67.19 in the New Testament, Eph. 4.8, the 'gifts' (δόματα) which Jesus gives are not associated with the new covenant or an internal law written on the heart, rather they are gifts of (Spirit-enabled) ministry (e.g. apostles, prophets, etc.).

This examination of the various arguments adduced in support of the claim that Luke (or the tradition he utilized) presents Pentecost as a 'new Sinai' has revealed that they are each deficient at crucial points. The evidence suggests that Luke neither shaped the Pentecost account with Sinai traditions in mind nor unconsciously used material significantly influenced by them. The Pentecost account indicates that Luke did not view the gift of the Spirit as the power of the new law of Christ. According to Luke, the Spirit of Pentecost is the source of prophetic inspiration and, as such, the Spirit of mission.

---

1. Lindars, *Apologetic*, pp. 52-53.

Chapter 11

THE DISCIPLES AND THE SPIRIT: THE PROPHETIC COMMUNITY

1. *Introduction*

I have argued that a careful analysis of the Pentecost narrative supports the thesis that Luke consistently portrays the Spirit as the source of prophetic power (producing special insight and inspired speech) which enables God's servants to fulfill their divinely appointed tasks. In Acts these servants are the disciples of Jesus and their ultimate task is to bear witness to the gospel of Jesus Christ unto 'the ends of the earth' (1.8). In the following chapter I shall examine texts from Acts relevant to this inquiry hitherto not (or only briefly) discussed and attempt to demonstrate that in Luke's perspective the Christian community is, by virtue of its reception of the Spirit, a prophetic community empowered for a missionary task.

The agenda for this chapter has been set by numerous attempts to establish a direct and necessary link between the gift of the Spirit and Christian initiation in Acts. Two contemporary New Testament exegetes are representative of this broad stream of scholarship: J. Dunn and J. Kremer. Both Dunn and Kremer argue that a thorough examination of Acts reveals that, for Luke, the Spirit is more than simply the source of prophetic power. Dunn asserts that for Luke 'the one thing that makes a man a Christian is the gift of the Spirit'.[1] Kremer contends that in several texts, most notably in Acts 2.38, by virtue of its close relationship to water baptism, the gift of the Spirit is presented as the 'means of salvation' and not principally as the source of prophetic power.[2] In order to assess the validity of these conclusions I shall examine each of the texts pertinent to the discussion as they occur in Acts: Acts 2.38; 8.4-25; 9.17-18; 10.44-48 (cf. 11.15-17; 15.8-10); 18.24-28; 19.1-7.

1. Dunn, *Holy Spirit*, p. 93.
2. Kremer, *Pfingstbericht*, p. 197. ET is my own. See also pp. 177-79, 197, 219-20, 273.

2. *Christian Initiation and the Gift of the Spirit in Acts*

2.1. *Acts 2.38*

It is often asserted that the collocation of repentance, baptism and the promise of the Spirit in Acts 2.38 demonstrates that Luke, like Paul and John, viewed reception of the Spirit as a necessary element in Christian initiation.[1] Acts 2.38 is thus offered as proof that for Luke the gift of the Spirit is the 'bearer of salvation', much more than a prophetic endowment.[2] Yet does Acts 2.38 support such a conclusion? The evidence suggests otherwise.

I have already noted that contextual considerations speak decisively against the interpretation outlined above. Consistent with Lk. 24.49, Acts 1.4 and 2.33, the promised gift of the Spirit in Acts 2.38 refers to the promise of Joel 3.1, and thus it is a promise of prophetic enabling granted to the repentant.

Furthermore, the collocation of baptism and reception of the Spirit in Acts 2.38 tells us little about the nature of the pneumatic gift. While it may indicate that for Luke the rite of water baptism is normally accompanied by the bestowal of the Spirit, Luke's usage elsewhere suggests that even this conclusion may be overstating the case. There is certainly nothing in the text which lends credence to Kremer's contention that the Spirit is presented here as the 'means of salvation and of life'.[3] Kremer would be on more solid ground if it could be established that the text presupposes an inextricable bond between water baptism and forgiveness of sins on the one hand and reception of the Spirit on the other. Yet this conclusion is clearly unwarranted. Since Luke fails to develop a strong link between water baptism and the bestowal of the Spirit elsewhere, and regularly separates the rite from the gift (Lk. 3.21-22; Acts 8.12-17; 9.17-18; 10.44; 18.24), the phrase καὶ λήμψεσθε τὴν δωρεὰν τοῦ ἁγίου πνεύματος ('and you will receive the gift of the Holy Spirit') should be interpreted as a promise that the Spirit shall be 'imparted to those who are already converted and baptized'.[4] In any case, the most that can be gleaned from the text is that repentance and

---

1. See for example J. Giblet, 'Baptism in the Spirit in the Acts of the Apostles', *OC* 10 (1974), p. 171; B. Sauvagant, 'Se repentir, être baptisé, recevoir l'Esprit, Actes 2,37 ss.', *FV* 80 (1981), p. 86; Dunn, *Holy Spirit*, pp. 90-92.
2. Dunn, *Holy Spirit*, p. 92.
3. Kremer, *Pfingstbericht*, p. 197. ET is my own.
4. Schweizer, 'πνεῦμα', p. 412.

water baptism are the normal prerequisites for reception of the Spirit, which is promised to every believer.

The evidence outlined above also highlights the improbable nature of Dunn's claim that in Acts 2.38 Luke portrays the gift of the Spirit as a necessary and climactic element in Christian initiation. As we have seen, this claim ignores important aspects of the immediate context; and, as I shall establish, it is inconsistent with Luke's usage elsewhere, most notably in Acts 8.12-17.

Luke undoubtedly viewed reception of the Spirit as a normal and important experience in the life of every Christian. Acts 2.38 suggests that repentance and water baptism constitute the normal prerequisites for receiving the Spirit and it may suggest that Luke viewed water baptism as the normal occasion for reception of the pneumatic gift. However, these conclusions cannot be adduced to support the assertion that Luke viewed the Spirit as 'the bearer of salvation' and, as such, a necessary element in Christian initiation. On the contrary, they are completely compatible with my contention that Luke portrays the Spirit as a prophetic enabling granted to those already converted. Indeed, the importance which Luke attaches to the gift of the Spirit does not bear witness to the purported integral role which it plays in conversion; it is a reflection of Luke's conviction that the church is a prophetic community with a missionary task.[1]

2.2. Acts 8.4-25

Acts 8.4-25 provides a real problem for those who argue that for Luke reception of the Spirit is a necessary element in Christian initiation. The narrative indicates that the Samaritans believed the preaching of Philip and were thus baptized by him (v. 12), yet they did not receive the Spirit until some time later (v. 15-17). The implications of this account for Luke's understanding of the Spirit are apparent. Since Luke considered the Samaritans to be Christians (i.e. converted) before they received the Spirit, it can hardly be maintained that he understood the Spirit to be either the 'means of salvation' or the 'one thing that makes a man a Christian'.

Those advocating a necessary link between reception of the Spirit and baptism/Christian initiation have attempted to mitigate the force of this text in a variety ways. It has been argued that the separation of the gift of the Spirit from the rite of baptism in Acts 8.4-25 does not represent

---

1. Schweizer, 'πνεῦμα', p. 413, and 'The Spirit of Power', p. 268.

historically reliable tradition; rather, the problematic text is the result of Luke's modification of his source material. This argument has generally taken one of two forms. It is claimed that Luke, either by conflating two originally independent sources,[1] or embellishing a traditional story originally about Philip's ministry in Samaria (including Simon's conversion) with fabricated material concerning Peter and John,[2] separated the gift from the baptismal rite and thus divided what in reality formed 'one indissoluble whole'.[3] This editorial activity, we are told, was motivated by a desire to link the new community to Jerusalem and highlight the authority of the apostles.

These theories have been severely criticized and must be judged improbable.[4] In any event, while offering possible explanations concerning how the narrative came to exist in its present form, these theories fail to deal with the crucial question concerning the implications of the text for Luke's pneumatology. It is unreasonable to assume that a man of Luke's editorial capabilities was unable to shape this account without contradicting his own pneumatology. Luke does not limit the bestowal of the Spirit to apostles (cf. 9.17).[5] And, even if he did intend to establish a link between the new community and Jerusalem, Luke's description of events in Antioch (Acts 11.22-24) indicates that he could have made the point without attributing the bestowal of the Spirit to the representatives of Jerusalem. The inescapable conclusion is that Luke simply did not feel that the text as it stands posed a problem. This judgment is confirmed by the fact that the 'problem' passage (vv. 14-17) is filled with themes and language characteristic of Luke.[6]

1. O. Bauernfeind, *Die Apostelgeschichte* (1939), pp. 124-25; D.-A. Koch, 'Geistbesitz, Geistverleihung und Wundermacht: Erwägungen zur Tradition und zur lukanischen Redaktion in Act 8.5-25', *ZNW* 77 (1986), pp. 64-82.

2. Dibelius, *Studies*, p. 17; Conzelmann, *Acts*, pp. 62-63; Haenchen, *Acts*, pp. 307-308; E. Käsemann, 'Die Johannesjünger in Ephesus', in *Exegetische Versuche und Besinnungen* (1960), I, pp. 165-66.

3. Haenchen, *Acts*, p. 308.

4. For criticism of source theories see R. Pesch, *Die Apostelgeschichte (Apg 1–12)* (1986), p. 271; Beasley-Murray, *Baptism*, pp. 115-17; Dunn, *Baptism*, pp. 60-62. Lampe calls recourse to the two-source theory of composition of the Samaritan account a 'desperate expedient' (*Seal of the Spirit*, p. 69).

5. K. Giles, 'Is Luke an Exponent of "Early Protestantism"? Church Order in the Lukan Writings (Part 1)', *EvQ* 54 (1982), p. 197; Marshall, *Acts*, p. 157; and Dunn, *Holy Spirit*, pp. 58-60.

6. Koch, 'Geistbesitz', pp. 69-71; Turner, *Luke and the Spirit*, p. 161.

Others have sought to ease the tension by describing the course of events narrated in Acts 8.4-25 as a unique exception necessitated by a new and decisive turning-point in the mission of the church: the Spirit was withheld until the coming of the apostles from Jerusalem in order to demonstrate to the Samaritans 'that they had really become members of the Church, in fellowship with its original "pillars"'.[1] Yet this view faces a number of serious objections. First, there is little reason to assume that this instance represents a unique exception, either historically or for Luke. Nothing in the text itself supports such a view[2] and, as I have noted, Luke regularly separates the gift from the rite. Secondly, the explanation offered for this purported exception is highly improbable. It is unlikely that the Samaritans would need any further assurance of their incorporation into the church after baptism. And, in similar decisive turning-points the assurance of incorporation into the church (as well as the reality itself) is not dependent on contact with representatives of Jerusalem (Acts 8.26-39; 9.17-18; 18.24–19.7) or their bestowal of the Spirit to the newly converted (Acts 11.22-24). Nevertheless, even if this theory is accepted, the 'problem' posed by the text is not eradicated. For however exceptional the event may have been (historically and for Luke), we must still account for Luke's carefully crafted interpretation of this event. Indeed, Luke's account betrays a pneumatology decidedly different from Paul or John, neither of whom could conceive of baptized believers being without the Spirit.

Fully aware that the implications for Luke's pneumatology which emerge from the two positions outlined above are incompatible with their respective attempts to tie reception of the Spirit to conversion-initiation (Dunn) and baptism (Beasley-Murray) in Luke–Acts, J. Dunn and G.R. Beasley-Murray offer alternative interpretations of Acts 8.4-25.

Beasley-Murray argues that Luke 'regarded these Christians as not without the Spirit but without the spiritual gifts that characterized the common life of the Christian communities'.[3] According to Beasley-Murray the πολλὴ χαρά ('great joy') of Acts 8.8 implies that the Samaritans received the Spirit when they were baptized, and the anarthrous use of πνεῦμα ἅγιον in Acts 8.15-16 suggests that apostles

---

1. Lampe, *Seal*, p. 70. Similar views are espoused by Chevallier, *Souffle*, pp. 201-202; Bruner, *Holy Spirit*, pp. 175-76; Marshall, *Acts*, pp. 153, 157.

2. J. Dunn, '"They Believed Philip Preaching (Acts 8.12)": A Reply', *IBS* 1 (1979), p. 180.

3. Beasley-Murray, *Baptism*, p. 119; see pp. 118-20 for his argument.

imparted spiritual gifts, not the Spirit itself. Neither of these arguments commends itself. The πολλὴ χαρά of Acts 8.8 results from the exorcisms and healings performed by Philip; it does not imply possession of the Spirit.¹ Nor can a neat distinction be made between τὸ πνεῦμα τὸ ἅγιον and πνεῦμα ἅγιον: they are equivalent titles.² However, the decisive objection against Beasley-Murray's thesis is Luke's explicit statement in v. 16: the Spirit 'had not yet fallen on any of them'.

Dunn seeks to establish that the Samaritans were not really Christians before they received the Spirit. He maintains that their 'initial response and commitment was defective' and that Luke 'intended his readers to know this'.³ The following arguments are produced in support of this claim: (1) Luke's description of Philip as preaching τὸν Χριστόν *simpliciter* (v. 5) and τῆς βασιλείας τοῦ θεοῦ ('the kingdom of God', v. 12) suggests that the Samaritans understood Philip's message in terms of their own nationalistic expectations of the Messiah and the kingdom he was to bring—expectations already 'roused to near fever-pitch' by the magician Simon. For the former phrase 'is always used in Acts of the Messiah of pre-Christian expectation' and the latter, when preached to non-Christians, always refers to the 'Kingdom of Jewish expectations'.⁴ (2) The Samaritans' response to Simon betrays a predilection for magic and a general lack of discernment. Luke indicates that their response to Philip was equally shallow through his use of προσέχω ('pay attention to'), a term descriptive of the Samaritan response to both Philip and Simon (vv. 6, 10-11). (3) Since πιστεύειν ('to believe') with the dative object usually signifies intellectual assent, the phrase ἐπίστευσαν τῷ Φιλίππῳ (rather than πιστεύειν εἰς or ἐπὶ κύριον) reveals that the Samaritan response was simply an assent of the mind and not reflective of genuine faith. (4) The comparison between the clearly defective experience of Simon and that of the other Samaritans (vv. 12-13) demonstrates that they 'all went through the form but did not experience the reality'.⁵

1.   Turner, 'Luke and the Spirit', p. 168. Turner, citing as examples Lk. 13.17 and 19.37, notes that 'such joy is frequently mentioned as the response to God's various saving acts throughout Luke–Acts'.

2.   See Dunn, *Holy Spirit*, pp. 56, 68-70; M. Turner, 'Luke and the Spirit', pp. 167-68.

3.   Dunn, *Holy Spirit*, p. 63; for his argument see pp. 63-68.

4.   Quotations from Dunn, *Holy Spirit*, p. 64.

5.   Dunn, *Holy Spirit*, p. 66.

Dunn's hypothesis has been subjected to intense criticism and must be rejected in view of the evidence.[1] Indeed, none of the arguments outlined above can be sustained. 1. There is nothing in Luke's account which would suggest that Philip's message was either deficient or misunderstood. On the contrary, Philip is presented as one of the group alluded to in Acts 8.4 who went about 'preaching the word' (εὐαγγελιζόμενοι τὸν λόγον). Since τὸν λόγον embodies the content of the kerygma (cf. Acts 2.41; 6.2; 8.14), it is quite evident that Luke understood Philip's preaching, variously described (vv. 5, 12), to be 'kerygmatic in the full sense'.[2] And there is nothing in the phrases 'he proclaimed τὸν Χριστόν' (v. 5) and 'the good news of the kingdom of God and the name of Jesus Christ' (τῆς βασιλείας τοῦ θεοῦ καὶ τοῦ ὀνόματος Ἰησοῦ Χριστοῦ, v. 12) which would suggest that the Samaritans misunderstood Philip's message. The phrase τὸν Χριστόν *simpliciter* appears frequently in Christian proclamation in Acts and with reference to the central elements of the kerygma: Christ's death (e.g. 3.18) and resurrection (e.g. 2.31).[3] In v. 5, as elsewhere in Acts (9.22; 17.3; 26.23; cf. 18.5, 28), the phrase serves as a summary of the kerygma.[4] Similarly, the phrase τῆς βασιλείας τοῦ θεοῦ καὶ τοῦ ὀνόματος Ἰησοῦ Χριστοῦ can scarcely mean less since it parallels the content of Paul's preaching in Rome (28.31). If the Samaritans had misunderstood Philip, we would expect the apostles to correct the deficiency through additional teaching (cf. 18.26), yet any reference to such activity is conspicuously absent.[5]

2. Dunn's attempt to dismiss the response of the Samaritans as merely a reflection of their predilection for magic is irreconcilable with the prominent place given to the proclamation of 'the word' in Luke's description of Philip's ministry (vv. 4-8, 12-13; cf. v. 14).[6] Miraculous

---

1. See for example E.A. Russell, '"They Believed Philip Preaching" (Acts 8.12)', *IBS* 1 (1979), pp. 169-76; Turner, 'Luke and the Spirit', pp. 163-67; H. Ervin, *Conversion-Initiation and the Baptism in the Holy Spirit* (1984), pp. 25-40; Marshall, *Acts*, p. 156; D. Ewert, *The Holy Spirit in the New Testament* (1983), pp. 118-19; M. Green, *I Believe in the Holy Spirit* (1975), p. 138; Carson, *Showing the Spirit*, p. 144; Stronstad, *Charismatic Theology*, pp. 64-65.

2. Russell, '"They Believed"', p. 170.

3. '"They Believed"', p. 170.

4. Roloff, *Die Apostelgeschichte*, p. 133; Turner, 'Luke and the Spirit', p. 163.

5. Marshall, *Acts*, p. 158; Turner, 'Luke and the Spirit', p. 164.

6. Note the occurrences of εὐαγγελίζομαι (vv. 4, 12), κηρύσσω (v. 5) and ἀκούω (v. 6).

signs do play an important role in the success of Philip's ministry (vv. 6-7, 13), but this emphasis is consistent with Luke's usage elsewhere: 'word and sign are complementary...both realities belong together in the missionary endeavour'.[1] Luke's use of προσέχω will hardly bear the weight of Dunn's argument: in v. 6 the Samaritans give heed to Philip's preaching (cf. 16.14);[2] in vv. 10-11 their attention is focused on the magician Simon. Also, rather than disparaging this 'attention' as shallow, Luke appears to underline the power of Simon's grip on the people and Philip's resounding triumph over it.

3. Dunn bases his claim that ἐπίστευσαν τῷ Φιλίππῳ ('they believed Philip', 8.12) is not descriptive of Christian commitment on two tenets, both of which are without foundation. First, Dunn implies that it is significant that the object of the verb ἐπίστευσαν is the preaching of Philip (τῷ Φιλίππῳ εὐαγγελιζομένῳ περί...) rather than κύριος or θεός. However, the description of Lydia's conversion in 16.14 indicates that Luke equates belief in the message of an evangelist with belief in God.[3] Secondly, Dunn insists that πιστεύειν with a dative object (rather than with the prepositions εἰς or ἐπί) signifies mere intellectual assent to a proposition. Yet Luke uses this construction elsewhere to describe genuine faith in God (Acts 16.34; 18.8). Furthermore, he does not distinguish between πιστεύειν with a dative object and πιστεύειν with εἰς or ἐπί. All three constructions appear with κύριος in descriptions of genuine faith.[4] That ἐπίστευσαν τῷ Φιλίππῳ does indeed refer to genuine faith is confirmed by the report that reached the apostles in Jerusalem: 'Samaria had accepted the word of God' (τὸν λόγον τοῦ θεοῦ, 8.14). A similar report heralds the conversion of Cornelius and his

---

1. O'Reilly, *Word and Sign*, p. 217.

2. Ervin correctly emphasizes the common elements in the accounts which describe the conversion of the Samaritans (8.6-7) and Lydia (16.14) respectively, 'Lydia "gave heed" (προσέχειν) to what was said by Paul and was baptized. The Samaritans "gave heed" (προσέχειν) to what was spoken by Philip, they believed and were baptized' (*Conversion-Initiation*, p. 32).

3. Acts 16.14: 'the Lord opened her heart to respond to Paul's message' (προσέχειν τοῖς λαλουμένοις ὑπὸ τοῦ Παύλου, cf. 8.6). For the use of πιστεύειν in a similar context see Acts 4.4.

4. Russell, '"They Believed"', p. 173. Russell notes that πιστεύειν and the object κύριος occur with the preposition εἰς (14.23), ἐπί (9.42), and simply with the dative object (18.8). He also points out that πιστεύειν is used in relation to the Scriptures with both the simple dative (24.14; 26.27) and the preposition ἐπί (Lk. 24.45).

household (11.1; cf. 2.41, 17.11). Since this latter report is not questioned, 'we should therefore find no reason to question the former'.[1] 4. Dunn's attempt to impugn the faith of the Samaritans by way of analogy with Simon's is also unconvincing, for the premise of Dunn's inference, that Simon's faith was defective, is demonstrably false. Dunn asserts that Simon's behavior reveals the true condition of his heart: he was never really converted. However, the example of Ananias and Sapphira (5.1-11) demonstrates the depth to which believers could sink in Luke's estimation. In all probability, Simon's sin, like that of Ananias and Sapphira, is considered 'so serious precisely because it is committed by a follower of Jesus'.[2] Central to Dunn's argument is Peter's indictment in v. 21: 'You have no part or share in this ministry' (ἐν τῷ λόγῳ τούτῳ)—a phrase which, according to Dunn, means that Simon 'never had become a member of the people of God'.[3] However, this interpretation is dubious. Two possibilities commend themselves, neither of which accords with Dunn's theory. First, E. Haenchen argues that the phrase forms part of a formula of excommunication[4]—a necessary corollary being that Simon was considered a Christian until this time. Secondly, noting that Haenchen's explanation fails to account for the demonstrative adjective (τούτῳ), Turner insists that the phrase refers to Simon's misguided attempt to buy the ability to confer the Spirit, and not to Simon's exclusion from the faith.[5] In view of contextual considerations, Turner's interpretation is to be preferred, although other elements within Peter's rebuke (8.20-23) indicate that Simon had apostatized.[6] That Simon's initial faith was sound is confirmed by the absolute use of πιστεύειν in v. 13. Elsewhere in Acts when πιστεύειν is used without an object it refers to genuine faith (2.44; 4.4; 11.21; 15.5).

---

1. Giles, 'Church Order (Part 1)', p. 197.

2. Turner, 'Luke and the Spirit', p. 165.

3. Dunn, *Holy Spirit*, p. 65. The phrase is reminiscent of Deut. 12.12 (LXX).

4. Haenchen, *Acts*, p. 305. Haenchen views the phrase ἐν τῷ λόγῳ τούτῳ as a reference to the Christian message.

5. Turner, 'Luke and the Spirit', p. 166. Turner contends that ἐν τῷ λόγῳ τούτῳ should be translated, 'in this matter', and refers to the apostles' authority to confer the Spirit.

6. The allusions to Ps. 77.37 (LXX: ἡ δὲ καρδία αὐτῶν οὐκ εὐθεῖα μετ' αὐτοῦ, cf. v. 21) and Deut. 29.17-18 (LXX: μὴ τίς ἐστιν ἐν ὑμῖν ῥίζα ἄνω φύουσα ἐν χολῇ καὶ πικρίᾳ, cf. v. 23), two OT texts which speak of the unfaithfulness of those within the covenant community, support the contention that Simon was guilty of apostasy, and as such, had abandoned his previous (genuine) profession of faith.

It has become apparent that the separation of Spirit-reception from baptism/Christian initiation in Acts 8.4-25 cannot be explained away as a piece of careless editorial work or disregarded as a unique exception. The former position is based on an implausible tradition-history of the text and the latter on a hypothetical reconstruction of the event; both ignore the significance of the existing narrative for Luke's pneumatology. Neither is it possible to eliminate the contradiction by postulating a 'silent' bestowal of the Spirit at baptism or impugning the faith of the Samaritans: the evidence speaks decisively against both views. Acts 8.4-25 poses an insoluble problem for those who maintain that Luke establishes a necessary link between baptism/Christian initiation and the gift of the Spirit.

This problem is resolved, however, when we recognize the distinctive character of Luke's prophetic pneumatology: the internal contradictions disappear and Luke is seen to be remarkably consistent. Indeed, it is quite evident that Luke viewed the gift of the Spirit received by the Samaritans (Acts 8.17) as of the same character as the Pentecostal gift; that is, as a prophetic endowment granted to the converted which enabled them to participate effectively in the mission of the church. This conclusion is supported by the following considerations.

1. The inescapable conclusion which emerges from the discussion above is that for Luke the gift of the Spirit does not constitute a Christian. On the contrary, the Spirit is a supplementary gift given to Christians, those who have already been incorporated into the community of salvation.[1]

2. It is abundantly clear from Luke's choice of language in Acts 8.15-19 that he considered the pneumatic gift received by the Samaritans to be identical to the Pentecostal gift. The terms descriptive of the Samaritan experience are also associated with Pentecost: λαμβάνειν πνεῦμα ἅγιον ('to receive', 2.38; 8.15, 17, 19; cf. 1.8); ἐπιπίπτειν τὸ πνεῦμα τὸ ἅγιον ('to come upon', 8.16; 11.15). It is also generally recognized that implicit within the narrative is the assumption that the Samaritans, upon reception of the Spirit, began to prophesy and speak in tongues as on the day of Pentecost (8.16-18; cf. 2.4-13; 10.45-46; 19.6).[2]

---

1. Schweizer, 'πνεῦμα', p. 412, and 'The Spirit of Power', pp. 267-68; Haya-Prats, *Force*, pp. 121-38; Bovon, *Luc le théologien*, p. 253; H. Flender, *Saint Luke: Theologian of Redemptive History* (1970), p. 138.
2. See for example J.D.M. Derrett, 'Simon Magus (Act 8.9-24)', *ZNW* 73 (1982), p. 54; Haenchen, *Acts*, p. 304; Dunn, *Holy Spirit*, p. 56, and 'I Corinthians

Thus the prophetic character of the gift received by the Samaritans is substantiated by the parallels with the Pentecostal gift, which we have already seen to be a prophetic endowment, and by the phenomena which Luke associated (implicitly) with its reception.

3. The association of the gift of the Spirit with the laying on of hands in Acts 8.17 suggests that Luke viewed the gift as an endowment for service in the mission of the church. There are two unambiguous contexts in which the laying on of hands occurs in the book of Acts: it is associated with healing (9.12, 17; 28.8) and with the commissioning of believers for service in the church's mission (6.6; 13.3; cf. 9.17). The laying on of hands also appears in conjunction with the bestowal of the Spirit in Acts 8.17, 19.6 and probably 9.17. However, it must be noted that the gift is often granted apart from the rite (2.38; 10.44) and the rite does not always confer the gift (6.6; 13.3).[1] This fact suggests that reception of the Spirit is not integral to the rite, but is rather a supplementary element. It appears that the primary focus of the rite can be either healing or commissioning, or, as in the case of Paul, both (9.17; cf. 22.14-15; 26.16-18). Since the rite is clearly not related to healing in Acts 8.17 and 19.6, it is not unreasonable to assume that in these instances it forms part of a commissioning ceremony.[2] I therefore suggest that Peter and John incorporate the Samaritans, not into the church, but into the missionary enterprise of the church.[3] This involves commissioning the nucleus of Samaritan believers for service in the church's mission through the laying on of hands. In this instance the gift of the Spirit accompanies the laying on of hands because those commissioned have not yet received the prophetic enabling necessary for effective service (cf. 9.17; 19.6), unlike the seven (6.6) or Paul and Barnabas (13.3). Thus the Samaritans are commissioned and empowered for the missionary task which lay before them. A prophetic community

15.45: Last Adam, Life-giving Spirit', in *Christ and Spirit in the New Testament* (1973), p. 132.

1. The laying on of hands which confers the Spirit is not limited to the apostles or to representatives of Jerusalem (cf. 9.17).

2. The laying on of hands as a Jewish rite was frequently used in the commissioning of a person for a special task: e.g. Num. 8.10; 27.19; Deut. 34.9 (Joshua is filled with the spirit of wisdom as a result of the rite); *Asc. Isa.* 6.3-5 (the rite results in prophetic speech); and *y. Sanh.* 1.19a (the rite is employed in the ordination of rabbis).

3. Lampe, *Seal*, pp. 70-78, and 'The Holy Spirit', p. 199; Bruce, *Book of Acts*, p. 183; and Hill, *Greek Words*, p. 264.

has been formed. A new center of missionary activity has been established (cf. 9.31).[1]

2.3. *Acts 9.17-18*

In the climax to Luke's account of Paul's conversion/call in Acts 9.1-19, Ananias lays his hands upon Paul and declares: 'Brother Saul, the Lord...has sent me so that you may see again and be filled with the Holy Spirit' (καὶ πλησθῇς πνεύματος ἁγίου, 9.17). Paul is immediately healed and subsequently baptized (9.18). Although the account fails to describe the actual bestowal of the Spirit, it is evident from Ananias's comment in 9.17 that Paul received the gift. In assessing the significance of the pericope for this inquiry, I shall seek to answer the vital question: is the gift of the Spirit presented here as the principal element in Paul's conversion, or is it rather an endowment which enables Paul to fulfill his missionary call? I shall begin the discussion with a few comments concerning methodology.

Paul's conversion/call was, without question, of great importance to Luke, for he recounts the event on three different occasions in Acts (9.1-19; 22.4-16; 26.12-18). A comparison of the three texts reveals considerable variation in form and content.[2] These variations led an earlier generation of source critics to postulate the existence of two or more underlying sources for the various accounts.[3] However, these theories have been largely rejected by contemporary critics.[4] It is now generally accepted that all three accounts are based on a single source and that the variations in the accounts are principally the result of Luke's literary method. The various accounts supplement and complement one

---

1. Lampe, *Seal*, p. 72. This conclusion is confirmed by the important summary in Acts 9.31: 'Then the church throughout Judea, Galilee and Samaria...encouraged by the Holy Spirit...grew in numbers' (τῇ παρακλήσει τοῦ ἁγίου πνεύματος ἐπληθύνετο).

2. For a summary of the main differences in the three accounts see K. Lönig, *Die Saulustradition in der Apostelgeschichte* (1973), p. 14.

3. See F. Spitta, *Die Apostelgeschichte* (1891), pp. 137-45, 270-77; J. Jüngst, *Die Quelle der Apostelgeschichte* (1895), pp. 83-95, 223-24; H.H. Wendt, *Die Apostelgeschichte* (1913), pp. 166-68.

4. See Dibelius, *Studies*, p. 158 n. 47; Haenchen, *Acts*, pp. 108-10; 325-29; Conzelmann, *Acts*, pp. 72-73; Lönig, *Die Saulustradition*, pp. 15-19; G. Lohfink, *The Conversion of St. Paul: Narrative and History in Acts* (1976), pp. 40-46, 81; C. Burchard, *Der dreizehnte Zeuge: Traditions- und kompositionsgeschichtliche Untersuchungen zu Lukas' Darstellung der Frühzeit des Paulus* (1970), p. 121.

another.[1] Thus, any attempt to reconstruct the theological perspectives which gave rise to the account of Paul's conversion/call recorded in Acts 9.1-19 must also take into consideration the parallel accounts in Acts 22.4-16 and 26.12-18. Paul's reception of the Spirit is closely linked to Ananias and, as such, it forms part of the Ananias episode of Acts 9.10-19. When this episode is compared with the parallel version in Acts 22.12-16 it becomes apparent that, in Luke's perspective, it is not the culmination of an account of Paul's conversion; rather, it is principally an account of Paul's commissioning as a missionary (cf. 22.14-15). Acts 26.12-18 confirms my contention that Paul's missionary call was foremost in Luke's mind, for here the Damascus event itself is viewed as the moment at which Paul receives his divine commission to engage in the mission to the Jews *and the Gentiles*.

There is abundant evidence of this perspective within the Ananias episode of Acts 9. The account exhibits many features of the 'commission form' prevalent in the Old Testament and other ancient Near Eastern texts.[2] And, although there is some question concerning which stage in the development of the tradition vv. 15-16 should be placed, it is evident that Luke penned these verses with reference to Paul's future missionary activity. Furthermore, this commission formula and the reference to the reception of the Spirit in v. 17 are linked to the statement concerning Paul's preaching activity in v. 20 by the preceding καὶ εὐθέως ('immediately'). In all probability the references to Paul's reception of the Spirit (v. 17) and his ensuing preaching activity (v. 20) are Lukan insertions:[3] the former understood to be the necessary prerequisite for the latter. Luke also indicates that Ananias laid his hands upon Paul (v. 17), a gesture which, in view of the considerations outlined above, must be viewed as the occasion for Paul's commissioning by Ananias (cf. Acts 22.14-15), as well as his healing. The text implies that the Spirit was conferred in conjunction with the laying on of hands, thus

1. C.W. Hedrick, 'Paul's Conversion/Call: A Comparative Analysis of the Three Reports in Acts', *JBL* 100 (1981), p. 432.

2. B.J. Hubbard, 'Commissioning Stories in Luke–Acts: A Study of their Antecedents, Form and Content', *Semeia* 8 (1977), pp. 103-26; T.Y. Mullins, 'New Testament Commission Forms, Especially in Luke–Acts', *JBL* 95 (1976), pp. 603-14; J. Munck, *Paul and the Salvation of Mankind* (1959), pp. 24-35.

3. Lönig, *Die Saulustradition*, pp. 45-47; Hedrick, 'Paul's Conversion/Call', p. 422; Burchard, *Der dreizehnte Zeuge*, p. 124.

Paul's reception of the Spirit is associated with his commissioning. The answer to my question is now apparent. In Acts 9.17 the gift of the Spirit is presented as an endowment which enables Paul to fulfill his missionary call. For Luke, Ananias's reluctant encounter with Paul is the occasion for a monumental event: Paul is commissioned and empowered to proclaim the gospel to, above all, the Gentiles.

2.4. *Acts 10.44-48*

The account of the Spirit-baptism of Cornelius's household (10.44-48) and the subsequent summaries of this dramatic event (11.15-17; 15.8-10) are frequently cited as evidence that, for Luke, the Spirit is the agent of 'forgiveness, cleansing, and salvation'.[1] For here, it is claimed, Luke equates the historic conversion of this initial band of Gentile Christians with their Spirit-baptism. On the face of it the assertion appears to be justified, for there can be little doubt that the conversion and Spirit-baptism of Cornelius's household are, at the very least, closely related chronologically. However, upon closer examination it becomes apparent that this interpretation is wide of the mark. The prophetic gift received by Cornelius and household is a 'sign of salvation', but not the 'means'.[2]

Questions of tradition and history, when applied to the Peter-Cornelius episode (10.1–11.18), have elicited a variety of conflicting responses. Nevertheless, there is a general consensus among scholars concerning the significance that Luke attached to the account: it demonstrates that the Gentile mission was initiated and validated by divine revelation.[3] The point is made through a profusion of heavenly visions, angelic visitations and interventions of the Spirit.[4] The decisive sign of God's favor on the Gentiles is their reception of the gift of the Spirit, manifested in inspired speech (10.46, λαλούντων γλώσσαις καὶ μεγαλυνόντων τὸν θεόν).[5]

---

1. Dunn, *Holy Spirit*, pp. 79-82, quote from p. 82; see also Kremer, *Pfingstbericht*, pp. 196-97; Bruce, 'The Holy Spirit', pp. 171-72.

2. *Contra* Kremer, who states that the gift of the Spirit is received 'als Zeichen und Mittel der Errettung und des Lebens' (*Pfingstbericht*, p. 197). ET is my own.

3. See Dibelius, *Studies*, p. 117 and virtually all of the commentators.

4. Thus Minear, with good reason, suggests that 'we should read the story of Peter and Cornelius (10.1–11.18; 15.6-11) as a clear instance of prophetic revelation' (*To Heal and to Reveal* [1976], p. 142).

5. The phrase λαλούντων γλώσσαις (10.46; cf. 19.6), unlike the λαλεῖν ἑτέραις γλώσσαις of 2.4, refers to unintelligible inspired utterance (cf. 1 Cor. 14.1-28). See Haenchen, *Acts*, p. 354; Schweizer, 'πνεῦμα', p. 410; George, 'L'Esprit', p. 509; Haya-Prats, *Force*, p. 107; J. Behm, 'γλῶσσα', *TDNT*, I, pp. 725-26.

It is this sign which astonishes Peter's circumcised companions (10.45-46) and results in his command to baptize the Gentile converts (10.47-48). It is also through reference to this sign that Peter justifies his table-fellowship with the uncircumcised (11.3, 15-17) and their admission into the church (15.8-9).

This emphasis on Spirit-baptism as a sign of God's acceptance accords well with Luke's distinctive pneumatology. Since according to Luke reception of the Spirit is the exclusive privilege of 'the servants' of God and generally results in miraculous and audible speech,[1] by its very nature the gift provides demonstrative proof that the uncircumcised members of Cornelius's household have been incorporated into the community of salvation. The sign-value of the prophetic gift is also emphasized in the Pentecost account (2.4-13, 17-20). Whether from the lips of a Jew in Jerusalem or a Gentile in Caesarea, the manifestation of inspired speech marks the speaker as a member of the end-time prophetic community.

The evidence suggests that Luke viewed the Gentiles' reception of the Spirit as the decisive sign of their acceptance by God. Luke's perspective is based upon the prophetic nature of the pneumatic gift and, as such, is entirely consistent with my description of his distinctive pneumatology. Although in this instance (in contrast to 8.17) reception of the Spirit accompanies conversion, the text does not imply that the gift is the means by which the uncircumcised are actually cleansed and forgiven. This unwarranted assumption is usually based on the summaries of the event recorded in 11.15-17 and 15.8-10.

Pointing to the similarities between 11.17a and 11.18b,[2] J. Dunn argues that the gift of the Spirit is 'God's gift of μετάνοια εἰς ζωήν' ('repentance unto life').[3] However, Dunn's equation must be rejected since elsewhere μετάνοια is a prerequisite for receiving the Spirit (Acts 2.38-39) and clearly distinguished from the gift itself (cf. 5.31-32).[4] The

---

1. Of the eight instances where Luke describes the initial reception of the Spirit by a person or group, five specifically allude to some form of inspired speech as an immediate result (Lk. 1.41; 1.67; Acts 2.4; 10.46; 19.6) and one implies the occurrence of such activity (Acts 8.15, 18). In the remaining two instances, although inspired speech is absent from Luke's account (Lk. 3.22; Acts 9.17), it is a prominent feature in the pericopes which follow (Lk. 4.14, 18-19; Acts 9.20).

2. Cf. v. 17a: 'So if God gave them the same gift as he gave us...'; v. 18b: 'So then, God has even granted the Gentiles repentance unto life'.

3. Dunn, *Holy Spirit*, p. 81; see also Bruner, *Holy Spirit*, p. 196.

4. Turner, 'Luke and the Spirit', p. 172; see also Haya-Prats, *Force*, pp. 122-25.

similarities between vv. 17a and 18b simply reflect the logic of Peter's argument: since God has granted the Gentiles the gift of the Spirit, it follows *a fortiori* that they have been granted μετάνοια εἰς ζωήν and are eligible for the baptismal rite.

Similarly, it is often claimed that 15.8 is synonymous with 15.9:[1]

v. 8: καὶ ὁ καρδιογνώστης θεὸς ἐμαρτύρησεν
αὐτοῖς δοὺς τὸ πνεῦμα τὸ ἅγιον καθὼς καὶ ἡμῖν
v. 9: καὶ οὐθὲν διέκρινεν μεταξὺ ἡμῶν τε καὶ αὐτῶν,
τῇ πίστει καθαρίσας τὰς καρδίας αὐτῶν.

v. 8: And God who knows the heart, showed that he accepted them
by giving the Holy Spirit to them, just as he did to us.
v. 9: He made no distinction between us and them,
for he purified their hearts by faith.

This assumption has led many to conclude that for Luke, 'God's giving of the Holy Spirit is equivalent to his cleansing of their hearts'.[2] But again Peter's argument speaks against this equation.[3] Verse 8 is the premise from which the deduction of v. 9 is drawn: God's bestowal of the Spirit bears witness (v. 8) to the reality of his act of cleansing (v. 9).[4] Peter's argument here is similar to that in 11.16-18. In each instance the logical distinction between the premise (gift of the Spirit) and deduction (repentance/cleansing) is apparent. My analysis is supported by the fact that Luke always attributes forgiveness (ἄφεσις), which is granted in response to faith/repentance, to Jesus—never to the Spirit (cf. 10.43).[5]

The decisive objection against the interpretations outlined above is that Luke equates the gift of the Spirit granted to Cornelius's household, not

Acts 5.31-32 is instructive: repentance (μετάνοια) and forgiveness (ἄφεσις) are attributed directly to Jesus, whom God has exalted to his right hand as σωτήρ; the Spirit, given to the obedient, bears witness to Jesus' true identity.

1. Dunn, *Holy Spirit*, p. 81; Bruce, 'The Holy Spirit', p. 171; and *Book of Acts*, pp. 306-307; Tiede, *Prophecy*, p. 50.

2. Dunn, *Holy Spirit*, pp. 81-82.

3. J.W. Taeger, *Der Mensch und sein Heil* (1982), p. 108.

4. It is noteworthy that the Spirit falls upon Cornelius and his household immediately after Peter declares that οἱ προφῆται μαρτυροῦσιν, ἄφεσιν ἁμαρτιῶν λαβεῖν διὰ τοῦ ὀνόματος αὐτοῦ ... (10.43). The conceptual parallels with 10.44-45, 11.17-18 and, above all, 15.8-9 are striking: by pouring out the Spirit of prophecy upon the Gentiles, God testifies that they have received ἄφεσιν ἁμαρτιῶν.

5. Forgiveness (ἄφεσις) is attributed to Jesus (Acts 5.31; 13.38), the name of Jesus (Lk. 24.47; Acts 2.38; 10.43) and faith in Jesus (26.18). See also Lk. 1.77; 3.3; 4.18 (2×).

with cleansing and forgiveness, but with the Pentecostal gift of prophetic inspiration.[1] Luke stresses the point through repetition: the Gentiles received the same gift granted to the Jewish disciples on Pentecost (10.47; 11.15, 17; 15.8). As I have noted, the significance that Peter attaches to the gift as a sign of God's acceptance is based on the prophetic nature of the gift. Indeed, the manifestation of the prophetic gift by the Gentiles is the climactic event in a series of divine interventions which serve to initiate and validate the Gentile mission. Since this is Luke's central concern, he does not pursue further at this point the significance of the gift for the missionary activity of this newly formed Christian community. However, we may presume that the prophetic band in Caesarea, like the communities in Samaria and Antioch, by virtue of the pneumatic gift participated effectively in the missionary enterprise (cf. 18.22; 21.8).

2.5. Acts 18.24-28; 19.1-7
Luke's record of the origins of the church in Ephesus includes the enigmatic and closely related pericopes dealing with Apollos (18.24-28) and the Ephesian disciples (19.1-7). The unusual description of Apollos as a powerful evangelist κατηχημένος τὴν ὁδὸν τοῦ κυρίου ('instructed in the way of the Lord') and yet knowing μόνον τὸ βάπτισμα 'Ιωάννου ('only the baptism of John') is matched by the peculiar portrait of the twelve Ephesians as μαθηταί ('disciples') who have received neither Christian baptism nor the gift of the Spirit. These perplexing texts have elicited a variety of explanations.

E. Käsemann has suggested that Luke, writing at a time when the church was battling against the heretics, modified his sources in order to present an idealized picture of a church without division, unified under the authority of the apostles.[2] According to Käsemann, Acts 18.24-28 is based on a tradition which recounted the exploits of Apollos, a noted freelance Christian missionary. In order to connect Apollos to the *una sancta apostolica*, Luke depicted him as deficient in understanding and in need of correction by Paul's associates. The denigration of Apollos was accomplished by the fabrication of 18.25c, a procedure suggested to Luke by the tradition underlying 19.1-7 which chronicled the conversion of members of the Baptist sect who 'knew only the baptism of John'.

---

1. Hill, *New Testament Prophecy*, pp. 96-97.
2. E. Käsemann, 'The Disciples of John the Baptist in Ephesus', in *Essays on New Testament Themes* (1964), pp. 136-48.

Luke heightened the parallels between Apollos and the disciples of the Baptist by transforming the latter into immature Christians. This transformation also enabled Luke to smooth over the rivalry which existed in the early days between the Baptist community and the church. Käsemann asserts that Acts 8.14-17 offers a parallel to this *Tendenz* in Luke's composition.

Käsemann's thesis has been criticized by, among others, Eduard Schweizer.[1] Pointing to Acts 15.39, 21.20, 21 and Luke's omission of any significant reference to Paul's collection for the Jerusalem church (11.27-30; 24.17; cf. Gal. 2.10), Schweizer challenges Käsemann's contention that Luke presents an idealized picture of the church unified under Jerusalem. Schweizer also questions Käsemann's treatment of Acts 8.14-17, 18.24-28 and 19.1-7. He insists that these pericopes— rather than reflecting a single theological *Tendenz*—have been shaped by a variety of factors. Acts 8.14-17 is the product of a conflation of two sources. The peculiar features of Acts 18.24-28 are explained as a case of misidentification. The original account related the conversion of a Jewish missionary. However, Luke misinterpreted τὴν ὁδὸν τοῦ κυρίου and ζέων τῷ πνεύματι as references to 'the teaching of *Jesus*' and 'the inspiration of the *Holy Spirit*', and thus erroneously presented Apollos as a Christian who simply received further instruction from Priscilla and Aquila. Schweizer notes that if Luke had intended to describe Apollos's incorporation into the *una sancta*, he would have had Paul baptize him. Schweizer acknowledges that in 19.1-7 Luke has transformed a Baptist group into immature Christians, nevertheless he insists that the error was inadvertent. The primary focus of the text is the displacement of water baptism by Spirit baptism. Thus Schweizer concludes that Luke is not interested in demonstrating that the individual churches in diverse locations form part of the *una sancta apostolica*. Luke's principal objective, reflected in these pericopes in varying degrees, is to emphasize the temporal continuity which characterizes salvation history as it moves from Judaism to Christianity.

Schweizer's criticism of Käsemann's thesis is telling. However, his own reconstruction of the tradition-history of Acts 18.24-28 and 19.1-7 is improbable.[2] Apollos is described as a Ἰουδαῖος, but this probably

---

1. E. Schweizer, 'Die Bekehrung des Apollos, Apg 18,24-26', in *Beiträge zur Theologie des Neuen Testaments: Neutestamentliche Aufsätze (1955–1970)* (1970), pp. 71-79.

2. Lüdemann, *Das frühe Christentum*, p. 216; Weiser, *Die Apostelgeschichte:*

indicates that he, like Aquila, was a Jewish Christian (18.2; cf. 10.28). This suggestion is supported by the fact that Paul knows nothing of a conversion of Apollos by Priscilla and Aquila (cf. 1 Cor. 1.12; 3.4-6, 22; 4.6; 16.12). Furthermore, the expression τὴν ὁδὸν τοῦ κυρίου, like much of the narrative, reflects Lukan style rather than a Jewish *Vorlage*. The phrase ἡ ὁδός is frequently used in Acts with reference to Christian belief and practice (9.2; 19.9, 23; 22.4; 24.14, 22), and κύριος naturally suggests the Lord Jesus. The phrase ζέων τῷ πνεύματι, whether Lukan or traditional, also suggests a Christian origin (cf. Rom. 12.11).

It appears that neither Käsemann nor Schweizer has presented a satisfactory explanation of the two accounts. Perhaps Luke has been more faithful to tradition and history than is often assumed. Both accounts have undoubtedly been significantly shaped by Luke, but this fact does not necessitate a negative assessment of the traditional and historical character of the essential elements in the narrative. It is not improbable that there existed, predominantly in Galilee, groups of former disciples of the Baptist who had come to believe in Jesus as the Coming One without receiving Christian baptism (i.e. in the name of Jesus) or instruction concerning the nature and availability of the Pentecostal gift.[1] This being the case, Luke's narrative is plausible: Apollos was converted by a member of such a group; and the twelve Ephesians were probably converted by Apollos. Luke relates the two accounts in order to retrace the origins of the church in Ephesus, the chief achievement of Paul's missionary career. Together, the two accounts emphasize that, while Apollos served as a precursor, Paul was the principal character in the establishment of the church in Ephesus. Although the Ephesians had come to believe in Jesus (presumably through the preaching of Apollos) before their encounter with Paul, it is Paul who persuades them to express their commitment to Jesus through Christian baptism and subsequently administers the rite. The baptismal rite, as the normal prerequisite for reception of the Spirit, leads to the climax of the second pericope: through the laying on of hands, Paul commissions the Ephesians as fellow-workers in the mission of the church and the twelve are thus endowed with the prophetic gift.[2]

Kapitel 13–28, p. 507; and Pesch, *Die Apostelgeschichte (Apg 13–28)*, p. 160.

1. Marshall, *Acts*, p. 304; Bruce, *Book of Acts*, pp. 381-82, and *New Testament History* (1982), p. 309; Beasley-Murray, *Baptism*, pp. 109-10; Hull, *Acts*, p. 112; Dunn, *Holy Spirit*, pp. 84-85.

2. For similar assessments see Lampe, *Seal*, pp. 75-76, and F. Pereira, *Ephesus:*

Two points emerge from this reconstruction which have a direct bearing on this inquiry into the nature of Luke's pneumatology and therefore deserve further examination: (1) the twelve Ephesians, like Apollos, were disciples of Jesus; (2) and, as a result of their encounter with Paul, they became his fellow-workers in the mission of the church. A number of factors suggest that Luke viewed Apollos and the twelve Ephesians as disciples of Jesus. Apollos's standing can hardly be questioned, for Luke indicates that he had been 'instructed in the way of the Lord' and ἐδίδασκεν ἀκριβῶς τὰ περὶ τοῦ Ἰησοῦ ('taught accurately about Jesus', 18.25). The former phrase indicates that, at the very least, Apollos was acquainted with the chief points of Jesus' ministry and teaching.[1] The latter phrase, descriptive of Paul's preaching in 28.31, suggests that Apollos preached the Christian gospel.[2] Moreover, Apollos's preaching was delivered under the inspiration of the Spirit (ζέων τῷ πνεύματι).[3] Since according to Luke the gift of the Spirit is not bound to the rite of baptism, there is no contradiction in his portrait of Apollos as a Spirit-inspired preacher who had not received Christian baptism. Similarly, Apollos's experience of the Spirit does not presuppose an awareness of the Pentecostal event or promise (cf. Lk. 1–2). Thus it does not preclude his contact with the Ephesian disciples, who had not heard of the availability of the Spirit. On the contrary, Luke has carefully constructed the narrative in order to emphasize the relationship between Apollos and the Ephesians (cf. 19.1), all of whom knew only 'the baptism of John' (18.25; 19.3).[4] The clear implication is that the twelve from Ephesus were converts of the inspired preacher active in the same city. It must therefore be concluded that in Luke's estimation

---

Climax of Universalism in Luke-Acts (1983), pp. 106-108.

1. C.K. Barrett, 'Apollos and the Twelve Disciples of Ephesus', in *The New Testament Age* (1984), p. 29; A.M. Hunter, 'Apollos the Alexandrian', in *Biblical Studies: Essays in Honour of William Barclay* (1976), p. 148.

2. Barrett, 'Apollos and the Twelve', p. 30. As Carson suggests, Apollos may have been aware of Jesus' death and resurrection (*Showing the Spirit*, p. 149).

3. See K. Aland, 'Zur Vorgeschichte der christlichen Taufe', in *Neues Testament und Geschichte* (1972), p. 6; Lampe, 'The Holy Spirit', p. 198; Beasley-Murray, *Baptism*, pp. 110-11; Giles, 'Church Order (Part 1)', p. 199.

4. The verb ἐπίσταμαι occurs frequently in Acts (10.28; 15.7; 18.25; 19.15, 25; 20.18; 22.19; 24.10; 26.26) and always with reference to factual knowledge rather than to religious commitment. Thus the phrase in Acts 18.25, ἐπιστάμενος μόνον τὸ βάπτισμα Ἰωάννου, simply indicates that Apollos's knowledge concerning baptismal practice was limited to the teaching of John the Baptist.

the Ephesians were, like Apollos, disciples of Jesus. This conclusion is supported by Luke's description of the Ephesians as μαθηταί (19.1), for when he employs the term without any further qualification it always refers to disciples of Jesus.¹ Moreover, since πίστις is the essence of discipleship,² the description of the Ephesians as 'believers' (19.2) confirms my findings.³

Several objections have been raised against the claim that Luke considered the Ephesians to be disciples of Jesus.

1. K. Haacker argues that 19.1-3, which contains one of the many cases of 'erlebter Rede' (interior monologue) in Luke–Acts, is written from the perspective of Paul and not reality as Luke perceived it: Paul initially *thought* that the Ephesians were 'disciples' and 'believers', but he quickly found that this was in fact not the case.⁴ Haacker's entire argument rests on the supposition that Luke could not conceive of 'disciples' or 'believers' as being without any knowledge of the Spirit. He rejects Acts 8.15-17 as a contradiction to this claim by insisting that 'there the conversion to Christianity is regarded as incomplete until the reception of the Spirit'.⁵ Yet, as I have already noted, Luke explicitly states that the Samaritans 'believed' (8.12) before they received the Spirit—the very point which Haacker must deny in order to put forth his 'erlebter Rede' thesis—and thus Haacker's argument falls to the ground.

2. J. Dunn also seeks to mitigate the force of Luke's description in 19.1-3. He asserts that Luke uses the relative pronoun (τινας) with μαθητής in 19.1 in order to highlight the Ephesians' lack of relation to the church in Ephesus: 'they are disciples, but they do not belong to *the* disciples'.⁶ However, since Luke uses the same pronoun in the singular with μαθητής in order to describe Ananias (Acts 9.10) and Timothy (Acts 16.1), we must reject this attempt to lessen the force of the phrase

1.   See Lk. 9.16, 18, 54; 10.23; 16.1; 17.22; 18.15; 19.29, 37; 20.45; 22.39, 45; Acts 6.1, 2, 7; 9.10, 19, 26, 38; 11.26, 29; 13.52; 14.20, 22, 28; 15.10; 16.1; 18.23, 27; 19.1, 9, 30; 20.1, 30; 21.4, 16. K. Haacker, 'Einige Fälle von "erlebter Rede" im Neuen Testament', *NovT* 12 (1970), p. 75: 'Der absolut Gebrauch von μαθητής wird von allen Auslegern als eine Bezeichnung für Christen erkannt'.

2.   See K.H. Rengstorf, 'μαθητής', *TDNT*, IV, p. 447.

3.   F.F. Bruce, *Commentary on the Book of Acts* (1984), p. 385.

4.   K. Haacker, 'Einige Fälle von "erlebter Rede" im Neuen Testament', *NovT* 12 (1970), pp. 70-77.

5.   Haacker, 'Erlebter Rede', p. 75. ET is my own.

6.   Dunn, *Holy Spirit*, pp. 84-85; quote from p. 85 (emphasis his).

in 19.1. Dunn also insists that Paul's question in 19.2 is 'one of suspicion and surprise': the Ephesians claimed to be men of faith, but Paul queries whether or not their claim is valid.[1] Dunn's argument at this point is based on the observation that the Paul of the epistles could not countenance the idea of 'believers' being without the Spirit (Rom. 8.9; 1 Cor. 12.3; Gal. 3.2; 1 Thess. 1.5-6; Tit. 3.5). However, this objection fails to take into account the fact that the narrative as it currently exists (particularly vv. 2-4) has been significantly shaped by Luke. The dialogue between Paul and the Ephesians is a Lukan construction[2] which highlights the Ephesians' need of the Spirit's enablement and its normal prerequisite, Christian baptism. Paul would undoubtedly have related the story differently,[3] for the potential separation of belief from reception of the Spirit *simpliciter* is presupposed by the question, 'Did you receive the Holy Spirit when you believed' (εἰ πνεῦμα ἅγιον ἐλάβετε πιστεύσαντες, 19.2)?

3. J.K. Parratt maintains that the Ephesians had heard the preaching of John second-hand and therefore, although they had received 'the baptism of John', they had not understood its full significance.[4] The thesis is based on Acts 19.4, where Paul recounts the significance of the Johannine rite. Parratt insists that only after Paul's instruction do the Ephesians comprehend that John had proclaimed repentance and faith in Jesus as Messiah. Having grasped the truth at last, the Ephesians are baptized. However, in view of the prior references to the Ephesians as 'disciples' and 'believers', it is unlikely that 19.4 ('that is, in Jesus') represents teaching of which the Ephesians were hitherto unaware. Rather, the verse should be seen as a summation of Paul's argument for the appropriateness and necessity of baptism in the name of Jesus, an argument which builds on what the Ephesians already knew: the Coming One which John proclaimed is Jesus.[5] For this reason Luke does not say, 'they believed and were baptized' (8.12, 13; 18.8; cf. 2.41; 16.14-15, 33-34); he simply states: ἀκούσαντες δὲ ἐβαπτίσθησαν εἰς

1. Dunn, *Holy Spirit*, p. 86. See also C.B. Kaiser, 'The "Rebaptism" of the Ephesian Twelve: Exegetical Study on Acts 19:1-7', *RefR* 31 (1977-78), p. 59.

2. Weiser, *Die Apostelgeschichte: Kapitel 13-28*, p. 513.

3. Perhaps Luke has compressed a more lengthy traditional account of the event. In any event, we need not question the essential features of Luke's account: he simply tells the story from his own theological perspective.

4. J.K. Parratt, 'The Rebaptism of the Ephesian Disciples', *ExpTim* 79 (1967-68), pp. 182-83.

5. Büchsel, *Geist Gottes*, p. 142 (n. 6 from p. 141).

τὸ ὄνομα τοῦ κυρίου Ἰησοῦ ('On hearing this, they were baptized into the name of the Lord Jesus', 19.5). Parratt's thesis, like that of Haacker and Dunn, must be rejected in view of the evidence. My conclusion that Luke viewed the Ephesians as disciples of Jesus is sustained.

This conclusion has significant implications for this inquiry into Luke's pneumatology, for it supports my contention that Luke does not view the gift of the Spirit as a necessary element in conversion. In Luke's perspective, conversion centers on God's gracious act of forgiveness (e.g. Acts 5.31-32; 10.43).[1] And, although faith-repentance and water baptism are usually closely linked, in terms of human response, faith-repentance is the decisive element in conversion,[2] for it forms the sole prerequisite for receiving the forgiveness of God (Lk. 5.20; 24.47; Acts 3.19; 5.31; 10.43; 13.38; 26.18).[3] Therefore, since forgiveness is given to faith, and Luke considered the Ephesians to be people of faith (disciples and believers) *before* they received the gift of the Spirit, he cannot have considered the gift to be the means by which God granted forgiveness to the Ephesians. In short, Luke separates the conversion (forgiveness granted in response to faith) of the twelve Ephesians from their reception of the Spirit.

This judgment, coupled with the prophetic manifestations associated with the Ephesians' reception of the Spirit (19.6, ἐλάλουν τε γλώσσαις καὶ ἐπροφήτευον),[4] indicates that Luke viewed the gift as a prophetic endowment granted to the converted. Furthermore, the association of the gift with the laying on of hands suggests that, according to Luke, the prophetic gift enabled the Ephesians to participate effectively in the mission of the church. The bestowal of the Spirit is God's response to Paul's incorporation of the Ephesians into the missionary enterprise of the church (accomplished through the laying on of hands). The

1. Marshall, *Luke: Historian and Theologian*, p. 169.
2. Dunn, *Holy Spirit*, pp. 96-98.
3. Dunn notes that whereas water baptism is never spoken of as the sole prerequisite to receiving forgiveness, Luke frequently speaks of repentance or faith as the sole prerequisite (*Holy Spirit*, p. 97).
4. The term ἐλάλουν τε γλώσσαις denotes unintelligible inspired speech and, in Luke's perspective, constitutes a special type of prophecy (see also Acts 2.17). Nevertheless, since προφητεύω designates a broad range of speech activity embracing both intelligible (cf. Lk. 1.67) and unintelligible inspired speech, the two terms should not be simply equated (so also Schneider, *Die Apostelgeschichte II. Teil*, p. 264). In this instance ἐπροφήτευον may imply that additional forms of inspired speech (intelligible) accompanied the manifestation of tongues-speech.

prophetic gift enables the Ephesians, like the Samaritans and Paul, to fulfill the task for which they have been commissioned and, in the prophetic manifestations which it inspires, it provides a sign that the twelve are members of the prophetic community.

My analysis is substantiated by the way in which Luke highlights the strategic role played by the Ephesian disciples in the missionary enterprise. The disciples remain in close company with Paul in Ephesus (19.9, 30; 20.1)[1] and were undoubtedly active in the remarkable missionary effort which took place during the two years Paul remained in Ephesus (19.10). In view of the charge given in 20.28, we may assume that the Ephesian twelve formed, at the very least, part of 'the elders of the church' in Ephesus (20.17) who traveled to Miletus to hear Paul's farewell address.[2] The charge itself, 'keep watch over…the flock of which the Holy Spirit has made you overseers' (v. 28), suggests that the Spirit came upon the Ephesian twelve (19.6) in order to equip them for the task which lay ahead—a task which in their case included sustaining the work in the region of Ephesus that Paul had initiated.

Therefore Luke's perspective is that the gift of the Spirit received by the Ephesians was of the same character as the gift received by the Samaritans, Paul, the household of Cornelius, and the disciples in Jerusalem on the day of Pentecost. In each instance the Spirit comes upon the individual or group as a prophetic endowment enabling the recipient(s) to participate effectively in the mission which has been entrusted to the prophetic people of God.

1.   Pereira, *Ephesus*, p. 112.
2.   This suggestion is supported by the fact that Paul addresses the elders from Ephesus 'as those first converted, who have been with Paul from the first day' (Haenchen, *Acts*, p. 590; see 20.18). It is also possible that the reference in 19.7 to the number of disciples being about twelve (ὡσεὶ δώδεκα) is Luke's way of emphasizing that these men formed the nucleus of the church in Ephesus.

CONCLUSION

This analysis of Luke–Acts has revealed that Luke consistently portrays the gift of the Spirit as a prophetic endowment which enables its recipient to fulfill a divinely ordained task. From the very outset of his two-volume work, Luke emphasizes the prophetic dimension of the Spirit's activity. The profusion of Spirit-inspired pronouncements in the infancy narratives herald the arrival of the era of fulfillment (Lk. 1.41-42, 67-79; 2.25-26). This era is marked by the prophetic activity of John, the ministry of Jesus, and the mission of his church, all of which are carried out in the power of the Spirit. Filled with the Spirit from his mother's womb (Lk. 1.15, 17), John anticipates the inauguration of Jesus' ministry. By carefully crafting his narrative, Luke ties his account of Jesus' pneumatic anointing (Lk. 3.22) together with Jesus' dramatic announcement at Nazareth (Lk. 4.18-19), and thus indicates that the Spirit came upon Jesus at the Jordan in order to equip him for his task as messianic herald. Literary parallels between the description of Jesus' anointing at the Jordan and that of the disciples at Pentecost suggest that Luke interpreted the latter event in light of the former: the Spirit came upon the disciples at Pentecost to equip them for their prophetic vocation. This judgment is supported by the Baptist's prophecy concerning the coming baptism of Spirit and fire (Lk. 3.16), for Luke interprets the sifting activity of the Spirit of which John prophesied as being accomplished in the Spirit-directed and Spirit-empowered mission of the church (Acts 1.5, 8). It is confirmed by Luke's narration of the Pentecost event (Acts 2.1-13), his interpretation of this event in light of his slightly modified version of Joel 3.1-5a (LXX), and his subsequent description of the church as a prophetic community empowered by the Spirit. Whether it be John in his mother's womb, Jesus at the Jordan, or the disciples at Pentecost, the Spirit comes upon them all as the source of prophetic inspiration, granting special insight and inspiring speech.

The distinctive character of Luke's prophetic pneumatology is particularly evident in his modification of primitive church tradition. Luke's nuanced use of δύναμις, particularly his integration of the term into the tradition of Jesus' birth by the Spirit, his omission of the phrase, ἰάσασθαι τοὺς συντετριμμένους τῇ καρδίᾳ, from the quotation of Isa. 61.1-2 (LXX) in Lk. 4.18-19, and his redaction of the Beelzebub Controversy tradition (Lk. 11.20; 12.10), all reflect his conviction that the activity of the Spirit is inextricably related to prophetic inspiration. Whereas the primitive church, following in the footsteps of Jesus, broadened the functions traditionally ascribed to the Spirit in first-century Judaism and thus presented the Spirit as the source of miracle-working power, Luke retained the traditional Jewish understanding of the Spirit as the source of special insight and inspired speech.

Luke, in accordance with the primitive church, does not present reception of the Spirit as necessary for one to enter into and remain with the community of salvation. Thus, in Luke's perspective, the disciples receive the Spirit, not as the source of cleansing and a new ability to keep the law, nor as the essential bond by which they (each individual) are linked to God, not even as a foretaste of the salvation to come; rather, the disciples receive the Spirit as a prophetic *donum superadditum* which enables them to participate effectively in the missionary enterprise of the church. As such, the gift of the Spirit is received principally for the benefit of others.

Therefore, with reference to pneumatology, Luke has more in common with the primitive church than with Paul or later Christian writers who reflect contact with Paul's perspective on the soteriological dimension of the Spirit's work (e.g. John and some of the Apostolic Fathers).[1] This fact, coupled with the Jewish nature of Luke's pneumatology, suggests that Luke–Acts was written at a relatively early date (AD 70–80). This judgment is also supported by the enthusiastic character of Luke's pneumatology. Far from representing an 'early catholic' perspective and institutionalizing the Spirit, in Luke's perspective the Spirit, frequently bestowed sovereignly by God or by figures outside of the apostolic circle, transforms the entire Christian community into a band of prophets.

Luke also anticipated that the prophetic Spirit would inspire the church of his day (Lk. 11.13; 12.10-12; Acts 2.38-39), as it had the church of the past (e.g. Acts 2.4). In light of this fact, I would suggest that one of the reasons Luke wrote was to offer theological and

---

1. See for example *2 Clem.* 14.3-5; *Ign. Eph.* 9.1; *Polycarp* 14.2; *Barn.* 11.11; 19.7; *Shepherd of Hermas* 1.3-5; 6.5-7.

methodological direction for the ongoing Christian mission. This thesis explains Luke's emphasis on the validity of the mission to the Gentiles, and the necessity of the Spirit's enabling.

Part III

THE SIGNIFICANCE OF LUKE'S PNEUMATOLOGY:
A PENTECOSTAL PERSPECTIVE

INTRODUCTION

The evidence I have presented challenges on assumption that has guided much of the modern discussion concerning the pneumatology of the early church, and particularly that of Luke. Most scholars have assumed that the early church, from its earliest days, uniformly viewed the Spirit as the source of Christian existence. My analysis suggests, however, that this was not the case: the pneumatology of the early church was not as homogeneous as most of the major post-Gunkel studies have maintained. Luke in particular represents a distinctive voice. Luke not only fails to refer to the soteriological aspects of the Spirit's work so prominent in the epistles of Paul, his narrative presupposes a pneumatology which excludes this dimension. Rather than presenting the Spirit as the source of Christian existence, Luke consistently portrays the Spirit as the source of prophetic inspiration.

This conclusion is not without significance for contemporary theological reflection and spiritual life. It is especially relevant for those wrestling with questions generated by the rise of the Pentecostal movement. Two issues in particular come to mind. Classical Pentecostals have long affirmed a baptism in the Holy Spirit (Acts 1.5; 2.4) 'distinct from and subsequent to' conversion, and that glossolalia is the 'initial physical evidence' of this experience.[1] These two affirmations concerning Spirit-baptism have generated considerable discussion and controversy. Yet much of the discussion has been predicated on the faulty assumption alluded to above. How does my reassessment of the character of early Christian pneumatology impact this discussion? More specifically, what are the implications of Luke's distinctive pneumatology for these tenets of Pentecostal doctrine? In the following two chapters I will seek to answer these questions. Chapter 12 focuses on the issue of 'subsequence' and dialogues with relevant portions of Gordon Fee's recent book,

---

1. *Minutes of the 44th Session of the General Council of the Assemblies of God* (Portland, Oregon, 6–11 August 1991), pp. 129-30.

Gospel and Spirit.[1] Chapter 13 centers on the 'initial evidence' question and interacts with various articles from the book edited by Gary McGee, *Initial Evidence.*[2]

---

1.   G.D. Fee, *Gospel and Spirit: Issues in New Testament Hermeneutics* (1991).
2.   G. McGee (ed.), *Initial Evidence: Historical and Biblical Perspectives on the Pentecostal Doctrine of Spirit Baptism* (1991).

Chapter 12

THE ISSUE OF SUBSEQUENCE

From the earliest days of the modern Pentecostal revival, Pentecostals have proclaimed that all Christians may, and indeed should, experience a baptism of the Holy Spirit 'distinct from and subsequent to the experience of new birth'.[1] This doctrine of subsequence flowed naturally from the conviction that the Spirit came upon the disciples at Pentecost (Acts 2), not as the source of new covenant existence, but rather as the source of power for effective witness. Although prominent Christian thinkers such as R.A. Torrey and A.J. Gordon also advocated a baptism of the Spirit subsequent to conversion, more recent biblical theologians have largely rejected the doctrine of subsequence, particularly in its Pentecostal form. Influenced largely by James Dunn's seminal work, *Baptism in the Holy Spirit*, non-Pentecostals have commonly equated the baptism of the Holy Spirit with conversion. Non-Pentecostals thus view Spirit-baptism as the *sine qua non* of Christian existence, the essential element in conversion-initiation.[2]

Although for years Pentecostals and non-Pentecostals were entrenched in their respective positions and seldom entered into dialogue, since 1970 this situation has changed dramatically. James Dunn's sympathetic but critical assessment of Pentecostal doctrine (alluded to above) marks a watershed in Pentecostal thinking, for it stimulated a burst of creative theological reflection by Pentecostals. As a result, the theological terrain of today is considerably different from that of 20 years ago. Yet, in spite of significant changes, the issue of subsequence still remains high on today's theological agenda. This fact is reflected in Gordon Fee's most

---

1. *Minutes of the 44th Session of the General Council of the Assemblies of God*, p. 129.

2. Although Pentecostals represent a diverse community, I shall distinguish between Pentecostals as those who affirm a baptism in the Spirit subsequent to conversion and non-Pentecostals as those who do not subscribe to this view.

recent book, *Gospel and Spirit*, which contains two (previously published but updated) articles featuring this issue.[1] A Pentecostal minister and noted biblical scholar, Fee has been an active and influential participant in the post-Dunn Pentecostal–Evangelical dialogue. While he speaks from inside the Pentecostal tradition, his viewpoint generally reflects prevailing Evangelical attitudes. I offer the following evaluation of Fee's position on the doctrine of subsequence with the hope that it might highlight the major issues in the discussion. Specifically, I will argue that Fee's discussion ignores important developments in New Testament and Pentecostal scholarship, and that when these developments are taken into consideration, Luke's intention to teach a baptism in the Spirit distinct from (at least logically if not chronologically) conversion for every believer—the essence of the doctrine of subsequence—is easily demonstrated.

1. *Fee's Critique of the Pentecostal Position*

Fee has established a reputation for acumen in the area of hermeneutics, and his sympathetic critique of the Pentecostal doctrine of subsequence focuses on shortcomings in this area. He notes that Pentecostals generally support their claim that Spirit-baptism is distinct from conversion by appealing to various episodes recorded in the book of Acts. This approach, in its most common form, appeals to the experience of the Samaritans (Acts 8), Paul (Acts 9) and the Ephesians (Acts 19) as a normative model for all Christians. But Fee, following the lead of many non-Pentecostals, maintains that this line of argumentation rests on a shaky hermeneutical foundation. The fundamental flaw in the Pentecostal approach is their failure to appreciate the genre of the book of Acts: Acts is a description of historical events. Unless we are prepared to choose church leaders by the casting of lots, or are willing to encourage church members to sell all of their possessions, we cannot simply assume that a particular historical narrative provides a basis for normative theology. Fee's concern is a legitimate one: how do we distinguish between those aspects of Luke's narrative that are normative and those that are not?

---

1. Fee, *Gospel and Spirit*. Chapters 6 and 7 are updated versions of the following articles: 'Hermeneutics and Historical Precedent—A Major Problem in Pentecostal Hermeneutics', in *Perspectives on the New Pentecostalism* (1976), pp. 118-32; 'Baptism in the Holy Spirit: The Issue of Separability and Subsequence', *Pneuma* 7 (1985), pp. 87-99.

Fee's answer is that historical precedent, if it is 'to have normative value, must be related to intent'.[1] That is to say, Pentecostals must demonstrate that Luke *intended* the various oft-cited episodes in Acts to establish a precedent for future Christians. Otherwise, Pentecostals may not legitimately speak of a Spirit-baptism distinct from conversion that is in any sense normative for the church. According to Fee, this is exactly where the Pentecostal position fails.

Fee describes two kinds of arguments offered by Pentecostals: arguments from biblical analogy; and arguments from biblical precedent. Arguments from biblical analogy point to Jesus' experience at the Jordan (subsequent to his miraculous birth by the Spirit) and the disciples' experience at Pentecost (subsequent to Jn 20.22) as normative models of Christian experience. Yet these arguments, as all arguments from biblical analogy, are problematic because 'it can seldom be demonstrated that our analogies are intentional in the biblical text itself'.[2] These purported analogies are particularly problematic, for the experiences of Jesus and the apostles—coming as they do prior to 'the great line of demarcation', the day of Pentecost—'are of such a different kind from succeeding Christian experience that they can scarcely have normative value'.[3]

Arguments from biblical precedent seek to find a normative pattern of Christian experience in the experience of the Samaritans, Paul and the Ephesians. Fee asserts that these arguments also fail to convince because it cannot be demonstrated that Luke intended to present in these narratives a normative model. The problem here is twofold. First, the evidence is not uniform: however we view the experience of the Samaritans and the Ephesians, Cornelius and his household (Acts 10) appear to receive the Spirit as they are converted. Secondly, even when subsequence can be demonstrated, as with the Samaritans in Acts 8, it is doubtful whether this can be linked to Luke's intent. Fee suggests that Luke's primary intent was to validate the experience of the Christians as the gospel spread beyond Jerusalem.[4]

This leads Fee to reject the traditional Pentecostal position. He concludes, a baptism in the Spirit distinct from conversion and intended for empowering is 'neither clearly taught in the New Testament nor

1. Fee, *Gospel and Spirit*, p. 92.
2. Fee, *Gospel and Spirit*, p. 108.
3. Fee, *Gospel and Spirit*, p. 94.
4. Fee, *Gospel and Spirit*, p. 97.

necessarily to be seen as a normative pattern (let alone the only pattern) for Christian experience'.[1] Yet this rejection of subsequence is, according to Fee, really of little consequence, for the central truth which marks Pentecostalism is its emphasis on the dynamic, powerful character of experience of the Spirit. Whether the Spirit's powerful presence is experienced at conversion or after is ultimately irrelevant, and to insist that all must go 'one route' is to say more than the New Testament allows.[2] In short, Fee maintains that although Pentecostals need to reformulate their theology, their experience is valid.

Before we move to an assessment of Fee's position, two points need to be made. First, although Fee suggests that his critique of subsequence does not impact the essentials of Pentecostalism, this claim is questionable. It should be noted that Fee's position is theologically indistinguishable from that of many other non-Pentecostal scholars, James Dunn in particular. His essential message is that Pentecostals have, in terms of theology, nothing new to offer the broader Christian world. While Pentecostal fervor serves as a reminder that Christian experience has a dynamic, powerful dimension, the theology which gives definition and expectation to this dimension is rejected. Furthermore, Fee's critique does not simply call into question the Pentecostal understanding of the timing of Spirit-baptism (i.e. whether it is experienced simultaneously with or after conversion), but it challenges the Pentecostal understanding of this experience at its deepest level.

The central issue is whether or not Spirit-baptism in the Pentecostal sense (Acts 2) can be equated with conversion. Non-Pentecostals affirm that the two are one, and Fee agrees, although he acknowledges that the dynamic, charismatic character of the experience (for a variety of reasons) in our modern context is often lacking. Fee's affirmation, qualified as it is, still undercuts crucial aspects of Pentecostal theology. Pentecostals, as I have noted, have generally affirmed that the purpose of Spirit-baptism is to empower believers so that they might be effective witnesses. This missiological understanding of Spirit-baptism, rooted in the Pentecost account of Acts 1–2, gives important definition to the experience. In contrast to Fee's vague descriptions of Spirit-baptism as 'dynamic', 'powerful' or even 'charismatic', Pentecostals have articulated a clear purpose: power for mission. When the Pentecostal gift is confused with conversion, this missiological (and I would add, Lukan) focus is lost.

1. Fee, *Gospel and Spirit*, p. 98.
2. Fee, *Gospel and Spirit*, p. 111.

Pentecostalism becomes Christianity with fervor (whatever that means?) rather than Christianity empowered for mission. Furthermore, this blurring of focus inevitably diminishes one's sense of expectation. For it is always possible to argue, as most non-Pentecostals do, that while all experience the soteriological dimension of the Pentecostal gift at conversion, only a select few receive gifts of missiological power. Fee's effort to retain a sense of expectation—though rejecting the distinction between Spirit-baptism and conversion—fails at this point.

The bottom-line is this: if Fee is right, Pentecostals can no longer proclaim an enabling of the Spirit which is distinct from conversion and available to every believer, at least not with the same sense of expectation, nor can Pentecostals maintain that the principle purpose of this gift is to grant power for the task of mission. To sum up, the doctrine of subsequence articulates a conviction crucial for Pentecostal theology and practice: Spirit-baptism, in the Pentecostal sense, is distinct from (at least logically, if not chronologically) conversion. This conviction, I would add, is integral to Pentecostalism's continued sense of expectation and effectiveness in mission.

A second point is also imperative to note. Although Fee focuses our attention on an important issue, the nature of Luke's theological intent, his critique is based on a fundamental presupposition. Fee repeatedly states that 'in the New Testament the presence of the Spirit was the chief element of Christian conversion'.[1] Indeed, Fee declares, 'what we must understand is that the Spirit was the chief element, the primary ingredient', of new covenant existence.[2] This is Paul's perspective *and also Luke's as well*! Fee confidently writes, 'on this analysis of things, it seems to me, all New Testament scholars would be in general agreement'.[3] Thus, in reality, Fee's article raises two important questions: first, did Luke intend for us to understand Spirit-baptism to be a gift distinct from conversion, granting power for effective witness, and available to every believer? And secondly, is it true that the the New Testament writers uniformly present the gift of the Spirit as the chief element of conversion-initiation? The remaining portion of this essay will seek to address these questions. I shall begin with the latter question, since this touches upon a presupposition fundamental to Fee's argument.

---

1. Fee, *Gospel and Spirit*, p. 98. See also pp. 94, 98, 109-17.
2. Fee, *Gospel and Spirit*, p. 114.
3. Fee, *Gospel and Spirit*, p. 115.

2. *The New Context: Defining the Crucial Issue*

As noted above, Fee's critique of the Pentecostal position centers on hermeneutical flaws, particularly the use of historical precedent as a basis for establishing normative theology. Fee skillfully demonstrates the weaknesses inherent in traditional Pentecostal arguments based on facile analogies or selected episodes from Acts. Here, we hear an echo of James Dunn's timely critique of arguments for subsequence based on a conflation of Jn 20.22 with Luke's narrative in Acts.[1] When originally published Fee's articles, painful though they might have been, served a valuable purpose: they challenged Pentecostals to come to terms with the new and pressing questions raised by their non-Pentecostal brothers. These questions were all the more urgent in view of the rapid assimilation of the Pentecostal movement in North America into mainstream Evangelicalism, a process which by the mid-70s was largely complete. Perhaps because of his position as an 'insider', Fee was thus able to give voice to a much needed message: no longer could Pentecostals rely on the interpretative methods of the nineteenth century holiness movement and expect to speak to the contemporary church world—a world which, with increasing vigor, was shaping the ethos of Pentecostalism.

Yet the theological landscape which Fee surveyed in the mid-70s and 80s has changed considerably. Simplistic arguments from historical precedent, though once the bulwark of Pentecostal theology, have been replaced with approaches that speak the language of modern hermeneutics. Although perhaps this is not entirely true when it comes to the question of tongues as initial evidence, it is certainly the case for the doctrine of subsequence. Roger Stronstad's *The Charismatic Theology of St. Luke* illustrates this fact. Published in 1984, it marks a key shift in Pentecostal thinking. Stronstad's central thesis is that Luke is a theologian *in his own right* and that his perspective on the Spirit is different from—although complementary to—that of Paul. My own study of Luke's pneumatology corroborates the findings of Stronstad. In previous chapters I have argued that unlike Paul, who frequently speaks of the soteriological dimension of the Spirit's work, Luke never attributes soteriological functions to the Spirit. Furthermore, his narrative presupposes a pneumatology which excludes this dimension (e.g. Lk. 11.13; Acts 8.4-17; 19.1-7). To put it positively, Luke describes the

---

1. Dunn, *Holy Spirit*, p. 39.

gift of the Spirit *exclusively* in charismatic (or, more specifically, in prophetic terms) as the source of power for effective witness. Luke's narrative, then, reflects more than simply a different agenda or emphasis: Luke's pneumatology is *different* from—although *complementary* to—that of Paul.

I have already analyzed the evidence which I believe substantiates this description of Luke's pneumatology, and I need not repeat the data here. Nevertheless, I would like to show how this assessment of Luke's pneumatology provides a biblical foundation for the doctrine of subsequence.

From a biblical perspective, the key question is: What is the nature of the Pentecostal gift (Acts 2)? As I have noted, it is abundantly clear that Luke *intended* his readers to understand that this gift (whatever its nature) was available to (and indeed, should be experienced by) everyone. Fee and virtually all non-Pentecostals assert that this gift is the chief element of conversion-initiation. Although most non-Pentecostals acknowledge that divine enabling is prominent in the narrative, this aspect of Luke's account is generally regarded as a reflection of his special emphasis. It is assumed that Luke and Paul shared essentially the same pneumatological perspective, and thus broader, soteriological dimensions of the Spirit's work are also understood to be present. The universal character of the Pentecostal gift is then easily explained: all should experience the gift because it is the means by which the blessings of the new covenant are mediated.

However, the description of Luke's pneumatology outlined above challenges this non-Pentecostal assessment of the Pentecostal gift. For if Luke views the gift of the Spirit exclusively in prophetic terms, then it is not possible to associate the Pentecostal gift with conversion or salvation. Indeed, by placing the Pentecost account within the framework of Luke's distinctive theology of the Spirit, Pentecostals are able to argue with considerable force that the Spirit came upon the disciples at Pentecost, not as the source of new covenant existence, but rather as the source of power for effective witness. And since the Pentecostal gift is prophetic rather than soteriological in character, it must be distinguished from the gift of the Spirit which Paul associates with conversion-initiation. Here, then, is a strong argument for a doctrine of subsequence—that is, that Spirit-baptism (in the Pentecostal or Lukan sense) is logically distinct from conversion. The logical distinction between conversion and Spirit-baptism is a reflection of Luke's distinctive theology of the Spirit.

Note that this argument is not based on biblical analogy or historical precedent. It does not seek to demonstrate that the disciples had received the Spirit, at least from Luke's perspective, prior to Pentecost. Nor is it dependent on isolated passages from the book of Acts. Rather, drawing from the full scope of Luke's two-volume work, it focuses on the nature of Luke's pneumatology and, from this framework, seeks to understand the character of the Pentecostal gift. The judgment that the gift is distinct from conversion is rooted in the gift's function: it provides power for witness, not justification or cleansing. The universal character of the gift established in Luke's narrative rather than historical precedent is the basis for its normative character.

All of this indicates that Fee's critique of Pentecostal hermeneutics, focused as it is on naive appeals to historical precedent, fails to address today's crucial question: Does Luke, in a manner similar to Paul, present the Spirit as the source of new covenant existence? Fee, as I have noted, assumes this to be the case, and confidently declares that on this point 'all New Testament scholars' would agree. Yet this confident statement, quite apart from my own study, ignores a significant group of New Testament scholars. Over a century ago Herman Gunkel reached very different conclusions; and he has been followed in more recent years by E. Schweizer, D. Hill, G. Haya-Prats and M. Turner, all of whom have written works which highlight the distinctive character of Luke's pneumatology.[1] The real issue centers not on hermeneutics and historical precedent, but rather on exegesis and the nature of Luke's pneumatology.

The question of Luke's intent, which looms so large in Fee's argument, is clearly subordinate to the more fundamental question outlined above. For if my description of Luke's 'distinctive' pneumatology is accurate, then Luke's intent to teach a Spirit-baptism distinct from conversion for empowering is easily demonstrated. One need only establish that Luke's narrative was designed to encourage every Christian to receive the Pentecostal gift. And, since Luke highlights Pentecost as a fulfillment of Joel's prophecy concerning an outpouring of the Spirit upon 'all flesh' (Acts 2.17-21), this appears to be self-evident. According to Luke the community of faith is, at least potentially, a community of

---

1. Gunkel, *Die Wirkungen*; Schweizer, 'πνεῦμα'; Hill, *Greek Words*; Haya-Prats, *Force*; and Turner, 'Luke and the Spirit'.

prophets; and it was his expectation that this potential would be realized in the church of his day as it had been in the past (Lk. 3.16; 11.13; 2.38-39).

3. Luke's Distinctive Pneumatology: A Response to Evangelical Objections

In his failure to address today's crucial issue, Fee does not stand alone. Two commonly held presuppositions have inhibited many Evangelical non-Pentecostals from considering the distinctive character of Luke's pneumatology. The first presupposition is associated with the inspiration of Scripture, the second stems from the conviction held by most Evangelicals that Luke traveled with Paul. I shall address the theological objection first, and then move to the historical one.

It is often assumed that since the Holy Spirit inspired each of the various New Testament authors, they must all speak with one voice. That is to say, each biblical author must share the same theological perspective. Thus to speak of Luke's distinctive pneumatology is to question the divine and authoritative character of Scripture.

Yet does an Evangelical or conservative view of Scripture demand such a view? In his helpful article, 'An Evangelical approach to "Theological Criticism"', I. Howard Marshall points out that a conservative doctrine of Scripture assumes that 'Scripture as a whole is harmonious'.[1] However, he notes that this assumption does not rule out theological differences between various biblical authors. Rather, it suggests that the differences which do exist are 'differences in harmonious development rather than irreconcilable contradictions'.[2] I would suggest therefore that a high view of Scripture demands, not that Luke and Paul have the same pneumatological perspective, but rather that Luke's distinctive pneumatology is ultimately reconcilable with that of Paul, and that both perspectives can be seen as contributing to a process of harmonious development.

It is imperative to note that when I speak of Luke's distinctive pneumatology I am not asserting that Luke's perspective is irreconcilable with that of Paul. On the contrary, I would suggest that the pneumatologies of Luke and Paul are different but compatible; and the

---

1. I.H. Marshall, 'An Evangelical Approach to "Theological Criticism"', *Themelios* 13 (1988), p. 81.
2. Marshall, 'Theological Criticism', p. 83.

differences should not be blurred, for both perspectives offer valuable insight into the dynamic work of the Holy Spirit. Clearly Paul has the more developed view for he sees the full richness of the Spirit's work. He helps us understand that the Spirit is the source of the Christian's cleansing (1 Cor. 6.11; Rom. 15.16), righteousness (Gal. 5.5, 16-26; Rom. 2.29, 8.1-17, 14.17) and intimate fellowship with God (Gal. 4.6; Rom. 8.14-17), as well as the source of power for mission (Rom. 15.18-19; Phil. 1.18-19). Paul attests to both the soteriological and the prophetic (as well as charismatic) dimensions of the Spirit's work. Luke's perspective is less developed and more limited. He bears witness solely to the prophetic dimension of the Spirit's work, and thus he gives us a glimpse of only a part of Paul's fuller view. Nevertheless, Luke, like Paul, has an important contribution to make. He calls us to recognize that the church, by virtue of its reception of the Pentecostal gift, is a prophetic community empowered for a missionary task. In short, not only are the pneumatological perspectives of Luke and Paul compatible, they are complementary: both represent important contributions to a holistic and harmonious biblical theology of the Spirit.

This leads us to another important point: if the differences between the perspectives of Luke and Paul are not recognized, the full richness of the biblical testimony cannot be grasped. This is why it is tragic when, in the name of biblical inspiration, legitimate theological diversity within the canon is repudiated. We must examine the biblical texts and be sensitive to the theological diversity which exists, for harmonization, when foisted upon the text, exacts a heavy price. In the case of Luke and Paul, that price is biblical support for a Pentecostal position on Spirit-baptism.

Evangelicals usually identify Luke as one who traveled with Paul. This being the case, it is understandable that some might be inclined to question whether Luke's pneumatology really could be different from Paul's. Would it have been possible for Luke to remain uninfluenced by the Apostle's soteriological perspective on the Spirit?

I would suggest that a thorough examination of Luke–Acts reveals this is precisely what happened. Several factors indicate that this conclusion should not surprise us even though Luke, as the traveling companion of Paul, probably spent a considerable amount of time with the apostle. First, it is generally recognized that Luke was not acquainted with any of Paul's epistles.[1] Thus Luke's contact with Paul's theology

---

1. M. Hengel, *Acts*, pp. 66-67; J.C. O'Neill, *The Theology of Acts in its Historical Setting* (1970), p. 135; C.K. Barrett, 'Acts and the Pauline Corpus',

was probably limited to personal conversation or secondary (oral or written) sources. It is also quite probable that Luke did not know Paul's epistles because they were not yet widely accessible or recognized in non-Pauline sectors of the church. This suggests that Paul's perspective had not yet significantly influenced these broader, non-Pauline elements of the early church.

Secondly, since other aspects of Paul's theology have not significantly influenced Luke, my suggestion is all the more credible. One example of Luke's theological independence from Paul (that is, that he does not slavishly imitate Paul) may be found in his rationale for salvation. While Luke emphasizes that salvation is found in Jesus because he is Lord and Messiah, he does not develop in a manner like Paul the full implications of the cross as the means of salvation.[1] Again we see that the perspectives of Luke and Paul complement one another: together they lead us into a deeper and fuller understanding of truth.

Thirdly, Luke's summaries of Paul's preaching—generally viewed as accurate representations of Paul's gospel by those who affirm that Luke traveled with Paul—do not contain any traces of Paul's soteriological pneumatology. This indicates that if, as is most probably the case, Luke heard Paul preach or entered into discussions with the apostle and thereby came to an accurate understanding of his gospel, it is entirely possible, indeed probable, that he did so without coming to terms with Paul's fuller pneumatological perspective.

These points are offered as a challenge to let the text of Luke–Acts speak for itself. Whatever we think of these specific points, one fact is undeniable: assumptions concerning the extent to which Luke was influenced by Paul must be judged in light of the evidence we have available to us, not on speculation of what might have been.

ExpTim 88 (1976), pp. 2-5; and R. Maddox, *The Purpose of Luke–Acts* (1982), p. 68. Of course Paul mentions Luke in three of his epistles (Col. 4.14; Phlm 24; 2 Tim. 4.11), all of which were probably written from Rome. While this suggests that Luke knew that Paul wrote these epistles, it does not indicate that Luke saw or read them. And since Luke–Acts does not reveal any contact with the epistles (quotations or allusions), it is unlikely that Luke had read them.

1.   Marshall, *Luke: Historian and Theologian*, p. 175.

4. *Conclusion*

Pentecostals are seeking to come to terms with the broader, more recent, and largely Evangelical dimensions of their heritage. Gordon Fee's recent book, *Gospel and Spirit*, represents the quest of one respected scholar. When the essays contained in this book were originally written, they provided a valuable service. They helped Pentecostals recognize their need to address the new and pressing questions raised by their non-Pentecostal brothers. Fee's quest encouraged others to make the journey. Yet the theological landscape has changed considerably since the initial publication of Fee's articles. And, although these articles have been updated, they do not show an awareness of the new terrain. Thus they address concerns that have little relevance. Today, the crucial issue centers not on hermeneutics and historical precedent, but rather on exegesis and the nature of Luke's pneumatology. If Fee and non-Pentecostal scholars wish to engage in meaningful dialogue with contemporary Pentecostal scholarship, they will need to address this issue.

Chapter 13

EVIDENTIAL TONGUES

1. *A Tale of Two Questions*

In the previous chapter, I suggested that Pentecostals have shed fresh light on an extremely important question: What is the nature of the Pentecostal gift? We now focus our attention on a second, separate question: What is the nature of the relationship between tongues (glossolalia) and the Pentecostal gift? It is imperative to recognize that these are two, distinct questions. Indeed, much of the confusion surrounding these questions stems from the failure to distinguish between them. On the one hand, this failure has led many Pentecostals erroneously to equate the Pentecostal gift with tongues. On the other hand, it is the reason why many non-Pentecostals, with tunnel vision, have focused on the hermeneutics of historical precedent and missed the fundamental question concerning the nature of Luke's pneumatology.

It is imperative to distinguish between these questions because they must be approached and ultimately answered in different ways. The question concerning the nature of the Pentecostal gift is a question of biblical theology. It is a question which Luke himself clearly addresses. Indeed, in previous chapters I examined evidence from Luke–Acts which supports my contention that Luke consistently presents the Pentecostal gift in prophetic terms as the source of power for effective witness; and furthermore, that he consciously encourages his readers to experience this gift. Here Luke's intent is clear. However, the question of tongues as initial evidence ushers us into the realm of systematic theology. In biblical theology, we focus on the agenda of the biblical authors. We seek to hear the questions they raise and the answers they offer. G.B. Caird has aptly described the task of biblical theology as one of listening to the dialogue of the biblical authors seated at a round table.[1] In biblical theology, we listen to their discussion. By way of

1.   Caird's approach is summarized by L.D. Hurst ('New Testament Theological

contrast, in systematic theology we frequently begin with the agenda and questions of our contemporary setting. We bring the pressing questions of our day to the biblical text and, as we wrestle with the implications that emerge from the text for our questions, we seek to answer them in a manner consistent with the biblical witness. In systematic theology, we do not simply sit passively, listening to the discussion at the round table. Rather, we bring our questions to the dialogue and listen for the various responses uttered. Ultimately, we seek to integrate these responses into a coherent answer.

The question concerning the relationship between tongues and Spirit-baptism is a question of systematic theology. Larry Hurtado correctly notes that 'the question of what constitutes "the initial evidence" of a person having received the "baptism in the Spirit" simply is not raised in the New Testament'.[1] Luke, as I shall emphasize, is no exception at this point. That is to say, neither Luke nor any other biblical author deliberately sets out to demonstrate that glossolalia is the initial physical evidence of that empowering experience (and dimension of the Spirit's activity) Pentecostals appropriately call, 'baptism in the Holy Spirit'. However, as Hurtado notes, this does not necessarily 'render the doctrine invalid' nor indicate that the questions associated with the doctrine are inappropriate.[2] Nevertheless, Hurtado goes on to suggest that in this instance the doctrine is invalid, but I shall treat his objections later. For the moment, it is important to note that it is not only legitimate, but often necessary, to bring our questions to the text or (as Caird might put it) to the dialogue at the round table. Here we must also carefully listen to the voice of Scripture. Although the biblical authors may not directly address our questions, our goal is to identify the implications for our questions which emerge from the various theological perspectives they represent.

2. *The Limitations of Biblical Theology*

The doctrine of evidential tongues is often treated purely in terms of the categories of biblical theology. This is true of Pentecostal presentations and non-Pentecostal evaluations. Pentecostals have generally supported

---

Analysis', in *Introducing New Testament Interpretation* [1989], p. 145).

1. L.W. Hurtado, 'Normal, but not a Norm: Initial Evidence and the New Testament', in *Initial Evidence* (1991), p. 191.

2. Hurtado, 'Normal', p 191.

the doctrine by arguing that the various accounts in Acts present a normative pattern for Christian experience. Although it is not always clearly articulated, implicit in this approach is the notion that Luke consciously crafted his narrative in order to highlight the normative character of evidential tongues. Yet, as Gordon Fee has pointed out, this sort of argument has not been persuasive.[1] In the previous chapter I noted that Fee's critique of arguments based on historical precedent was significant because it challenged Pentecostals to deal with this fact.

The inability of Pentecostals to offer clear theological support for the doctrine of evidential tongues is nowhere more clearly demonstrated than in the recent publication of *Initial Evidence*.[2] The articles by Hurtado and J. Ramsey Michaels represent further elaborations of the basic message voiced by Fee over a decade ago.[3] Pentecostals have failed to convince because they have not been able to demonstrate that Luke intended to present in the key narratives of Acts a normative model of Christian experience. The problem again is twofold. First, the evidence is not uniform: if Luke intended to teach evidential tongues as normative, why does he not consistently present tongues as the immediate result of Spirit-baptism (e.g. Acts 8.17; 9.17-18)? Secondly, even when glossolalia is connected to Spirit-baptism, it is doubtful whether this connection is made in order to present evidential tongues as a normative doctrine. In other words, it is difficult to argue that Luke, through his narrative, intended to teach this doctrine as articulated by modern Pentecostals. This does not appear to be his concern.

As noted above, we should be careful not to jump to the unwarranted conclusion that this judgment necessarily invalidates the doctrine of evidential tongues. Nevertheless, this is precisely the conclusion that is usually drawn. The reason is clearly articulated by Fee, who suggests that normative theology at this point must be grounded in Luke's 'primary intent' or 'intention to teach'.[4] But surely this is overly

---

1.   Fee, 'Hermeneutics and Historical Precedent', pp. 118-32; see also 'The Issue of Separability and Subsequence', pp. 87-99.

2.   This is the case in spite of D.A. John's excellent article, 'Some New Directions in the Hermeneutics of Classical Pentecostalism's Doctrine of Initial Evidence', in *Initial Evidence* (1991), pp. 145-67. John's article focuses on methodology and thus, by design, represents a provisional statement.

3.   Hurtado, 'Normal', pp. 189-201, and J.R. Michaels, 'Evidences of the Spirit, or the Spirit as Evidence? Some Non-Pentecostal Reflections', in *Initial Evidence*, pp. 202-18.

4.   Fee, 'Hermeneutics and Historical Precedent', pp. 83-99.

restrictive. Not all questions of normative teaching are rooted directly in the intention of the author. Hurtado notes the oft-cited illustration of the doctrine of the Trinity, which is not taught explicitly in the New Testament but developed on the basis of inferences from biblical teaching. Is it not valid to inquire about the character of Luke's pneumatology, and then to wrestle with the implications which emerge from his pneumatology for our contemporary questions? Only 'the most severe form of biblicism' would deny the validity of this sort of exercise.[1]

An exclusive focus on an author's 'primary intent' or 'intention to teach' too often leads to a form of tunnel vision which ignores the implications of an individual text for the theological perspective of the author. This myopia is illustrated in Fee's treatment of the Samaritan episode in Acts 8.4-17.[2] He argues that this passage is ultimately irrelevant to discussions concerning the doctrine of subsequence for Luke's 'primary intent' lies elsewhere. Now, the primary intent of the narrative, as Fee suggests, may be to stress that the expansion of the gospel beyond the bounds of Judaism had 'divine and apostolic approval'. And, I would agree, it is unlikely that Luke consciously sought to teach here that the gift of the Spirit is normally separate from saving faith. Yet this does not allow us to ignore the clear implications of the narrative for Luke's pneumatology. Indeed, the fact that Luke *does* separate the gift of the Spirit from saving faith clearly reveals his distinctive pneumatological perspective. Paul would not—indeed, could not—have interpreted and narrated the event in this way. Furthermore, this separation refutes the commonly accepted interpretation of the Lukan gift as 'the climax of conversion-initiation'. In other words, the value of a passage for assessing the theological perspective of a given author cannot be reduced to its 'primary intent'. A passage must be understood in terms of its original setting and intention, but the theological freight it carries may transcend its 'primary intent'. Each piece of evidence must be taken seriously as we seek to reconstruct the theological perspective of the biblical author.

This leads to an important conclusion regarding theological method. The quest for normative theology is often a twofold task, embracing both the disciplines of biblical and systematic theology. First, we must reconstruct the theological perspective of the biblical authors, thereby

---

1. Hurtado, 'Normal', p. 191.
2. G.D. Fee, *How to Read the Bible for All its Worth* (1982), pp. 94-96; see also Fee, *Gospel and Spirit*, p. 97.

enabling them to take their rightful places at the round table. This task of reconstruction cannot be limited to a survey of the 'primary intent' of isolated passages; rather, it calls for a careful analysis of the theological significance of the author's entire work. Secondly, after the task of theological reconstruction is finished, we must bring our questions to the round table and listen attentively to the ensuing dialogue. Here we seek to hear the answers (by inference) to our questions which emerge from the various theological perspectives of the biblical authors. In the following sections I shall seek to employ this twofold method in an attempt to evaluate the Pentecostal doctrine of evidential tongues.

3. The Contributions of Biblical Theology

Let us then gather the biblical authors together at the round table. For my purposes Luke and Paul will be sufficient. However, before we raise our question, it would be well for us simply to listen. We must listen to their discussion of significant matters related to the manifestation of tongues and prophetic speech. Paul is the first to respond. And, although his statement is not definitive for our question, it is significant nonetheless. Paul affirms that *every Christian may—and indeed should—be edified through the private manifestation of tongues.*

This statement is significant, for some have suggested that Paul limits tongues-speech to a few in the community who have been so gifted. Don Carson's comments in *Showing the Spirit* are representative of this position.[1] On the basis of the rhetorical question in 1 Cor. 12.30 ('Do all speak in tongues?'), Carson argues that it is inappropriate to insist that all may speak in tongues: not all have the same gift. This principle is central to Carson's dismissal of tongues as evidence of a distinctive post-conversion experience. Yet Carson fails to acknowledge the complexity of the issue: 12.30 must be reconciled with 14.5 ('I would like everyone of you to speak in tongues'). Furthermore, he does not consider whether the reference in 12.30 is limited to the public manifestation of tongues. If, as the context suggests, this is the case, then the way is open for every believer to be edified personally through the private manifestation of tongues. It is striking that Carson fails to discuss this exegetical option when he acknowledges that, although all are not prophets (12.29), all may prophesy (14.31).[2] Paul's comment in 14.18

1. Carson, *Showing the Spirit*, pp. 49-50.
2. Carson, *Showing the Spirit*, pp. 117-18.

('I thank God that I speak in tongues more than all of you'), coupled with the reference in 14.5 noted above, indicates that Paul considered the private manifestation of tongues to be edifying, desirable and available to every Christian.[1] It would appear that Carson has misread Paul and inappropriately restricted tongues-speech to a select group within the Christian community.

We now turn our attention to Luke. His contribution is multi-faceted. First, Luke reminds us of *the prophetic character of the Pentecostal gift*. I have noted that Luke describes the gift of the Spirit *exclusively* in prophetic terms as the source of power for effective witness. That is to say, Luke does not, in a manner analogous to Paul, present the Spirit as a soteriological agent (the source of cleansing, justification or sanctification). If we ask more specifically concerning the impact of the Spirit in Luke–Acts, we see that Luke's perspective is quite similar to that of the Judaism of his day. First-century Judaism, as I have noted, identified the gift of the Spirit as the source of prophetic inspiration. This view was dominant for the Judaism which gave birth to the early church, with Wisdom and the hymns of Qumran providing the only exceptions. Thus, for example, Isa. 44.3 ('I will pour out my Spirit on your offspring') was interpreted by the rabbis as a reference to the outpouring of the Spirit of prophecy upon Israel; and the transformation of the heart referred to in Ezek. 36.26-27 was viewed as a prerequisite for the eschatological bestowal of the Spirit, generally interpreted in light of Joel 2.28-29 as the restoration of the Spirit of prophecy.

As the source of prophetic inspiration, the Spirit grants special revelation and inspired speech. These twin functions are exemplified by the many instances where the rabbis speak of 'seeing' or 'speaking *in the Spirit*'. One early citation I noted, *ARN* A.34, is also illustrative: 'By ten names was the Holy Spirit called, to wit: parable, metaphor, riddle, speech, saying, glory, command, burden, prophecy, vision'.[2] Notice here how the various 'names' identified with the Holy Spirit feature charismatic revelation (e.g. 'prophecy', 'vision') and speech (e.g. 'speech', 'saying', 'command').

I have argued above that Luke also presents the Spirit as the source of prophetic inspiration. This is apparent from the outset of his Gospel, which features outbursts of prophetic speech by Elizabeth (Lk. 1.41-42), Zechariah (Lk. 1.67), and Simeon (Lk. 2.25-28). It is highlighted in the

---

1. Note also 1 Cor. 14.4: 'He who speaks in a tongue edifies himself...'
2. ET from J. Goldin, *The Fathers*.

programmatic accounts of Jesus' sermon at Nazareth (Lk. 4.18-19) and
Peter's sermon on the day of Pentecost (Acts 2.17-18). Both accounts
indicate that the Lukan gift of the Spirit is intimately connected to
inspired speech. Furthermore, references to Spirit-inspired speech punc-
tuate Luke's two-volume work (e.g. Lk. 10.21; 12.10-12; Acts 4.31;
6.10). Thus, when Luke reminds us of the prophetic character of the gift
of the Spirit, he is in fact affirming that the Pentecostal gift is intimately
linked to inspired speech.

4. *The Contributions of Systematic Theology*

We are now in a position to press beyond the initial and foundational
contributions of biblical theology, and particularly Paul and Luke. We
must now put our questions before them: What is the nature of the
relationship between tongues (glossolalia) and the Pentecostal gift? More
specifically, is tongues the 'initial physical evidence' of the baptism in
the Holy Spirit (Acts 1.5; 2.4)?

Paul must remain silent at this point. I have already noted that Paul's
theology does not stand in contradiction to evidential tongues.
Nevertheless, since Paul does not speak specifically of the Pentecostal
gift we are unable to reconstruct his contribution to the discussion at this
point.

Luke, however, has much to say. Concerning the question of 'initial
physical evidence', one might be inclined to hear in his answer an allusion to charismatic revelation and inspired speech, including both intelligible and unintelligible (glossolalia) utterances. Certainly Luke presents
the Pentecostal gift as the source of prophetic inspiration, and this
inspiration includes all three of these activities (charismatic revelation,
intelligible speech and glossolalia). Yet as we reflect on the question and
listen attentively, we can hear that Luke's answer is more precise. After
all, 'physical evidence' suggests visible or audible signs which verify
reception of the Pentecostal gift. Thus, we can, without further ado,
eliminate charismatic revelation from Luke's response. Charismatic
revelation, unless uttered in some way, cannot serve as 'physical
evidence', for it lacks a visible or audible dimension. Furthermore, how
is one to distinguish inspired intelligible speech from that which is
uninspired? Although we may all be able to think of instances when
intelligible speech was uttered in a manner which indicated the inspiration of the Spirit (spontaneous, edifying, appropriate), the point is that

judgments of this kind are rather tenuous or approximate. Tongues-speech, however, because of its unusual and demonstrative character (the very reason it is both often maligned or over-esteemed), is particularly well suited to serve as 'evidence'. In short, if we ask the question concerning 'initial physical evidence' of Luke, tongues-speech uniquely 'fits the bill' because of its intrinsically demonstrative character.

There is evidence, apart from Luke's larger pneumatology, that suggests that this conclusion is harmonious with Luke's perspective. The decisive sign of God's favor on the Gentiles is their reception of the gift of the Spirit, manifested in tongues-speech (Acts 10.46). It is this sign which astonishes Peter's circumcised companions and results in his command to baptize the Gentile converts (Acts 10.45-48). This emphasis on the sign value of tongues-speech is rooted in Luke's prophetic pneumatology. Since according to Luke reception of the Spirit is the exclusive privilege of 'the servants' of God and produces miraculous and audible speech, by its very nature tongues-speech provides demonstrative proof that the uncircumcised members of Cornelius's household have been incorporated into the community of salvation. The sign-value of tongues-speech is also emphasized in the Pentecost account (2.4-5, 17-20). Whether from the lips of a Jew in Jerusalem or a Gentile in Caesarea, the manifestation of tongues-speech marks the speaker as a member of the end-time prophetic community.

I am now in a position to summarize my findings. I have argued that the doctrine of 'tongues as initial evidence', although not explicitly found in the New Testament, is an appropriate inference drawn from the prophetic character of the Pentecostal gift and the evidential character of tongues-speech. Although tongues-speech, as a form of inspired or prophetic speech, is integral to the Pentecostal gift, Paul makes a significant contribution to the discussion by highlighting the potentially universal character of tongues-speech. I will now make an evaluation of my approach and findings.

5. *The Limitations of Systematic Theology*

My approach to the 'tongues' question is not based on arguments from historical precedent. I have not, on the basis of an analysis of isolated passages from the book of Acts, sought to demonstrate that Luke intended to teach evidential tongues. Rather, drawing from the full scope of Luke's two-volume work, I have focused on the nature of Luke's pneumatology and, from this theological framework, sought to answer our contemporary question concerning 'initial evidence'. Significant evidence from Paul has also been considered. The normative character of evidential tongues thus emerges, not from Luke's primary intent, but rather as an implication from Luke's prophetic pneumatology and Paul's complementary perspective.

Larry Hurtado, as I have noted, acknowledges that doctrines cannot be judged invalid simply because they are not explicitly taught in Scripture. In principle, it is valid to base doctrine on inferences drawn from the text. And in practice, although I acknowledge that the doctrine of the Trinity is not explicitly taught in Scripture, I affirm its validity. However, Hurtado suggests that the doctrine of evidential tongues cannot be compared to that of the Trinity, and that while the latter is valid, the former is not. The Christian movement, from its earliest stages, 'was engaged in attempting to understand God in the light of Christ'.[1] Thus later Trinitarian statements represent the culmination of a process which can traced back to the apostolic age. Hurtado contrasts the apostolic origins of Trinitarian thought with the relatively modern origin of evidential tongues: 'the question of whether there is a separate level of Spirit empowerment subsequent to regeneration, with a required "evidence" of it, seems not to be reflected at all in the New Testament'.[2]

Yet Hurtado's judgment needs to be re-examined. As I have noted, a careful analysis of Luke–Acts indicates that from its earliest days the early church was cognizant of 'a separate level of Spirit empowerment subsequent to regeneration'. This level of empowerment was described by Luke in terms of the Pentecostal gift and promise. Furthermore, a process of development in the early church's understanding of the work of the Spirit is clearly reflected in the writings of Mark, Matthew, Luke, Paul and John. The evidence suggests that Paul was the first Christian to attribute soteriological significance to the gift of the Spirit and that his insight did not impact non-Pauline sectors of the early church until after the writing of Luke–Acts (probably around AD 70). This means that from its earliest days the church knew only of 'a level of Spirit empowerment subsequent to [or at least logically distinct from] regeneration'. Paul's fuller understanding had to be integrated with this more primitive perspective. This indicates that the Pentecostal

1. Hurtado, 'Normal', p. 192.
2. Hurtado, 'Normal', p. 192.

doctrine of Spirit-baptism also has apostolic roots.

I would acknowledge that 'initial physical evidence' is a relatively recent theological formulation. Indeed, even the wording of the phrase is conditioned by historical circumstances. The focus on 'evidence' reminds us of a day in which the scientific method had seized the imagination of the American people. Nevertheless, this modern formulation is related to a process of doctrinal development which is reflected in the New Testament and which has been largely ignored by modern exegetes. What is the nature of the Pentecostal gift? This question has been with the church since that first Pentecost day. The question with which I have been wrestling in this chapter, 'What is the nature of the relationship between tongues (glossolalia) and the Pentecostal gift?', undoubtedly generated considerable discussion among Peter's colleagues. Thus it is virtually certain that it accompanied the expansion of the church among the Gentiles.[1] And it appears to be an inevitable question for those who would try to reconcile Paul's gift language with Luke's Pentecostal gift. It appears that the pedigree of Pentecostal doctrine is not as shabby as Hurtado would suggest.

This is not to suggest that modern Pentecostal formulations are inspired. All theological formulations are the product of human beings and thus, for better or for worse, are human attempts to come to terms with the significance of the Word of God. All such formulations stand under the judgment of the Word of God. The phrase 'initial physical evidence', as all theological formulations, has its limitations. The focus on 'evidence' can easily lead to a confusion of the gift with the sign. The Pentecostal gift is not tongues. It is rather an empowering which enables its recipient to participate effectively in the mission of God. The manifestation of tongues is an evidence of the Pentecostal dimension of the Spirit's work, but not the gift itself. An inordinate focus on 'evidence' may result in Christians who, looking back into the distant past, can remember the moment they 'got it', but for whom the Pentecostal dimension of power for witness is presently unknown.[2]

Yet this human formulation also captures well the sense of expectation called for by Luke and Paul: tongues-speech is an integral part of the Pentecostal gift, edifying and universally available; therefore, when one receives the gift, one would *expect* to manifest tongues. Furthermore,

1. P.F. Esler, 'Glossolalia and the Admission of Gentiles into the Early Christian Community', *BTB* 22 (1992), pp. 136-42.
2. The phrase 'accompanying sign' is a possible useful alternative.

the manifestation of tongues is a powerful reminder that the Church is, by virtue of the Pentecostal gift, a prophetic community empowered for a missionary task.

This, of course, does not exhaust the theological significance of glossolalia. Frank Macchia, in a stimulating article, appropriately calls for further reflection on the theological significance of tongues-speech.[1] In my judgment, Macchia highlights three areas of special significance. *Missiology*: Is it not significant that tongues-speech accompanies (and is a decisive 'sign' of) God's initiative in breaking through racial and economic barriers?[2] *Eschatology*: The manifestation of tongues reminds us that we, like those on that first Pentecost, live in the 'last days'—that period of God's gracious deliverance which immediately precedes the Day of the Lord (Acts 2.17)—and that God has called us to be a part of his glorious plan of salvation. *Ecclesiology*: Tongues has been described as a Pentecostal 'sacrament' (a visible sign of a spiritual reality), but one that is not bound to clergy or institution, and therefore one which has a powerful democratizing effect on the life of the church. Is it purely coincidental that tongues-speech has frequently accompanied renewed vision for ministry among the laity?

6. Conclusion

I have argued that the Pentecostal doctrine of evidential tongues is an appropriate inference drawn from the prophetic character of Luke's pneumatology (and more specifically, the Pentecostal gift) and Paul's affirmation of the edifying and potentially universal character of the private manifestation of tongues. My argument may be summarized as follows:

1. Paul affirms that the private manifestation of tongues is edifying, desirable and universally available. In short, all should speak in tongues.

2. Luke affirms that the Pentecostal gift is intimately connected to inspired speech, of which tongues-speech is a prominent form, possessing a unique evidential character.

1. F.D. Macchia, 'The Question of Tongues as Initial Evidence: A Review of *Initial Evidence*, edited by Gary B. McGee', *JPT* 2 (1993), pp. 117-27.
2. See M. Dempster, 'The Church's Moral Witness: A Study of Glossolalia in Luke's Theology of Acts', *Paraclete* 23 (1989), pp. 1-7.

3. Therefore, when one receives the Pentecostal gift, one should *expect* to manifest tongues, and this manifestation of tongues is a uniquely demonstrative sign (evidence) that one has received the gift.

Although the doctrine of evidential tongues is formulated in modern language and addresses contemporary concerns, it is linked to a process of doctrinal development which extends back into the apostolic age. Indeed, the question it addresses undoubtedly accompanied the expansion of the church among the Gentiles and it appears to be unavoidable for those who would try to reconcile Paul's gift language with Luke's Pentecostal gift. The doctrine calls us to retain a biblical sense of expectancy, for it reminds us that the manifestation of tongues is an integral part of the Pentecostal gift, edifying and universally available. Above all, the manifestation of tongues is a powerful reminder that the Church is, by virtue of the Pentecostal gift, a prophetic community called and empowered to bear witness to the world.

Chapter 14

CONCLUSION

No-one would deny that Paul attributes soteriological significance to the gift of the Spirit. According to Paul, reception of the Spirit enables one to enter into and remain within the community of salvation. For, in Paul's perspective, the Spirit reveals to each Christian the true meaning of the death and resurrection of Jesus Christ, and progressively transforms him or her into the image of Christ. Thus Paul declares that the Spirit is the source of the Christian's cleansing, righteousness, intimate fellowship with God, and ultimate transformation through the resurrection.

Yet I have noted that the soteriological dimension of the Spirit's activity which forms such a prominent part of Paul's pneumatology appears infrequently in the literature of intertestamental Judaism. The literature is united in its description of the Spirit as a prophetic endowment. As the source of special insight and inspired speech, the Spirit enables the prophet, sage or Messiah, to fulfill special tasks. Thus the gift of the Spirit is presented as a *donum superadditum* rather than a soteriological necessity. The only significant exceptions to this perspective are found in later sapiential writings: Wisdom and the hymns of Qumran.

The soteriological dimension is entirely absent from the pneumatology of Luke. In accordance with the Jewish perspective outlined above, Luke consistently portrays the gift of the Spirit as a prophetic endowment which enables its recipient to fulfill a particular task. The Spirit equips John for his role as the prophetic precursor, Jesus for his task as messianic herald, and the disciples for their vocation as witnesses. Furthermore, we have seen that Luke not only fails to refer to soteriological aspects of the Spirit's work, but his narrative presupposes a pneumatology which excludes this dimension. Therefore, it cannot be maintained that Luke recognized the soteriological significance of the pneumatic gift, but simply chose to emphasize the prophetic and missiological implications of the gift. Luke's 'prophetic' pneumatology must be distinguished from the 'soteriological' pneumatology of Paul.

We have observed that the traditions of the primitive church utilized by Luke also fail to attribute soteriological functions to the Spirit. Although the primitive church, following the lead of Jesus, broadens the functions traditionally ascribed to the Spirit in first-century Judaism and thus presents the Spirit as the source of miracle-working power (as well as prophetic inspiration), the 'charismatic' pneumatology of the primitive church is otherwise essentially the same as the 'prophetic' pneumatology of Luke. The gift of the Spirit is viewed as an endowment for special tasks granted to those already within the community of salvation.

These observations suggest that Paul was the first Christian to attribute soteriological functions to the Spirit; and furthermore, that this soteriological element of Paul's pneumatology did not influence wider (non-Pauline) sectors of the early church until after the writing of Luke–Acts (AD 70–80). This should not surprise us given the striking fact that Luke apparently was not acquainted with Paul's epistles. And, since other distinctive aspects of Paul's theology have not significantly influenced Luke or the other synoptic evangelists, this suggestion is all the more credible.

One must therefore affirm that the pneumatology of the early church was not as homogeneous as most of the major post-Gunkel studies have maintained. On the contrary, the evidence indicates that three distinct pneumatological perspectives co-existed: the 'charismatic' pneumatology of the primitive church, the 'prophetic' pneumatology of Luke, and the 'soteriological' pneumatology of Paul. The differences between the pneumatologies of the primitive church and Luke on the one hand, and the perspective of Paul on the other, are particularly acute.

This conclusion has important implications for the theological reflection of the contemporary church. It indicates that the task of articulating a holistic biblical theology of the Spirit is more complex than is often assumed. More specifically, it calls into question attempts at theological synthesis which do not adequately account for the distinctive pneumatological perspectives of the primitive church (Mark, Matthew), and particularly Luke–Acts. Indeed, as we re-examine the foundations upon which our theologizing is built, we are reminded that the church, by virtue of its reception of the Pentecostal gift, is a prophetic community empowered for a missionary task.

Appendix

THE SPIRIT OF GOD IN ACTS

Of the 59 references to the Spirit of God in Acts, 36 are unequivocally linked to prophetic activity. Although the distinction between the two activities listed below is at times arbitrary since they often overlap, Luke's usage in Acts may be conveniently summarized as follows: the Spirit is the agent of inspired speech (1.8, 16; 2.4, 14, 17, 18, 33; 4.8, 25, 31; 5.32; 6.10; 7.51; 9.31; 10.44, 45; 13.9; 18.25; 19.6; 28.5) and special revelation through which it directs the mission of the church (1.2; 7.55; 8.29; 10.19; 11.12, 28; 13.2, 4; 15.28; 16.6, 7; 19.21; 20.22, 23; 21.4, 11). On the basis of my analysis in the previous chapters, one may affirm that the connection between the Spirit and prophetic activity is implicit in the remaining 23 references (1.5; 2.38; 5.3, 9; 6.3, 5, 10; 8.15, 17, 18, 19, [39]; 9.17; 10.38, 47; 11.15, 16, 24; 13.52; 15.8; 19.2, 12; 20.28). Four groups of texts are often cited as proof that Luke viewed the Spirit as the source of the religious and ethical life of the Christian;[1] however, these texts are consistent with the affirmation made above.

Acts 2.42-47. As Haya-Prats notes, there is no indication that Luke considered the diverse aspects of community life mentioned in this summary (so also 4.31-36; 5.11-16) to be the direct result of the Spirit's activity.[2]

Acts 5.1-11. Luke's narrative at this point presupposes that the Spirit of prophecy is operative in Peter; thus he is aware of the deception perpetrated by Ananias and Sapphira and describes it as an offense against the Spirit (5.3, 9). Although here the Spirit undoubtedly influences the religious and ethical life of the Christian community, the Spirit does so as the Spirit of prophecy, giving voice to special revelation which in turn directs the actions of the various constituents of the church. The gift of the Spirit is never presented as the direct and principal source of moral transformation in the individual; rather, it remains for Luke a prophetic *donum superadditum* which directs the community (indirectly through the prophet) in special instances.

Acts 6.3, 5, 10; 11.24. The description of the deacons as 'full of the Spirit and wisdom' and of Stephen and Barnabas as 'full of faith and of the Holy Spirit'

---

1. See for example von Baer, *Der heilige Geist*, pp. 188-90; Bovon, *Luc le théologien*, p. 232; and Dunn, *Holy Spirit*, pp. 50-51.
2. Haya-Prats, *Force*, pp. 150-56.

indicates that these men were endowed with the prophetic gift (an *Amtscharisma* vital for the fulfillment of their calling) through which they received special wisdom and confidence. This Spirit-inspired wisdom and faith enabled Stephen (6.10) and Barnabas (11.23-24) to speak authoritatively.

Acts 13.52. The χαρά ('joy') in this instance is remarkable and attributed to the Spirit because it is experienced in the face of persecution (Acts 13.50; 14.19-20). Here, as in Acts 4.31, the Spirit comes upon a persecuted band of disciples in order to equip them with boldness for the task of mission (cf. Acts 13.49). Luke probably penned Acts 13.52 with the promise of Lk. 12.12 in mind. This conclusion not only accords well with the immediate context, but it is suggested by Luke's use of πίμπλημι with the Spirit, which elsewhere in Acts is always associated with an endowment of power for mission resulting in inspired speech (2.4; 4.8, 31; 9.17; 13.9; cf. Lk. 1.41, 67). The parallels between this summary statement and that of Acts 4.31 are particularly striking.

BIBLIOGRAPHY

Adler, N., *Das erste christliche Pfingstfest: Sinn und Bedeutung des Pfingstberichtes Apg. 2,1-13* (Münster: Aschendorff'sche Verlagsbuchhandlung, 1938).

Aland, K., 'Zur Vorgeschichte der christlichen Taufe', in *Neues Testament und Geschichte: Historisches Geschehen und Deutung im Neuen Testament* (FS for O. Cullmann; ed. H. Baltensweiler and B. Reicke; Tübingen: J.C.B. Mohr, 1972), pp. 1-14.

Alexander, P.S., 'Rabbinic Judaism and the New Testament', *ZNW* 74 (1983), pp. 237-46.

Allen, L.C., *The Books of Joel, Obadiah, Jonah and Micah* (NICOT; Grand Rapids: Eerdmans, 1976).

Andersen, F.I., '2 (Slavonic Apocalypse of) Enoch', in Charlesworth (ed.), *Pseudepigrapha*, I, pp. 91-221.

Anderson, A.A., 'The Use of "Ruah" in 1QS, 1QH, and 1QM', *JSS* 7 (1962), pp. 293-303.

Anderson, H., '4 Maccabees', in Charlesworth (ed.), *Pseudepigrapha*, II, pp. 531-64.

Baer, H. von, *Der heilige Geist in den Lukasschriften* (Stuttgart: Kohlhammer, 1926).

Barrett, C.K., *The Holy Spirit and the Gospel Tradition* (London: SPCK, 1947).

—'Acts and the Pauline Corpus', *ExpTim* 88 (1976), pp. 2-5.

—'Apollos and the Twelve Disciples of Ephesus', in *The New Testament Age: Essays in Honor of Bo Reicke* (ed. W.C. Weinrich; Macon, GA: Mercer University Press, 1984), I, pp. 29-39.

Bauernfeind, O., *Die Apostelgeschichte* (THKNT, 5; Leipzig: Deichert, 1939).

Beasley-Murray, G.R., *Baptism in the New Testament* (Exeter: Paternoster Press, 1962).

—'Jesus and the Spirit', in *Mélanges Bibliques* (ed. A. Déscamps and A. de Halleux; Gembloux: Duculot, 1970), pp. 463-78.

Behm, J., 'γλῶσσα', *TDNT*, I, pp. 719-27.

Best, E., 'The Use and Non-Use of Pneuma by Josephus', *NovT* 3 (1959), pp. 218-25.

—'Spirit-Baptism', *NovT* 4 (1960), pp. 236-43.

Billerbeck, P., 'Ein Synagogengottesdienst in Jesu Tagen', *ZNW* 55 (1965), pp. 143-61.

Black, M. (ed.), *Apocalypsis Henochi Graece* (PVTG, 3; Leiden: Brill, 1970).

—*The Book of Enoch* (Leiden: Brill, 1985).

Bloch, R., 'Methodological Note for the Study of Rabbinic Literature', in *Approaches to Ancient Judaism: Theory and Practice* (ed. W.S. Green; Missoula, MT: Scholars Press, 1978), pp. 51-75.

Bock, D.L., *Proclamation from Prophecy and Pattern: Lucan Old Testament Christology* (JSNTSup, 12; Sheffield: JSOT Press, 1987).

Bornkamm, G., *Jesus of Nazareth* (trans. I. McLuskey and F. McLuskey with J.M. Robinson; London: Hodder & Stoughton, 1960).

Bovon, F., *Luc le théologien: Vingt-cinq ans de recherches (1950-1975)* (Paris: Delachaux & Niestlé, 1978).

—'Aktuelle Linien lukanischer Forschung', in *Lukas in neuer Sicht* (BTS, 8; Neukirchen-Vluyn: Neukirchener Verlag, 1985), pp. 9-43.

Bowker, J., *The Targums and Rabbinic Literature* (Cambridge: Cambridge University Press, 1969).

Brandenburger, E., *Fleisch und Geist: Paulus und die dualistische Weisheit* (WMANT, 29; Neukirchen-Vluyn: Neukirchener Verlag, 1968).

Braude, W.G., *The Midrash on Psalms* (2 vols.; New Haven: Yale University Press, 1959).

—*Pesikta Rabbati: Discourses for Feasts, Fasts, and Special Sabbaths* (2 vols.; New Haven: Yale University Press, 1968).

Braumann, G., 'Das Mittel der Zeit', *ZNW* 54 (1963), pp. 117-45.

Broer, I., 'Der Geist und die Gemeinde: Zur Auslegung der lukanischen Pfingstgeschichte (Apg 2,1-13)', *BibLeb* 13 (1972), pp. 261-83.

Brown, R.E., *The Birth of the Messiah: A Commentary on the Infancy Narratives in Matthew and Luke* (London: Geoffrey Chapman, 1977).

—'Luke's Method in the Annunciation Narratives of Chapter One', in *Perspectives on Luke-Acts* (ed. C.H. Talbert; Edinburgh: T. & T. Clark, 1978).

Bruce, F.F., *The Acts of the Apostles: The Greek Text with Introduction and Commentary* (London: Tyndale Press, 1951).

—*Commentary on the Book of Acts* (NICNT; repr.; Grand Rapids: Eerdmans, 1984 [1954]).

—'The Holy Spirit in the Acts of the Apostles', *Int* 27 (1973), pp. 166-83.

—'The Speeches in Acts: Thirty Years After', in *Reconciliation and Hope* (ed. R. Banks; Grand Rapids: Eerdmans, 1974), pp. 53-58.

—*New Testament History* (Basingstoke: Pickering & Inglis, 1982).

Bruner, F.D., *A Theology of the Holy Spirit: The Pentecostal Experience and the New Testament Witness* (Grand Rapids: Eerdmans, 1970).

Buber, S., *Midrasch Tanchuma* (Wilna, 1885).

Büchsel, F., *Der Geist Gottes im Neuen Testament* (Gütersloh: C. Bertelsmann, 1926).

Bultmann, R., *The History of the Synoptic Tradition* (trans. J. Marsh; Oxford: Blackwell, 1968).

—'ἀγαλλιάομαι', *TDNT*, I, pp. 19-21.

Burchard, C., *Der dreizehnte Zeuge: Traditions- und kompositionsgeschichtliche Untersuchungen zu Lukas' Darstellung der Frühzeit des Paulus* (FRLANT, 103; Göttingen: Vandenhoeck & Ruprecht, 1970).

Burrows, M., *More Light on the Dead Sea Scrolls* (New York: Viking, 1958).

Busse, U., *Das Nazareth-Manifest Jesu: Eine Einführung in das lukanische Jesubild nach Lk 4,16-30* (SBS, 91; Stuttgart: Katholisches Bibelwerk, 1977).

Carson, D., *Showing the Spirit: A Theological Exposition of 1 Corinthians 12-14* (Grand Rapids: Baker Book House, 1987).

Charles, R.H., *The Book of Jubilees* (London: A. & C. Black, 1902).

—*The Book of Enoch* (Oxford: Clarendon Press, 1912).

Charlesworth, J.H. (ed.), *The Old Testament Pseudepigrapha* (2 vols.; London: Darton, Longman, & Todd, 1983, 1985).

Chevallier, M.A., *L'Esprit et le Messie dans le bas-judaïsme et le Nouveau Testament* (EHPR, 49; Paris: Presses Universitaires de France, 1958).

—*Souffle de dieu: Le Saint-Esprit dans le Nouveau Testament* (PTh, 26; Paris: Editions Beauchesne, 1978).

Chilton, B., 'Announcement in Nazara: An Analysis of Luke 4.16-21', in *Gospel Perspectives: Studies of History and Tradition in the Four Gospels* (ed. R.T. France and D. Wenham; Sheffield: JSOT Press, 1981), II, pp. 147-72.

Collins, J.J., 'Artapanus', in Charlesworth (ed.), *Pseudepigrapha*, II, pp. 889-903.

Colson, F.H., and G.H. Whitaker, *Philo* (10 vols. and 2 suppl. vols.; ed. R. Marcus; LCL; London: Heinemann, 1929–1962).

Conzelmann, H., *The Theology of St Luke* (trans. G. Buswell; Philadelphia: Fortress Press, 1961).

—*Die Apostelgeschichte* (HNT, 7; Tübingen: J.C.B. Mohr, 1963), ET, *Acts of the Apostles* (Herm; Philadelphia: Fortress Press, 1987).

Cranfield, C.E.B., *The Gospel according to Saint Mark* (CGTC; Cambridge: Cambridge University Press, 5th edn, 1977).

Crockett, L., 'Luke IV. 16-30 and the Jewish Lectionary Cycle: A Word of Caution', *JJS* 17 (1966), pp. 13-46.

Danby, H., *The Mishnah* (Oxford: Clarendon Press, 1933).

Davies, W.D., *Paul and Rabbinic Judaism: Some Rabbinic Elements in Pauline Theology* (London: SPCK, 1948).

—'Paul and the Dead Sea Scrolls: Flesh and Spirit', in *The Scrolls and the New Testament* (ed. K. Stendahl; London: SCM Press, 1958), pp. 157-82.

Davis, J.A., *Wisdom and Spirit: An Investigation of 1 Corinthians 1.18–3.20 against the Background of Jewish Sapiential Tradition in the Greco-Roman Period* (Lanham, MD: University Press of America, 1984).

Delobel, J., 'La rédaction de Lc., IV, 14-16a et le "Bericht vom Anfang"', in *L'évangile de Luc: Problèmes littéraires et théologiques* (Mémorial Lucien Cerfaux; ed. F. Neirynck; Gembloux: J. Duculot, 1973), pp. 203-23.

Dempster, M., 'The Church's Moral Witness: A Study of Glossolalia in Luke's Theology of Acts', *Paraclete* 23 (1989), pp. 1-7.

Denis, A.M. (ed.), *Fragmenta Pseudepigraphorum Quae Supersunt Graeca* (PVTG, 3; Leiden: Brill, 1970).

Derrett, J.D.M., 'Simon Magus (Act 8.9-24)', *ZNW* 73 (1982), pp. 52-68.

Dibelius, M., *A Fresh Approach to the New Testament and Early Christian Literature* (Hertford: Stephen Austin & Sons, 1936).

—*Studies in the Acts of the Apostles* (trans. M. Ling; London: SCM Press, 1956).

—'The Speeches in Acts and Ancient Historiography', in *Studies in the Acts of the Apostles* (London: SCM Press, 1956).

Diez Macho, A., *Neophyti I* (6 vols.; Madrid: Consejo Superior de Investigaciones Científicas, 1968).

Dunn, J.D.G., *Baptism in the Holy Spirit: A Re-examination of the New Testament Teaching on the Gift of the Spirit in Relation to Pentecostalism Today* (London: SCM Press, 1970).

—'Spirit-Baptism and Pentecostalism', *SJT* 23 (1970), pp. 397-407.

—'Spirit and Kingdom', *ExpTim* 82 (1970), pp. 36-40.

—'Spirit-and-Fire Baptism', *NovT* 14 (1972), pp. 81-92.

—'I Corinthians 15.45: Last Adam, Life-giving Spirit', in *Christ and Spirit in the New Testament: In Honour of Charles Francis Digby Moule* (ed. B. Lindars and S.S. Smalley; Cambridge: Cambridge University Press, 1973), pp. 127-42.

—*Jesus and the Spirit: A Study of the Religious and Charismatic Experience of Jesus and the First Christians as Reflected in the New Testament* (London: SCM Press, 1975).

—'The Birth of a Metaphor: Baptized in the Spirit', *ExpTim* 89 (1977), pp. 134-38, 173-75.

—*Unity and Diversity in the New Testament: An Inquiry into the Character of Earliest Christianity* (London: SCM Press, 1977).

—' "They Believed Philip Preaching (Acts 8.12)": A Reply', *IBS* 1 (1979), pp. 177-83.

—'Baptism in the Spirit: A Response to Pentecostal Scholarship on Luke–Acts', *JPT* 3 (1993), pp. 3-27.

Dupont, Jacques, *The Sources of Acts: The Present Position* (trans. K. Pond; London: Darton, Longman & Todd, 1964).

—*Les tentations de Jésus au désert* (SN, 4; Paris: de Brouwer, 1968).

—*Nouvelles études sur les Actes des Apôtres* (LD, 118; Paris: Cerf, 1984).

—'La nouvelle Pentecôte (Ac 2, 1-11)', in *Nouvelles études*, pp. 193-98.

—'Ascension du Christ et don de l'Esprit d'après Actes 2,33', in *Nouvelles études*, pp. 199-209.

Eisler, R., *The Messiah Jesus and John the Baptist according to Flavius Josephus' Recently Rediscovered 'Capture of Jerusalem' and the Other Jewish and Christian Sources* (London: Methuen, 1931).

Ellis, E.E., *The Gospel of Luke* (NCB; London: Oliphants/Marshall, Morgan, & Scott, 1974).

Epstein, I. (ed.), *The Babylonian Talmud* (35 vols.; London: Soncino, 1935-52).

Ervin, H., *Conversion-Initiation and the Baptism in the Holy Spirit* (Peabody, MA: Hendrickson, 1984).

Esler, P.F., 'Glossolalia and the Admission of Gentiles into the Early Christian Community', *BTB* 22 (1992), pp. 136-42.

Etheridge, J.W., *The Targums of Onkelos and Jonathan Ben Uzziel on the Pentateuch* (New York: Ktav, 1968).

Ewert, D., *The Holy Spirit in the New Testament* (Kitchener, Ontario: Herald Press, 1983).

Farris, S.C., 'On Discerning Semitic Sources in Luke 1-2', in *Gospel Perspectives: Studies of History and Tradition in the Four Gospels* (ed. R.T. France and D. Wenham; Sheffield: JSOT Press, 1981), II, pp. 201-37.

—*The Hymns of Luke's Infancy Narratives: Their Origin, Meaning and Significance* (JSNTSup, 9; Sheffield: JSOT Press, 1985).

Fee, G.D., 'Hermeneutics and Historical Precedent—A Major Problem in Pentecostal Hermeneutics', in *Perspectives on the New Pentecostalism* (ed. R.P. Spittler; Grand Rapids: Baker, 1976), pp. 118-32.

—'Baptism in the Holy Spirit: The Issue of Separability and Subsequence', *Pneuma* 7 (1985), pp. 87-99.

—*The First Epistle to the Corinthians* (NICNT; Grand Rapids: Eerdmans, 1987).

—*Gospel and Spirit: Issues in New Testament Hermeneutics* (Peabody, MA: Hendrickson, 1991).

Fee, G.D., and D. Stuart, *How to Read the Bible for all its Worth* (Grand Rapids: Zondervan, 1982).

Fitzmyer, J.A., *The Gospel according to Luke* (2 vols.; AB, 28; New York: Doubleday, 1981, 1985).

Flender, H., *Saint Luke: Theologian of Redemptive History* (trans. R.H. Fuller and I. Fuller; London: SPCK, 1970).

Flew, R.N., *Jesus and his Church* (London: Epworth Press, 1960 [1938]).

Flusser, D., 'The Dead Sea Scrolls and Pre-Pauline Christianity', in *Aspects of the Dead Sea Scrolls* (ed. C. Rabin and Y. Yadin; SH, 4; Jerusalem: Magnes, 1967), pp. 215-66.

Foakes-Jackson, F.J., and K. Lake (eds.), *The Beginnings of Christianity* (5 vols.; London: Macmillan, 1920–33).

Foerster, W., 'Der heilige Geist im Spätjudentum', *NTS* 8 (1961–62), pp. 117-34.

Freedman, H., and M. Simon, *The Midrash Rabbah* (5 vols.; London: Soncino, 1977).

Gasque, W.W., '"The Speeches of Acts: Dibelius Reconsidered', in *New Dimensions in New Testament Study* (ed. R.N. Longenecker and M.C. Tenney; Grand Rapids: Zondervan, 1974), pp. 232-250.

George, A., 'L'Esprit Saint dans l'œuvre de Luc', *RB* 85 (1978), pp. 500-42.

Giblet, J., 'Baptism in the Spirit in the Acts of the Apostles', *OC* 10 (1974), pp. 162-71.

Giles, K., 'Is Luke an Exponent of "Early Protestantism"? Church Order in the Lukan Writings (Part 1)', *EvQ* 54 (1982), pp. 193-205.

—'Salvation in Lukan Theology', *RTR* 42 (1983), pp. 10-16, 45-49.

Ginsberger, M., *Pseudo-Jonathan* (Berlin: Calvary, 1903).

Gloël, J., *Der heilige Geist in der Heilsverkündigung des Paulus* (Halle: Niemeyer, 1888).

Goldberg, A.M., *Untersuchungen über die Vorstellung von der Schekhinah in der frühen rabbinischen Literatur* (SJ, 5; Berlin: de Gruyter, 1969).

Goldin, J., *The Fathers according to Rabbi Nathan* (YJS, 10; New Haven: Yale University Press, 1955).

Goldschmidt, L. (ed.), *Der Babylonische Talmud* (8 vols.; Leipzig: Otto Harrassowitz, 1897–1922).

Green, M., *I Believe in the Holy Spirit* (Grand Rapids: Eerdmans, 1975).

Grundmann, W., *Das Evangelium nach Lukas* (THKNT, 3; Berlin: Evangelische Verlagsanstalt, 1961).

Gunkel, H., *Die Wirkungen des heiligen Geistes nach der populären Anschauung der apostolischen Zeit und nach der Lehre des Apostels Paulus* (Göttingen: Vandenhoeck & Ruprecht, 1888), ET, *The Influence of the Holy Spirit: the Popular View of the Apostolic Age and the Teaching of the Apostle Paul* (trans. R.A. Harrisville and P.A. Quanbeck II; Philadelphia: Fortress Press, 1979).

Guthrie, D., *New Testament Theology* (Leicester: Inter-Varsity Press, 1981).

Haacker, K., 'Einige Fälle von "erlebter Rede" im Neuen Testament', *NovT* 12 (1970), pp. 70-77.

Haenchen, E., 'Schriftzitate und Textüberlieferung in der Apostelgeschichte', *ZTK* 51 (1954), pp. 153-67.

—*The Acts of the Apostles* (trans. B. Noble and G. Shinn; Oxford: Basil Blackwell, 1971).

Hamerton-Kelly, R.G., 'A Note on Matthew XII.28 Par. Luke XI. 20', *NTS* 11 (1964–65), pp. 167-69.

Harrington, D.J., 'Pseudo-Philo', in Charlesworth (ed.), *Pseudepigrapha*, II, pp. 297-377.

Harrington, D.J., and A.J. Saldarini, *Targum Jonathan of the Former Prophets* (ArBib, 10; Edinburgh: T. & T. Clark, 1987).

Haya-Prats, G., *L'Esprit force de l'église: Sa nature et son activité d'après les Actes des Apôtres* (trans. J. Romero; LD, 81; Paris: Cerf, 1975).

Hedrick, C.W., 'Paul's Conversion/Call: A Comparative Analysis of the Three Reports in Acts', *JBL* 100 (1981), pp. 415-32.

Hengel, M., *Judaism and Hellenism: Studies in their Encounter in Palestine during the Early Hellensitic Period* (2 vols.; trans. J. Bowden; London: SCM Press, 1974).

—*Acts and the History of Earliest Christianity* (trans. J. Bowden; London: SCM Press, 1979).

Hill, D., *Greek Words and Hebrew Meanings: Studies in the Semantics of Soteriological Terms* (SNTSMS, 5; Cambridge: Cambridge University Press, 1967).

—'The Rejection of Jesus at Nazareth (Lk 4.16-30)', *NovT* 13 (1971), pp. 161-80.

—*New Testament Prophecy* (London: Marshall, Morgan, & Scott, 1979).

—'The Spirit and the Church's Witness: Observations on Acts 1:6-8', *IBS* 6 (1984), pp. 16-26.

Holm-Nielsen, S., *Hodayot: Psalms from Qumran* (AThD, 2; Aarhus: Universitetsforlaget, 1960).

Holst, R., 'Re-examining Mk 3.28f. and its Parallels', *ZNW* 63 (1972), pp. 122-24.

Holtz, T., 'Christliche Interpolationen in "Joseph und Aseneth"', *NTS* 14 (1967–68), pp. 482-97.

—*Untersuchungen über die alttestamentlichen Zitate bei Lukas* (TU, 104; Berlin: Akademie Verlag, 1968).

Horst, P.W. van der, 'Pseudo-Phocylides', in Charlesworth (ed.), *Pseudepigrapha*, II, pp. 565-82.

Hubbard, B.J., 'Commissioning Stories in Luke–Acts: A Study of their Antecedents, Form and Content', *Semeia* 8 (1977), pp. 103-26.

Hull, J.H.E., *The Holy Spirit in the Acts of the Apostles* (London: Lutterworth, 1967).

Hurst, L.D., 'New Testament Theological Analysis', in *Introducing New Testament Interpretation* (ed. S. McKnight; Grand Rapids: Baker, 1989), pp. 133-61.

Hurtado, L.W., 'Normal, but Not a Norm: Initial Evidence and the New Testament', in McGee (ed.), *Initial Evidence*, pp. 189-201.

Isaac, E., '1 (Ethiopic Apocalypse of) Enoch', in Charlesworth (ed.), *The Old Testament Pseudepigrapha*, I, pp. 5-89.

Isaacs, M., *The Concept of Spirit: A Study of Pneuma in Hellenistic Judaism and its Bearing on the New Testament* (HM, 1; London: Heythrop College, 1976).

Jeremias, J., *The Prayers of Jesus* (London: SCM Press, 1967).

—*New Testament Theology: The Proclamation of Jesus* (trans. J. Bowden; London: SCM Press, 1971).

—*Die Sprache des Lukasevangeliums: Redaktion und Tradition im Nicht-Markusstoff des dritten Evangeliums* (KEKNT, Sonderband; Göttingen: Vandenhoeck & Ruprecht, 1980).

Jervell, J., *The Unknown Paul: Essays on Luke–Acts and Early Christian History* (Minneapolis: Augsburg, 1984).

Johns, D.A., 'Some New Directions in the Hermeneutics of Classical Pentecostalism's Doctrine of Initial Evidence', in McGee (ed.), *Initial Evidence*, pp. 145-67.

Jüngst, J., *Die Quelle der Apostelgeschichte* (Gotha: Friedrich Andreas Perthes, 1895).

Kaiser, C.B., 'The "Rebaptism" of the Ephesian Twelve: Exegetical Study on Acts 19:1-7', *RefR* 31 (1977–78), pp. 57-61.

Käsemann, E., 'Die Johannesjünger in Ephesus', in *Exegetische Versuche und*

Besinnungen (Göttingen: Vandenhoeck & Ruprecht, 6th edn, 1970), I, ET, 'The Disciples of John the Baptist in Ephesus', in *Essays on New Testament Themes* (SBT, 41; London: SCM Press, 1964).

Keck, L.E., 'The Spirit and the Dove', *NTS* 17 (1970), pp. 41-68.

Klein, M.L., *The Fragment-Targums of the Pentateuch according to their Extant Sources* (2 vols.; AnBib, 76; Rome: Biblical Institute Press, 1980).

Knibb, M.A., 'Martyrdom and Ascension of Isaiah', in Charlesworth (ed.), *Pseudepigrapha*, II, pp. 143-76.

—*The Qumran Community* (Cambridge: Cambridge University Press, 1987).

Knox, W.L., *The Acts of the Apostles* (Cambridge: Cambridge University Press, 1948).

Koch, D.-A., 'Geistbesitz, Geistverleihung und Wundermacht: Erwägungen zur Tradition und zur lukanischen Redaktion in Act 8.5-25', *ZNW* 77 (1986), pp. 64-82.

Kremer, J., *Pfingstbericht und Pfingstgeschehen: Eine exegetische Untersuchung zur Apg 2,1-13* (SBS, 63-64; Stuttgart: KBW, 1973).

Kuhn, H.W., *Enderwartung und gegenwärtiges Heil: Untersuchungen zu den Gemeindeliedern von Qumran* (SUNT, 4; Göttingen: Vandenhoeck & Ruprecht, 1966).

Kuhn, K.G., 'πειρασμός-ἁμαρτία-σάρξ im Neuen Testament und die damit zusammenhängenden Vorstellungen', *ZTK* 49 (1952), pp. 200-22.

—*Konkordanz zu den Qumrantexten* (Göttingen: Vandenhoeck & Ruprecht, 1960).

Lampe, G.W.H., *The Seal of the Spirit* (London: Longmans, Green & Co., 1951).

—'The Holy Spirit in the Writings of St Luke', in *Studies in the Gospels* (ed. D.E. Nineham; Oxford: Basil Blackwell, 1957), pp. 159-200.

—*God as Spirit: The Bampton Lectures, 1976* (Oxford: Clarendon Press, 1977).

La Potterie, I de, 'L'onction du Christ: Etude de théologie biblique', *NRT* 80 (1958), pp. 225-52.

Laurentin, A., 'Le pneuma dans la doctrine de Philon', *ETL* 27 (1951), pp. 390-437.

Laurentin, R., *Les évangiles de l'enfance du Christ: Vérité de noël au-delà des mythes* (Paris: Desclée, 1982).

Le Déaut, R., 'Pentecost and Jewish Tradition', *DL* 20 (1970), pp. 250-67.

Legrand, L., 'L'arrière-plan néotestamentaire de Lc. 1,35', *RB* 70 (1963), pp. 161-92.

Leisegang, H., *Der heilige Geist: Das Wesen und Werden der mystich-intuitiven Erkenntnis in der Philosophie und Religion der Griechen* (Leipzig: B.G. Teubner, 1919).

—*Pneuma Hagion: Der Ursprung des Geistbegriffs der synoptischen Evangelien aus der griechischen Mystik* (Leipzig: J.C. Hinrichs, 1922).

Lentzen-Deis, F., *Die Taufe Jesu nach den Synoptikern: Literarkritische und gattungsgeschichtliche Untersuchungen* (Frankfurt am Main: Josef Knecht, 1970).

Levey, S.H., *The Targum of Ezekiel* (ArBib, 13; Edinburgh: T. & T. Clark, 1987).

Liebermann, S., *Midrash Debarim Rabbah: Edited for the First Time from the Oxford ms. No. 147 with an Introduction and Notes* (Jerusalem: Bamberger & Wahrmann, 1940).

Lincoln, A.T., 'Theology and History in the Interpretation of Luke's Pentecost', *ExpTim* 96 (1984–85), pp. 204-209.

Lindars, B., *New Testament Apologetic* (London: SCM Press, 1961).

Lohfink, G., *The Conversion of St. Paul: Narrative and History in Acts* (trans. B.J. Malina; Chicago: Franciscan Herald Press, 1976).

Lohmeyer, E., *Das Evangelium des Markus* (Göttingen: Vandenhoeck & Ruprecht, 1959).

Lohse, E., 'Lukas als Theologe der Heilsgeschichte', in *Die Einheit des Neuen Testament* (Göttingen: Vandenhoeck & Ruprecht, 1973), pp. 145-64.

—'πεντηκοστή', *TDNT*, VI, pp. 44-53.

—'Die Bedeutung des Pfingstberichtes im Rahmen des lukanischen Geschichtswerkes', in *Die Einheit des Neuen Testament* (Göttingen: Vandenhoeck & Ruprecht, 1973), pp. 178-92.

—(ed.), *Die Texte aus Qumran: Hebräisch und deutsch* (Munich: Kösel, 1971).

Longenecker, R., *Paul: Apostle of Liberty* (New York: Harper & Row, 1964).

Lönig, K., *Die Saulustradition in der Apostelgeschichte* (NTA NS, 9; Münster: Aschendorff, 1973).

Lüdemann, G., *Das frühe Christentum nach den Traditionen der Apostelgeschichte* (Göttingen: Vandenhoeck & Ruprecht, 1987).

Macchia, F.D., 'The Question of Tongues as Initial Evidence: A Review of *Initial Evidence*, edited by Gary B. McGee', *JPT* 2 (1993), pp. 117-27.

Maddox, R., *The Purpose of Luke–Acts* (FRLANT, 126; Göttingen: Vandenhoeck & Ruprecht, 1982).

Mandelbaum, B., *Pesikta de Rab Kahana* (New York: The Jewish Theological Seminary of America, 1962).

Manns, F., *Le symbole eau-esprit dans le judaïsme ancien* (SBF, 19; Jerusalem: Franciscan Printing Press, 1983).

Manson, T.W., *The Sayings of Jesus* (London: SCM Press, 2nd edn, 1949).

—*The Teaching of Jesus* (Cambridge: Cambridge University Press, 1952).

Margulies, M., *Midrash Haggadol on the Pentateuch, Genesis* (Jerusalem: Mossad Harev Kook, 1947).

Marmorstein, A., *Studies in Jewish Theology* (ed. J. Rabbinowitz and M.S. Lew; London: Oxford University Press, 1950).

Marshall, I.H., 'Hard Sayings: VII. Lk 12.10', *Theology* 67 (1964), pp. 65-67.

—*Luke: Historian and Theologian* (Grand Rapids: Zondervan, 1970).

—'The Meaning of the Verb "to Baptize"', *EvQ* 45 (1973), pp. 130-40.

—*The Origins of New Testament Christology* (Leicester: Inter-Varsity Press, 1976).

—'The Significance of Pentecost', *SJT* 30 (1977), pp. 347-69.

—*The Gospel of Luke: A Commentary on the Greek Text* (NIGTC; Grand Rapids: Eerdmans, 1978).

—*The Acts of the Apostles: An Introduction and Commenatry* (TNTC, 5; Leicester: Inter-Varsity Press, 1980).

—'Luke and his "Gospel"', in *Das Evangelium und die Evangelien* (ed. P. Stuhlmacher; WUNT, 28; Tübingen: J.C.B. Mohr, 1983), pp. 289-308.

—'An Evangelical Approach to "Theological Criticism"', *Themelios* 13 (1988), pp. 79-85.

McGee, G. (ed.), *Initial Evidence: Historical and Biblical Perspectives on the Pentecostal Doctrine of Spirit Baptism* (Peabody, MA: Hendrickson, 1991).

McNamara, M., *Palestinian Judaism and the New Testament* (GNS, 4; Wilmington, DE: John Carroll University Press, 1983).

Menzies, R.P., 'Spirit and Power in Luke-Acts: A Response to Max Turner', *JSNT* 49 (1993), pp. 11-20.

—'James Shelton's *Mighty in Word and Deed*: A Review Article', *JPT* 2 (1993), pp. 105-15.

—'Luke and the Spirit: A Reply to James Dunn', *JPT* 4 (1994), pp. 115-38.

Metzger, B., *A Textual Commentary on the Greek New Testament* (London: United Bible Societies, 2nd edn, 1975).

—'The Fourth Book of Ezra', in Charlesworth (ed.), *Pseudepigrapha*, I, pp. 517-59.

Michaels, J.R., 'Evidences of the Spirit, or the Spirit as Evidence? Some Non-Pentecostal Reflections', in McGee (ed.), *Initial Evidence*, pp. 202-18.

Minear, P.S., 'Luke's Use of the Birth Stories', in *Studies in Luke–Acts* (ed. L.E. Keck and J.L. Martyn; London: SPCK, 3rd edn, 1978), pp. 111-30.

—*To Heal and to Reveal: The Prophetic Vocation According to Luke* (New York: Seabury, 1976).

Montague, G.T., *The Holy Spirit: Growth of a Biblical Tradition* (New York: Paulist Press, 1976).

Moore, C.A., *Daniel, Esther, and Jeremiah: The Additions* (AB, 44; New York: Doubleday, 2nd edn, 1978).

Morgenthaler, R., *Die lukanische Geschichtsschreibung als Zeugnis: Gestalt und Gehalt der Kunst des Lukas* (2 vols.; ATANT, 15; Zürich: Zwingli-Verlag, 1949).

Morrice, W.G., *Joy in the New Testament* (Exeter: Paternoster Press, 1984).

Morris, L., *The New Testament and Jewish Lectionaries* (London: Tyndale Press, 1964).

Müller, D., 'Geisterfahrung und Totenauferweckung: Untersuchung zur Totenauferweckung bei Paulus und in den ihm vorgegebenen Überlieferungen' (unpublished PhD dissertation, Christian-Albrecht-Universität zu Kiel, 1980).

Mullins, T.Y., 'New Testament Commission Forms, Especially in Luke–Acts', *JBL* 95 (1976), pp. 603-14.

Munck, J., *Paul and the Salvation of Mankind* (Atlanta: John Knox, 1959).

Mussner, F., 'In den letzen Tagen (Apg 2,17a)', *BZ* 5 (1965), pp. 263-65.

Neusner, J., 'The Teaching of the Rabbis: Approaches Old and New', *JJS* 27 (1976), pp. 23-35.

—*The Tosefta: Translated from the Hebrew* (6 vols.; New York: Ktav, 1977-86).

Nickelsburg, G.W.E., *Jewish Literature between the Bible and the Mishnah: A Historical and Literary Introduction* (London: SCM Press, 1981).

Noack, B., 'The Day of Pentecost in Jubilees, Qumran, and Acts', *ASTI* 1 (1962), pp. 73-95.

Nötscher, F., 'Heiligkeit in den Qumranschriften', *RevQ* 2 (1960), pp. 315-44.

Oliver, H.H., 'The Lucan Birth Stories and the Purpose of Lk–Acts', *NTS* 10 (1964), pp. 202-26.

O'Neill, J.C., *The Theology of Acts in its Historical Setting* (London: SPCK, 2nd edn, 1970).

O'Reilly, L., *Word and Sign in the Acts of the Apostles: A Study in Lucan Theology* (AnGreg, 243; Rome: Editrice Pontificia Università Gregoriana, 1987).

O'Toole, R.F., 'Acts 2:30 and the Davidic Covenant of Pentecost', *JBL* 102 (1983), pp. 245-58.

Otzen, B., 'צר', *ThWAT*, III, pp. 830-39.

Parratt, J.K., 'The Rebaptism of the Ephesian Disciples', *ExpTim* 79 (1967–68), pp. 182-83.

Pearson, B.A., *The Pneumatikos-Psychikos Terminology in 1 Corinthians: A Study in the Theology of the Corinthian Opponents of Paul and its Relation to Gnosticism* (SBLDS, 12; Missoula, MT: SBL, 1973).

Pereira, F., *Ephesus: Climax of Universalism in Luke–Acts. A Redaction-Critical Study* of Paul's Ephesian Ministry (Acts 18.23–20.1) (JTF, 10.1; Anand, India: Gujarat Sahitya Prakash, 1983).

Perrot, C., 'Luc 4, 16-30 et la lecture biblique de l'ancienne Synagogue', *RSR* 47 (1973), pp. 324-40.

Pesch, R., *Die Apostelgeschichte* (2 vols.; EKKNT; Zürich: Benzinger Verlag, 1986).

Pfleiderer, O., *Paulinism: A Contribution to the History of Primitive Christian Theology* (trans. E. Peters; 2 vols.; London: Williams & Norgate, 1877).

—*Das Urchristenthum: Seine Schriften und Lehren in geschichtlichem Zusammenhang* (Berlin: Georg Reimer, 1887).

Potin, J., *La fête juive de la Pentecôte* (LD, 65; Paris: Cerf, 1971).

Rahlfs, A. (ed.), *Septuaginta* (Stuttgart: Deutsche Bibelgesellschaft, 2nd edn, 1979).

Reicke, B., 'Jesus in Nazareth—Lk 4,14-30', in *Das Wort and die Wörter* (FS for Gerhard Friedrich; ed. H. Balz and S. Schulz; Stuttgart: W. Kohlhammer, 1973), pp. 47-55.

Rengstorf, K.H., *Das Evangelium nach Lukas* (NTD, 3; Göttingen: Vandenhoeck & Ruprecht, 1937).

—'μαθητής', *TDNT*, IV, pp. 390-461.

Rese, M., *Alttestamentliche Motive in der Christologie des Lukas* (SNT, 1; Gütersloh: Gütersloher Verlagshaus, 1969).

Robinson, W.C., *Der Weg des Herrn* (trans. G. Strecker and G. Strecker; WBKEL, 36; Hamburg: Herbert Reich Evangelischer Verlag, 1964).

Rodd, C.S., 'Spirit or Finger', *ExpTim* 72 (1960–61), pp. 157-58.

Roebeck, C.M., 'The Gift of Prophecy in Acts and Paul, Part I', *StBT* 5 (1975), pp. 15-38.

Roloff, J., *Die Apostelgeschichte* (NTD; Göttingen: Vandenhoeck & Ruprecht, 1981).

Runia, D.T., *Philo of Alexandria and the Timaeus of Plato* (PA, 44; Leiden: Brill, 1986).

Russell, D.S., *The Method and Message of Jewish Apocalyptic* (London: SCM Press, 1964).

Russell, E.A., ' "They Believed Philip Preaching" (Acts 8.12)', *IBS* 1 (1979), pp. 169-76.

Rylaarsdam, J.C., *Revelation in Jewish Literature* (Chicago: The University of Chicago Press, 1946).

—'Feast of Weeks', *IDB*, IV, pp. 827-28.

Sandmel, S., 'Parallelomania', *JBL* 81 (1962), pp. 1-13.

Sauvagant, B., 'Se repentir, être baptisé, recevoir l'Esprit, Actes 2,37 ss.', *FV* 80 (1981), pp. 77-89.

Schäfer, P., 'Die Termini "Heiliger Geist" und "Geist der Prophetie" in den Targumim und das Verhältnis der Targumim zueinander', *VT* 20 (1970), pp. 304-14

—*Die Vorstellung vom heiligen Geist in der rabbinischen Literatur* (SANT, 28; Munich: Kösel-Verlag, 1972).

Schlier, H., 'Zu Röm 1,3f', in *Neues Testament und Geschichte: Historisches Geschehen und Deutung im Neuen Testament* (FS for O. Cullmann; ed. H. Baltensweiler and B. Reicke; Tübingen: J.C.B. Mohr, 1972), pp. 207-18.

Schnabel, E.J., *Law and Wisdom from Ben Sira to Paul: A Tradition Historical Enquiry into the Relation of Law, Wisdom, and Ethics* (WUNT, 2.16; Tübingen: J.C.B. Mohr, 1985).

Schneider, G., 'Jesu geistgewirkte Empfängnis (Lk 1,34f)', *TPQ* 119 (1971), pp. 105-16.

—*Die Apostelgeschichte* (2 vols.; HTKNT, 5; Freiburg: Herder, 1980, 1982).

—'Die Bitte um das Kommen des Geistes im lukanischen Vaterunser (Lk 11,2 v.1)', in *Studien zum Text und zur Ethik des Neuen Testaments: Festschrift zum 80. Geburtstag von Heinrich Greeven* (ed. W. Schrage; Berlin: de Gruyter, 1986), pp. 344-73.

Schramm, T., *Der Markus-Stoff bei Lukas: Eine Literarkritische und Redaktionsgeschichtliche Untersuchung* (SNTSMS, 14; Cambridge: Cambridge University Press, 1971).

Schürer, E., *The History of the Jewish People in the Age of Jesus Christ* (rev. and ed. G. Vermes, F. Millar and M. Black; 3 vols.; Edinburgh: T. & T. Clark, 1973–86).

Schürmann, H., 'Der "Bericht vom Anfang": Ein Rekonstruktionsversuch auf Grund von Lk 4,14-16', in *Traditionsgeschichtliche Untersuchungen zu den synoptischen Evangelien* (Düsseldorf: Patmos, 1968), pp. 69-80.

—*Das Lukasevangelium, 1. Teil: Kommentar zu Kap. 1,1–9,50* (HTKNT, 3; Freiburg: Herder, 1969).

—'Zur Traditionsgeschichte der Nazareth-Perikope Lk 4,16-30', in *Mélanges Bibliques* (ed. A. Déscamps and A. de Halleux; Gembloux: Duculot, 1970), pp. 187-205.

—'Die geistgewirkte Lebensentstehung Jesu', in *Einheit in Vielfalt* (FS for Hugo Aufderbeck; ed. W. Ernst and K. Feiereis; Leipzig: St Benno, 1974), pp. 156-69.

Schweizer, E., 'The Spirit of Power: The Uniformity and Diversity of the Concept of the Holy Spirit in the New Testament' (trans. J. Bright and E. Debor), *Int* 6 (1952), pp. 259-78.

—'πνεῦμα', *TDNT*, VI, pp. 389-455.

—'Die Bekehrung des Apollos, Apg 18,24-26', in *Beiträge zur Theologie des Neuen Testaments: Neutestamentliche Aufsätze (1955–1970)* (Zürich: Zwingli Verlag, 1970), pp. 71-79.

Scroggs, R., 'Paul: ΣΟΦΟΣ and ΠΝΕΥΜΑΤΙΚΟΣ', *NTS* 14 (1967), pp. 33-55.

Seccombe, D.P., 'Luke and Isaiah', *NTS* 27 (1981), pp. 252-59.

Shelton, J.B., *Mighty in Word and Deed: The Role of the Holy Spirit in Luke–Acts* (Peabody, MA: Hendrickson, 1991).

Sloan, R.B., *The Favorable Year of the Lord: A Study of Jubilary Theology in the Gospel of Luke* (Austin, TX: Schola Press, 1977).

Smalley, S.S., 'Redaction Criticism', in *New Testament Interpretation: Essays on Principles and Methods* (ed. I.H. Marshall; Grand Rapids: Eerdmans, 1977), pp. 181-95.

Sperber, A., *The Bible in Aramaic* (4 vols.; Leiden: Brill, 1959–68).

Spitta, F., *Die Apostelgeschichte: Ihre Quellen und deren geschichtlicher Wert* (Halle: Waisenhaus, 1891).

Spittler, R.P., 'Testament of Job', in Charlesworth (ed.), *Pseudepigrapha*, I, pp. 829-68.

Stählin, G., *Die Apostelgeschichte* (NTD, 5; Göttingen: Vandenhoeck & Ruprecht, 1970).

Stemberger, G., *Der Leib der Auferstehung: Studien zur Anthropologie und Eschatologie des palästinischen Judentums im neutestamentlichen Zeitalter (ca. 170 v. Chr.-100 n. Chr.)* (AnBib, 56; Rome: Biblical Institute Press, 1972).

Stenning, J.F., *The Targum of Isaiah* (repr.; Oxford: Clarendon Press, 1953 [1949]).

Strack, H.L., *Introduction to the Talmud and Midrash* (Philadelphia: Jewish Publication Society of America, 1931).

Strack, H.L., and P. Billerbeck, *Kommentar zum Neuen Testament aus Talmud und Midrasch* (4 vols.; Munich: Becksche, 1922-28).

Streeter, B.H., *The Four Gospels: A Study in Origins* (London: Macmillan, 1924).

Stronstad, R., *The Charismatic Theology of St Luke* (Peabody, MA: Hendrickson, 1984).

Tachau, P., 'Die Pfingstgeschichte nach Lukas: Exegetische Überlegungen zu Apg. 2,1-13', *EE* 29 (1977), pp. 86-102.

Taeger, J.W., *Der Mensch und sein Heil: Studien zum Bild des Menschen und zur Sicht der Bekehrung bei Lukas* (SNT, 14; Gütersloh: Gütersloher Verlagshaus, 1982).

Talbert, C.H., *Literary Patterns, Theological Themes, and the Genre of Luke–Acts* (SBLMS, 20; Missoula, MT: SBL and Scholars Press, 1974).

—'Shifting Sands: The Recent Study of the Gospel of Luke', in *Interpreting the Gospels* (ed. J.L. Mays; Philadelphia: Fortress Press, 1981), pp. 197-213.

Talmon, S., 'The Calendar Reckoning of the Sect from the Judaean Desert', in *Aspects of the Dead Sea Scrolls* (ed. C. Rabin and Y. Yadin; SH, 4; Jerusalem: Magnes, 1967), pp. 162-99.

Tannehill, R.C., *The Narrative Unity of Luke–Acts: A Literary Interpretation. I. The Gospel according to Luke* (Philadelphia: Fortress Press, 1986).

Tatum, W.B., 'The Epoch of Israel: Luke I–II and the Theological Plan of Luke–Acts', *NTS* 13 (1966-67), pp. 184-95.

Taylor, V. *The Passion Narrative of St Luke: A Critical and Historical Investigation* (SNTSMS, 19; Cambridge: Cambridge University Press, 1972).

Thackeray, H.J., and R. Marcus (eds.), *Josephus with an English Translation* (9 vols.; LCL; London: W. Heinemann, 1926-65).

Tiede, D.L., *Prophecy and History in Luke–Acts* (Philadelphia: Fortress Press, 1980).

—'The Exaltation of Jesus and the Restoration of Israel in Acts 1', *HTR* 79 (1986), pp. 278-86.

Treves, M., 'The Two Spirits of the Rule of the Community', *RevQ* 3 (1961), pp. 449-52.

Trites, A.A., *The New Testament Concept of Witness* (SNTSMS, 31; Cambridge: Cambridge University Press, 1977).

Tuckett, C., 'Luke 4,16-30, Isaiah and Q', in *Logia: Les paroles de Jésus—The Sayings of Jesus* (ed. J. Delobel; BETL, 59; Leuven: Leuven University Press, 1982), pp. 343-54.

Turner, M.M.B., 'The Significance of Spirit Endowment for Paul', *VE* 9 (1975), pp. 56-69.

—'Luke and the Spirit: Studies in the Significance of Receiving the Spirit in Luke–Acts', unpublished Ph.D. dissertation; University of Cambridge, 1980.

—'Spirit Endowment in Luke–Acts: Some Linguistic Considerations', *VE* 12 (1981), pp. 45-63.

—'Jesus and the Spirit in Lucan Perspective', *TynBul* 32 (1981), pp. 3-42.

—'The Spirit of Christ and Christology', in *Christ the Lord* (ed. H.H. Rowdon; Leicester: Inter-Varsity Press, 1982), pp. 168-90.

—'Spiritual Gifts then and now', *VE* 15 (1985), pp. 7-64.

—'The Spirit and the Power of Jesus' Miracles in the Lukan Conception', *NovT* 33 (1991), pp. 124-52.

—'The Spirit of Prophecy and the Power of Authoritative Preaching in Luke-Acts: A Question of Origins', *NTS* 38 (1992), pp. 66-88.

Vaux, R. de, *Ancient Israel: Its Life and Institutions* (trans. J. McHugh; London: Darton, Longman, & Todd, 1961).

Verbeke, G., *L'évolution de la doctrine du Pneuma du Stoicisme à S. Augustin* (Paris: Desclée de Brouwer, 1945).

Vermes, G., *Scripture and Tradition in Judaism: Haggadic Studies* (SPB, 4; Leiden: Brill, 2nd edn, 1973).

—*Jesus the Jew: A Historian's Reading of the Gospels* (London: Collins, 1973).

—'Jewish Studies and New Testament Interpretation', *JJS* 31 (1980), pp. 1-17.

—*The Dead Sea Scrolls in English* (Sheffield: JSOT Press, 3rd edn, 1987).

Violet, B., *Die Esra-Apokalypse (IV. Esra)* (GCS, 18; Leipzig: Hinrichs, 1910).

Vos, J.S., *Traditionsgeschichtliche Untersuchungen zur paulinischen Pneumatologie* (Assen: Van Gorcum, 1973).

Weiser, A., *Die Apostelgeschichte* (2 vols.; ÖTKNT, 5; Gütersloh: Gütersloher Verlagshaus, 1981).

Weiss, B., *Lehrbuch der biblischen Theologie des Neuen Testaments* (Berlin: Hertz, 2nd edn, 1873).

Wendt, H.H., *Die Begriffe Fleisch und Geist im biblischen Sprachgebrauch* (Gotha, 1878).

—*Die Apostelgeschichte* (KEKNT, 3; Göttingen: Vandenhoeck & Ruprecht, 1913).

Wernberg-Møller, P., 'A Reconsideration of the Two Spirits in the Rule of the Community', *RevQ* 3 (1961), pp. 413-41.

Wilckens, U., *Die Missionsreden der Apostelgeschichte: Form- und traditions-geschichtliche Untersuchungen* (WMANT, 5; Neukirchen–Vluyn: Neukirchener Verlag, 3rd edn, 1974).

Wintermute, O.S., 'Jubilees', in Charlesworth (ed.), *Pseudepigrapha*, II, pp. 35-142.

Wolff, H.W., *Joel and Amos* (ET; Herm; Philadelphia: Fortress Press, 1977).

Wolfson, A., *Philo* (2 vols.; Cambridge, MA: Harvard University Press, 1948).

Worrell, J.E., 'Concepts of Wisdom in the Dead Sea Scrolls' (unpublished PhD dissertation, Claremont Graduate School, 1968).

Wright, R.B., 'Psalms of Solomon', in Charlesworth (ed.), *Pseudepigrapha*, II, pp. 639-70.

Yadin, Y., *The Temple Scroll: The Hidden Law of the Dead Sea Sect* (London: Weidenfeld & Nicolson, 1985).

Yates, J.E., 'Luke's Pneumatology and Luke 11.20', in *Studia Evangelica. II. Papers Presented to the Second International Congress on New Testament Studies* (ed. F.L. Cross; TU, 87; Berlin: Akademie Verlag, 1964), pp. 295-99.

Ziegler, J. (ed.), *Duodecim prophetae: Septuaginta Vetus Testamentum Graecum* (Göttingen: Vandenhoeck & Ruprecht, 1967), XIII.

Zuckermandel, M.S., *Tosefta unter Zugrundelegung der Erfurter und Wiener Handschriften* (Trier: Fr. Lintz'schen Buchhandlung, 1882).

INDEXES

INDEX OF REFERENCES

OLD TESTAMENT

TARGUMS

JOSEPHUS

CHRISTIAN AUTHORS

INDEX OF AUTHORS

Lightning Source UK Ltd.
Milton Keynes UK
UKOW021510021211

183110UK00010B/11/A